The Netflix Effect

The Netflix Effect

Technology and Entertainment in the 21st Century

Edited by
Kevin McDonald and Daniel Smith-Rowsey

Bloomsbury Academic India
An imprint of Bloomsbury Publishing Inc

BLOOMSBURY
NEW DELHI • LONDON • OXFORD • NEW YORK • SYDNEY

BLOOMSBURY INDIA
Bloomsbury Publishing India Pvt. Ltd
Second Floor, LSC Building No. 4, DDA Complex, Pocket C–6&7,
Vasant Kunj, New Delhi 110070

BLOOMSBURY, BLOOMSBURY ACADEMIC INDIA and the Diana logo are
trademarks of Bloomsbury Publishing Plc

First published in India 2024
First published 2016

This edition published with permission from Bloomsbury Publishing Plc,
50 Bedford Square, London, WC1B3DP, UK

British Library Cataloguing-in-Publication Data
A catalogue record for this book is available from the British Library

Library of Congress Cataloging-in-Publication Data
A catalog record for this book is available from the Library of Congress

ISBN: 978-93-93715-59-3

Typeset by Integra Software Services Pvt. Ltd.
Printed and bound in India by Replika Press Pvt. Ltd.
To find out more about our authors and books
visit www.bloomsbury.com and sign up for our newsletters

Contents

List of Figures

List of Tables

Acknowledgments

This collection grew out of a series of workshops and panels held at the 2014 Society of Cinema and Media Studies annual conference in Seattle. We thank everyone who participated in those events for their interest in the topic and for the valuable insights that they provided. We also thank everyone at Bloomsbury, especially Katie Gallof, whose initial interest in the project really got the ball rolling, and Mary Al-Sayed, who diligently helped us navigate every step of the process. Of course, this collection would not have been possible without the hard work of our contributors. We sincerely thank all of them for their dedication to this project and for making Netflix such a vibrant and productive topic. Daniel would love to thank his extremely patient wife, Irena, and their wonderful kids. Kevin would like to thank Kris Fallon and Ben Stork for providing him with an opportunity at the 2011 Visible Evidence conference in New York to first think about Netflix from a critical perspective. He would also like to thank his family and Gina Giotta for their never-ending support.

Contributors

Neta Alexander is a doctoral student in the Department of Cinema Studies at New York University (NYU), researching streaming technologies and digital spectatorship through the lens of failure, breakdown, and "noise." She has published articles and reviews in *Film Quarterly*, *Film Comment*, and *Media Fields Journal*, among other venues. Her book chapters are forthcoming in the anthologies *Compact Cinematics* (Bloomsbury Publishing) and *Anthropology and Film Festivals* (Cambridge Scholars Publishing).

Sarah Arnold works for the Social TV company Axonista and previously worked as Senior Lecturer in Film and Television at Falmouth University. She is currently working on the book *Television, Technology and Gender: New Platforms and New Audiences*. Her previous books include *Maternal Horror Film: Melodrama and Motherhood* and the coauthored book *The Film Handbook*.

Sheri Chinen Biesen is Associate Professor of Radio, Television, and Film Studies at Rowan University and author of *Blackout: World War II and the Origins of Film Noir* (2005) and *Music in the Shadows: Noir Musical Films* (2014) at Johns Hopkins University Press. She received her PhD from the University of Texas at Austin, her MA and BA from the University of Southern California, and has taught at University of Southern California (USC), the University of California, the University of Texas, and in England. She has contributed to the BBC documentary *The Rules of Film Noir* and has published work in *Film and History*, *Quarterly Review of Film and Video*, and *Popular Culture Review*, and has served as an editor of *The Velvet Light Trap*.

Lyell Davies is a documentary video maker and professor of film and media at the City University of New York. His documentaries have aired on PBS and screened at film festivals internationally, and he has facilitated participatory media-making projects engaging youth, recent immigrants, the homeless, and workers. His scholarly research focuses on media and social change, media justice, and documentary filmmaking. He earned his PhD in Visual and Cultural Studies from the University of Rochester.

Brittany Farr is a doctoral student at the University of Southern California. Her work examines the ways in which different kinds of violence are commodified and the intersections between this commodification and postfeminism. Her research interests are postfeminism, neoliberalism, race and ethnicity, and feminist theory.

Cameron Lindsey is a doctoral student at the University of Texas. He holds an MA Arts in Cinema Studies from NYU and has worked as an editor and writer of *The Storyville Post* and *On the Media*. His research focuses on youth media and new digital media.

Casey J. McCormick is a PhD candidate at McGill University, completing a dissertation on TV finales, digital distribution, and social viewing. She has contributed to *Time in Television Narrative* (University of Mississippi Press, 2012) and has forthcoming contributions to *Participations: International Journal of Audience Research* (2016 special issue) and *A Companion to Fandom and Fan Studies* (Wiley-Blackwell, 2017). She teaches Cultural Studies courses at McGill and coorganizes the Future Humanities project at the Institute for the Public Life of Arts and Ideas.

Kevin McDonald teaches in the Communication Studies Department at Cal State Northridge. He received his PhD from the University of Iowa. His research focuses on film theory, contemporary Hollywood, and media industries. His work has appeared in *Jump-Cut* and *Alphaville*.

Alison N. Novak is Assistant Professor of Public Relations and Advertising at Rowan University. She received her PhD in Communication, Culture, and Media from Drexel University. Her research explores the future of media regulation, political discourses of voter engagement, and youth civic practices. Her research has been featured in *Wired magazine* and *The Huffington Post*. She has been published in *Review of Communication* and *Journal of Race and Policy*. She is also the coeditor of *Defining Identity and the Changing Scope of Culture in the Digital Age* and the author of *Media, Millennials, and Politics*.

Sudeep Sharma is Director of Public Programs for the Academy of Motion Picture Arts and Sciences in Los Angeles. He received his PhD in Cinema and Media Studies from University of California, Los Angeles. He has also served as Associate Programmer for documentaries at the Sundance Film Festival and Programmer for the Indian Film Festival of Los Angeles. His dissertation focuses on 1990s' cable television news and its use of history.

Gerald Sim is Associate Professor of Film Studies at Florida Atlantic University, and the author of *The Subject of Film and Race: Retheorizing Politics, Ideology, and Cinema* (Bloomsbury Academic, 2014). His writing on new media includes an essay in *Projections* about the industrial transition to digital cinematography. The contribution to this volume seeds future work on big data's effects on subjectivity and its place in software studies.

Daniel Smith-Rowsey is Instructor of Film at Sacramento State. His book *Star Actors in the Hollywood Renaissance* was published in 2013 by Palgrave MacMillan, and nominated for a Best First Book Award by the Society of Cinema and Media

Studies. His recent publications include "Dustin Hoffman: As Artistic as Possible" in Rutgers University Press' *New Constellations: Movie Stars of the 1960s* as well as " 'You Know Billy, We Blew It': Historical Influences on the 'Rough Rebels' and How the Counterculture Was Excluded from Hollywood" in *Bright Lights Film Journal*. His feature film *Fish, Chips, and Mushy Peas* (2012) won the Silver Screen Award at the 2012 Nevada Film Festival.

Zachary Snider teaches writing, literature, film, and speech classes at Bentley University in Massachusetts, and previously taught similar courses for New York University. He completed his PhD in Postmodern Literature and Creative Writing at London Metropolitan University. Before becoming a professor, he worked as an entertainment journalist in New York City, Los Angeles, and across Europe. Now he publishes fiction, creative nonfiction, and scholarly essays about television and film, postmodern fiction and theatre, pedagogical composition studies, among other interdisciplinary fields.

Christian Stiegler is Professor of Media Management, Consumer Culture and New Media and Head of the Degree Program of International Media Management at Karlshochschule International University in Karlsruhe, Germany. He worked for several years as a journalist in TV, radio, print, and online and has lectured on Entertainment and Media Industry Studies.

Sam Ward received his PhD from the University of Nottingham in 2015. His research focuses on the role of transnational industrial connections in the branding of digital television channels and technologies. He has taught at the University of Roehampton and is currently Associate Lecturer at the University of Derby.

Introduction

Kevin McDonald and Daniel Smith-Rowsey

In 1988, John and JoAnn McMahon founded Murphy's Express, a California video store with an innovation: its drivers delivered videocassettes to customers' homes. Thousands of households in Berkeley, Oakland, and nearby towns were outfitted with key-operated plastic boxes that remain affixed to the walls of many East Bay porches to this day. Despite its prescience, the business closed in 1994 due to the growing number of competing media options and various logistical roadblocks. Shortly thereafter, Stuart Skorman founded Reel, a dotcom that promised to combine its recommendation system, "Reel Genius," with the convenience of home delivery. By 1998, as the internet bubble began to mushroom, this proved so enticing that Skorman sold Reel.com to Hollywood Video for $100,000,000. However, the cost of mailing VHS tapes proved to be logistically prohibitive, and Hollywood Video shut down its Reel.com branch shortly after the "dotcom bust" in 2000. Looking over its shoulder, Blockbuster Video saw the $100 million snafu as evidence that online rentals and sales weren't worth the trouble.

In one sense, these businesses paved the way for Netflix, which launched in 1997 and, unlike them, made a foundational decision to rent and sell DVDs only, hitching its star to the newer format and never looking back. Two years later, Netflix adopted a subscription-only model, becoming the only national service that could promise customers no late fees; this combination proved so successful that by 2006, Netflix served as *Wired* editor Chris Anderson's leading example of Long Tail economics—that is, because of lower overhead, internet companies can afford a wider variety of specialization and personalization. In another sense, however, the exigencies of Murphy's Express and Reel.com—and eventually, Hollywood Video and Blockbuster Video, which both filed for bankruptcy in 2010—remind us that the rise of Netflix was hardly inevitable, that contingency played a key role in the rise of the company that boasted America's fastest-growing stock price between 2010 and 2015, and that the future of Netflix is similarly not yet written.

Even with that caveat, Netflix has had a transformative effect in the relationship between consumers and content providers in the twenty-first century. With well over 65 million subscribers worldwide (and many more accessing the service through friends, family members, and other illegal proxies), Netflix accounts for up to one-third of North American internet traffic at any given time. As a result, Netflix has not only achieved remarkable financial success, but, like Amazon, Facebook, Google, and a handful of other internet-based companies, has become synonymous with the growing, pervasive impact of technology. Unlike these other firms, Netflix is primarily devoted to high-quality media content, the type of entertainment that has been traditionally produced by the Hollywood studios and major television networks. To the extent that Netflix has contributed to changes in existing distribution and exhibition models—in many ways realizing long-held predictions of a future in which all media is available on-demand across multiple platforms—the major media conglomerates have been less appreciative of its aptitude for technological innovation, often viewing Netflix more as a disruptive interloper than as a savvy competitor. If there is a singular Netflix effect, it may simply be that technology and entertainment are merging at an accelerating rate and seriously impacting the business and economics of mass media. This collection illustrates how this effect is connected to other larger developments, but also makes the case that examining the specificity of Netflix provides key insights into how these developments will shape media, technology, and society moving forward.

With its popularity and financial success, Netflix has become a convenient avatar widely cited by business analysts, media and technology experts, and the popular press more generally as a way to demonstrate what Henry Jenkins terms "convergence culture." For instance, much of Netflix's success is due to advances in technological convergence—the success of its streaming service closely coincided with the growing adoption of high-speed internet connections (which surpassed 50 percent in the United States in 2008 and 70 percent in 2013). During this time, high-speed or broadband internet became increasingly accessed in conjunction with other communications technologies—packaged together with services provided by cable companies, direct-broadcast satellites, and wireless mobile phone networks. The convergence of these technologies in turn accelerated several other trends that would benefit Netflix. The rise of cable television, for example, expanded the number of available programming choices and promoted the idea that content should be tailored to niche audiences. The proliferation of smartphones and wireless connections (as well as digital video recorders) shifted expectations about accessibility and convenience, popularizing presumptions that culture circulates best on an on-demand basis.

Convergence is just as important for Netflix from an industrial or business standpoint. Headquartered in Los Gatos at the southernmost reaches of Silicon Valley, it is as though Netflix has always been reaching toward Hollywood in an attempt to bridge California's two most famous industries. And while Netflix has built its reputation on doing just that, there is still a good deal of contention among competing interests. The "Big Six" media companies—Disney, Fox/News Corp., NBC/Comcast, Warners/HBO, Viacom/Paramount, and Sony—have had considerable reason to lament Netflix's rise. Their studio branches, following the windfall spawned by DVDs, blamed Netflix for spoiling plans to harness subsequent generations of digital media, either through a high-definition physical format (i.e., Blu-ray) or by developing their own proprietary video-on-demand (VOD) platforms. Their television networks were wary of new media in general—a broad distinction that included video games, interactive technologies, and web-based competitors like Netflix—as they struggled with declining ratings and fragmenting audiences. Despite these concerns, Emmy voters awarded Netflix the first Emmy for a web-based content provider (for *House of Cards*) and the Big Six rushed to renegotiate their leasing terms with the company, not unreasonably speculating that if Netflix was earning record profits, they were earning too little. Now Netflix is remaking itself into a studio, financing and producing its own content, expanding beyond television programming to feature-length films, and working with A-list talent (e.g., Brad Pitt, Idris Elba, Adam Sandler, Angelina Jolie) to bring small-scale, cutting-edge passion projects to a global audience. In this respect, Netflix continues to be a thorn in the side of existing media industries, sometimes beating the Big Six at their own game.

While it is unclear whether Netflix will stand the test of time or that it alone is capable of summing up certain changes, the company is at this point deeply intertwined with the same kind of transformation that we now associate with film's adoption of sound technologies in late 1920s, the widespread adoption of television in the 1950s, the introduction of home video, specifically the VCR, in the 1980s, and the rise of the internet in the 1990s. These changes, like Netflix itself, map out a gradual shift from the relationship between Hollywood and technology to a much broader shift to the merging of media, technology, and entertainment. The Hollywood studios have a long history of being wary of new technologies, but both in the case of television and VCR they negotiated the arrival of these new competitors in a way that was ultimately advantageous. This has become less obviously true with the rise of twenty-first-century technologies like DVRs and ubiquitous high-speed or broadband internet connections.

Although the business of media convergence means that competing interests will regularly butt heads, the growing importance of bringing together entertainment and technology has also prompted a diverse array of new and dynamic partnerships. One example of this is Apple's iTunes, the digital distribution platform that proved the importance of linking popular media to accessible, user-friendly computer software that operates across multiple devices. This was a product that, somewhat similar to the video game consoles introduced by Sony and Microsoft, linked software to hardware in ways that were designed to mutually reinforce one another. This was also true for Netflix, though in a slightly different sense. Netflix incorporated recommendation and personalization software into its interface. This strategy typified the way in which many web-based businesses began to rely on user-generated information or metadata—details about how users interact within and between different websites. For Netflix, these programs were primarily used to enhance its service, directing users to related films and other programming that they might enjoy based on various algorithmic calculations, rather than as a way to monetize that information either through advertising or other means. While winning over consumers with its technological proficiency, Netflix proved similarly adept at combining old and new media. This was true in its use of new filtering software to drive its users to older movie titles and in its combination of new internet technologies with the seemingly anachronistic postal system as part of its DVD-by-mail service. Even today, as Netflix has embraced its position as nonpareil streaming service, it continues to deliver DVDs—a format that some liken to eight-track cassettes—to over 5 million customers, remaining one of the few competitors, along with automated kiosks like Redbox, operating in the still-profitable physical rental market.

If analysts have often commented on Netflix's luck in remaking itself first from an online video store to a streaming service, then from a service to a studio, they have less often noted its knack for self-made serendipity. In the first decade of the twenty-first century, tens of millions of Americans became familiar with its red envelopes which regularly entered, lingered around, and departed domestic spaces, enabling what advertisers call a "brand penetration" that few other brands can claim. Netflix may well have been tempted to plaster the outsides of its envelopes with advertisements, but instead generally left its trademark red undiluted, a classroom-ready case of steadily building a brand and logo. While the name "Netflix" appeared to be on the brink of anachronism—recalling companies like Netscape and other casualties of the deflated internet bubble, it suddenly regained relevance in the midst of a new Golden Age in television. More than just a "net of movies" or "internet flicks," it now suggests a new kind of television "network," heralding the company's putative future in production. Netflix has made this type of reversal part of its modus operandi. As an internet company, for example, it regularly turns bugs into features, as when, on a monthly basis, it keeps its name in active news search results by naming the titles being released *and withdrawn* from the service. And yet it thwarts standard assumptions about monetizing digital content by releasing TV seasons all at once, obviating the added value of widely trafficked weekly recaps of shows on channels like HBO, AMC, FX, and Showtime. Netflix can be both hermeneutically rich and hermetically sealed, empowering and dominating, a model for technological innovation and a wildcard that seemingly defies commonsense.

As part of its willingness to experiment with these new strategies, Netflix has demonstrated how convergence is altering traditional relationships in the production and consumption of media. In this regard, scholars like Jenkins have focused on how convergence lends itself to more active forms of participation by audiences and consumers. This indeed has been an important part of Netflix's rhetoric with CEO Reed Hastings and other company representatives repeatedly emphasizing how its service empowers users, liberating them from a previous era of gatekeeper-restricted media access. While it is clearly the case that audiences have greater control in determining when and how they consume certain types of media, larger questions of power and shifting paradigms are more complex. Perhaps owing to its historically antagonistic relationships with Blockbuster and the Big Six media companies, Netflix often accentuates its status as an outsider, upstart, disruptor, underdog, and even as a direct threat or "game changer" to the entire status quo. One characteristic example is Netflix's experiment with day-and-date releases—the simultaneous release of a film across different exhibition platforms including video-on-demand—that have infuriated traditional gatekeepers of the theatrical window. From Netflix's marketing perspective, the Netflix effect may be the broadening of consumer choices and better-enabled individuation; from others' perspective, the Netflix effect may be seen as this same personalization restricted to that which benefits Netflix.

If newer strategies challenge existing paradigms, some of them also emulate the approach of what many view as Netflix's closest competitors, premium channels like HBO. Like Netflix, HBO is a hybrid channel offering premium Hollywood films, signature television series, and other original programming options, packaged together in a way that differentiates the service as a "quality" media brand. And as HBO moves to compete more directly with Netflix—launching HBO Now, its internet-only service, in 2015—it has the advantage of being part of the larger media conglomerate, Time Warner. Although conglomeration and horizontal integration have not always produced the benefits that they once promised, these relationships remain an important factor in generating strategic convergences. This is also why streaming services like Hulu, an enterprise co-owned by three of the Big Six media companies, video-sharing websites like YouTube, a subsidiary of Google, and Amazon Instant Video, an add-on VOD service bundled with an Amazon Prime subscription, are all viewed as serious adversaries despite the fact that they represent very different business models and have only had varying degrees of success thus far. Netflix has likewise struggled with these questions in its uneasy relationship with internet and cable service providers like Comcast. At times, Netflix has openly clashed with Comcast and its ilk, celebrating its capacity to promote "cord cutting"—the discontinuation of one's cable subscription—and actively participating in a campaign to bolster net neutrality, the principle that all data be treated equally. On the other hand, Netflix has also partnered with these same service providers, paying to ensure that delivery of its content continues unabated. Contrary to its insurrectionary overtures, this is an example of how media monopolies take priority over individual users and the principles of fair use.

The complexity of these different relationships and the shifting status of convergence illustrate the importance of developing new scholarly strategies both in understanding the specific impact of Netflix and the evolution of media industries in the twenty-first century more generally. Recent work in subfields like reception studies, which has drawn heightened attention to how audiences and individual users actively engage with technology and media, and media industry studies, which aims to historicize the business of entertainment, provide important points of reference. However, the different approaches undertaken as part of this collection stress the need for versatility and synthesis more than any one particular disciplinary methodology. Understanding the relationship between technology and entertainment, in other words, requires new perspectives that are capable of analyzing both film and television, that appreciate the technical requirements that separate competing distribution platforms, that address the intersection between production and reception, that recognize how social, political, legal, and industrial factors can all play a decisive role, and that know when and how to mobilize the appropriate critical rubric in order to elucidate the effect of this relationship.

To this end, this collection consists of three parts that collectively aim to explain Netflix's effect on technology and entertainment. The first part addresses "Technology, Innovation, and Control." As much as Netflix encompasses a range of hybrid practices, the company is ultimately an internet-based service, one that depends on preconditions ranging from the physical infrastructures on which information circulates to the accessibility of consumer electronics and advances in the integration of software applications. In the first chapter of this section, Lyell Davies analyzes Netflix's role in the ongoing debates on net neutrality. These debates highlight the growing tensions and shifting alliances among different stakeholders as technology becomes more deeply ingrained in our lives. In many ways, this tension is most palpable in the strained relationship between internet service providers—the major corporations like Comcast that control the so-called pipes that connect individual consumers to the internet—and services like Netflix that offer content that must travel through those pipes. At the same time debates about net neutrality recall larger questions about whether communications technologies are supposed to serve public interests or if private commercial interests should take precedence. The last forty years have witnessed the rise of neoliberal economics and a climate of government deregulation, circumstances that have generally favored private interests and that have been embraced by Silicon Valley and the rest of the high-tech industry as a necessary condition of innovation. Despite this tendency, Netflix strategically aligned itself with open internet and social justice advocates appealing to policy makers in support of net neutrality. As Davies shows, this alliance is more likely than not a short-lived matter of convenience, part of a relentless effort to keep up with its competitors rather than a sign of Netflix's altruistic commitment to fairness or democracy.

Alison N. Novak, in the following chapter, is likewise concerned with how policy makers affect technological progress. Her approach, however, focuses on a very different challenge: how policy makers and politicians understand or frame Netflix within existing discourses about technology, politics, and regulatory imperatives. Novak's investigation shows that Netflix has become a convenient focal point in discussions that will shape future policy debates, but that this does not necessarily work in Netflix's favor. In fact, this dilemma demonstrates the difficulties that accompany technological innovation. By industry standards, Netflix's first decade represents a gradual process. For government regulators and policy makers, however, Netflix represents a drastic turn of events. There is no basis for comparison and this makes it difficult to establish precedents with regard to regulation, policy, and general reception. As a result, Netflix is subject to exaggeration, disparagement, and ignorance within ongoing public debates about the changing nature of media and technology. It is largely for this reason that Netflix has made such a concerted effort to have a hand in shaping its reception through other avenues—like lobbying, marketing, and public relations. Netflix knows that by generating enough public support it might eventually sway political officials and regulators to support its agenda. This reflects the importance of being in a position to shape future debate and to elicit the kinds of positive reinforcement that can overcome the current state of political uncertainty.

The second part of this section shifts the focus to how Netflix utilizes specific technologies within its service and how these technologies in turn structure the way its subscribers access and engage media. In this regard, the last three chapters in this section all address an underlining contradiction in the success of Netflix. As part of the broader commercial growth of the internet, start-ups like Netflix promised to use technology to create efficiencies in their business operations and to better serve consumers through enhanced choice, convenience, and customization. Much of Netflix's reputation developed around its ability to incorporate filtering software that contributed to both of these goals. That is to say, through its various recommendation and personalization systems, Netflix was able to understand and control its inventory—DVDs in its early period and now predominantly streaming video—in a more cost-effective way while celebrating its ability to empower viewers, enabling them to see more of what they want, whenever and wherever they want. Both Sarah Arnold and Neta Alexander challenge these simple accounts, arguing instead that the way Netflix tailors content to individual preferences in fact disempowers users. In Chapter 3, Arnold demonstrates that Netflix measures audience engagement in ways that render their behavior abstract, shifting control away from human agency in conjunction with a broader neoliberal ideology that seeks to replace uncertainty with depersonalized predictability.

Daniel Smith-Rowsey explores a similar incongruity in relation to Netflix's classification systems, particularly its use of genre, and posits that the service intentionally engenders instability within these systems as part of its shift away from its earlier Long Tail business model. Genre presents an especially interesting case here because it has nearly always existed at the intersection between media producers—the way studios, for instance, describe and market their films—and media users—the way audiences understand these texts. Similar to Arnold and Alexander, Smith-Rowsey shows that Netflix controls this process in a way that obscures its own criteria for genre classification while also limiting the ability of users to participate in ongoing debates about genre. At the same time, he argues that Netflix's classification system demonstrates how new distribution platforms are affecting the relationship between producers and consumers, and that this development provides an opportunity to update and expand the work of genre theorists within the field of film and media studies. Alexander ties together threads from Arnold and Smith-Rowsey as she focuses on Cinematch, Netflix's proprietary recommendation system that briefly garnered widespread attention as part of a 2006–9 open competition to improve the company's predictive algorithm. Alexander considers the degree to which very little is known about software applications like Cinematch and further argues that these technologies devalue taste as a form of cultural currency, relegating many viewers to an insular bubble that reifies existing preferences and encourages instant gratification. As a result, Netflix's recommendation systems increasingly cater to what viewers want—or are willing—to watch "right now" rather than as a means of guiding viewers to discover edifying or interesting materials that actually align with their individual preferences.

After launching its "Watch Instantly" option in 2007, Netflix began a period of significant transition. It wasn't that it became any less devoted to technology. In fact, quite the contrary, as Netflix shifted its focus to streaming—introducing a separate "streaming only" plan in 2010 which by the end of 2012 had surpassed its DVD-by-mail option in total number of subscribers—it necessarily became more concerned with technological issues like net neutrality. However, there was a major shift at this time in how Netflix as a business was perceived. It was no longer associated with mere video rental—a somewhat lowly and subsidiary retail business—but instead began to more fully establish itself as a distinct entertainment service. As part of this transition, its focus shifted from movies to licensing the rights to television programming—which by the end of 2011 accounted for approximately 60 percent of the content streamed by Netflix subscribers—and then to financing and producing its own original series. The second section, "Changing Entertainment," addresses this shift to television and original productions along with the ways that this type of content has prompted new forms of accelerated or intensified media consumption. These new forms of engagement mark something of an unexpected development. While Netflix has made on-demand a nominal reality, the result is not that viewers consume less entertainment in more discerning ways—watching *only* what they want when and where they want—but that this new platform has somehow triggered an insatiable appetite to consume more. In this regard, Netflix has become inextricably intertwined with the phenomenon known as binge-watching.

There is a great deal of speculation that Netflix used the data provided by its recommendation and personalization systems (and other access points) to inform its transition to television and the type of programming it invested in. This type of speculation dovetails with more general suspicions about Netflix and technology, suspicions that often encourage sweeping generalizations about the negative effects of binge-watching. Although the essays in this section certainly acknowledge the perils of this new phenomenon, they also indicate its complexity and ambiguity, underscoring the need for further analysis and debate. Casey J. McCormick, in the first chapter in this section, details the influence of binge-watching as both a thematic undercurrent and narrative structuring device in Netflix's original series, *House of Cards*. Through a combination of textual and narrative analysis of the series' first three seasons, McCormick identifies cues within the program that simultaneously guide and comment on the viewing experience. She goes on to argue that in heightening viewers' attention to these details shows like *House of Cards* mark a new type of engagement, one that is fundamentally different from earlier patterns associated with television or DVD viewing.

Zachary Snider, by contrast, takes a more critical approach to the phenomenon of binge-watching. He explores the topic from a cognitive psychology perspective and enumerates the detrimental effects of consuming television shows in rapid succession. More specifically, he argues that certain types of television programs require a high degree of psychological investment—as a matter of following complex plotlines and in identifying with ambivalent or unscrupulous characters—and that as this investment intensifies by virtue of binge-watching, this phenomenon has the power to create emotional confusion and to blur the line between fiction and reality. Despite foregrounding these dangers, Snider also makes his own binge-watching experience the primary example in his consideration, meaning that he is careful not to condemn this activity but instead draws attention to the need for further reflection on the social and psychological effects of new platforms like Netflix.

Whereas most discussions of binge-watching concern recent programming like Netflix's original series, Sheri Chinen Biesen considers it in relation to film noir. As an older genre, noir is more commonly associated with Netflix's Long Tail business model, with its ability to drive viewers to older, more specialized types of content that is cheaper to license and therefore a more cost-effective business strategy. Nonetheless, Biesen argues that the formation of film noir as a critical distinction was contingent on new modes of intensified spectatorship—ones that demanded acute attention to stylistic and narrative details across multiple narratives and cultural texts—and that these behaviors coalesce with the recent rise of binge-watching. She further notes that this may explain why some of the most popular contemporary serial dramas have incorporated noir elements into both their narrative configuration and visual aesthetics. While these connections promise to renew interest in film noir and to recreate the culture of connoisseurship that has long preserved it, Netflix also illustrates a more precarious mediascape in which older titles come and go with great frequency and on-demand undermines the effort required to seek out rare and hard-to-find titles.

This ambivalence is likewise evident in Sudeep Sharma's account of the relationship between Netflix and documentary filmmaking. Documentary represents another important specialty genre for Netflix—one that, again, has been primarily associated with its Long Tail strategy rather than binge-watching but that illustrates its need to have a diverse selection of content as part of a larger effort to maintain viewer engagement. In some ways, Netflix's commitment to documentary evokes the many promises of how technology and new VOD platforms would be a boon to independent filmmakers, helping to expand the range of available media while also engendering a better-informed and more democratic public sphere. As Sharma details, this type of rhetoric fails to grasp Netflix's fundamental premise as a commercial enterprise. By extension, he explains that as much as documentary filmmakers appreciate the emergence of new opportunities for distribution and exhibition, they remain cautious of Netflix's overall objectives. In this regard, it seems that Netflix treats documentary in the same way that it treats all content—not as a commitment to art or ideas but as a carefully calculated means of augmenting its overall business interests.

In the last chapter in this section, Brittany Farr analyzes *Orange Is the New Black*, the other original series that much like *House of Cards* has become emblematic of Netflix's successful foray into production. Farr continues the shift away from binge-watching per se but maintains this section's focus on the ways in which shifting conditions of production and reception influence contemporary television programming. In particular, she shows that the "edgy" overtones and multicultural cast in *Orange Is the New Black* are in fact part of a strategy devoted to risk aversion, an example of Netflix's use of data analysis to finance safe projects that promise a profitable return on its investment. Farr further investigates this logic in relation to *Orange's* focus on underrepresented minorities, mapping this in relation to the ideological uses of blackness in popular culture and the mass incarceration of African Americans as part of an evolving neoliberal security apparatus. This analysis, along with the other chapters in this section, demonstrates that while Netflix may have fostered new ways of producing and consuming entertainment, representations in this new era continue to demand critical attention with regard to the social and historical circumstances that underlie their production.

While the first two sections focus on Netflix's relationship to technology and entertainment, it should be clear that these relationships are simultaneously inflected with manifold economic interests. In the third section, "The Business of Media Convergence," these interests are explored in greater detail with an emphasis on the contradictions in Netflix's current success and the challenges it must face as part of its global expansion. In analyzing Netflix from a business perspective, many of the ambiguities that surfaced in earlier sections—for example, questions as to whether its technological innovations in fact empower audiences and the value of new forms of viewer engagement like binge-watching—are once again apparent. On the one hand, Netflix suggests a kind of corporate outlier, one that—by many counts, most especially its own—aims to buck the status quo. On the other hand, Netflix is in many ways a paragon of global capitalism in the twenty-first century. In the first chapter of this section, Cameron Lindsey explores this quandary by showing that Netflix's success may in fact help its competitors to reclaim the VOD market and that as the economic stakes increase, larger media conglomerates are likely to regain leverage. At the same time, Lindsey complicates matters by considering piracy as another looming threat. With the demise of physical media, streaming services such as Netflix have acclimated consumers to a more fluid and conspicuous marketplace, one in which expediency often takes priority over prudence. If more viewers are willing to navigate the increasingly porous boundaries between legal and extra-legal platforms, this could have serious repercussions for Netflix as well as its competitors.

The following two chapters similarly interrogate Netflix's current status, drawing attention to the ideological underpinnings associated with new media and the shifting business practices that are emerging across different media industries. In Gerald Sim's analysis, it is not only Netflix that warrants scrutiny, but the entire discursive framework that is perpetuated in the hollow business jargon so often repeated by media pundits and cultural critics alike. Moreover, as part of an argument that recalls Brittany Farr's critique of *Orange Is the New Black*, Sim links praise for Netflix and its signature programs with a broader tendency in new media scholarship to uncritically celebrate the illusory promise of individual freedom. For Sim, this intersection evokes the most pernicious features of what the Frankfurt School once labeled "the culture industry." Kevin McDonald, in the chapter that follows, addresses Netflix's transition from a DVD-by-mail service to one that describes itself as a global internet TV network. He situates this transition in relation to the changing value of home entertainment and to the growing importance of brand equity for services like Netflix. McDonald also provides an overview of the company's turn to international expansion and how this strategy may undermine its long-term success.

Aside from Netflix's shift to television and original programming, the most important development in its recent history has been its commitment to global expansion. In the last part of this section both Sam Ward and Christian Stiegler address this development and demonstrate the complexities of entering new international markets. In his chapter on Netflix's arrival in Britain, Ward elucidates the post-broadcast landscape there and how it is different from the United States. He shows that even though the British marketplace had matured prior to Netflix's arrival, the new service has nonetheless had considerable success. Ward attributes this to the way Netflix positioned itself as a complementary service rather than one designed to replace existing services. He goes on to detail how this approach is evident in the promotional materials of both Netflix and direct competitors like Sky. Christian Stiegler examines the introduction of Netflix in Germany by adopting an industrialization of culture model that emphasizes the interrelationship between mandates, cultural conditions, and existing technological practices. In doing so, he provides a valuable portrait of a non-Anglophone market as well as the challenges that Netflix faces in negotiating unfamiliar social traditions, tastes, and preferences. Like Ward, Stiegler identifies important variations within Netflix's business model as the company adapts to these different environments. These variations will become a more prominent factor as Netflix continues its international expansion, and as it comes to rely more and more on a global audience to maintain its growing subscriber base.

Looking forward today, it is easy to see a future in which Netflix, HBO, Comcast, and Google dominate media and entertainment. But it is just as easy to see a future in which Netflix, or any of these others, has completely disappeared, written out of history by some future, unforeseeable competitor that changes the course of how media and technology are understood. This is the challenge of writing a history of the present, a history of a company like Netflix that has fundamentally affected the present while remaining uncertain for the future. However, this much is clear: Netflix and its competitors will face new challenges as media, technology, and entertainment industries continue to evolve. The perspectives presented by the scholars throughout this collection are designed to understand these larger processes and to provide a foundation for developing further scholarship addressed to the complexities of hybrid endeavors like Netflix and the conflicting developments of the current field. In ten years, whether Netflix has become Blockbuster, America's most profitable studio/platform, or something in between, there will remain much to be gleaned from its steps and missteps as chronicled in this collection.

Part One

Technology, Innovation, and Control

1

Netflix and the Coalition for an Open Internet

Lyell Davies

Toward the end of 2013, subscribers to Netflix's video-on-demand (VOD) service noticed a slowing in the speed at which videos they selected to watch were delivered to their viewing devices. Netflix reported that subscribers who had previously been watching the company's streamed content at high-definition (HD) quality levels were now viewing it at resolutions close to Video Home System (VHS) quality, and charged that broadband internet service provider (ISP) Comcast was responsible for the declining video quality.[1] Netflix argued that by deliberately slowing the transfer of its content, Comcast was discriminating against Netflix by favoring the content, applications, or services offered to the public by other internet companies, as well as interfering with the choices made by internet users who had paid for broadband service with the expectation that they would to be able to access any content without discrimination.

Launched in 1997 as a DVD-by-mail service, today a majority of Netflix's users access the company's content via the internet, a shift that has positioned Netflix as one of the internet's most prominent "edge providers"—a term that denotes the companies or other entities that provide content, applications, or other online services over the internet.[2] To stream video to its subscribers, Netflix has built a content delivery network (CDN) comprised of a nationwide network of servers which interconnect to the networks operated by broadband ISPs, the latter being the "last mile" providers that deliver the internet to homes or businesses.[3] During peak periods, Netflix's servers are the source of about 30 percent of all the internet traffic delivered to U.S. residential customers.[4] But the company rejects that this heavy bandwidth use means that it should pay a toll to broadband ISPs to carry the content, since consumers who subscribe to broadband ISPs have paid for internet access and should be able to access whatever content they want, irrespective of its source.[5] Nonetheless, with its VOD service compromised, in February 2014 Netflix entered into a deal with Comcast where it agreed to pay for improved access to the broadband ISP's network. Within days of the deal, the quality of Netflix's video streaming returned to HD-quality levels.[6] Soon thereafter, Netflix made similar deals with other broadband ISPs. A new era seemed to have arrived for the internet: one where edge providers pay tolls to broadband ISPs in order to see their content delivered to users.

Most of the time, the general public does not give much thought to matters of media policy: the media we consume and the devices and services we use to access it are largely accepted off the shelf, and "most of us know little about the policies that structure the media surrounding us."[7] When not satisfied by the media content that is available to us, the speed of our internet connection, or the quality of our phone or cable TV service, we may complain to customer service representatives or shop around for a different service vendor, if one is available. But our day-to-day dissatisfaction with these matters does not typically lead to an examination of the media policies that govern the media landscape we inhabit. This is in part due to a common perception that media policy is too complex and technical for the general public to understand, and that it therefore belongs in the hands of government experts or corporate decision makers.[8] This thinking is reinforced by the way the mainstream news media consigns media policy issues to the business or technology folios. Another factor leading to public disengagement with media policy is the illusion of our own media power: while the multitude of devices available to us *seem* to create opportunities for us to participate directly in the media arena, we forget that "these platforms are owned and controlled by media and telecom corporations whose agenda focuses on profit and corporate interests rather than participation, empowerment, and social justice."[9] In light of these conditions, it is common for U.S. lawmakers to escape public scrutiny as they introduce policies that have far-reaching impact on the communications arena and society at large.

In 2014 and early 2015, there was a break in this trajectory. Public engagement spiked during this period and media policy became one of the most contentious and far-reaching issues of our time with questions about net neutrality and an open internet in particular prompting serious debate and political activism. The slowing of Netflix's video stream and the deals the company struck with broadband ISPs drew public attention to a policy issue that has been unfolding for more than a decade, as the Federal Communications Commission (FCC) has sought to develop rules to govern the internet. It is an issue that has engaged a diversity of constituencies. On the one hand, pressing for the strong net neutrality rules are the following: edge providers, large and small; civil society and media justice and reform organizations; and individual, concerned, internet-using members of the public. On the other side of the issue are broadband ISPs, with their extensive lobbying and public relations apparatuses and a practiced history of influencing lawmakers. Central to the issue is a theme that has been contested since the invention of electronic communications networks in the nineteenth century: should our society's communications infrastructure be the private domain of the business interests active in this arena, or is it a public sphere, servicing a public interest?

In this chapter, I discuss Netflix's role in the organizing efforts that took place in support of an open internet, noting that the California-based VOD company was an early lightning rod on the issue, drawing public and media attention to how moves were afoot that would dramatically alter the internet. I provide an outline of how Netflix participated in a loose, national coalition committed to ensuring that the internet is operated in such a way that all data traffic is delivered to users with equal priority. While describing the activities of this coalition, I ultimately argue that communications policy must not be set to meet the needs, present or future, of Netflix or other powerful edge providers. The internet is the preeminent communications platform of our age; therefore, the rules that govern its operation must ensure that it serves the public interest above all else.

Net neutrality and an open internet

Internet legal scholar Tim Wu coined the term "net neutrality" to describe a state where all data traffic carried by broadband ISPs on their networks is treated equally.[10] Thanks to the efforts of public interest advocates, internet developers, scholars, and concerned members of the public, the basic principle of net neutrality is broadly embraced in U.S. society and there is the tacit expectation that all internet traffic will be treated neutrally.[11] Net neutrality is a prerequisite for an open internet, defined by the FCC as conditions where "consumers can go where they want, when they want… innovators can develop products and services without asking for permission… and broadband providers cannot block, throttle, or create special 'fast lanes' for that content."[12] However, broadband ISPs have not universally been required to uphold net neutrality on their networks, and they have not always done so.[13]

The arguments presented in favor of an open internet are numerous. They include those that stress the role of the internet in fostering technological and product innovation, catalyzing economic growth, strengthening democratic processes, and advancing social justice. Integral to these arguments is a belief that the dynamism of the internet resides in two constituent spheres. On the one hand, it rests with the edge providers that generate the heterogeneous array of content, services, or applications that are available through the internet. On the other hand, it rests with the internet's users, who freely exercise their choice as they select from the offerings presented to them by edge providers. Describing the power vested in the hands of internet users, developer Vinton Cerf argues, "[w]ith the Internet, decisions were made to allow the control and intelligence functions to reside largely with users at the 'edges' of the network… This is precisely the opposite of the traditional telephony and cable networks."[14] Advocates for an open internet argue that without net neutrality, control of the internet shifts from edge providers and users into the hands of broadband ISPs, who could operate as content-gatekeepers, demanding pay-to-play tolls from edge providers, and thereby determining what information or services users can access. In this scenario, the internet could start "to look like cable TV" with a handful of massive companies "deciding what you get to see and how much it costs."[15] Pressing for an open internet, Netflix's CEO Reed Hastings argues that the "essence of net neutrality" is that users' choices, not decisions by corporate gatekeepers, determine what flourishes on the internet.[16]

Others who argue for the introduction of strong net neutrality rules stress the role of open communication to the well-being of democracy. Thus, the citizen advocacy organization Common Cause argues that an open internet is needed, since "voters inform themselves online, advocates organize themselves online, and citizens debate issues online."[17] Taking a stance that highlights the connections between internet access and social justice, the United Church of Christ (UCC)—an organization with a history of grassroots organizing on media policy issues stretching back to the civil rights era—proffers ten reasons why net neutrality is important. These range from UCC's everyday operational needs (faith-based organizations need an affordable means to reach their constituents), to concern that without net neutrality the digital divide will deepen, ending the internet's role as an "equalizer" that provides "a space for voices that have historically been relegated to the sidelines, like people of color and the LGBT community."[18] There are many precedents for instituting polices that guarantee an open internet: Wu argues that net neutrality "is no different than ... promoting fair evolutionary competition in any privately owned environment, whether a telephone network, operating system, or even a retail store."[19]

While Netflix and its CEO Hastings are vocal on the importance of strong net neutrality rules, some commentators question whether Netflix's dispute with Comcast is really a matter of net neutrality. The slowing of Netflix's content did not occur once it was in transit on a broadband ISP's network. Instead, it occurred at the point of "interconnection" where it enters Comcast's network. Thus, some commentators argued that it is erroneous to depict Comcast's demand for an interconnection fee as an end to net neutrality. Instead, interconnection fees should be seen as one among the many financial transactions that occur between the various providers as they bring content to users.[20] The internet is composed of numerous autonomously operated networks: interconnecting with the last mile broadband ISPs are CDNs and long-distance internet transit providers, which operate in concert through settlement-free "peering" agreements or fee-based transit agreements. These agreements are not typically thought to pose a threat to net neutrality. The difference between paying for an improved connection to a broadband ISP's network at an interconnection point as Netflix did, and paying for preferential treatment once on that network, is significant both legally and in principle. It is a difference noted by Hastings when he stressed that Netflix was not paying "for priority access against competitors, just for interconnection."[21] But while there are differences between interconnection fees and the creation of fast and slow lanes on a broadband ISP's network, Netflix argued that the practical outcome would be the same. Thus, Hastings proposed that rules are needed to ensure that at the point of interconnection, broadband ISPs "provide sufficient access to their network without charge," thereby supporting the needs of "services like Netflix, YouTube, or Skype" as well as those of internet transit providers and CDNs such as "Cogent, Akamai or Level 3."[22]

All media companies face the challenge of distributing their content to users. For Netflix today, distribution means access to broadband networks, and from the outset a potential Achilles' heel of the company's business model is that without an open internet there "is no guaranteed level playing field for reaching an audience of cable high-speed-data subscribers."[23] The relationship between Netflix and broadband ISPs is complex: web surfing, sending emails, and similar online activities constitute only a trickle of all internet data traffic. In contrast, VOD services use considerable bandwidth. It is the public's demand for access to bandwidth-heavy "long-form, professional online video ... half-hour- or hour-long shows with continuing narratives and high production values" of the kind offered by Netflix, that has fueled demand for high-speed broadband internet services.[24] Thus, with some authority, Netflix can argue that its VOD service has created demand for the high-speed services offered by Comcast and the other broadband ISPs.[25] Conversely, while Netflix may be generating demand for Comcast's broadband services, the company's VOD offerings compete with Comcast's cable TV offerings. For broadband ISPs facing the possibility that their cable TV revenues could wither in the face of competition from VOD services, a way to increase revenue and moderate the impact of a competitor's services could be to put in place interconnection or a pay-to-play fees. Meanwhile, for Netflix, interconnection fees or even pay-to-play fees, if they were introduced, are unlikely to pose a major threat since the company is in a position to pass any increase in its operating expenses on to subscribers by raising subscription fees. Thus, the edge providers most likely to be hurt by an end to net neutrality are start-up companies offering previously unknown products, those serving highly specialized constituencies, or operating as low- or non-profit entities. Hastings acknowledges that Netflix can afford to pay interconnection fees, but he notes, "imagine the plight of smaller services today and in the future."[26]

From the perspective of broadband ISPs, the benefit of operating without net neutrality is simple. It allows them to favor their own content or applications, or to introduce a tiered pay-to-play system where edge providers must pay in order to see their content reach users. Opponents of net neutrality rules argue that broadband ISPs own the internet's physical infrastructure and should be allowed to charge for its use as they see fit. In addition, adherents to this way of thinking argue that future innovation and improvement of internet services will most effectively occur if broadband ISPs have a free hand in how they operate their networks. If individual ISPs do a poor job in providing services, so this argument goes, their failings will be corrected by marketplace competition. Critics of these arguments counter that in many regions individual broadband ISPs operate as a monopoly, with no competition to press them to deliver quality service, reasonable pricing, or the content users seek.[27] Others opposed to the introduction of net neutrality rules argue that it de facto already exists, since broadband ISPs have typically treated all internet traffic equally. Taking this position, FCC commissioner Ajit Pai argues that the present system works, and therefore "[n]et neutrality has always been a solution in search of a problem."[28]

The FCC

In the beginning years of the twenty-first century, several laws designed to strengthen net neutrality rules were proposed in Washington, but all died in committee or on the floor of Congress. Still seeking to put strong net neutrality rules in place, in December 2010 the FCC, under Chairman Julius Genachowski, released the Open Internet

Order.[29] This stated that broadband ISPs must not block or unreasonably discriminate against lawful internet traffic, and must put in place transparent network management practices so that their adherence to these rules can be monitored. The FCC's rules faced rapid opposition from broadband ISPs, and in a case brought by Verizon, the U.S. Court of Appeals for the D.C. Circuit ruled in January 2014 that the FCC had overreached its authority.[30] The court determined that under the existing FCC rules, since broadband ISPs are "information service" providers governed by Title I of the Telecommunications Act of 1996, the FCC is not permitted to stipulate the nature of the content carried by them.[31] However, the court also determined that the FCC does possess regulatory authority over the internet, and could reclassify broadband ISPs under Title II of the Telecommunications Act. So reclassified, broadband ISPs would be a "common carrier" utility service, and be required to treat all data equally—just as telephone companies must treat all phone calls equally.[32]

Following the court's ruling, advocates for an open internet charged that the FCC had seriously erred in the method it had used in its effort to enforce net neutrality: Craig Aaron, president of the media reform organization Free Press, called the commission's 2010 order a "grave mistake" that failed "to ground its Open Internet rules on solid legal footing."[33] The five FCC commissioners were divided in their response to the court's ruling, with liberal commissioners Jessica Rosenworcel and Mignon Clyburn expressing support for further efforts to put strong net neutrality rules in place, and conservative commissioners Pai and Mike O'Rielly stating that the FCC should take no further action on the issue.[34]

In April 2014, FCC chairman Tom Wheeler released a revised net neutrality proposal using as its framework Section 706 of the Telecommunications Act of 1996.[35] This proposal would require broadband ISPs to provide a basic level of unfettered internet service, while also allowing the creation of a tiered system where major edge providers could pay to see their content favored. In response to the announcement the *New York Times* reported, "[t]he principle that all Internet content should be treated equally as it flows through cables and pipes to consumers looks all but dead."[36] In May, the FCC voted to move forward considering two options: Wheeler's proposal and reclassification under Title II. This decision opened a 60-day period for the filing of public comments on the two proposals, followed by a second period for rebuttal comments.[37]

Opposition to Wheeler's proposal was immediate. Wu reports, "[i]f the Internet can be said to have a street, it erupted—with tens of thousands of angry e-mails, phone calls, Reddit rants … investigations by young reporters at Vice and The Verge, and the Internet's forte, amusing online videos."[38] More than a hundred internet companies wrote to the FCC expressing dissatisfaction with the proposal, "from smaller tech firms like Etsy and Tumblr up to older authorities like Google, Microsoft, and eBay."[39] In comments submitted by Netflix, the company pressed the FCC to reclassify broadband ISPs under Title II, arguing that "section 706 authority by itself is a recipe for 'weak tea' that is likely to prove both legally unsatisfying to the courts and substantively unsatisfying to Internet users."[40] The company also pressed the FCC to create strong rules "not only on the last mile, but also at the point of interconnection to the last mile."[41] If the latter did not occur, Hastings proposed, "[i]t would be better to have no rules than the ones being proposed."[42]

While reclassification of the internet as a Title II utility has long been the goal of public interest–minded media reformers, Netflix's decision to press the FCC to reclassify broadband ISPs illustrates a significant shift in thinking about government regulation on the part of a Silicon Valley edge provider. Early in 2014, Hastings indicated that he would like to avoid government regulation of the internet if broadband ISPs would agree to net neutrality in their terms of service. Although, he also conceded, "[w]e don't have anything close to that level of agreement."[43] Silicon Valley's high-tech media companies have commonly opposed government regulation of the internet, arguing that it functions better with a minimum of regulatory oversight. Drawing on a vague anti-establishment ethos, these companies have cultivated the image that their way of doing business offers an alternative to the lumbering ways of government bureaucracies and nefarious, corporate big business. It's an image that does not fit well with calls for assertive government regulation of the internet. As if to illustrate Netflix's reluctance to be seen to call on the government for internet regulation, in an article published in the tech magazine *Wired* after Netflix submitted its comments to the FCC, Hastings depicts Netflix as a company doing battle with "big ISPs."[44] He lambasts AT&T, Comcast, and Verizon's demand that Netflix pay interconnection fees, as well as Comcast's moves to purchase Time Warner Cable, but no mention is made of Netflix pressing the FCC for regulation of the internet under Title II.[45]

A coalition for an open internet

Battles over media policy are not new to U.S. life: antecedents for the present-day struggle for net neutrality can be found in nineteenth-century calls for regulation of the telegraph;[46] the radio broadcast reform movement of the 1920s and 1930s;[47] and challenges to media ownership and mainstream media representation of minorities during the 1960s.[48] Since the turn of the millennium, sustained advocacy efforts have been launched in support of strong net neutrality rules and other internet freedoms. These include, by 2006, widespread support for the Free Press' Save The Internet campaign,[49] as well as more recent broad-based opposition to the passing of the stifling copyright infringement laws, Stop Online Piracy Act (SOPA) and Protect IP Act (PIPA). Responding to what seemed the impending end to net neutrality, in Spring 2014 a loose coalition of edge providers and organizations came together to press the FCC to introduce strong net neutrality rules. These included, in addition to Netflix, leading edge providers such as Kickstarter, Meetup, Reddit, Tumblr, Etsy, and Vimeo; civil society organizations including Common Cause, Consumers Union, and Demand Progress; and media justice and reform organizations including the Center for Media Justice (CMJ), Free Press, Public Knowledge, Fight for the Future, The National Hispanic Media Coalition, and the UCC.

With regard to the edge providers involved, the campaign is illustrative of a struggle for marketplace hegemony between new internet-based companies and long-established communications industry companies (the cable TV and telephone companies now turned broadband ISPs). These two industries pressed their agendas in different ways: the broadband ISPs accelerated their lobbying and public relations activities in an effort to sway lawmakers, while internet edge providers placed significant emphasis on appealing directly to their users for support. Liba Rubenstein, director of social impact and public policy at the social media company Tumblr, stated that "[w]e don't have an army of lobbyists to deploy. We don't have financial resources to throw around," but "[w]hat we do have is access to an incredibly engaged, incredibly passionate user base, and we can give folks the tools to respond."[50] Rubenstein's comments illustrate a repeated motif of the edge providers' campaign; that their interests and the public's interest are synergistic. Taking a similar position, Etsy's global policy director Althea Erickson argues that the internet companies involved in the coalition were acting as "community organizers," and that at Etsy "we see ourselves as activists for our seller community."[51] At face value, these arguments suggest the presence of a corporate–public partnership on media policy issues, and the possibility of synergist political campaign work by these two constituencies. But this is a notion that needs further scrutiny, to explore whether an alliance of this kind can meaningfully serve the public interest over the long term; particularly since some of the large edge providers are moving to become political powerbrokers in their own right. For instance, in an effort to influence lawmakers, Netflix employs "the services of nearly two-dozen registered lobbyists, including in-house advocates and those from three lobbying firms."[52]

Others in the coalition pressed for net neutrality rules using their ability to mobilize grassroots constituents for publicity-gathering protests or rallies. In early December 2014, Free Press positioned a large video screen across the street from a location where Chairman Wheeler was being honored by telecommunications industry lawyers and lobbyists. The videos presented on the screen included, "homemade YouTube videos, images from Net neutrality rallies and testimonials from public hearings that the FCC chairman and his fellow commissioners declined to attend."[53] In another instance, the group Fight for the Future acquired the direct telephone numbers of about thirty FCC officials. A torrent of more than 55,000 phone calls followed, until the group turned off the protest.[54] Nor were the politically savvy media justice and reform groups limited to staging protests: in November 2014, a delegation of representatives from CMJ's Media Action Grassroots Network (MAG-Net), Color of Change, Presente.org, Free Press, and others met with Commissioner Clyburn to deliver a letter signed by more than ninety racial justice and civil rights organizations in support of an open internet.[55]

Public awareness of the unfolding battle around net neutrality was increased in other ways, such as by the "fake" television news shows that now compete with conventional news programming to shape national political agendas.[56] During a thirteen-minute segment airing on the Home Box Office show "Last Week Tonight," host and satirist John Oliver ridiculed Chairman Wheeler and the broadband ISPs, while calling on viewers to submit comments to the FCC in support of net neutrality. The show generated more than 45,000 comments in support of reclassification,[57] overwhelming the FCC's electronic comments filing system leading to its temporary shutdown.[58] Describing how the varied constituents that made up the coalition worked together, Free Press' Aaron argues that "people forgot how to play their own roles," and were willing to embrace each other's agendas and strategies.[59] He recalls, coalition partners would think, "some people are really good at creative online organizing, let's have them do that… Some people are really good lawyers, let the lawyers do that, and their was enough trust that it survived."[60]

Shared ideals?

For commercial edge providers like Netflix, an open internet is important to the operation of their business model, but a feature of how many of these companies framed the net neutrality issue is that they claimed that larger, non-commercial principles underlie their thinking. For instance, Hastings argues, "[t]he Internet is improving lives everywhere—democratizing access to ideas, services and goods. To ensure the Internet remains humanity's most important platform for progress, net neutrality must be defended and strengthened."[61] The zeal of this statement illustrates that for Hastings and other similarly minded internet entrepreneurs, "idealistic and moralistic claims" regarding the structure and operation of the internet are present in their thinking.[62] To borrow a term used in the study of social movements, if groups or individuals are to work together, they must adopt a "collective action frame" encompassing a shared diagnosis that there is a problem that needs to be addressed, a prognosis of how to do this, and the motivation needed to take action.[63] By framing the issue in idealist terms, edge providers found common ground with the coalition's civil society- and social justice–driven participants. Thus, Hastings' comments dovetail, at least superficially, with the democracy-centered policy agenda of media justice and reform organizations such as Free Press or CMJ—the latter of which argues that an open internet is a civil rights issue, since the internet offers low income and minority communities a "powerful vehicle" through which to have a "political voice."[64]

But while the idealistic statements of commercial edge providers provide some common ground for the open internet coalition partners, they should be treated with caution. As Wu argues, for Silicon Valley edge providers "the argument for network neutrality must be understood as a concrete expression of a system of belief about innovation"; what he calls an "evolutionary model" of thinking where "adherents view the innovation process as a survival-of-the-fittest competition among developers of new technologies."[65] Under close examination, this way of thinking has little in common with the public interest or social justice-advancement arguments put forward by civil society organizations. Nonetheless, the practical necessity of pressing for an open internet brought together strange allies, trumping an exploration of ideological differences among those involved. CMJ's Steven Renderos acknowledges that the various entities participating in the campaign were motivated differently, but argues that from the point of view of his organization "working with unlikely allies is just part of what we do … there are going to be times in which our messaging and our strategy diverges, and at those points we have to be OK with disagreeing."[66]

The FCC rules

As the end of the period for public comments to the FCC drew near in mid-September, under the banner "Battle for the Net," the coalition called for an "Internet Slowdown" day. Organized primarily by Free Press, Fight for the Future, Demand Progress, and Engine Advocacy, for the day of protest edge providers were asked to add a rotating "download loading" icon called the "spinning wheel of death" to their websites, to symbolize the slowed access consumers could experience if edge providers do not pay for priority status. Nearly 10,000 websites participated in the protest.[67] On Netflix's website, the protest's rotating icon was accompanied by the words, "[p]rotect Internet freedom. Defend Net neutrality." Visitors to the site could click on a "take action" link that led them to a website operated by Battle for the Net. Here, Comcast, Verizon, Time Warner Cable, and AT&T were targeted for "attacking the Internet … with plans to charge websites arbitrary fees and slow (to a crawl) any sites that won't pay up. If they win, the Internet dies."[68] The site states that the only option to prevent broadband ISPs from "breaking the key principles of the Internet we love" is Title II reclassification.[69]

When the period for public comments closed, the FCC reported that nearly four million submissions had been received on the open internet docket, with 2.5 million more submitted during the reply period, the most ever submitted on a single issue.[70] Commissioner Clyburn stated, "[t]hese numbers speak volumes of the tremendous impact the Internet has on our society."[71] She also indicated that she sought to extend the framework of the FCC's consideration of net neutrality to include mobile devices. On November 10, President Barack Obama released a statement indicating, "the FCC should reclassify consumer broadband service under Title II of the Telecommunications Act."[72] Then, in a reversal that could not confidently have been anticipated a year earlier, in January 2015 Wheeler signaled that he intended to introduce "bright line" rules to protect net neutrality, reclassifying broadband ISPs under Title II.[73]

On February 26, the FCC adopted open internet rules that redefine broadband ISPs as "telecommunication service" rather than as "information service" providers, placing them under Title II of the Communications Act. The rules state,

> [a]ny person engaged in the provision of broadband Internet access service … shall not unreasonably interfere with or unreasonably disadvantage (i) end users' ability to select, access, and use broadband Internet access service or the lawful Internet content, applications, services, or devices of their choice, or (ii) edge providers' ability to make lawful content, applications, services, or devices available to end users. Reasonable network management shall not be considered a violation of this rule.[74]

In a second major shift, the FCC included mobile devices, as well as fixed-wire broadband services, in the ruling. The *New York Times* called the FCC's move on title reclassification, "perhaps the biggest policy shift since the Internet became a reality."[75] Free Press' Aaron noted the massive turnaround that had occurred, writing "[e]ven a few months ago this victory didn't seem possible… It's an incredible turnaround that wouldn't have happened without every single phone call, email, rally, Facebook post, tweet, meeting with Congress and everything else activists have been part of in the fight to save the Internet."[76] In a brief press release Netflix stated, "[t]he net neutrality debate is about who picks winners and losers online: Internet service providers or consumers. Today, the FCC settled it: Consumers win."[77] On interconnection, the FCC's ruling was less decisive. The FCC asserted that it has authority to regulate interconnection, but states, "this Order does not apply the open Internet rules to interconnection."[78] The commission proffered that it intends to be attentive to the interconnection issue. However, it was also reluctant because of the changing nature of internet traffic due to growing VOD usage and the "degradation resulting from commercial disagreements, perhaps most notably in a series of disputes between Netflix and large last-mile broadband providers."[79] For the time being, "we find that the best approach is to watch, learn, and act as required, but not intervene now, especially not with prescriptive rules."[80]

Conclusion

In early 2014, there were indications that net neutrality was soon to become a thing of the past. After a year of advocacy efforts by media justice and reform organizations, civil society organizations, edge providers, and members of the general public, a different future for the internet seems possible. The effort brought together diverse constituents, with "groups using their own creative strength and reaching out to their own constituents around this goal of convincing the FCC to reclassify Internet access providers."[81] The involvement of high-profile edge providers played an important role in bringing the public's attention to the issue, but it would be a mistake to believe, as one reporter in the *New York Times* proposes, that the pressure on the FCC was "driven by Internet companies… Netflix, Twitter, Mozilla and Etsy."[82] More accurately, a broad coalition was active on the issue. Stressing the role grassroots efforts played in the campaign, David Segal of Demand Progress argues, "[o]nce it became clear that the grassroots were demanding Title II and the strongest rules possible, politicians and companies started sticking their necks out and helped propel Americans forward."[83] With regard to the media policy the coalition pressed for, it is noteworthy that media justice and reform organizations have long proposed that the most secure way to ensure the existence of an open internet is the classification of broadband ISPs under Title II. Edge providers like Netflix came to this conclusion only reluctantly. Indeed, in March 2015, Netflix's CFO stated that the company would have preferred "a non-regulated solution."[84] While some of the leading edge providers that participated in the coalition are far better known to the public than the media justice, media reform, or other civil society organizations that participated in the effort, it is the latter that provided the campaign's ideological thrust and most cogently articulated its most elemental principle—a belief that an open internet is essential to the existence of a just and democratic society.

As of 2015, the struggle for an open internet is not over: media policy is constantly renegotiated and "always in flux to varying degrees."[85] Illustrating the ongoing nature of the open internet issue, within weeks of the FCC's ruling, a flurry of moves were made in Washington to prevent the new rules from taking effect.[86] Time will tell if the broadband ISPs, by tapping their ability to influence lawmakers and an overarching hegemony of neoliberal economic thought, are able to stymie moves for an open internet. As Crawford hazards, even regulators who press for policies friendly to the public interest are often "outmaneuvered" by corporate agendas.[87] Nonetheless, the campaign work that was carried out in 2014–15 for an open internet is illustrative of how effective, broad-based organizing efforts by an array of motivated constituents *can* prevail over entrenched, communications industry interests. What does the FCC's ruling mean for Netflix? Reclassifying the internet as a utility under Title II establishes that edge providers like Netflix will not see their content blocked or throttled once it enters a network operated by a broadband ISP. For Netflix, this is a victory. The matter of interconnection fees is less clearly resolved: for the time being, the FCC states that it intends to be attentive to what is happening at the point of interconnection, perhaps introducing rules later based on the trends they observe. Early in 2014, Netflix's interconnection payments to broadband ISPs drew public and media attention to the net neutrality issue, and as a campaign for an open internet unfolded, the company was among the many players that pressed for strong net neutrality rules. When the FCC ruled on the issue, Netflix was among the winners.

Notes

1 See Markham C. Erickson et al., "Comments of Netflix, Inc.," prepared for the Federal Communications Commission, July 16, 2014. http://blog.netflix.com/2014/07/netflix-submits-fcc-comments-on.html (accessed September 17, 2014), 13.

2 Companies such as Amazon.com, Facebook, Google, or YouTube are among the most prominent edge providers, but the term also applies to the tens of thousands of other operations, large or small, that provide content for the internet. The FCC states, the term "edge provider" is used because operations such as these "generally operate at the edge rather than the core of the network"—the latter being the domain of ISPs, transit providers, and related entities (2010).

3 The "last mile" is an industry term referring to the cable or wireless network operated by broadband ISPs to deliver connectivity to subscribers.

4 Erickson et al., "Comments of Netflix, Inc.," 16.

5 See Reed Hastings, "Internet Tolls and the Case for Strong Net Neutrality," *Netflix US & Canada Blog*, March 20, 2014. http://blog.netflix.com/2014/03/internet-tolls-and-case-for-strong-net.html (accessed August 26, 2014).

6 See Glenn Peoples, "Netflix-Comcast Battle Shows Net Neutrality Has Real Consequences," *Billboard*, August 29, 2014. http://www.billboard.com/articles/business/6236490/netflix-comcast-battle-net-neutrality-consequences (accessed September 1, 2014).
7 Victor Pickard, *America's Battle for Media Democracy: The Triumph of Corporate Libertarianism and the Future of Media Reform* (New York: Cambridge University Press, 2015), 1.
8 See Stefania Milan, *Social Movements and Their Technologies: Wiring Social Change* (New York: Palgrave Macmillan, 2013), 4.
9 Ibid., 1.
10 See Tim Wu, "Network Neutrality, Broadband Discrimination," *Journal of Telecommunications and High Technology Law* 2 (2003): 141–179. http://ssrn.com/abstract=388863 or http://dx.doi.org/10.2139/ssrn.388863 (accessed September 1, 2014).
11 The "common carrier" principle has been applied to a variety of industries including telephony, railroads, and shipping.
12 See "Open Internet," FCC, n.d. http://www.fcc.gov/openinternet (accessed April 23, 2015).
13 See Peter Svensson, "Comcast Blocks Some Internet Traffic," *Washington Post*, October 19, 2007. http://www.washingtonpost.com/wp-dyn/content/article/2007/10/19/AR2007101900842.html (accessed August 23, 2014).
14 Vinton Cerf, "Prepared Statement of Vinton G. Cerf, Vice President and Chief Internet Evangelist, Google Inc.," prepared for U.S. Senate Committee on Commerce, Science, and Transportation Hearing on "Network Neutrality," February 7, 2006. http://www.commerce.senate.gov/pdf/cerf-020706.pdf (accessed August 23, 2014).
15 Lawrence Lessig and Robert W. McChesney, "No Tolls on the Internet," *Washington Post*, June 8, 2006. http://www.washingtonpost.com/wp-dyn/content/article/2006/06/07/AR2006060702108.html (accessed September 4, 2014).
16 Hastings, "Internet Tolls."
17 "Preserving the Internet," *Common Cause* (website), n.d. http://www.commoncause.org/issues/media-and-democracy/preserving-the-internet/ (accessed April 23, 2015).
18 Kimberly Knight, "10 Reasons Net Neutrality Matters to Progressive Christians," United Church of Christ: UCC Media Justice Update, January 17, 2014. http://www.uccmediajustice.org/o/6587/p/salsa/web/blog/public/?blog_entry_KEY=7124 (accessed August 21, 2014).
19 Wu, "Network Neutrality, Broadband Discrimination," 142.
20 See Kevin Werbach and Phil Weiser, "The Perfect and the Good on Network Neutrality," *Huffington Post*, April 27, 2014. http://www.huffingtonpost.com/kevin-werbach/network-neutrality_b_5221780.html (accessed August 23, 2014).
21 Hastings, "Internet Tolls."
22 Ibid.
23 Susan Crawford, *Captive Audience: The Telecom Industry and Monopoly Power in the New Gilded Age* (New Haven, CT: Yale University Press, 2013), 121.
24 Ibid., 110.
25 See Hastings, "Internet Tolls."
26 Ibid.
27 Cerf, "Prepared Statement of Vinton G. Cerf."

28 "Statement of Commissioner Ajit Pai on FCC Internet Regulation," FCC Press Release, February 19, 2014. http://www.fcc.gov/document/commissioner-pai-statement-fcc-internet-regulation (accessed December 22, 2014). See also footnote 13 for a notable example of how this is not always the case.
29 "Report and Order: In the Matter of Preserving the Open Internet," prepared for the Federal Communications Commission, December 23, 2010. https://apps.fcc.gov/edocs_public/attachmatch/FCC-10-201A1_Rcd.pdf (accessed September 17, 2014).
30 Verizon Communications Inc. *v.* Federal Communications Commission (2014).
31 The Communications Act of 1934 as amended consists of seven sections or "titles," each governing a feature of the U.S. communications arena.
32 The Telecommunications Act of 1996 made a distinction between "telecommunications service," to indicate offering phone or similar services to the public for a fee and falling under Title II common carrier rules, and "information service," indicating offering services with the capability for generating, acquiring, storing, transforming, processing, retrieving, utilizing, or making available information via telecommunications (FCC 1996).
33 Quoted in Adi Robertson, "Federal Court Strikes Down FCC Net Neutrality Rules," *The Verge*, January 14, 2014. http://www.theverge.com/2014/1/14/5307650/federal-court-strikes-down-net-neutrality-rules (accessed September 6, 2014).
34 See "Statement of Commissioner Ajit Pai on D.C. Circuit's Decisions Striking Down Net Neutrality Rules," FCC, January 14, 2014. http://www.fcc.gov/document/commissioner-pais-statement-dc-circuits-net-neutrality-decision (accessed December 22, 2014); "Statement of Commissioner Mike O'Rielly on the D.C. Circuit's Decision Striking Down Net Neutrality Rules," FCC, January 14, 2014. http://www.fcc.gov/document/commissioner-oriellys-statement-net-neutrality-decision (accessed December 22, 2014); "Statement of FCC Commissioner Jessica Rosenworcel on Open Internet Announcement," FCC, February 19, 2014. https://apps.fcc.gov/edocs_public/attachmatch/DOC-325673A1.doc (accessed December 22, 2014); and "Statement of Commissioner Mignon L. Clyburn on Open Internet Announcement," FCC, February 19, 2014. http://www.fcc.gov/document/stmt-commissioner-mignon-l-clyburn-open-internet-announcement (accessed December 22, 2014).
35 Section 706 addresses preventing a digital divide in broadband access. The act directs the FCC to "take immediate action to accelerate deployment" of broadband services if it is not "being deployed to all Americans in a reasonable and timely fashion." See "The Telecommunications Act of 1996," FCC. http://transition.fcc.gov/Reports/tcom1996.txt (accessed April 5, 2015).
36 Edward Wyatt, "F.C.C., in a Shift, Backs Fast Lanes for Web Traffic," *New York Times*, April 23, 2014. http://www.nytimes.com/2014/04/24/technology/fcc-new-net-neutrality-rules.html (accessed August 23, 2014).
37 See "FCC Launches Broad Rulemaking On How Best to Protect and Promote the Open Internet," FCC, May 15, 2014. http://www.fcc.gov/document/fcc-launches-broad-rulemaking-protect-and-promote-open-internet (accessed December 29, 2014).
38 Tim Wu, "The Solution to the F.C.C.'s Net-Neutrality Problems," *The New Yorker*, May 9, 2014. http://www.newyorker.com/tech/elements/the-solution-to-the-f-c-c-s-net-neutrality-problems (accessed February 26, 2015).

39 Ibid.

40 Erickson et al., "Comments of Netflix, Inc.," 21.

41 Ibid., ii.

42 Reed Hastings, "How to Save the Net: Don't Give In to Big ISPs," *Wired*, August 19, 2014. http://www.wired.com/2014/08/save-the-net-reed-hastings/ (accessed December 10, 2014).

43 Quoted in Dawn Chmielewski, "Netflix CEO Reed Hastings Talks Net Neutrality," *Re/code*, May 29, 2014. http://recode.net/2014/05/29/netflix-ceo-reed-hastings-talks-net-neutrality-liveblog/ (accessed August 26, 2014).

44 Hastings, "How to Save the Net."

45 Ibid.

46 See Menahem Blondheim, "Rehearsal for Media Regulation: Congress Versus the Telegraph-News Monopoly, 1866–1900," *Federal Communications Law Journal* 56.2, Article 3. http://www.repository.law.indiana.edu/fclj/vol56/iss2/3 (accessed August 4, 2014): 299–327.

47 See Robert W. McChesney, *Telecommunications, Mass Media, & Democracy: The Battle for the Control of U.S. Broadcasting, 1928–1935* (New York: Oxford University Press, 1993).

48 See Patricia Aufderheide, *Communications Policy and the Public Interest: The Telecommunications Act of 1996* (New York: The Guildford Press, 1996).

49 See Lessig and McChesney, "No Tolls on the Internet."

50 Quoted in Jonathan Weisman, "F.C.C. Net Neutrality Rules Clear Hurdle as Republicans Concede to Obama," *New York Times*, February 24, 2015. http://www.nytimes.com/2015/02/25/technology/path-clears-for-net-neutrality-ahead-of-fcc-vote.html (accessed December 22, 2014).

51 Althea Erickson, "How the Net (Neutrality Battle) Was Won," *Personal Democracy Forum*, June 4–5, 2015, Panel Discussion.

52 Dave Levinthal, "Netflix Forms PAC," *Politico*, April 7, 2012. http://www.politico.com/news/stories/0412/74929.html (accessed December 29, 2014).These lobbying efforts are primarily designed to influence laws regarding copyright, telecommunications, consumer protection, tax policy, and the internet. See also Erica Chang, "Netflix's New Political Actions Committee: FLIXPAC," *International Business Times*, April 9, 2012. http://www.ibtimes.com/netflixs-new-political-actions-committee-flixpac-435204 (accessed December 29, 2014).

53 "Free Press Parks Pro-Net Neutrality Jumbotron Outside Gala for the FCC Chairman," *Free Press*, December 4, 2014. http://www.freepress.net/press-release/106678/free-press-parks-pro-net-neutrality-jumbotron-outside-gala-fcc-chairman (accessed December 22, 2014).

54 See Weisman, "F.C.C. Net Neutrality Rules Clear Hurdle as Republicans Concede to Obama."

55 Steven Renderos, "FCC, Deliver the Internet We Deserve," Media Action Grassroots Network, November 21, 2014. http://mag-net.org/2014/11/fcc-deliver-internet-deserve/ (accessed December 2, 2014).

56 See Zoe M. Oxley, "More Sources, Better Informed Public? New Media and Political Knowledge," in *iPolitics: Citizens, Elections, and Governing in the New Media Era*, eds Richard L. Fox and Jennifer M. Ramos (Cambridge: Cambridge University Press, 2011), 25–47.

57 Lee Fang, "Net Neutrality Is Here—Thanks to an Unprecedented Guerrilla Activism Campaign," *The Intercept*, February 26, 2015. https://firstlook.org/theintercept/2015/02/26/net-neutrality-thanks-unprecedented-guerrilla-activism-campaign/ (accessed February 28, 2015).

58 See Joan E. Solsman, "John Oliver's Net Neutrality Response Swamps FCC," *CNET*, June 3, 2014. http://www.cnet.com/news/john-olivers-net-neutrality-rallying-cry-swamps-fcc/ (accessed March 3, 2015).

59 Craig Aaron, "How the Net (Neutrality Battle) Was Won," *Personal Democracy Forum*, June 4–5, 2015. Panel Discussion.

60 Ibid.

61 Hastings, "Internet Tolls."

62 John Lofland, *Social Movement Organizations: Guide to Research on Insurgent Realities* (New York: Aldine de Greyter, 1996), 2–3.

63 See Jeff Goodwin, James M. Jasper, and Francesca Polletta, "Introduction: Why Emotions Matter," in *Passionate Politics: Emotions and Social Movements*, eds Jeff Goodwin, James M. Jasper, and Francesca Polletta (Chicago: University of Chicago Press, 2001), 6, 1–26.

64 Steven Renderos, "FCC, Deliver the Internet We Deserve."

65 Wu, "Network Neutrality, Broadband Discrimination," 145–146.

66 Steven Renderos, October 28, 2014, personal interview.

67 See Emily Peck, "Why Netflix Looks Different Today: It's Fighting for Net Neutrality," *Huffington Post*, September 10, 2014. http://www.huffingtonpost.com/2014/09/10/internet-slowdown-day_n_5797966.html (accesses September 14, 2014).

68 Battle for the Net, September 10, 2014, website, https://www.battleforthenet.com/sept10th/ (accessed September 14, 2014).

69 Ibid.

70 Gigi B. Sohn and David A. Bray, "Setting the Record Straight on Open Internet Comments," FCC, December 23, 2014. http://www.fcc.gov/blog/setting-record-straight-open-internet-comments (accessed December 26, 2014).

71 "Opening Statement of Commissioner Mignon Clyburn Federal Communications Commission Before the Congressional Forum On Net Neutrality," FCC, September 24, 2014. https://apps.fcc.gov/edocs_public/attachmatch/DOC-329579A1.pdf (accessed December 22, 2014).

72 "Net Neutrality/President Obama's Plan for a Free and Open Internet," The White House, November 10, 2014. http://www.whitehouse.gov/net-neutrality (accessed December 22, 2014).

73 Candace Clement, "You Won't Believe This," *Free Press*, January 8, 2015. http://www.freepress.net/blog/2015/01/08/you-wont-believe (accessed March 21, 2015).

74 "Report and Order on Remand, Declaratory Ruling, and Order: In the Matter of Protecting and Promoting the Open Internet," prepared for the Federal Communications Commission, March 12, 2015. http://transition.fcc.gov/Daily_Releases/Daily_Business/2015/db0312/FCC-15-24A1.pdf (accessed March 24, 2014).

75 Weisman, "F.C.C. Net Neutrality Rules Clear Hurdle as Republicans Concede to Obama."

76 Craig Aaron, "Net Neutrality Victory," *Free Press*, February 26, 2015. http://www.freepress.net/blog/2015/02/26/net-neutrality-victory (accessed February 26, 2015).

77 "Netflix Says Consumers Win Today's FCC Decisions on Net Neutrality, Community Broadband," Netflix, February 26, 2015. https://pr.netflix.com/WebClient/getNewsSummary.do?newsId=1941 (accessed February 26, 2015).
78 "Report and Order (2015)," 10.
79 Ibid., 10–11.
80 Ibid., 11.
81 Fang, "Net Neutrality Is Here."
82 Weisman, "F.C.C. Net Neutrality Rules Clear Hurdle as Republicans Concede to Obama."
83 Quoted in Fang, "Net Neutrality Is Here."
84 Todd Spangler, "Netflix CFO Says Pressing FCC for Title II Broadband Regs Was Not Its Preferred Option," *Variety*, March 4, 2015. http://variety.com/2015/digital/news/netflix-cfo-pleased-with-fcc-title-ii-ruling-although-its-preference-would-have-been-no-broadband-regulation-1201446282/ (accessed April 14, 2015).
85 Pickard, *America's Battle for Media Democracy*, 1.
86 See Candace Clement, "The Many Ways Congress Could Mess Up Net Neutrality," *Free Press*, March 16, 2015. http://www.freepress.net/blog/2015/03/16/many-ways-congress-could-mess-net-neutrality (accessed March 18, 2015).
87 Crawford, *Captive Audience*, 16.

2

Framing the Future of Media Regulation through Netflix

Alison N. Novak

In a January 2015 speech on broadband access, President Barack Obama told a group of utility workers in Cedar Falls, Iowa, that today's debate over the future of technology is about more than complex and abstract policies. He states: "Today, high-speed broadband is not a luxury, it's a necessity. This isn't just about making it easier to stream Netflix or scroll through your Facebook newsfeed—although that's fun, and it's frustrating if you're waiting for a long time before the thing finally comes up."[1] The president's quote, while humorous and drawing a laugh from the otherwise critical audience, denotes larger discourses surrounding the future of media regulation, broadband rights, and, of course, online streaming through Netflix. As Netflix has developed over the past fifteen years as one of the most popular and well-known distributors of film, television, and original content, increasing attention has been paid to the role the company will have in media regulation. Netflix's size and dominance within the market has challenged traditional forms and mediums of entertainment.[2] In doing so, political and public attention, like President Obama's speech, has turned to discussing the need for policy on bandwidth use, net neutrality, and the selling of spectrum for broadcasting wirelessly through Federal Communications Commission (FCC) auctions as they relate to Netflix's growing presence.

Shortly before and concurrent with Netflix's growth, much of the late 1990s and 2000s were spent changing government and policy regulations of the media and technology industries. The Telecommunications Act of 1996, designed to protect local television stations and outlets, ultimately failed to address many of the needs and demands of digital producers, resulting in what Pila called competitive and anti-consumerist behaviors only known to "the Wild-West" of home-streaming providers.[3] Regulatory provisions and policies since the 1996 Act have been critiqued for being too lenient on providers and technology companies as prices for these services increase, and consumer protection decreases.[4] While these practices extend beyond Netflix, the company has become the poster child of contemporary and ongoing debates because of its wide-scale recognition and dominance in online content distribution.[5] Additionally, Netflix has become the central concern of government and policy makers as increasing news media attention is paid to lawsuits pending by and against the company, such as its 2012 multi-million-dollar class-action lawsuit on the privacy of past rentals. In turn, this complex intersection of new media technologies, the evolving role of the government in streaming regulations, and the growing popularity of Netflix demands scholarly attention to understand how the future of media organizations is impacted by today's actions.

This chapter is one of the first studies of how policy makers and government leaders frame Netflix as a part of government regulations and policy. To study how Netflix is a part of ongoing regulation debates, the C-SPAN archives will be examined to ascertain how government leaders, policy makers, and politicians debate, discuss, and analyze the future of the growing company. Specifically, this study will look at how these policy makers frame Netflix as a part of the greater debates over the future of media regulation. It will address questions such as, How do policy makers, journalists, and industry leaders discuss the past and future of Netflix's effects on the media industry?

Review of the literature: Netflix and media regulation

Hillard and Keith write that throughout American history media regulation has often been described and designed through the lens of current, powerful organizations.[6] Early telecommunications policy in the 1920s and 1930s was directed toward the quickly growing and powerful AT&T, and recent policies in the 1990s were created based on online service providers such as AOL and Microsoft's success. In following this trajectory, new media regulations and policies will likely follow a similar format, reacting to growing twenty-first-century companies and new digital technologies.[7] Previous research indicates that Netflix, as one of the fastest growing online platforms today, may be one of the companies that similarly impacts future policy issues.[8] These policy issues include spectrum auctions and bandwidth use, especially considering the everyday access of Netflix by the public. As such, Netflix's expansion and popularity has been the focus of international policy questions and revision, thus making it an important topic for research on the framing of future media regulations.

Netflix was founded in 1997 as a DVD delivery service for users to watch movies without fear of late fees.[9] By 2007, the public company began to move away from delivery service and into an online streaming model. Rather than wait for DVDs to be delivered, users could now watch a selection of films on their computers, greatly increasing the number of daily and hourly visitors to the site.[10] Through its embracing of algorithms and a 2006 Netflix contest awarding people who could increase the accuracy of user recommendations, the company was identified as a leader and innovator in online content streaming and digital platforms by journalists.[11]

It was this sudden surge in activity and popularity (as of January 2015, nearly one in five Americans had access to Netflix) that also attracted government media regulators.[12] Brenner notes that Netflix's presence in the digital world drew concerns from lawmakers because of its potential ability to impact other forms of media engagement, such as download speeds, use of bandwidth, and the financial models of online service providers.[13] Simultaneously, government and regulatory organizations such as the FCC announced their intentions to issue a ruling on net neutrality and the principles of an open internet model. This led to what Jennings et al. call a virtual Pandora's box of legal problems and policy changes.[14]

The convergence of Netflix's growth and ongoing policy debates presents a unique opportunity to look at how a media platform is used discursively as a part of larger regulatory conversations. While previous research suggests that using organizations like Netflix in debates by policy makers is common, few studies have centrally explored how these media institutions are framed, and what implications this might have for a growing platform.[15] This study looks at how Netflix, the largest and most used online subscription-based streaming platform in the world, is invoked and framed within these debates.

Contemporary media regulations have the potential to seriously impact Netflix and its business model. In 2014, Netflix and service provider Comcast reached an undisclosed financial agreement that would maintain online streaming quality of the site for Comcast customers. This drew criticisms of unfair partnerships and even claims of antitrust violations.[16] Combined with the secrecy shrouding Netflix's government lobbying and data storing efforts, politicians and other public figures have voiced their concern over the practices of the popular platform.[17] Upcoming decisions in late 2015 regarding net neutrality, spectrum auctions, and bandwidth use have the potential to greatly impact Netflix's ability to provide online streaming content and partnerships with online service providers like Comcast. Examining Netflix's role in debates about the future of media regulation will therefore offer insight into what actions the company might take next.

Political framing of regulation

Earlier research has identified that the framing of the future of public policy, government action, and regulations has an impact on the public or audience's view on the issue, organization, or political body.[18] In media regulations and public policy, frames are a tool used by a speaker to identify, describe, and orient an issue within a larger context.[19] Frames are used as a means to insert an opinion or a particular view while alienating or distancing an alternative perspective on a topic.[20] Scholarship has found that frames are powerful devices within speeches, interviews, and conversations that can be used to subtly persuade the audience to adopt a particular view in situations that often do not allow for explicit or personal (subjective) statements to be issued.[21]

Allen argues that frames have a direct impact on the public's view of a media platform as well as any policies or laws tied to that platform.[22] As the audience listens to a speaker describe or invoke a media platform, they internalize that description and use it to form opinions on that specific technology, or others like it. This is particularly true when a technology is in the early phases of the adoption curve.[23] While many studies have asserted the directness and strength of these framing effects, little previous research outside of Allen's study have looked directly at this relationship within the context of a media technology such as Netflix. Dong-Hee argues that more research on the use of media platforms as examples within public policy debates is vital.[24] This has also been identified in the framing of previous technologies such as the VCR and music file sharing. These government discourses often drive public opinion and have been viewed as a catalyst for changing the public's views on particularly controversial topics and business models such as Napster. However, since this research, few studies have looked at how framing affects presentations of other forms of media technologies.

Framing media regulation is a particularly difficult task because the speaker must first describe why a proposed regulation is necessary and then make it applicable to the public to gain support.[25] Delshad and Raymond note that there is an ongoing interplay between the frames used by politicians and frames used by the media to describe upcoming policies, regulations, and government actions.[26] Speeches made by politicians use carefully crafted frames on these topics because the media frequently re-uses and adopts the frame in their own reporting on the topic.[27] Through the use of quotes, sound bites, and on-air interviews, the frames used by politicians are reinforced by their repetition by journalists and other members of the press. Framing also extends beyond the audience that hears the original speech, to those that encounter it as part of the media coverage of the speech. Moriearty demonstrated that this repetition and continuous use of political frames in the media can impact the public's perception of an issue and even the eventual approval and adoption of a public policy within government.[28] Otway and Ravetz argue that this creates a linear effect in media regulation where political frames are adopted by the media, then adopted by the audience who consumed the media's coverage and use of the political frames, thus translating into larger public approval percentages for policies and regulations.[29] One important question stemming from this model regards its presence and potential impact on the current Netflix and regulation debates. This study does not provide evidence of audience reception of these frames, but instead identifies the rhetorical framing of Netflix regulation so that later work on audience adoption and support of the linear model may be completed.

Although the linear model of direct effect between media use and public adoption of frames has been an important tool in understanding the effects of framing, few studies have explored how this process is articulated within a contemporary media environment. Yates, Gulati, and Weiss identified that this linear model was present in policy debates on mobile broadband diffusion and the media's adoption of politicians' framing was critically important to the passing of mobile policy and laws in 2012.[30] Their study also identified that politicians and journalists regularly invoke and use the names of large media companies, such as Netflix, as a way to describe how abstract policies may impact the public. They request more research on the use of these companies and how they impact the framing of larger policy issues. To understand how the framing of media regulation circulates among politicians, journalists, and the public, it is necessary to find a dataset that involves all three groups.

C-SPAN's role

C-SPAN is an important hybrid between the media, the political process, and the model of framing described in the previous section. The channel features 24/7 coverage of national, international, and local government, as well as regular interviews and commentary by members of the press and technology/media industry leaders. Since its 1979 launch, the network has broadcasted unedited live sessions of Congress, its own original programming such as *The Communicators*, and breaking news coverage of political events. Its integration of political actions and press coverage makes it an ideal source for examining the first part of the linear model of media regulation as well as how specific media organizations are framed within its coverage.

Previous research has identified that C-SPAN has a unique relationship with Congress and political news. As the first network allowed to broadcast Congressional votes in the 1990s, the network has since expanded, including multiple other channels and broadcasting formats (e.g., C-SPAN 2, BookTV). C-SPAN does not receive money from corporate advertisers, but instead relies on government funding and small donations. Thus, the network is not tied to a profit-seeking model like other corporate channels. Other work has studied C-SPAN's coverage of topics ranging from African American rights to the framing of technology. These critical studies suggest the ongoing importance of the network and scholarship related to the topic.

In addition, C-SPAN has been identified as a force within government affairs and public policies. The nonprofit network has used its continuous coverage to highlight and bring to light topics that are usually excluded from profit-driven news networks, such as policies on organ donation.[31] Popkin identified C-SPAN as an important part of the media landscape (one often overlooked by media scholars) because of its continued presence and recording of previously private political exchanges, votes, and debates.[32] This coverage helps ensure that this study looks at the complete corpus of mentions of Netflix within the debates over the future of media regulation because of the variety of people, events, and issues broadcast on the network.

Methods

To see how Netflix was framed as a part of media regulation, this study analyzes the C-SPAN digital archives for mentions of the company. Using the advanced search options in the digital archives, transcripts of all C-SPAN content were crawled for uses of "Netflix" or the alternative spelling "Net-Flix" (occasionally used in Congressional hearings). The C-SPAN digital archives house all on-air content of C-SPAN and its affiliate channels since 1992. Because Netflix was not established as a company until 1997, the archives house all mentions of Netflix airing on C-SPAN.

In total, Netflix is mentioned 2,954 times on C-SPAN in the period between December 1, 1999, and March 1, 2015. Through the C-SPAN digital library and advanced platform tools, each of the mentions was archived as a part of a larger clip. Clips include the speech surrounding the word's use, such as a question by an interviewer and the rest of the response. Therefore, this analysis was able to include the context of the mention, thus helping the qualitative forming of each frame. Each of the mentions was exported including its audio, visual, and closed-captioning content (or official speech, if provided). The term was used in a variety of contexts including Congressional hearings, journalist interviews, speeches by the president, and FCC hearings. While a more detailed report on the programming context would be an important addition, this chapter examines the qualitative results of a framing analysis to provide detailed insight into the overall usage of the company's name and to draw deeper conclusions regarding how media institutions are invoked in regulatory discussions.

Each of the 2,954 mentions was investigated with an eye toward patterns in the way the company was used, such as tone, context, or comparisons. After the entire corpus of Netflix clips were watched, a set of frames were developed and detailed below. This chapter reports on three of the most common frames: disparagement, futurist, and dramatic. While other frames were developed as part of a larger study, in the interest of time and relevance to the topic, these three will be detailed below. For reliability purposes, each frame includes examples of quotes using the frame and a hyperlink in the footnotes for ease of access.

Disparagement

The first and most frequent frame used to describe Netflix was in disparaging terms, often using the company as an example of larger, more serious problems or issues. This frame was frequently used by members of Congress addressing their peers on issues such as net neutrality, spectrum auctions, and the growth of smaller local media businesses. For example, Senator Maria Cantwell (D-WA) spoke just days before the FCC issued its February 2015 Net Neutrality ruling, urging her fellow senators to consider how net neutrality could positively impact the smaller businesses in their home district. "The commission is expected to vote on this rule later this month, and I hope that all of our colleagues would be paying attention to this decision. Because this decision is not just whether I can download or use Netflix. It's about equal access to the marketplace."[33] Cantwell's quote demonstrates the use of Netflix as a small, yet relatable, example of the larger ongoing issues that need political attention. Her use of "not just" is emblematic of the frequent practice of using Netflix as a humorous example within an otherwise serious and critical speech. Similarly, President Obama used Netflix (and Facebook) as a humorous example of larger broadband issues at the start of this chapter. While in both these examples the crowd and the speaker smile and quietly laugh, they are meant rhetorically to bond the speaker with the audience over common frustrations. In doing this, they position Netflix as just a symptom of the issue, not the issue itself. This disparages the topic as less important than what they identify as the "real" topic that needs to be addressed.

It is critical to note that there is an inherent contradiction in the usage of the disparagement frame to identify Netflix's place in society and government. The frequency of the use of Netflix in this context challenges the disparagement frame. It prompts the audience to ask: if Netflix is not the real issue, then why is it so often cited in this context? Netflix's continued presence within the speeches made by political leaders suggests that at the very least it is a recognizable facet of the technology industry, especially because it is often used to bond the speaker and audience. However, despite its frequency, the statements still reinforce the inferior position of Netflix to what is described as the real issue. Consider Paul Barbagallo, a journalist with the *Washington Journal*, who uses Netflix as an example in his interview on the future of bandwidth: "This is really about who pays for the infrastructure and how much the largest content providers have to pay to the largest ISP's. Because things like Netflix, things like Instagram, they make a lot of congestion online."[34] Barbagallo and others demonstrate that disparagement can also refer to the description of the Netflix platform as a part of the problem with the larger issues of infrastructure and ISP finances. Netflix is not just a sign of the larger regulatory issues that need to be addressed by the government, but instead it is creating a problem. New regulations are necessary because of Netflix's use and (as others call it) abuse of existing bandwidth and data. As part of the disparagement frame, the accuracy of these claims is not entirely supported.

While Barbagallo's quote still fits within the disparagement frame, it is important to note the difference and diversity within the category. While disparagement is demonstrated through the rhetorical inferiority in addressing and using Netflix, the company is also discussed as problematic for the larger digital structure and system. It is not that Netflix is unimportant, but rather that its impact is problematic or only part of a larger issue. Netflix is not alone in this use; other online platforms are similarly used in these contexts such as Facebook, Instagram, and Pinterest.

Disparagement has a long history in media framing research. As identified by Gitlin, disparagement is a technique used by a media producer to devalue or create a sense of inferiority surrounding a topic or issue.[35] However, the use of disparagement in these cases is somewhat different than the historical model described by Gitlin. Disparagement here represents a range of possible views on the topic (described in the above paragraph). While previously disparagement reflected the intention of belittling a group or issue, here the frame is combined with the use of humor and problematizing the effects of Netflix on digital media and technology. Perhaps this is because of the futurist connotation within the mentioning and use of Netflix on C-SPAN, a context which introduces its own frame described in the next section.

Futurist

While Netflix was disparaged in debates about current social and political policy, there was a stark difference in how its future impact was framed. Unlike the disparagement frame, the futurist frame does not have a previous theoretical framework, but rather emerged from this dataset specifically. The futurist frame described Netflix as a visionary for the upcoming media industry and economic models, one that was not always understood by the policy makers and speakers. For example, Larry Irving, a former National Telecommunication and Information Administrator of the FCC (1993–99), described Netflix as having an almost mystical yet powerful effect: "What's happening with Netflix and their stock going up, HBO saying we are going to go extra cable and go over the top, and then CBS over the top again. Five years, I bet you the media landscape will be markedly different than it is now. How, I can't tell you."[36] The futurist frame credits Netflix and other media platforms with upcoming large-scale changes to the media industry, but rarely identifies the company's history or past experiences as a mechanism for this effect. The focus is on how Netflix will drive future business, not current events or industry practices. Importantly, this is also coupled with a mysterious connotation. Irving adds that he is unsure what the future will look like, but he is sure that it will be a result of innovations by Netflix and other media producers.

This mystery supports the futurist frame as it contributes to larger social discussions about anxieties over what actions need to be taken now to ensure the best possible future. It is also reflective of the overall context of C-SPAN and the variety of perspectives housed within. Because C-SPAN airs content by government and policy makers, as well as companies and advocate groups, all of which are fighting for some control over the future media landscape, the futurist frame embraces the mystery and uncertainty of what that future looks like. John M. Peha, a professor at Carnegie Mellon University, described his own confusion over Netflix's relationship with other media partners in a panel sponsored by the Progressive Policy Institute: "Let me bring to the most controversial discussion in this world which is the Comcast and Netflix discussion. Start with a caveat. I have no idea what is going on with Comcast and Netflix."[37] The futurist frame challenges the earlier disparagement one because it recognizes Netflix as having an important place in the future of media. While disparagement belittles Netflix's present-day role, most of the speakers featured in the 2,954 mentions identified its potential power and effect in the future. Importantly, a timeline for this future was never identified on C-SPAN. It is unclear if these changes are happening tomorrow or in the next few years. The lack of specificity within the frame underscores the mysterious context of these potential future effects.

This is also visible in the connection of Netflix and other online streaming technologies being connected to the next generation of media customers: the millennials, sometimes referred to as cord-cutters. Many segments identified Netflix as emblematic of the new media landscape that is being articulated and embraced by young people under the age of 30. In a *Communicators* interview with Craig Moffett, a partner and senior Research Analyst with Moffett-Nathanson Research, Netflix was repeatedly identified as a part of the future media landscape as dictated by the interests and lifestyles of millennials.

> The impact of some of the ones that are already here, like Netflix, has already been very profound. I think what we are seeing here is a real change in the viewing habits of Millennials. They are simply watching TV in a very different way than

> my generation watched TV, and you are starting to see all the media companies embrace that and recognize that they can't sort of circle the wagons and just try to protect the existing ecosystem anymore. They actually have to reach out to that set of customers.[38]

Netflix, again, is identified as having an impact on the future of media, especially as it is discursively juxtaposed to other media companies who have not embraced online technologies or streaming. Later in the interview, CBS is identified as one of these slow-reacting companies. Netflix is described as an industry visionary who embraced future markets before other companies recognized that cord-cutting and online streaming were more than just a short fad, but instead a long-term trend.

This is not to say that all mentions of the future of Netflix are filtered through a positive lens. Alternatively, other speakers employ the futurist frame to describe their concerns over the future of media or even government regulation. While in conversation with Peha, Hal Singer, a senior fellow with the Progressive Politics Institute, stated: "I'm actually worried that we're learning about the interconnection debate through the prism of the Netflix, really the Netflix wars. Whether it's Netflix/Comcast, Netflix/Whomever. And Netflix may not be all that average representative of your content provider. So I'm concerned that regulation is going to be spawned through a prism that might be a false one."[39] Singer ties these concerns to the way that Netflix interacts with other major players in the media. Previous research on Comcast's role in regulation suggests that the organization is largely framed as a negative lobbying group that prevents appropriate media legislation from being enacted and even fully considered.[40] Through the continued discursive connection of Netflix to companies such as Comcast, the futurist frame is used to describe concerns over the future ability of lawmakers to regulate and control the difficult media industry.

The futurist frame is also used when interviewing industry leaders. In a 2014 interview on C-SPAN, CEO of Cisco, John Chambers, was asked what he thought some of the largest looming questions were that impacted the future of the media industry. He answered, "If you watch what Netflix is doing, is it where [Netflix] is going to get revenue streams?"[41] Again, the futurist frame is paired with mystery, as Chambers asks the audience a rhetorical question meant to reinforce the uncertainty of Netflix's future actions and what impact this may have. Netflix, in this frame, is a tool used by the speaker to encourage the audience to question the motivations, impact, and personal effect the future of the company may have. Importantly, in the 250 hours of C-SPAN coverage watched in this research, Comcast was the only other media organization discussed using the futurist frame. While it is difficult to say why Netflix is singled out in this capacity, this may partially be informed by the third frame: dramatic.

Dramatic

The dramatic frame, which often appears in segments alongside the futurist frame, depicts Netflix as an overly emotional, entitled company that causes unnecessary problems for the media industry and government. Similar to the futurist frame, the dramatic frame emerged directly from the dataset rather than from previous scholarly work. However, unlike the futurist frame, this frame focuses on Netflix's current role in culture, often using terms such as "immature," and "nuisance." The company and its technology are looked upon as a problem because of the disproportionate public demand for its service and the company's lack of desire to cooperate with traditional regulations.

This is different from the disparagement frame that identifies the company as weak, because in these sentiments the company's dramatic tendency is only allowed and tolerated because of its massive public backing. In fact, through this frame, Netflix's industry power is identified as being a direct result of public demand and platform usage. For example, Brendan Sasso, a Technology Correspondent for the *Washington Journal* identified Netflix's ability to challenge the FCC's policies as a result of its huge market share and customer use. "And a huge portion of internet traffic, something like 30%, is just Netflix... If Netflix feels it is being this extended or that the charges are unreasonable, the FCC could deal with that for the first time."[42] As Sasso explains, Netflix is a frequent challenger of industry norms and regular practices. The company does not hesitate to challenge FCC policies, such as the cost of bandwidth, often citing the high demand of their platform as a reason for this outlook. The dramatic frame then is used to identify these challenges as being unnecessary and reactionary.

In addition, the dramatic frame is used to describe the reactions of the FCC and other media regulating groups to Netflix's increasing presence in the industry. Often, these governing bodies are characterized as operating too slowly to keep up with the ongoing innovations of technology companies. Ongoing debates within the FCC and Securities and Exchange Commission (SEC) are characterized through the dramatic frame as being something problematic for the companies as well. In a 2014 roundtable of the Congressional Internet Caucus Advisory Committee, Matthew Brill, a communications and appellate law attorney, described the SEC as operating too slowly because of ongoing debates over the constitutionality of networks working together (like Netflix and Comcast), thus causing the companies to exist and operate outside of existing laws. He states, "We will have a debate over whether such an arrangement might be reasonable. The interconnection between networks and Netflix directly Comcast and between Comcast with an intermediary is something that the SEC has set it outside of these rules."[43] Other members of the roundtable reinforced Brill's analysis, adding that because regulating bodies like the FCC and SEC have taken too long to issue clear decisions or policies on topics like net neutrality (before the 2015 decision), companies are forced to form partnerships that may not have government approval, but are necessary for the good of the customer. This focus on the customer, instead of financial profits or market shares, is a critical piece of the dramatic frame.

By simultaneously invoking its large customer base and cultural impact (i.e., 30 percent of broadband usage), as well as the overly dramatic tendencies, the media suggests that Netflix is acting on the public's behalf. In this sense, the ongoing debates, as Brill suggests, are positioned as harmful to the public and customers because they are described as taking longer than they should, thus not active enough to help in immediate situations. One of these ongoing debates surrounds the topic of "Open Internet," a frequent area of conversation for C-SPAN guests. In a 2014 interview, Lynn Stanton, a senior editor of the *Washington Journal*, explained why the open internet was taking so long, and how Netflix (among other digital companies) has been impacted by the indecisions of the FCC.

> They want their services to be sold, but other companies like Netflix, they have interest in restricting them in addition to that. They can restrict how you use your Internet connection, they restrict you from running personal servers. There are some big issues with how we do Internet in this country, and we really need to separate out those with a vested interest in selling us content from providing us the Internet pipes.[44]

As Stanton suggests, the overly drawn-out debate has given companies such as Netflix more control over the users' internet and digital capacities. She mentioned before that it is the FCC's lack of swift and early decision on open internet policies that ultimately shape the current behaviors of companies such as Netflix. The dramatics of both Netflix and the ongoing debates within the media industry have a direct impact on the customer and public.

Reflection

When used together, these three frames identify Netflix as a complicated yet frequently used example of current and upcoming problems with media regulation. Critical to the investigation of media frames is the potential impact these may have on the audience. While an audience analysis is outside the scope of this study, there are important connections made through the disparagement, futurist, and dramatic frames that may have long-term implications on future developments. Through the disparagement frame, Netflix is described as an inferior media organization and platform, one that is emblematic of real issues, but not the issue itself. Netflix is also used as a rhetorical device to bond the speaker and audience together over common struggles such as the quality and timing of streaming content. The dramatic frame provides an interesting context for disparagement, as the effect of these large institutions and ongoing "real issues" impact the customer and wider public. When considered together, disparagement and dramatic frames reinforce Netflix as a popular online provider, yet one that is wrapped up in debates over net neutrality, open internet, and bandwidth usage. Netflix is a vehicle for the on-air speakers to address complicated and difficult current problems with digital technologies and internet policy. As noted with the disparagement frame, the humor often used to describe Netflix (like in President Obama's remarks noted earlier in this chapter), may be a helpful means for the speaker to help make these often abstract debates feel relevant for the audience and public. This is one area of potential future research when considering the framing of media regulation.

In addition, the futurist frame also deserves more inquiry and investigation. Particularly relevant to this study is the reference to mystery in descriptions of how Netflix may be impactful in the future. Many speakers hedged their analyses with statements of uncertainty regarding how Netflix may be a part of the future of media regulation. When coupled with the disparagement frame, this suggests that there is a difference in the perception of current and future Netflix action. Mystery may also explain why Netflix's actions were sometimes described as dramatic, because the speakers were unsure about what or how these ongoing debates might end.

The findings of this study also support the presence of the first stages of the linear model of the future of media regulation, as the journalists and members of the press featured on C-SPAN often adopt and integrate the frames used by politicians. While a longitudinal study is necessary to understand how the audience may or may not adopt these frames, it is likely, based on earlier regulation research, that these frames can have a lasting effect on the public's views of the Netflix platform. Netflix's use continued to grow throughout the 2010s, and although one of the frames is largely negative, it is possible that the positivity and futurist-connotation of the frames may support ongoing audience use of the platform.

This also brings up an important disparity between popular and government views of Netflix. Previous research has identified that the public largely approves of and supports the company's goals and direction.[45] This popularity may suggest the ineffectiveness of the disparagement frame, or the power of the futurist or dramatic frames. Again, although more audience-focused studies would be needed to examine the use of these frames by the public, it does seem as if the public approval of the company most closely matches futurist and dramatic framing.

The use of C-SPAN in this chapter also contributed to its findings and their potential generalizability. As described earlier, C-SPAN provides a place for journalists, policy makers, government employees, and politicians to come together to discuss issues with technology. A more statistical approach to framing may help to analyze if there are pronounced differences in the ways each category of individuals reflected on Netflix. It should also be noted that no employee or leader from Netflix has ever been interviewed or present on C-SPAN, thus leaving an important voice outside of the dataset. This may also partially impact the reactions and framing of the company by content hosts or regular personalities.

While this project represents the beginning of an investigation into how platforms such as Netflix are invoked and used in the debates over the future of media regulation, there is much more research that needs to be done. The three frames identified here seemingly support the linear model of the future of media regulation; however, more quantitative studies will need to verify this. As C-SPAN continues to record live political acts and broadcast industry and press reactions, it can serve as an important research tool for scholars examining how the future of media regulation is discussed.

Notes

1 Barack H. Obama, "Remarks on Broadband Access, presentation, Cedar Falls Facility, Cedar Falls, Iowa," Recorded January 14, 2015. CSPN. http://www.c-span.org/video/?323783-1/president-obama-remarks-broadband-access&start=402 (accessed July 10, 2015).

2 Lyne Stanton and John Curran, "Analysts See Comcast's Netflix Deal as Smoothing TWC Merger," *Telecommunication Reports* 80 (2014): 20.

3 Josha N. Pila, "They're Already Regulating the Internet?" *Communications Lawyer* 29 (2012): 12.

4 Scott J. Wallsten, "Is Xfinity TV Anticompetitive? Let the Courts, Not Regulators, Decide," *The Economists' Voice* 9 (2012): 3.

5 Stanton and Curran, "Analysts," 22. See also Simon Dumenco, "Netflix Must Die! And Hulu and YouTube Too!" *Advertising Age* 84 (2013): 50.

6 Robert L. Hillard and Michael C. Keith, *The Broadcast Century and Beyond: A Biography of American Broadcasting* (New York: Focal Press, 2013), 100.

7 Tim Wu, *The Master Switch* (New York: Vintage Press, 2011), 15.

8 Grace Allen, Dorothee Feils, and Holly Disbrow, "The Rise and Fall of Netflix: What Happened and Where Will It Go from Here?" *Journal of the International Academy for Case Studies* 20 (2014): 119.

9 Julie A. DeCesare, "The Mass Market and Consumer Tools," *Library Technology Reports*, 50 (2014): 33.

10 Philip M. Napoli, "Automated Media: An Institutional Theory Perspective on Algorithmic Media Production and Consumption," *Communication Theory* 24 (2014): 340.

11 Napoli, "Automated," 340.

12 Netflix.com, About, 2015. www.netflix.com/about (accessed July 10, 2015).

13 Daniel L. Brenner, "Explaining Yourself: Thirty Years After a Marketplace Approach to Broadcast Regulation," *Administrative Law Review* 65 (2013): 743.

14 Susan Evans Jennings, Justin R. Blount, and M. Gail Weatherly, "Social Media—A Virtual Pandora's Box: Prevalence, Possible Legal Liabilities, and Policies," *Business and Professional Communication Quarterly* 77 (2014): 96.

15 Hillard and Keith, *The Broadcast Century*, 102.

16 Eriq Gardner, "Netflix Beats Antitrust Class Action at Appeals Court," *The Hollywood Reporter*, February 27, 2015. http://www.hollywoodreporter.com/thr-esq/netflix-beats-antitrust-class-action-778300 (accessed July 10, 2015).

17 Alison N. Novak, "Narrowcasting Netflix: The Personalization of Genre in Digital Media Streaming," *The Netflix Reader* (Philadelphia: Lexington Press, 2015).

18 Lee Edwards et al. "Framing the Consumer: Copyright Regulation and the Public," *Convergence* 19 (2012): 9.

19 Edwards et al., "Framing," 9.

20 Leonhard Dobusch and Sigrid Quack, "Framing Standards, Mobilizing Users: Copyright Versus Fair Use in Transnational Regulation," *Review of International Political Economy* 20 (2013): 52.

21 Dobusch and Quack, "Framing Standards," 55. See also Colin Gavaghan, "A Whole New … You? 'Personal Identity', Emerging Technologies and the Law," *Identity in the Information Society* 3 (2010): 423.

22 Jonathan P. Allen, "Who Shapes the Future?: Problem Framings and the Development of Handheld Computers," *Computers and Society* 28 (1998): 3.
23 Allen, "Who Shapes," 3.
24 Shin Dong-Hee, "Convergence of Telecommunications, Media and Information Technology, and Implications for Regulation," *Information* 8 (2006): 42–56.
25 Andra Seceleanu and Aurel Papari, "Presentation of Media Discourse of Information on Social Issues Through the Construction of the Agenda Setting and Framing," Paper presented at the Economic Development and Research Conference 62 (2013): 17.
26 Ashlie Delshad and Leigh Raymond, "Media Framing and Public Attitude Towards Biofuels," *Review of Policy Research* 30 (2013): 190.
27 Delshad and Raymond, "Media Framing," 190.
28 Perry L. Moriearty, "Framing Justice: Media, Bias, and Legal Decision Making," *Maryland Law Review* 69 (2010): 849.
29 Harry Otway and Jerome Ravetz, "On the Regulation of Technology: Examining the Linear Model," *Futures* 16 (1984): 217.
30 David J. Yates, Gurish J. Gulati, and Joseph W. Weiss, "Understanding the Impact of Policy, Regulation and Governance on Mobile Broadband Diffusion," *System Sciences (HICSS), 2013 46th Hawaii International Conference* (Wailea, Maui, Hawaii, USA, 2013): 2852.
31 LaShara Davis, Lisa Chewning, Tyler Harrison, Mark DiCorcia, and Susan Morgan, "Entertainment (Mis)education: The Framing of Organ Donation in Entertainment Television," *Health Communication* 22 (2007): 143–151.
32 Samuel L. Popkin, "Changing Media, Changing Politics," *Perspectives on Politics* 4 (2006): 327.
33 Maria Cantwell, "Senate Session, Part 1: Homeland Security Spending," Recorded February 4, 2015. C-SPAN. http://www.c-span.org/video/?324183-1/us-senate-legislative-business&start=5158 (accessed July 10, 2015).
34 Paul Barbagallo, "Net Neutrality: Washington Journal," Recorded November 13, 2014. C-SPAN. http://www.c-span.org/video/?322634-5/washington-journal-paul-barbagallo-net-neutrality&start=830 (accessed July 10, 2015).
35 Todd Gitlin, *The Whole World Is Watching: Mass Media in the Making and Unmaking of the New Left*, 2nd ed. (Berkeley: University of California Press, 2003).
36 Larry Irving, "1934 Communications Act and Modern Technology," Recorded October 22, 2014. C-SPAN. http://www.c-span.org/video/?322250-1/discussion-communications-act-1934&start=4621 (accessed July 10, 2015).
37 John M. Peha, "FCC Open Internet Policy," Recorded May 27, 2014. C-SPAN. http://www.c-span.org/video/?319582-1/open-internet-policy&start=6072 (accessed July 10, 2015).
38 Craig Moffett, "Communications with Craig Moffett and Michael Nathanson," Recorded December 10, 2014. C-SPAN. http://www.c-span.org/video/?323145-1/communicators-craig-moffett-michael-nathanson (accessed July 10, 2015).
39 Hal Singer, "FCC Open Internet Policy," Recorded May 27, 2014. C-SPAN http://www.c-span.org/video/?319582-1/open-internet-policy&start=6072 (accessed July 10, 2015).
40 Emily R. Roxberg, "FCC Authority Post-Comcast: Finding a Happy Medium in the Net Neutrality Debate," *The Journal of Corporation Law* 37 (2011): 223.

41 John Chambers, "Wall Street Journal Viewpoints Breakfast with John Chambers," Recorded September 24, 2014. C-SPAN. http://www.c-span.org/video/?321694-1/wall-street-journal-viewpoints-breakfast-john-chambers&start=2377 (accessed July 10, 2015).

42 Brendan Sasso, "FCC Net Neutrality Proposal," Recorded February 15, 2014. C-SPAN. http://www.c-span.org/video/?324071-3/washington-journal-brendan-sasso-fcc-net-neutrality-proposal&start=1445 (accessed July 10, 2015).

43 Matthew Brill, "Open Internet Rules," Recorded May 16, 2014. C-SPAN. http://www.c-span.org/video/?319434-1/open-internet-rules&start=3115 (accessed July 10, 2015).

44 Lynn Stanton, "FCC and Net Neutrality," Recorded May 16, 2014. C-SPAN. http://www.c-span.org/video/?319338-5/washington-journal-fcc-net-neutrality&start=1407 (accessed July 10, 2015).

45 Novak, "Narrowcasting," 12.

3

Netflix and the Myth of Choice/ Participation/Autonomy

Sarah Arnold

The success of Netflix has resulted in debates about its radical adjustment of the film and television viewing experience (see Carr,[1] Auletta,[2] and Madrigal[3]), and the company is often (self-) promoted as an enhancement of the personalized viewing already offered by DVDs, time-shifting devices, and other streaming technologies. This personalization is enabled by Netflix's analysis of vast quantities of user data, generated through the monitoring and interpretation of users' interactions with Netflix while viewing content. Netflix posits the use of data mining systems as beneficial for the consumer and suggests that such systems allow the company to better understand and respond to audience tastes through its recommendation system.[4] This represents a shift in audience measurement and interpretation from the notion of the depersonalized mass to the personalized, the individuated, and the autonomous.

Historically, the audience, as conceptualized by media institutions, has been discursively produced.[5] Knowledge of the audience was limited by the technologies available to account for these viewers and, as a result, the audience was reduced to characteristics, attributes, and a narrow set of identities. As Ien Ang suggests, the information generated by audience measurement systems became a "truth" of sorts that was acted upon by media producers and broadcasters.[6] In turn, media institutions and producers sought to know and influence the audience in order to guarantee reasonable audience viewing figures for their content. These media producers and broadcasters sought to capture the widest audience and, in the context of commercial broadcast, the most valuable audiences. The audience was consequently figured as "depersonalized" and "part of a whole" but, paradoxically, a powerful mass that exercised relatively free choices (of limited content options) that were subject to later sampling and analysis.[7]

Traditional television audience measurement was, therefore, somewhat speculative, "desperately seeking the audience"[8] but unable to locate or identify those outside of sample groups. Measurement organizations—from in-house audience research carried out by networks and broadcasters to independent measurement companies such as Nielsen and BARB—could not measure the "actual audience,"[9] one that remained difficult to capture and manage. The by-product of this was, I would suggest, audience agency, whereby media organizations could only pursue but never quite govern audience behavior and attention. In the era of IPTV and internet television, however, new forms of measurement are enabled and enacted through datafication, ones that manage to capture and influence the audience in unprecedented ways. Like traditional television audience measurement, this is framed as in the service of the audience, producing a more enhanced means of personalizing the viewing experience: "what you want, when you want it."[10] Services such as Netflix, then, make a special claim to knowledge about the identity and personhood of the individual members of its audience. While the discourse of individualized and personal service might point to a sense of audience autonomy, I would suggest that this instead reveals datafication's propensity for what Mark Andrejevic claims as exploitation[11] and Antoinette Rouvroy has understood as an "algorithmic governmentality."[12] These new forms of measurement use data gleaned from online user interactions as a way of profiling and controlling the behavior of every individual. This datafication of audience measurement represents a significant shift from following the lead of audiences to predicting and governing future audience behavior.[13] It represents a move from a measurement model that understands audience identity as culturally produced (and brought to the viewing experience) to audience identity as produced through data (and defined by data algorithms). To date, there has been little consideration of the institutional and social significance of this shift toward datafication, particularly in the context of its effect on audience agency, identity, and autonomy. In this chapter, I consider such issues in respect of the increased forms of measurement enabled by datafication as compared to traditional television audience measurement. I suggest that while datafication might allude to the liberation of the individual from the mass, it equally masks more profound forms of individual manipulation and governance manufactured through data algorithms used by online television platforms such as Netflix.

Is Netflix television?

Netflix has become a significant provider of television content through its streaming platform. This provision of television content—ranging from drama series to reality television—has been concomitant with an increase in digital and online viewing.[14] Not only does it distribute content, but Netflix has also entered the field of production. This situates Netflix within the same institutional landscape of television and makes it a competitor with the television industries for television viewers. A broader paradoxical discourse has emerged, one that imagines Netflix as television but also as the company that will sound the death knell of television. Reviewers, business analysts, audience measurement agencies, and the public more broadly have continued to both align Netflix with television and to perceive it as a challenge to television, distinguishing between linear and new, internet-based television.

There are some obvious and fundamental differences between Netflix and linear television. Netflix is not transmitted live and refrains from streaming content that depends on the experience of liveness such as chat shows, news, and sports. Netflix's provision of content remains largely post-broadcast, although release windows are narrowing. Netflix identifies itself as distinct from linear television, claiming that internet television is not simply a competitor of linear television but that it will eventually replace it.[15] Finally, Netflix provides a substantially different viewing experience than linear television. Rather than a fixed linear flow of content, Netflix provides a finite catalogue of content from which the viewer selects. Though the interface suggests a schedule of sorts, "recommendations," the viewer can alternatively browse the catalogue. Once in play, the content is uninterrupted by brand messages or advertisements, though as of 2015 this is evolving.[16] All this necessitates a different form of viewer interaction than that of linear TV, which, in turn, requires Netflix to produce a user-friendly interface that maintains the perception of choice but also directs the viewer toward content more likely to keep them engaged and subscribed. Netflix, in this respect, follows linear television practice in developing strategies and tools to understand how and why viewers watch.

Traditional television audience measurement

It is, of course, imperative and inevitable that content providers such as Netflix endeavor to understand their audiences. The business model of both linear and internet television is dependent on capturing the largest audience market for any content. As Napoli suggests, media industries are not simply producers of content; they are at the same time producers of audiences.[17] Thus, content providers not only provide access to their product—the content—but they also work as audience providers. Where content is provided to the audience, the audience, in turn, is provided to a range of industries, businesses, and commercial interests. The financial model of the linear television industry works by initially offering a predicted audience to advertisers, then costing advertising in relation to the measured audience as determined by measurement companies such as Nielsen.[18] Television organizations, therefore, depend on Nielsen ratings of audience size and composition since this forms the basis for future advertising revenue. This is how the U.S. television industry was initially supported: free at the point of access for the viewer and charged to the advertiser. In later years, content was also provided to cable and satellite audiences who, in turn, were provided to subscription companies. Today, internet television uses both approaches, with Netflix providing content to audiences who pay a subscription fee to it. In all cases, it is important that content providers attract audiences. For Napoli, content providers do not simply deal in audiences; they more specifically deal in audience attention:

> Human attention resists the type of exact verification and quantification that typify the transactions that take place in most other industries. Steel is weighed, insurance is expressed in specific dollar amounts of coverage, and legal advice generally is

> measured in terms of the amount of time spent producing and delivering it. Thus when measurement is in pounds, dollars, or hours, reasonably precise and stable measurement systems facilitate these transactions, and the products of them are reasonable tangible.[19]

Measuring human attention, then, is less achievable since attention is not a quantifiable object like steel. The media industry has worked to develop close enough methods of quantification that can reasonably reflect audience attention. Media organizations have different and sometimes competing reasons for measuring audiences, yet all are invested in generating knowledge of their audience. Television organizations are perhaps more closely associated with audience measurement given that the business model largely depends on the relationship between viewer engagement and content. As Barrie Gunter suggests, "within the television industry, audience measurement is important to judge the performance of programs, to guide decisions about program scheduling, and for advertising planning and trading."[20] This knowledge is sometimes pursued by the media companies as a way of confirming the success of particular programming. More often, the generation of knowledge about an audience is part of the commercial process of advertising. In this case, separate audience measurement companies such as Nielsen sell data to television organizations so that the latter can more effectively price its advertising space. Subscription-based television operators such as HBO and Netflix do not depend on advertising revenue, but they still retain an investment in audience measurement, since continuous audience engagement secures subscriptions.

Despite significant investment in generating knowledge of audience engagement, the tools available to measure audiences remain limited. Audience measurement systems and organizations have historically tried to negotiate between volume and value. In other words, they were tasked with generating data on overall audience size and demographic as well as personal and individual engagements with media. In the early years of audience measurement, sampling was used in order to overcome the issue of volume. Since it was impossible to assess exactly how many people were listening at a given time, representative samples were used to determine or estimate overall audience listenership. As Webster, Phalen, and Lichty note, telephone sampling was used in the 1930s, whereby listeners were asked to recall what they had engaged with the previous day.[21] Since this system depended on direct engagement with individual listeners, such measurement tools were produced by participation and consent. Audiences were asked to provide feedback. In subsequent years, listeners were asked to reveal what they were watching at that moment, because listener recall proved unreliable.

In both cases, however, the amount of data generated was both thin and often inaccurate. For example, measurement was limited to those with a household television, thus narrowing the genuine audience of radio and television. Diaries were later used to overcome this. The diary could be sent to a wider sample of the population and more detailed and accurate feedback generated. In addition, demographic information could be included. This, again, relied on the participation of respondents and on the memory, accuracy, and honesty of them in their feedback. Given the susceptibility of this to human error, measurements increasingly turned toward more abstract and scientific data collection methods. The meter became the tool used to bypass the direct participation of the respondent. The television set-top meter, for example, collected data straight from the television, meaning that the respondent was not tasked with representing their responses; their viewing was automatically recorded. Where the set-top meter did not account for who was viewing, the development of the peoplemeter attempted to overcome this. It required that individuals press a button to indicate who in the household was watching. Meters were (and continue to be) installed in a selection of households rather than on all television sets since they are expensive to install on a larger scale. So, where more detailed data on viewing behaviors and demographics might be possible, the sample remained (and remains) small.

The datafication of the audience

More recent television and internet streaming technologies have monitoring tools already embedded within them. The turn toward datafication means that there are now ways of measuring not just a representative sample, but of all activity pertaining to a particular website or online media platform. Webster, Phalen, and Lichty have referred to this as a shift from user-centric to server-centric measurement.[22] Where traditional techniques situate the user at the center of measurement (in other words, where members of the household have their engagement with television measured), service-centric measurement situates the server at the center of measurement (what is measured is the extent of server interactions by users). Measurement companies can draw from both traditional and new methods to measure internet audiences. Nielsen, for example, uses a desktop meter to measure the internet usage of 230,000 people, one of the largest samples to date.[23] This type of measurement draws from panel data (considers who the user is) as well as direct data (usage, location, platforms). Elsewhere, individual providers can bypass audience measurement companies and self-generate knowledge and understanding of their audience through direct data mining, tracking data generated by user interactions with a specific service. Netflix more closely reflects the latter model of measurement. From data generated through user interactions, Netflix gains insights on, and develops recommendation models for, individual subscribers. In addition, it acquires insights on overall, total audience patterns and behaviors. It can assess the performance of individual assets (TV shows or films) much more closely and with much greater accuracy. With large amounts of data on overall user engagement with individual shows, films, or genres, it can more quickly act (to purchase or remove content). It can, in theory, target content to users more effectively, based on the way in which such data can be used to predict viewing patterns.

Thus Netflix overcomes many of the pitfalls of traditional audience measurement. It solves the issue of sample size since it can measure all its subscribers in real time. It can assess individual user engagement with great detail, measuring how users engaged (through interactions such as scroll, select, pause, return to interface). It does not contend with the issue of interviews and diaries, whereby human error can spoil samples. It overcomes the limits of the peoplemeter by incentivizing individual profiling, where use of the individual profile results in personalized recommendations. In addition, the Netflix subscriber is invited to participate by rating content according to their tastes and values. Where individual value judgments in traditional audience measurement systems had little impact on future scheduling, Netflix's data algorithms will tailor content to the individual user.

Netflix bypasses, then, the need for the generation of knowledge on audience composition and constitution—including size, demographic profile, interests, or lifestyle. It overcomes many of the limits of empirical research that sought to account for all of these. Indeed, industry-produced traditional audience measurement techniques have been subject to a great deal of criticism. Ang, for example, points to the significant contextual lack of television audience measurement systems, which tend to ignore or miss the "subjective practices and experiences of actual audience."[24] For her, efforts to classify and identify the audience through the use of narrow frameworks such as "size and demographic composition" resulted in a misconception of the audience as consistent and knowable.

> The matching of factors such as age, sex, race, income, occupation, education and area of residence with viewing behaviour variables (e.g. amount of viewing and programme choice) results in the statistical determination of relatively stable "viewing habits"—a set of imputed behavioural routines that form a perfect merger of the objective and the subjective.[25]

However, this "map" of the audience served to reduce it to a set of somewhat arbitrary classifications, none of which were guaranteed to account for viewing behaviors. Equally, and related to the latter point, the institutional map of audiences neglected the specificities of viewing behaviors: the pleasures, motivations, and meanings for viewers. That Netflix has developed a system that seems to resolve these issues might seem beneficial to viewers as well as media industries. Its model of prediction and recommendation does not depend on or draw from actual user demographics (at least, so far as can be ascertained[26]). It can assess a comprehensive history of viewing behaviors at the level of the individual, including pleasures, interests, and dislikes. It is interactive in that it allows the user to "speak back" to the service through a ratings system. This mechanism for providing feedback recalls the use of previous audience research such as telephone polls and panels, but with the added advantage of being thoroughly representative of individual viewing preferences rather than a reflective sample of a given population. Netflix seems to have erased the ambiguities and guesswork of traditional audience measurement, producing more accurate, detailed, and specific data on individual users.

The predictable audience

However, I wish to claim that the Netflix model of measurement and prediction effaces the context, experiences, and identities of its users even more so than traditional measurement systems. The type of knowledge produced by Netflix works to negate the sense of a public, of a socially shared experience, and of human agency. No longer conceived of as an audience or a collection of individuals, the Netflix user becomes classified as a set of data and the information drawn from this data becomes the primary form of knowledge produced by Netflix. In this sense, Netflix engages with what Antoinette Rouvroy calls "data behaviorism," marked by:

> producing knowledge about future preferences, attitudes, behaviours or events without considering the subject's psychological motivations, speeches or narratives, [instead] relying on *data*. The "real time operationality" of devices functioning on such algorithmic logic spares human actors the burden and responsibility to transcribe, interpret and evaluate the events of the world. It spares them the meaning-making processes of transcription or representation, institutionalization, convention and symbolization.[27]

Data behaviorism refers, therefore, to the way in which data itself becomes knowledge-generating. Empirical research, interpretation, judgment, and analysis are no longer relevant or necessary. Data speaks for itself through the algorithm. Data mining's promise of "personalization" and "individuality" operates in tandem with a system that strips away human agency, personality, and character. Where traditional audience measurement systems formed knowledge of the audience by mapping data onto human activity and sociality, the Netflix model's method of knowledge production reduces humans to digital traces or events. Here, data is knowledge itself. Meaning is not made of data, rather data is all meaning. As Rouvroy suggests, "'Data behaviourism' spares the burden of testing, questioning, examining, evaluating actual facts and persons of flesh and blood, it avoids making persons appear … in order to test or question their causes or intentions."[28] In the case of Netflix, the knowledge formed through its data mining enables it to exert power over the user, who becomes less autonomous, the more their interactions are exploited by the service (since the algorithm increasingly determines the range of content offered to that user).

The knowledge produced via user digital interactions has no referent in the personhood of the user: their tastes, social values, or other non-digital behaviors and expressions. It represents "not the attempt to get at an underlying demographic 'truth', but the ongoing search for productive correlations"[29] that produces a data truth regime that discursively produces the person as profile. This data-generated knowledge, for Rouvroy, does not extend out into the world, but stems "from the digital world."[30] In other words, the data mined by Netflix is not used to infer anything about the human agent interacting with the service; instead it finds correlations between profiles and data interactions. The user is subjected to the digital identity inferred by a personalization and recommendations system (PRS) generated through algorithms rather than an autonomous subject who governs their own behavior. For example, if a Netflix user watches an episode of *Orange Is the New Black*, data traces feed into the PRS that determines the likely pattern of behavior/viewing of this user. This results in a series of new recommendations for this user on his/her next login. This process continues, modifying recommendations according to the user's behaviors. Each time the user logs in, s/he encounters a more algorithmically specified catalogue of content. And, given that the PRS continues to adapt to the new interactions, the range of content becomes more self-fulfilling. The PRS becomes increasingly deterministic, producing a user profile as much informed by its own logic than of genuine and autonomous open interactions by the user. Thus, what is being measured is not spontaneous and willful engagement by the user; rather measurement is compromised by the way in which the PRS shapes behavior.

This algorithmic determinism produces what Cheney-Lippold terms an "algorithmic identity."[31] This identity is generated by organizations that map, collate, and then make algorithmic sense of user data traces in order to understand the identity of that user, not in the sense of actual personhood but as a digital identity or profile. A key point here is that identity is disembodied and, therefore, need not have any actual relevance to the embodied person. However, the algorithm also designates identity using programmed classifications in order to make sense of the data traces left by the user. While Netflix's PRS does not draw from user demographics, such demographics are built into its design and its system of tagging genres. In this sense, the promise of personalization and autonomy is undone since Netflix simply shifts such demographic markers to genre tags. Identity is displaced from the user to the content. In other words, the user does not bring their identity—along with the complexities that inform it—to the platform, rather the platform has determined what these mean. The PRS can then steer the user toward this content, thus ghettoizing the user in a prescribed category of demographically classified content.

This is apparent elsewhere in the way marketers and advertisers use cookies to track a user's online activity. Often algorithms are used to match online data with offline demographic data and work to build a personal profile of that user. This allows advertisers to target their adverts to a profile inferred through a set of social classifications assumed by the online activity and offline social status of that user. For example, if a search engine is used to find information on a cosmetic product, this will likely result in a range of advertisements on other websites and social media—advertisements that infer a specific social body in terms of age, sex, or social class. For Cheney-Lippold, this algorithmic identity, stemming from mathematical algorithms, uses:

> Statistical commonality models to determine one's gender, class or race in an algorithmic manner at the same time as it defines the actual meaning of gender, class or race themselves. … it moves the practice of identity into an entirely digital, and thus measurable, plane.[32]

Thus, while the online world seems to propose the possibility of identity as fluid, transformative, and self-determined, in fact the use of algorithms (by media corporations) work to establish identities as fixed and stable. In addition, the identities inferred by algorithms do much to perpetuate problematic representational effects, whereby "normative" identities are rendered invisible (assumed) and "difference" is labeled. For example, Amazon's online bookstore has a number of categories pertaining to sexual identity—"Gay and Lesbian" and "Women Writers and Fiction"—but these tend to allude to the marginal status of such identities.[33]

A similar compartmentalization of identities exists on Netflix. Its use of identity classifications is apparent in its reference to recommended categories and tagged subgenres such as those with the suffix "with a strong female lead." Here, Netflix infers from previous user interactions that viewing behavior has been determined by gender. In other words, if a user watches a television program that happens to have an assertive female protagonist, the PRS takes this to mean that the user identifies with or engages with the program *because* of gender (of the user or of the protagonist). It is not so much that the PRS works to identify the user as female but that notions of gender are a significant factor determining how the user makes judgments about, and ascribes value to, that particular program.

Netflix's PRS creates distinctions between such classifications and, like Amazon, insists on articulating only those identities culturally coded through "difference." Its use of tags as a means of generating subgenres works to map taste onto demographic categories, but only for those "non-normative" identities. Users are addressed through their difference. For example, race appears as one such subgenre, produced through the tagging of genres ("African-American Movies," "Violent African-American Action and Adventure," "Raunchy African American Comedies," and "Emotional African American Dramas"[34]). Similar tags do not exist for whiteness or white Americans. Femaleness is tagged to genres but not maleness. In this sense, socially marginalized identities are politicized through their separation from non-marginalized identities. These identities are produced through otherness and alterity, whereby whiteness, maleness, and American-ness are assumed as dominant and pervasive (and, therefore, not in need of positioning) and non-white, non-male, non-American identities as distinct and "Other." Netflix's PRS operates on the assumption that race, sex, and nationality shape the identities of some more than others.

Netflix, therefore, makes reductive claims about its users. The Netflix PRS works to enact and prescribe identities it has already produced. However scattered, contradictory, and diverse user iterations might be, its algorithms produce commonalities and, through profiling, generate and assign these commonalities to specific—often socially overdetermined—identities. For example, imagine a user has a preference for crime dramas. The user may select to watch *The Bridge*, *Top of the Lake*, and *The Good Wife*. Any number of reasons might have informed their decision to watch each; however, the Netflix PRS will likely note a pattern of assertive female protagonists. This will then form the basis for future recommendations, thereby subjecting the user to an algorithmic identity. The discourse produced by the recommendations, as they appear on the platform, makes claims about identity: womanhood as the non-normative counterpart to manhood, female strength as the non-normative counterpart to female weakness. Thus, Netflix maps complex data onto reductive demographic categories with the result that it "regulates certain categories" and user identities through what Cheney-Lippold calls "statistical stereotyping."[35]

Not only does Netflix infer identity from user interactions, but it also resists and dismisses attempt by users to self-determine taste preferences and judgments. Netflix assigns different values to different types of data: the more invisible and automatic data are prioritized over self-reflective data offered by the user. The company distinguishes between user behavior and user expression (of taste, interests, and identity). It sees user expression (via taste preferences and ratings) as poor data, as it doesn't correlate as neatly with actual interactions and behavior. The context offered by the user, namely the knowledge they produce about their personhood through wish lists and personalization, is secondary to the knowledge produced by algorithms. The PRS works to produce consistency, coherency, and predictability. Although the user's expressions of preferences and tastes might reflect their spontaneity, diversity of taste, or their mood at a particular moment, this cannot easily be measured and does little to help Netflix coordinate and control the user experience.

Those at Netflix have indicated their resistance to user expression and defended the emphasis on recommendation algorithms centered on behavior. A vice president of product innovation, Todd Yellin, has claimed that:

> most of our personalization right now is based on what [users] actually watch, and not what they say they like... because you can give five stars to *An Inconvenient Truth* because it's changing the world, but you might watch *Paul Blart: Mall Cop 2* three times in a few years... so what you actually want and what [you] say you want are very different.[36]

Netflix does, in some cases, use traditional audience measurement and research, from interviews to surveys. However, its preference for knowledge produced via data algorithms ultimately reveals a "big data mindset" whereby data is figured as a neutral and accurate measurement of human behavior and identity without considering the extent to which the procurement of such data shapes such behavior and identity.[37]

Algorithms and human agency

The regulation of identity—both through the inscription of identity onto profiles and the dismissal of user self-definition in favor of abstract data behavior—has implications for human agency. According to Giddens, human agency can be understood as "concerning the events of which an individual is the perpetrator, in the sense that the individual could, at any phase in a given sequence of conduct, have acted differently."[38] Agency thus refers to the capacity to act (or not act) and this confers power, power here being "the capability to intervene in a given set of events so as in some ways to alter them."[39] It is precisely this form of agency at stake when algorithms increasingly determine one's capacity to act. While data might be "created by users," it is "not controlled by users, who have little choice over how and when this data is generated and little say in how it is used."[40] Netflix, through its PRS, predicts and determines how a user might interact with its content. Through algorithmic predictions, it takes actions on behalf of (or away from) the user. It is telling that studies show that users bypass the recommendations only 25 percent of the time.[41] This suggests that the regulatory power exercised by Netflix does impact on human agency. The effect of such regulatory power on human agency—produced as it is from data-generated knowledge—results in what Rouvroy has termed "algorithmic governmentality." Rouvroy contrasts this with "ordinary" governmentality that regulates through law, a law that depends on the compliance of the subject but, crucially, cannot determine the actions of the subject. The subject, knowing of the law and the consequences of its transgression, may choose to be compliant or not.[42] In this understanding of human agency, the subject retains the capacity to self-determine actions and behaviors. In comparison, "the 'force' of algorithmic government consists in separating subjects from their ability to do or not do certain things. Its target—as its focus on prediction and preemption attests—is *contingency as such*, the conditional mode of the formula 'what a body *could* do.'"[43]

Although Netflix's brand identity centers on notions of user choice, its algorithms work to actively negate choice. Human agency is infringed on through the discreet operations of the PRS, which masks its own operations. The user's ability to act, to determine among the totality of the Netflix service and without reference to their profile, is impeded. The PRS commandeers choice so that the user will not experience the burden of self-definition and autonomy. Netflix acts so that the user does not have to. Human agency, here, is posited as an encumbrance, something best surrendered so that the user is not overwhelmed with uncertainty and, in the worst case, indecision. In exchange for the convenient service offered by Netflix through its PRS, the user foregoes the labor required by autonomous action and independent choice and unwittingly submits to another form of less burdensome labor: that of being subjected to an ongoing process of data monitoring.

> Algorithmic governmentality thus exhibits a new strategy of uncertainty management consisting in minimizing the uncertainty associated with human agency: the capacity humans have to do or not do all they are physically capable of. Effected through the reconfiguration of informational and physical architectures and/or environments within which certain things become impossible or unthinkable, and throwing alerts or stimuli producing reflex responses rather than interpretation or reflection, it affects individuals in their agency that is, in their *inactual, virtual* dimension of potentiality and spontaneity.[44]

It is this spontaneity that traditional audience measurement systems had to contend with. Although figured as a failing of the measurement tools, the inability of measurement and research organizations—and the media companies that relied on their data—to impede on viewing activities and behaviors in the same way meant that the subject retained a degree of human agency. The use of Big Data, therefore, represents a fundamental shift in the ways that audiences are known and acted upon. Traditional audience measurement systems can speculate but cannot predict audience actions. That television broadcasters "battle for the audience" and compete to gain audience attention suggests that the audience retains some form of power. As Ang suggests, for television broadcasters the audience remains "extremely difficult to define, attract and keep."[45] Television broadcasters continuously promote and advertise themselves and they continue to provide full schedules of varied and diverse content. They attempt a form of discipline and control through the use of audience measurement but must also contend with the fact that such measurement is always lacking in information and, as a result, they cannot develop full knowledge of, or enact power over, the audience. The ability of television industries to regulate audiences and stifle their agency is limited.

This is not to suggest that the historical relationship between media companies, audience measurement companies, and audiences should be idealized in a utopian fantasy that included audience autonomy. Rather, one might consider the implications of the failure of audience measurement systems to fulfill their ambition of knowing the audience and, through this, their failure to constitute identity and encroach on human agency. Algorithms, which yield radically more detailed measures of audience behavior and identity, produce new forms of knowledge about the audience. Those used by Netflix, in particular, allow for a reconceptualization of the viewing body, not as a member of an audience but as unique profile. Thus, the use of Big Data promises a unique and individual viewing experience.

However, we have seen that the forms of knowledge generated, and the enactment of this knowledge in the form of recommendations, have effects on human agency, identity, and autonomy. The algorithmic identity produced through recommendations is disembodied, depersonalized, and dehumanized. The Netflix user becomes a measurable and predictable set of data, always produced, and then acted on, by the PRS. The user is no longer a person in the world with a complex and spontaneous relationship to the many events, situations, interfaces it interacts with. The user is no longer embodied in, and expressive of, an identity structured over time and in relation to an endless series of encounters and actions; the user is instead subjected to identities and interactions, governed and expressed by the PRS. Netflix is not, of course, alone in this. It represents a much broader trend in the measurement of human activity. Yet, as the case of Netflix illustrates, the move toward datafication as a new form of measurement should be subject to reflection and interpretation, something that an algorithm cannot achieve.

Notes

1 David Carr, "TV Foresees Its Future. Netflix Is There," *The New York Times*, July 21, 2013. http://www.nytimes.com/2013/07/22/business/media/tv-foresees-its-future-netflix-is-there.html (accessed June 20, 2015).

2 Ken Auletta, "Outside the Box: Netflix and the Future of Television," *The New Yorker*, February 3, 2014. http://www.newyorker.com/magazine/2014/02/03/outside-the-box-2 (accessed June 20, 2015).

3 Alexis C. Madrigal, "How Netflix Reverse Engineered Hollywood," *The Atlantic*, January 2, 2014. http://www.theatlantic.com/technology/archive/2014/01/how-netflix-reverse-engineered-hollywood/282679/ (accessed June 20, 2015).
4 "Netflix Taste Preferences & Recommendations." *Netflix*. https://help.netflix.com/en/node/9898 (accessed June 20, 2015).
5 Ien Ang, *Desperately Seeking the Audience* (London & New York: Routledge, 1991); Philip M. Napoli, *Audience Evolution: New Technologies and Transformations of Media Audiences* (New York: Columbia University Press, 2011).
6 Ang, *Desperately Seeking the Audience*, 21.
7 Ibid., 36.
8 Ibid., preface.
9 Philip M. Napoli, *Audience Economics: Media Institutions and the Audience Marketplace* (New York: Columbia University Press, 2003), 33–34.
10 "Netflix 'What You Want, When You Want' Promo" YouTube video, posted January 8, 2013. https://www.youtube.com/watch?v=A-90OwZtzT4 (accessed June 20, 2015).
11 Mark Andrejevic, "Surveillance and Alienation in the Online Economy," *Surveillance & Society* 8.3 (2011): 278–287.
12 Antoinette Rouvroy, "The End(s) of Critique: Data-Behaviourism vs. Due-Process," in *Privacy, Due Process and the Computational Turn: The Philosophy of Law Meets the Philosophy of Technology*, eds Mireille Hildebrandt and Ekatarina De Vries (New York: Routledge, 2013), 143–168.
13 Andrejevic, "Surveillance and Alienation," 281.
14 Cynthia Littleton, "Linear TV Watching Down, Digital Viewing Up in Nielsen's Q3 Report," *Variety*, December 3, 2014. http://variety.com/2014/tv/news/linear-tv-watching-down-digital-viewing-up-in-nielsens-q3-report-1201369665/ (accessed June 12, 2015).
15 Jay Yarow, "Netflix CEO on the TV Industry: It Had a Great 50-Year Run, but It's Over Now," *Business Insider UK*, April 26, 2015. http://www.businessinsider.com/netflix-ceo-on-the-tv-industry-2015-4 (accessed June 10, 2015).
16 Alison Griswold, "Netflix Is Running Ads That It Insists Aren't Ads," *Slate*, June 1, 2015. http://www.slate.com/blogs/moneybox/2015/06/01/netflix_is_running_ads_for_its_own_content_says_they_re_not_really_ads.html (accessed June 10, 2015).
17 Napoli, *Audience Economics*, 3.
18 Ibid.
19 Ibid., 5.
20 Barry Gunter, *Media Research Methods: Measuring Audiences, Reactions and Impact* (London: Sage, 2000), 116.
21 James G. Webster et al., *Ratings Analysis: Audience Measurement and Analytics*, 4th ed. (New York: Routledge, 2014), 22.
22 Ibid., 38.
23 "Nielsen Launches Largest, Most Representative Online Audience Measurement Panel in the U.S," *Nielsen*, July 13, 2009. http://www.nielsen.com/us/en/press-room/2009/Nielsen_Launches_Largest__Most_Representative_Online_Audience_Measurement_Panel.html (accessed June 11, 2015).
24 Ang, *Desperately Seeking the Audience*, 62.
25 Ibid.

26 "Netflix Goes Beyond Demographics," *Warc*, March 27, 2015. https://www.warc.com/LatestNews/News/Netflix_goes_beyond_demographics.news?ID=34519 (accessed June 13, 2015).
27 Rouvroy, "The End(s) of Critique: Data-Behaviourism vs. Due-Process," 143.
28 Ibid., 149.
29 Andrejevic, "Surveillance and Alienation," 281.
30 Rouvroy, "The End(s) of Critique: Data-Behaviourism vs. Due-Process," 147.
31 John Cheney-Lippold, "A New Algorithmic Identity: Soft Biopolitics and the Modulation of Control," *Theory, Culture & Society* 28.6 (2011): 164–181.
32 Ibid., 165.
33 Amazon UK, 2015.
34 Agid, *Netflix Genres*. https://docs.google.com/spreadsheets/d/1eISFvq42Sll10xekyV-XQdwoG7_gjZpreNG40Pz8G0k/edit?pli=1#gid=1310164220 (accessed June 12, 2015).
35 Cheney-Lippold, "A New Algorithmic Identity," 170.
36 Josh Lowinsohn, "The Science Behind Netflix's First Major Redesign in Four Years," *The Verge*, May 22, 2015. http://www.theverge.com/2015/5/22/8642359/the-science-behind-the-new-netflix-design (accessed June 11, 2015).
37 José van Dijck, "Datafication, Dataism and Dataveillance: Big Data Between Scientific Paradigm and Ideology," *Surveillance and Society* 12.2 (2014): 197–208.
38 Anthony Giddens, *The Constitution of Society* (Berkeley: University of California Press, 1984), 9.
39 Anthony Giddens, *The Nation-State and Violence* (Berkeley: University of California Press, 1987), 7.
40 Andrejevic, "Surveillance and Alienation," 286.
41 Blake Hallinan and Ted Striphas, "Recommended for You: The Netflix Prize and the Production of Algorithmic Culture," *New Media & Society* 18.1 (January 2016): 130.
42 Rouvroy, "The End(s) of Critique: Data-Behaviourism vs. Due-Process," 155.
43 Ibid.
44 Ibid., 155–156.
45 Ang, *Desperately Seeking the Audience*, preface.

4

Imaginative Indices and Deceptive Domains: How Netflix's Categories and Genres Redefine the Long Tail

Daniel Smith-Rowsey

Introduction

In Chris Anderson's 2006 book *The Long Tail: Why the Future of Business Is Selling Less of More*, the editor-in-chief of *Wired* explained that compared with previous business models, the "granular data mining" employed by internet companies caters to customers' tastes far more precisely, enabling niche offerings as easily as mass-market products.[1] However, as Astra Taylor and others have since written, in practice, the Long Tail strategy suppresses creative freedom and user choices, directing users less to their self-curated gardens and more to advertisements that support oligarchic internet companies like Google, Apple, Facebook, Amazon, and Netflix.[2] One way to elucidate the problems with this shift is to examine one of these companies, deconstruct one crucial aspect of its business, and show how the Long Tail has become something of a Tall Tale.

In 2006, Anderson supported his arguments with interviews with Reed Hastings, chief executive officer of Netflix, which has since emerged as the definitive media company of the twenty-first century, perhaps best exemplifying the synergy *and* tension between Silicon Valley and Hollywood. Netflix is one of the leading providers of digitally delivered media content and is continually expanding access across the screen platforms and mobile devices of its subscribers, who now number more than sixty-five million worldwide. Once the poster child for the Long Tail strategy, now Netflix's own home page and envelope advertisements—which promote big hits as well as Netflix-produced entertainment—offer evidence of how the strategy has been warped by corporate interests. This transformation has troubling implications for leading internet media companies like Google, Apple, Facebook, and Amazon, as well as the "Big Six" media companies—Warners/HBO, Universal/Comcast, Viacom/Paramount, Disney, Sony, and Fox. If, as contemporary trade pieces in places like *Wired* and *Variety* would have it, all ten of these companies stand to mimic or surpass current Netflix's ostensible Long Tail strategies (i.e., catering to consumers instead of telling them what they want), those policies deserve closer scrutiny.

I wish to emphasize that as a distribution platform, Netflix is programmed with what I call *intentional instability*. I argue herein that on Netflix, the information provided by Long Tail–style granular data collection rests uneasily with both capitalist imperatives and hierarchies produced by Netflix's somewhat Bourdieuan authority. Pierre Bourdieu argued that our tastes are directed by those who position us toward our social aspirations, and Netflix indeed positions us this way, which Harold Bloom suggests remains necessary for society to function[3]—even as Netflix also pushes us in less predictable directions. I find the company's intentional instability most clearly demonstrated through Netflix's re-definition of genre, genre being a core aspect of Netflix's business model and projected appeal to consumers, as indicated by the search-field suggestions on its home page (through 2015): "Titles, People, Genres." Thus, I begin with a brief overview of genre and how scholars such as Rick Altman explain the power of such distinctions, continue with an exploration of the advantages and disadvantages of Netflix's broader genre categories, examine "micro-genres," and conclude with reflections on how the Long Tail has been curtailed.

Imaginative solutions and deceptive non-solutions

Rick Altman writes that platforms of distribution and exhibition exert a deterministic power over how audiences perceive genres.[4] Netflix features a "Complete Genre Listing" of 19 umbrella categories, roughly 400 subcategories, and about 73,000 so-called micro-genres (e.g., "Visually Striking Father-Son Movies"). Netflix asserts a sort of capitalist-driven postmodernism, in that studios can, to a limited extent, pay to have films/shows pop up where they should not be. Netflix refuses to let users understand this process at the same time as it diminishes certain well-researched indices. What we might call the "effacement level" is high on Netflix and Facebook; a little lower on Amazon, where links are shown as sponsored but recommendations are left opaque; somewhat lower on Google, where the first three links of your search are marked as sponsored, and subsequent links are "pure" results (though also based on your location and previous searches); and particularly low on Wikipedia, where one can see histories of all user changes. While effacing its recommendation processes, Netflix in effect privileges some films and shows and types of viewership, and to some degree re-constitutes what Netflix's sixty million users *think* when they think of film and TV.

A surfeit of genre criticism presumes two major groups who label genres—studios and audiences. The powers of video stores and other distributors are sometimes acknowledged, but rarely as a third, determinative labeling agent. Steve Neale,[5] Yvonne Tasker,[6] and other scholars chart an ontological course between studios and audiences, reminding us of the shifting capitalist imperatives of the former and the shifting "usability" imperatives of the latter. Yet Netflix, a lowly distributor, presents a rather rigorous, seemingly exhaustive index of genres without quite adhering to either of these groups. In the past, studios, critics, and audiences articulated genre discursively, yet by ceding ground to a distributor, Netflix, genre has become intertwined with technical distinctions, term coding, tags/links functionality, and most importantly, Netflix's business model. Clearly, Netflix shares the capitalist imperatives of the studios, but they do not see eye to eye, not least because Netflix does not wish to lose market share to, for example, foreign distributors or websites—including YouTube, Hulu, Vimeo, and Vine—who offer monetizable content that the studios neither approve of nor distribute. Though Netflix markets itself as a customer-oriented experience, it is hardly as user-curated as, say, Instagram, Imgur, Reddit, or Pinterest. Considering the wide, increasing reach of Netflix, future genre criticism would do well to consider this third source of genre definition.

Altman establishes a binary of two different strains of genre criticism. For Altman, ritual critics see films offering *imaginative* solutions to real-world problems, but ideological/Marxist critics see films offering *deceptive* non-solutions that serve governmental/corporate purposes. Part of the power of Netflix lays in its ostensible appeal to the imaginative, or as Altman puts it,

> Following the example of primitive or folk narrative, the ritual approach considers that audiences are the ultimate creators of genres, which function to justify and organize a virtually timeless society. According to this approach, the narrative patterns of generic texts grow out of existing social practices, imaginatively overcoming contradictions within those very practices. From this point of view, audiences have a very special investment in genres, because genres constitute the audience's own method of assuring its unity and envisioning its future. [This approach is] particularly welcome to champions of popular culture because of its ability to lend meaning to a previously neglected or condemned domain.[7]

Yet this may be a case of a deceptive wolf wearing an imaginatively rendered sheep's clothing. Altman says that some indices of genres are indeed both at once, and Netflix's 19 umbrella categories and 400 subcategories provide further evidence to this effect, suggesting and encouraging leaps of imagination as well as extensions of deception. As examples, in the next section I point to genres that are effaced or diminished by Netflix, a development that threatens these genres' very existence in an increasingly Netflixed world. If the curator at New York's Museum of Modern Art exercises considerable discretion over what counts as Modern Art, we may say that Netflix curators tell us what counts as types of movies, and even movies themselves.

The 19 and the 400

To understand how Netflix turned the vaunted Long Tail into something less inclusive, begin with Netflix's list of 19 umbrella genres/categories: Action and

Adventure, Anime and Animation, Children and Family, Classics, Comedy, Documentary, Drama, Faith and Spirituality, Foreign, Gay and Lesbian, Horror, Independent, Music and Musicals, Romance, Sci-Fi and Fantasy, Special Interest, Sports and Fitness, Television, and Thrillers. Yes, some of the hyperlinks for the subgenres appear under more than one header: for example, the hyperlink for Classic Dramas can be found under Classics or under Dramas, and the link takes you to the same list. After eliminating doubles like these, I have arrived at the rough number of 400 subcategories (see Table 4.1 at the end of this chapter for Netflix's complete genre list).

Here I would like to note several well-researched genres that do not appear in the umbrella 19 *or* the 400: gangster, melodrama, road movies, buddy movies, chick flicks, women's pictures, pornography, soft-core porn, torture porn, J-horror, K-horror, scenics, newsreels. (No doubt I am missing many more.) Once, Rick Altman asked Leonard Maltin to settle the question: is *Thelma and Louise* "a chick-flick, a buddy film, a road movie, or something else?"[8] For Netflix, it is none of these, because Netflix has none of those three categories. *Thelma and Louise*'s two genres on Netflix are Drama and Crime Dramas. (I speculate that Netflix's "Drama" category is meant to encompass "Melodrama" without alienating viewers who would picture a mustachioed villain tying a blonde to train tracks, and that the "Mobster" subgenre, listed under the main genre of "Thrillers," is meant to "sub" for "Gangster" without connoting anything close to "gangster rap." But replacement does not equal 1-to-1 substitution.)

Of course, most Netflix titles are tagged with more than one genre/category. As Jacques Derrida put it, all texts participate in one or several genres.[9] Probably, studios would prefer that most of its product fall into no fewer than three categories. What is troubling for them and for genre scholars is the fact that Netflix genre/category associations are not restrictive; some films (e.g., *Lord of the Rings: The Fellowship of the Ring*) are tagged with as many as seven genre/categories, and thus it is hard to see how films would be hurt by being tagged/hyperlinked with, say, melodrama or certain kinds of horror. *Easy Rider* would not lose "Drama" or "Independent" or anything else if it also took on "road movies." But because Netflix has judged this subcategory unnecessary, it has moved users ever-so-slightly toward a similar consideration.

The problem of exclusion is abetted by the fact that as a distribution platform, Netflix is programmed with *intentional instability*. As chapters by Sarah Arnold and Neta Alexander in this collection make clear, any user's "recommendations list" is an uneasy, combustible product of that user's taste and Netflix's authority to create that user's taste. Netflix maintains an algorithm of what its users prefer, but then intentionally offers content that both follows and subverts that algorithm. (As an example, I searched for George Clooney and my top choice was a Rosemary Clooney show collection in which George does not appear. None of my previous Netflix choices would lead anyone to think that I prefer Rosemary to George; quite the opposite, in fact.) If Netflix is so bold as to refine my results for its own reasons, why not permit broader pathways of cross-referencing?

Intentional instability, of course, refers to Netflix's intentions, not those of users, who, unlike on sites like Wikipedia or IMDb, are excluded from curating their Netflix "recommendations" experience. Users cannot just create an umbrella "chick flick" genre if desired. Users also cannot understand the parameters surrounding category distinctions; for example, we cannot be sure (as of this writing) how many titles one requires to constitute a subcategory. "Healing and Reiki" (a sub under "Mindfulness and Prayer," which is in turn a group under the "Faith and Spirituality" umbrella) produces exactly twenty titles. Many others (particularly around the "Mindfulness and Prayer" area) are likewise associated with fewer than 100 titles. It is hardly crazy to speculate that hypothetical Netflix genres like Gangster or Melodrama could be used to tag more than 100 titles. In fairness, this problem of genre reconfiguration is not limited to Netflix. Marieke Jenner uses Jason Mittell's "discursive cluster" approach to television genre as a broad framework for questioning video-on-demand (VOD) reconfiguration of genre more generally. Jenner, aware that TV and film genres have a problematic relationship, nonetheless raises crucial questions about medium, scheduling, and the above-mentioned "micro-genres": are different viewing devices, viewer autonomy, and personalized genres favoring, disfavoring, or re-defining established genres?[10]

It may be that Netflix is abetting a semantic evolution of the very term *genre*. Its users may not find Netflix's list of 19 or 400 to be truly definitive; some of the categories in the umbrella 19—for example, Gay and Lesbian, Special Interest, Sports and Fitness—do not really correspond to "genre" in Altman's sense of audiences accepting certain genres. However, this may only be a matter of time. And Netflix, more than IMDb or Wikipedia or Metacritic or Rotten Tomatoes, may find itself, indeed already does find itself, settling some old arguments, for example, about "thrillers" (its own umbrella) and "Blaxploitation" (under Action and Adventure) and "mockumentaries" (under Comedies *and* Documentary). How regular people define "Classics" or even "classical" may evolve because Netflix currently includes films from the twenty-first century (like *Y Tu Mama Tambien* [2001]) in its "Classics." As a subcategory under "Classics," the commonalities of "Silent Films" may be massively oversimplified to the point of absurdity. There have already been scholarly arguments about using terms like "Television,"[11] "Documentary,"[12] "Foreign,"[13] and "Animation"[14] as generic categories; these were signified during Brad Bird's acceptance speech at the 2005 Academy Awards, when upon receiving the Award for Best Animated Feature (for *The Incredibles*, 2004), he shouted "Animation is *not* a genre!" Nonetheless, these are 4 of the 19 umbrella terms of Netflix's page headlined "Complete Genre Listing."

However, Brad Bird may yet have the last laugh. Because "Anime and Animation" includes mostly foreign films and quirky one-offs (e.g., Adam Sandler's *Eight Crazy Nights*)—and none of the cartoons in the top 300 all-time box-office earners (e.g., *Toy Story, Shrek, Despicable Me, Frozen*)—Netflix nudges us, along with its (sometimes erstwhile) corporate allies Disney, Pixar, and DreamWorks Animation, to think of those studios' hallmark films less as animation and more as "Children and Family" films, the umbrella category that contains them. In fact, in "Children and Family," the subcategory "Cartoons" refers only to collections of shorts. Here Netflix seems less intentionally unstable, and more intentionally predisposed against certain kinds of animation.

"Disney," "Nickelodeon," and "Saturday Night Live" seem to be the only three of the 400 subgenres named directly for corporate entities, and thus these brands succeed here in almost de-branding themselves, making themselves as natural as westerns and romantic comedies. Furthermore, Netflix extends these three brands/genres in a manner that the heads of Disney's rivals, like Paramount, Universal, and Warner Bros. (which are not Netflix genres unto themselves), could only dream about. Clicking "Disney" in July 2013, my top row appeared as *The Muppets*, *Tron: Legacy*, *Chimpanzee*, and *The Proposal* (with Sandra Bullock and Ryan Reynolds). Clicking "Nickelodeon" also in July 2013, I found a wide array of their (limited) product, like *iCarly*, *SpongeBob*, *The Penguins of Madagascar*, and *Max & Ruby*. Clicking "Saturday Night Live" around the same time revealed dizzying brand extension: the offerings include *SNL* collections (e.g., *The Best of Amy Poehler*, *The Best of Eddie Murphy*), as well as films starring *SNL* alums that have no other significant connection to the show.

Many critics have applied Fredric Jameson's observations about postmodernism and capitalism to the internet—in a world where the digital is real, capitalism and private enterprise conspire to shift definitions so often and regularly that private definitions are obliterated.[15] Yet this dictum can oversimplify the complex way in which corporate interests function against the supposed Long Tail strategy. In Orwell's *1984*, a citizen of Oceania could do well simply by recalling the opposite of a governmental dictum—for example, canards like War is Peace, Freedom is Slavery, Ignorance is Strength. However, in Netflix's brave new world, half the signifiers make sense and the other half shift—but one does not know which are shifting at which time. This is one significant marker of Netflix's intentional instability.

For example, I go to the Action and Adventure genre and click on "Blockbusters," a term with various definitions, but we may tentatively use Steve Neale's two sets: intended blockbusters, which are among the highest-budgeted films of their time, and accidental blockbusters, which rank among their year's top earners despite modest budgets.[16] Alongside the first page's somewhat predictable *Hunger Games*, *Avengers*, *Sherlock Holmes*, and *Mission Impossible*, I also see *The Help*, *The Vow*, and *The King's Speech*—not exactly what anyone would consider Action and Adventure Blockbusters. The natural retort is that the category is akin to box-office overperformers, but the front page also includes *The Expendables*—not a bomb by any means, but hardly a runaway smash. As studios shift support, signifiers shift as well; users are carefully satisfied and not satisfied, directed to what they would like and re-directed to what they might consider. Of course, users can supplement their Netflix searches with more authoritative services like instantwatcher.com or film-fish.com, but that merely offers a new set of malleable signifiers. In the end, Netflix users (like everyone else) will often accept the postmodern sprawl, shrug and decide that nothing can be trusted—hardly the sort of reaction that enables something like the diverse, personalized array of choices promised by Anderson in *The Long Tail.*

If Anderson suggested in *The Long Tail* that Netflix was becoming a sort of amazon.com of screen content, that ambition seems to have been curtailed in favor of certain priorities for the company. As an example, Netflix seems to maintain a bias toward content than *can or will be* available on DVD. Netflix does not seem to offer many TV shows that *are not* coming out on DVD, like the vast majority of game shows, reality shows, morning shows, talk shows, legal shows, soap operas, and quotidian sports (and video games). Hulu, by contrast, offers all of this TV-based content in spades. Hulu is much closer to TV-on-demand, while Netflix's streaming service is closer to what would happen if one could stream every DVD ever printed. Perhaps the idea, well in line with its original content like *House of Cards, Orange Is the New Black, Daredevil, The Unbreakable Kimmy Schmidt,* and *Arrested Development,* is to keep Netflix just a bit more prestigious, even if Hulu is perhaps cozier or less pretentious. This sort of branding is probably related to the absence of genres like body horror and pornography.

Micro-genres

None of Netflix's 19 umbrella genres or 400 subgenres are dated to any specific period, furthering Altman's notion that genre is transhistorical and synchronic. Thus, Netflix helps to refute Jane Feuer's notion of a "life cycle" for genres.[17] Instead, Netflix confirms Altman's suggestion that "in the genre world, however, every day is Jurassic Park day," meaning that genres can be cross-fertilized at any time with any genre that ever existed.[18] In theory, Netflix could actively endeavor to create new genres and new classification systems. However, in practice, since 2006, when it redeveloped its Cinematch recommendations algorithm(s), Netflix has left most potential cross-fertilization undone… at least, at the level of the 19 umbrella categories and 400 subcategories. But these are not the only way in which Netflix denotes its massive catalog. There are descriptions that pop up as a curated shelf of (usually five) sample suggestions ostensibly based on user tastes—for example: Cerebral Con-Game Thrillers, Visually-Striking Father-Son Movies, Violent Nightmare-Vacation Movies, Understated Independent Workplace Movies, and Emotional Drug Documentaries. Reporters and scholars working on these tags have not always been clear that they are *not* part of a film's home page on Netflix but instead part of a subtler recommendations function, and thus part of a process that works to obscure Netflix's intentional instability—and to reify the necessity of Netflix functioning as our "ghost in the machine." These wordy categories are called "micro-genres" by Alexis Madrigal, who in the January 2014 *Atlantic,* published "How Netflix Reverse Engineered Hollywood," in which he identified 76,897 micro-genres. (For the record, none of the 76,897 are "gangster" or "body horror.") But this is where Netflix periodizes, as Feuer might have hoped, because part of the expanding corpuses is through dangling modifiers like "from the 1950s" or "from the 1980s." Madrigal elaborates:

> Using large teams of people specially trained to watch movies, Netflix deconstructed Hollywood. They paid people to watch films and tag them with all kinds of metadata. This process is so sophisticated and precise that taggers receive a 36-page training document that teaches them how to rate movies on their sexually suggestive content, goriness, romance levels, and even narrative elements like plot conclusiveness. They capture dozens of different movie attributes. They even rate the moral status of characters.[19]

But can Bourdieuan notions of taste truly be translated into mathematical or even pseudo-mathematical formulas for millions of users? Favoring formulas not so unlike the classical Hollywood storytelling technique that can be found in any screenwriting manual, micro-genres seem to offer a revolutionary way to categorize, filter, and disseminate visual content in the manner Anderson suggested in *The Long Tail*. However, Neta Alexander argues in her chapter in this collection that micro-genres really create "filter bubbles" that feed us formulistic products and therefore pose a threat to originality and creative freedom.

Unlike Alexander or myself, Madrigal managed to interview Netflix's Todd Yellin, the man who supervises this process. As a business, Netflix, much like Hollywood itself, does not offer you *exactly* what you think you want—instead it offers some of exactly what you want, and a little more that you might like if you tried. If I were Madrigal I might have asked about *those* numbers. For example, as a user, do I have an A-tier of likely preferences, and then a B-tier, and then a C-tier? Does Netflix offer me, say, 50 percent of my A-tier, 25 percent of my B-tier, 20 percent of my C-tier, and 5 percent that I've indicated zero preference for? If not, those percentages, which ones are closer? And what is the formula for the latter group—to reference my earlier example, exactly how do you decide to give George Clooney lovers his aunt instead of, say, Brad Pitt?

Netflix's intentional instability no doubt runs on certain precepts, and as of this writing, users have no way to know what those are. Madrigal's 5,000-word article manages to leave most of the important questions unanswered. For example: How much and how often do studios pay to get their films into categories? How often do the films in the categories rotate? How long do studios pay for? A week, a month, a year? Is there any plan to give Netflix users more power over categorization itself? What if I, as a user, am not happy with the Comcast-like array of category choices, and I want something more binary? What if I want to categorize films into two groups, domestic and foreign? Or made-for-cinema and made-for-TV? Or animated and non-animated? Or fiction and non-fiction? Or even three-act-formula bound or not? Is there any plan to make Netflix more user-controlled in any areas?

Netflix does offer users the *apparent* ability to build their own micro-genres; the easiest way to access this function is by clicking one of the adjectives in a given film's home page. Under the given film's list of associated genres is a line that says "This Film Is:"; afterward it might say Gritty, Exciting, Witty, or at least 200 other adjectives. The user clicks the adjective's hyperlink, and is taken to a screen to ask for "more like this." Here the user chooses by clicking bubbles next to terms, among a few (perhaps four or five) descriptors in one column, and then in another column, and then in yet another. The interface is not unlike the stereotypical Chinese-food menu: a little bit from Column A, a little bit from Column B, a little bit from Column C. Unsurprisingly, your result often takes you to a "shelf" of sponsored releases with only tangential relation to the micro-genre you have just asked for. And the shelves under your ostensibly self-curated shelf may offer even less association with the instructions you attempted to provide. BuzzFeed recently published a list of twenty-three Netflix micro-genres that lead to exactly one film.[20] The first genre on their list, Raunchy TV Comedies Featuring a Strong Female Lead, leads only to Netflix's own *Orange Is the New Black*. Each of these twenty-three is what we might call a particularly corporate-friendly deceptive domain; we are told of a plural ("comedies," "dramas") and the set has turned out to feature exactly one figure.

A bright side

If Netflix's genre categories demonstrate distortion of the Long Tail strategy, might the categories yield other benefits to users? To begin to answer this, let me postulate that many, perhaps all, film scholars of a certain age have had the experience of walking into an independent video store and observing that some anonymous, creative clerk has conjured up an entirely original category that causes a smile. I recall once seeing a shelf of films exclusively populated by boxes featuring 1980s' poster images of men lowering their Ray-Ban sunglasses to the bridge of the nose. Blogs and Tumblrs may well provide twenty-first-century equivalents of such groupings. We may call this an imaginative index in Altman's terms—while it may not solve a real-world problem, it does speak to our instinctive, evolutionary desire to categorize and group together like objects, particularly ones that our neighbors may not have thought to group. Many of Netflix's 400 subcategories suggest commonalities that might have been heretofore heterodox: under the Horror umbrella, one can click Vampires, Werewolves, Zombies, and even Teen Screams; under Children and Family, one sees subs like Book Characters and Dinosaurs; under Music, a person can click Gospel Music, Show Tunes, World Fusion, Reggae, and separately Reggaeton; under Special Interest, users are offered Sculpture, Tap and Jazz Dance, Hunting, Magic and Illusion, Wine and Beverage Appreciation, Performance Art and Spoken Word, Shakespeare, as well as Healing and Reiki. As a general rule, film scholarship has barely scratched the surface of instructional videos and non-persuasive documentaries, particularly on sports; Netflix's list suggests continents of possible trailblazing. Netflix's Top 19 umbrella genres are probably a relief for scholars of Comedy, Horror, and Sci-Fi and Fantasy. The 19 genres *may* be read as particular vindication to those who have carved out generic, semantic/syntactic space for Romance, Thrillers, and even Independent films. And the 19 umbrella categories do suggest work to be done or re-done. "Children and Family" and "Faith and Spirituality" are two particularly under-researched indices, considering their prominence in people's lives.

Genre criticism—and most book-length film criticism—faces the problem of *caprice*: why these films and not other films? A scholar might reply that foundational work was done on such-and-such films, and thus it makes sense to extend that work… but would it not make just as much sense to build a new foundation? How can influence truly be measured? Or quality? Box office numbers represent something tangible, at least with the requisite caveats about adjusted dollars, but few, perhaps no, researchers claim to study the Top 10 or Top 50 or Top 100 highest-earning films ever made in a given genre. Nonetheless, genre studies tend to single out a few formative films with an often under-examined presumption of synecdoche—that the part stands for the whole. Testing such presumptions against Netflix's list may in fact prove productive.

For an example, I return to the first of Netflix's 19 umbrella genres, Action and Adventure, and compare Netflix's offerings to recent scholarship. In Barna William Donovan's 2010 book *Blood, Guns, and Testosterone: Action Films, Audiences, and a Thirst for Violence*, Donovan cites appropriate antecedents: Yvonne Tasker, John Cawelti, John Fiske, Mark Gallagher, Neal King, Will Murray, Gina Marchetti, and others. Using their work and his own, he runs through foundational franchises to define the "Modern American Action Film": James Bond, *Dirty Harry*, *Rambo*, *The Terminator*, *Lethal Weapon*, *Die Hard*, *Mission: Impossible*, *The Matrix*, *Batman*, *Spider-Man*, *Iron Man*, and a few others. Donovan particularly favors films starring Sylvester Stallone, Arnold Schwarzenegger, and Bruce Willis. He finds that questions about the supposed crisis of masculinity lie at the heart of understanding modern action. He concludes his epistemic chapter: "Action films function as morality tales of modernity and postmodernity, with men in the absolutist, modernist camp and women in the world of rising postmodernity. Male heroes of the action genre are often lonely figures, their reason for existence becoming their crusades as families and lovers cast them by the wayside. But, ultimately, the genre is about aggression and the male capacity for it. The films foreground the visual spectacle of destruction."[21]

Like scholars of the horror film, the musical, the western, and other genre films, Donovan has not premised his observations on any indexing of the highest-earning or highest-budgeted films. (In Donovan's case, such a list would include films from the franchises *Pirates of the Caribbean*, *Lord of the Rings*, *Men in Black*, several Pixar/Disney cartoons, and *Harry Potter*, only the latter of which merits even a cursory mention.) This is normal for scholars; some sort of picking and choosing is necessary. The question is not about outliers who happened to have earned the most profits, but more about whether scholarly generalizations that begin "The action film is about… " can withstand anything like the entire Netflix-denoted (American, in Donovan's case) corpus of such films. In light of Netflix's growing reach, the new question to ask Donovan, and many genre scholars like him, is: can your observations about the salient properties of your genre hold true when checked against a reasonable sample of films denoted by Netflix as part of this genre? In the case of Donovan and "Action and Adventure" (allowing that Action and Adventure may be separate entities), are these films really mostly about lonely men resolving internal crises through external crises? Or does this fail to hold up against the films in Netflix's subcategories under the Action umbrella like "Action Comedies," "African-American Action," "Heist Films," "Martial Arts," "Military and War Action," and "Super Swashbucklers"? Netflix's list of 400 subgenre terms represents a potential path for achievable scholarship that offers the promise of slightly less privileging of the same old texts.

Steve Neale points out that many definitions of genre presume Hollywood and American culture as a base referent, and indeed, on Netflix, foreign-language films are somewhat ghettoized, without all of the same distinctions that English-language films get, thus further decreasing the likelihood that any foreign genre-busting film will succeed in American theaters.[22] Still, while the foreign section may not be authoritative, one could do worse than checking academic assumptions about comedy, drama, horror, musicals, romance, sci-fi, and thrillers against Netflix's hyperlinks to lists of Foreign Comedies, Foreign Dramas, Foreign Horror, Foreign Musicals, Foreign Romance, Foreign Sci-Fi, and Foreign Thrillers (respectively). And the denotations of foreign lands and foreign languages could yet serve as useful complication to reams of scholarship about genres.

Conclusion

In summary, Netflix's reconfiguration of genre refutes much of the optimism offered by Chris Anderson's ideas about a Long Tail. Instead, Netflix well represents the latest in internet-based postmodern capitalism, ostensibly tailored to users but actually designed with an intentional instability that keeps users partly satisfied and partly redirected to corporate interests. Netflix's 19 umbrella genres, 400 subgenres, and 76,897 micro-genres threaten to diminish extant scholarship even as they offer new opportunities for less capricious, more data-based academic work. Netflix itself has many questions to answer, particularly regarding the nature of its algorithms and its plans for greater user input. Perhaps never before has a distributor occasioned so many reasons for re-thinking contemporary trends in cinema and new media.

Table 4.1 Netflix's complete genre list (numbering does not appear in original version)

1. Action & adventure	2. Anime & animation	3. Children & family
1. Action Classics	17. Animation for Grown-ups	27. Ages 0–2
2. Action Comedies	18. Anime Action	28. Ages 2–4
3. Action Thrillers	19. Anime Comedy	29. Ages 5–7
4. Adventures	20. Anime Drama	30. Ages 8–10
5. African-American Action	21. Anime Fantasy	31. Ages 11–12
6. Blaxploitation	22. Anime Feature Films	32. Animal Tales
7. Comic Books and Superheroes	23. Anime Horror	33. Book Characters
8. Crime Action	24. Anime Sci-Fi	34. Cartoons
9. Deadly Disasters	25. Anime Series	35. Coming of Age
10. Espionage Action	26. Kids' Anime	36. Dinosaurs
11. Foreign Action and Adventure		37. Disney
12. Heist Films		38. Education & Guidance
13. Martial Arts		39. Family Adventures
14. Military & War Action		40. Family Animation
15. Super Swashbucklers		41. Family Classics
16. Westerns		42. Family Dramas
		43. Family Sci-Fi & Fantasy
		44. Kids' Music
		45. Kids' TV
		46. Nickelodeon
		47. Teen Comedies
		48. Teen Dramas
		49. Teen Romance
4. Classics	**5. Comedy**	**6. Documentary**
50. Classic Comedies	63. African-American Comedies	79. African-American Docs
51. Classic Dramas	64. Best of British Humor	80. Biographical Docs
52. Classic Sci-Fi & Fantasy	65. Cult Comedies	81. Crime Documentaries
53. Classic Thrillers	66. Dark Humor & Black Comedies	82. Faith & Spirituality Docs
54. Classic War Stories	67. Foreign Comedies	83. Inspirational Biographies
55. Classic Westerns	68. Latino Comedies	84. Religion & Mythology Docs
56. Epics	69. Political Comedies	85. Spiritual Mysteries
57. Film Noir	70. Romantic Comedies	86. Foreign Documentaries
58. Foreign Classics	71. Saturday Night Live	87. HBO Documentaries
59. Foreign Classic Comedies	72. Screwball	88. Historical Documentaries
60. Foreign Classic Dramas	73. Slapstick	89. Indie Documentaries
61. Foreign Silent Films	74. Spoofs and Satire	90. Military Documentaries
62. Silent Films	75. Sports Comedies	91. Miscellaneous Docs
	76. Stand-Up	92. PBS Documentaries
	77. Mockumentaries	93. Political Documentaries
	78. Showbiz Comedies	94. Rocumentaries
		95. Science and Nature Docs
		96. Social & Cultural Docs
		97. Sports Documentaries
		98. Travel & Adventure Docs
		99. Mockumentaries

Source: http://dvd.netflix.com/AllGenresList

7. Drama	8. Faith & spirituality	9. Foreign
100. African-American Dramas	125. Faith & Spirituality Feature Films	146. Foreign Actin & Adventure
101. Biographies	126. Inspirational Stories	147. Foreign Art House
102. Courtroom Dramas	127. Religious & Myth Epics	148. Foreign Children & Family
103. Crime Dramas	128. Religious & Spirituality Dramas	149. Foreign Comedies
104. Dramas Based on Real Life	129. Religious Comedies & Stories	150. Regional–Africa
105. Dramas Based on the Book	130. Inspirational Biographies	151. Regional–Argentina
106. Dramas Based on Bestsellers	131. Spiritual Mysteries	152. Regional–Australia & New Zealand
107. Dramas Based on Classis Literature	132. Inspirational Music	153. Regional–Belgium
108. Dramas Based on Contemporary Literature	133. Gospel Music	154. Regional–Brazil
109. Foreign Dramas	134. Inspirational Rock & Pop	155. Regional–China
110. Gambling Dramas	135. New Age	156. Regional–Czech Republic
111. Gay & Lesbian Dramas	136. Sacred Classical Music	157. Regional–Eastern Europe
112. Indie Dramas	137. Sacred Talk & Traditional Music	158. Regional–France
113. Latino Dramas	138. Judaica	159. Regional–Germany
114. Medical Dramas	139. Kids' Inspirational	160. Regional–Greece
115. Military & War Dramas	140. Inspirational Sing-Alongs	161. Regional–Hong Kong
116. Period Pieces	141. Inspirational Stories for Kids	162. Regional–India
117. Pre-Twentieth Century Period Pieces	142. Mindfulness & Prayer	163. Regional–Iran
118. Twentieth Period Pieces	143. Healing & Reiki	164. Regional–Israel
119. Political Drams	144. Meditation & Relaxation	165. Regional–Italy
120. Romantic Dramas	145. Prayer & Spiritual Growth	166. Regional–Japan
121. Showbiz Dramas		167. Regional–Korea
122. Social Issue Dramas		168. Regional–Latin America
123. Sports Dramas		169. Regional–Mexico
124. Tearjerkers		170. Regional–Middle East
		171. Regional–Netherlands
		172. Regional–Philippines
		173. Regional–Poland
		174. Regional–Russia
		175. Regional–Scandinavia
		176. Regional–Southeast Asia
		177. Regional–Spain
		178. Regional–Thailand
		179. Regional–United Kingdom
		180. Language by Region
		181. Foreign Musicals
		182. Foreign Must–See
		183. Foreign Romance
		184. Foreign Steamy Romance
		185. Foreign Television
		186. Bollywood

Source: http://dvd.netflix.com/AllGenresList

(*continued*)

10. Gay & lesbian	11. Horror	12. Independent
187. Gay & Lesbian Comedies 188. Gay & Lesbian Dramas 189. Gay & Lesbian Romance 190. Foreign Gay & Lesbian 191. Indie Gay & Lesbian 192. Gay 193. Lesbian 194. Bisexual 195. LOGO	196. B-Movie Horror 197. Creature Features 198. Cult Horror 199. Foreign Horror 200. Asian Horror 201. Italian Horror 202. Frankenstein 203. Horror Classics 204. Monsters 205. Satanic Stories 206. Slashers & Serial Killers 207. Supernatural Horror 208. Teen Screams 209. Vampires 210. Werewolves 211. Zombies	212. Experimental 213. Indie Action 214. Indie Classics 215. Indie Comedies 216. Indie Dramas 217. Indie Gay & Lesbian 218. Indie Romance 219. Indie Suspense & Thriller
13. Music & musicals	**14. Romance**	**15. Sci-Fi & fantasy**
220. Classical Music 221. Classical Choral Music 222. Classical Instrumental 223. Opera & Operetta 224. Country & Western/Folk 225. American Folk & Bluegrass 226. Classic Country & Western 227. New Country 228. Inspirational Music 229. Gospel Music 230. Jazz & Easy Listening 231. Afro-Cuban & Latin Jazz 232. Classic Jazz 233. Contemporary Jazz 234. Jazz Greats 235. Swing & Big Band 236. Vocal Jazz 237. Vocal Pop 238. Karaoke 239. Latin Music 240. Brazilian Music 241. Latin Pop 242. Reggaeton 243. Rock en Espanol 244. Traditional Latin Music 245. Music Lessons 246. Musicals 247. Classic Movie Musicals 248. Classic Stage Musicals 249. Contemp. Movie Musicals 250. Contemp. Stage Musicals 251. Foreign Musicals 252. Must-See Musicals 253. Show Tunes 254. Music Genres (e.g., Rock) 255. Must-See Concerts 256. World Music by Region	257. African-American Romance 258. Foreign Romance 259. Indie Romance 260. Romance Classics 261. Romantic Dramas 262. Steamy Romance	263. Action Sci-Fi & Fantasy 264. Alien Sci-Fi 265. Classic Sci-Fi & Fantasy 266. Fantasy 267. Foreign Sci-Fi & Fantasy 268. Sci-Fi Adventure 269. Sci-Fi Cult Classics 270. Sci-Fi Dramas 271. Sci-Fi Horror 272. Supernatural Sci-Fi

Source: http://dvd.netflix.com/AllGenresList

16. Special interest	17. Sports & fitness	18. Television
273. Art & Design	310. Baseball	353. British TV
274. Computer Animation	311. Basketball	354. British TV Comedies
275. Painting	312. Extreme Sports	355. British TV Dramas
276. Photography	313. Extreme Combat & MMA	356. Kids' TV
277. Sculpture	314. Extreme Motorsports	357. TV Action & Adventure
278. Career & Finance	315. Extreme Snow & Ice Sports	358. TV Classics
279. Dance	316. Mountain Biking	359. Classic TV Comedies
280. Ballet & Modern Dance	317. Mountaineering & Climbing	360. Classic TV Dramas
281. Bellydance	318. Skateboarding	361. Classic TV Sci-Fi & Fantasy
282. Dance Workouts	319. Stunts & General Mayhem	362. TV Comedies
283. Hip-Hop & Contemp. Dance	320. Football	363. Must-See TV Comedies
284. Latin & Ballroom Dance	321. Golf	364. TV Animated Comedies
285. Tap & Jazz Dance	322. Boxing & Wrestling	365. TV Sitcoms
286. World Dance	323. General Martial Arts	366. TV Sketch Comedies
287. Food & Wine	324. Karate	367. TV Documentaries
288. Cooking Instruction	325. Kung Fu	368. HBO Documentaries
289. Food Stories	326. Self-Defense	369. PBS Documentaries
290. Wine & Bev. Appreciation	327. Tai Chi & Qigong	370. TV Science & Nature
291. Hobbies & Games	328. Auto Racing	371. TV Dramas
292. Boating & Sailing	329. Motorcycles & Motocross	372. Must-See TV Dramas
293. Car Culture	330. Bodybuilding	373. TV Courtroom Dramas
294. Fishing	331. Cycling	374. TV Crime Dramas
295. Hunting	332. Horse Racing	375. TV Dramedy
296. Magic & Illusion	333. Tennis	376. TV Family Dramas
297. Poker & Gambling	334. Snow & Ice Sports	377. TV Medical Dramas
298. Home & Garden	335. Ice Hockey	378. TV Soaps
299. Entertaining	336. Skiing & Snowboarding	379. TV Teen Dramas
300. Home Improvement	337. Soccer	380. TV Miniseries
301. Pets	338. Sports Stories	381. TV Mysteries
302. Homework Help	339. Olympics & Other Games	382. TV Reality Programming
303. English & Language Arts	340. Sports Comedies	383. TV Sci-Fi & Fantasy
304. History & Social Studies	341. Triumph of the Underdogs	384. TV Variety & Talk Shows
305. Math & Science	342. Women in Sports	385. TV War & Politics
306. Language Instruction	343. Water Sports	386. TV Westerns
307. IMAX	344. Surfing & Boardsports	387. Made-for-TV Movies
308. Mind & Body	345. Abs & Glutes Workouts	
309. Healthy Living	346. Cardio & Aerobics	
	347. Strength & Flexibility	
	348. Kids' Fitness	
	349. Low-Impact Workouts	
	350. Pilates & Fitness Ball	
	351. Pregnancy Related Fitness	
	352. Yoga	

Source: http://dvd.netflix.com/AllGenresList

(*continued*)

19. Thrillers		
387. Action Thrillers 388. Classic Thrillers 389. Crime Thrillers 390. Erotic Thrillers 391. Espionage Thrillers 392. Foreign Thrillers 393. Indie Suspense & Thriller 394. Mobster 395. Mystery 396. Political Thrillers 397. Psychological Thrillers 398. Sci-Fi Thrillers 399. Supernatural Thrillers 400. Suspense		

Source: http://dvd.netflix.com/AllGenresList

Notes

1 Chris Anderson, *The Long Tail: Why the Future of Business Is Selling Less of More* (New York: Hatchette Books, 2006).

2 Astra Taylor, *The People's Platform: Taking Back Power and Culture in the Digital Age* (New York: Metropolitan Books, 2014), 15.

3 Harold Bloom, *The Western Canon: The Books and Schools of the Ages* (New York: Riverhead Trade, 1994).

4 Rick Altman, *Film/Genre* (London: British Film Institute, 1999), 33.

5 Steve Neale, *Genre and Hollywood* (London: Routledge Books, 2000), 12.

6 Yvonne Tasker, *The Action and Adventure Cinema* (London: Routledge, 2004), 73.

7 Altman, 35.

8 Ibid., 51.

9 Jacques Derrida, "The Law of Genre," *Critical Inquiry* 7.1 (Autumn, 1980): 55–81. (Translated by Avital Ronell).

10 Marieke Jenner, "Is This TVIV? On Netflix, TVIII and Binge-Watching," *New Media & Society*, July 7, 2014. http://nms.sagepub.com/content/early/2014/07/03/1461444814541523 (accessed July 14, 2015).

11 Jason Mittell, *Genre and Television: From Cop Shows to Cartoons in American Culture* (London: Routledge, 2004).

12 Michael Renov, "Toward a Poetics of Documentary," in *Theorizing Documentary*, ed. Michael Renov (London: Routledge, 1993).

13 Andrew Lapin, "Foreign Is Not a Film Genre," *Michigan Daily Film*, 2009. http://www.michigandaily.com/content/film-column-foreign-films (accessed July 21, 2015).

14 Amid Amidi, "NY Times Unaware That Animation Is a Medium," *Cartoon Brew*, 2010. http://www.cartoonbrew.com/ideas-commentary/ny-times-doesnt-know-animation-is-a-medium-27566.html (accessed July 21, 2015).

15 Fredric Jameson, "Postmodernism, or, the Cultural Logic of Late Capitalism," originally in *New Left Review*, 1984. http://www.marxists.org/reference/subject/philosophy/works/us/jameson.htm (accessed September 25, 2014).

16 Steve Neale, "Hollywood Blockbusters: Historical Dimensions," in *Movie Blockbusters*, ed. Julian Stringer (London: Routledge, 2003), 47–60.

17 Jane Feuer, "Genre Study and Television," in *Channels of Discourse, Reassembled: Television and Contemporary Criticism*, ed. Robert C. Allen (Chapel Hill: The University of North Carolina Press, 1992), 138–160.

18 Altman, 62.

19 Alexis Madrigal, "How Netflix Reverse-Engineered Hollywood," *The Atlantic*, January 2, 2014. http://www.theatlantic.com/technology/archive/2014/01/how-netflix-reverse-engineered-hollywood/282679/ (accessed September 25, 2014).

20 Hunter Schwarz, "23 Oddly Specific Netflix Categories That Only Have One Show You Can Watch." *BuzzFeed*, January 11, 2014. http://www.buzzfeed.com/hunterschwarz/23-oddly-specific-netflix-categories-that-only-have-one-show#pk9igq (accessed September 25, 2014).

21 Barna William Donovan, *Blood, Guts, and Testosterone: Action Films, Audiences, and a Thirst for Violence* (New York: Scarecrow Books, 2009).

22 Neale, *Genre and Hollywood*, 77.

5

Catered to Your Future Self: Netflix's "Predictive Personalization" and the Mathematization of Taste

Neta Alexander

The "eye" is a product of history reproduced by education.

Pierre Bourdieu[1]

We don't have opinions here, we have hypotheses. And we test them to make sure we're acting in our clients' best interest.

Eric Colson, Netflix's former chief data analyst[2]

Introduction

Writing in 1996, one year before Netflix was founded in California by Marc Randolph and Reed Hastings, Susan Sontag famously eulogized the concept of "cinephilia" and warned the readers of the *New York Times* that the commercialization of cinema makes it more and more difficult to encounter "great films." In Sontag's words, these are "works based on the actual violations of the norms and practices that now govern movie making everywhere in the capitalist and would-be capitalist world—which is to say, everywhere."[3] By identifying criteria for exemplary art, Sontag applied a modernist sensibility to what she called "The Decay of Cinema." More importantly, she foreshadowed one of the central paradoxes that developers of algorithmic-based recommendation systems are facing: the greatest films also tend to be the most difficult to classify or to easily break down into tags and categories.

Taking this paradox as its point of origin, this chapter will provide a better understanding of how Netflix translates the numerous titles in its content library into what the company calls "microtags" and "altgenres." This, in turn, will lead to a careful examination of the proprietary set of algorithms Netflix calls "Cinematch," as well as the dangers and prospects of shaping cultural preferences based on methods such as data mining and collaborative filtering.[4]

Since 2011, Netflix not only tags existing films and television shows but also produces original content based on the data collected via the website's (at least) sixty-five million subscribers. These nascent modes of production, exhibition, and consumption of audiovisual content raise an intriguing set of questions: Can an elusive category such as "taste" be translated into an empirical, mathematically based formula? In what ways can an algorithms-based system replace the cultural expert or mediator? And, finally, do "altgenres" and "microtags" offer a revolutionary way to distribute and consume moving images, or do they create "filter bubbles" that feed us with the same formulistic products and therefore pose a threat to both the culture of cinephilia and filmmakers' creative freedoms?

To start unpacking these questions, this chapter will be structured around a set of paradoxes, with the first being the tension between "taste" as a subjective, personal, and consistent set of preferences manifested via the consumption of cultural goods (clothes, food, furniture, art works, books, etc.), and "taste" as a cultural construct that can be manipulated and shaped by media oligopolies and their ever-increasing advertising budgets.

The question of how taste is acquired and shaped has been the focus of a rich literature on aesthetics and the distinction between the "good" and the "beautiful," which can be traced back to David Hume's "Of the Standard of Taste" and Immanuel Kant's *Critique of Judgment* (originally titled *Critique of Taste*).[5] Theirs is an ideal, normative perception of taste that prevailed throughout the eighteenth-century "Age of Reason" which, as Henry Allison reminds us, was also known as "the Century of Taste." Writing in 2001, Allison outlines the shift from Kant's theory of taste—which weaves together aesthetics, ethics, and morality—to the twenty-first century's *zeitgeist* of relativism and individual preference:

> Whereas to us to say that a question or evaluation is a matter of taste is to imply that it is merely a private, subjective matter lacking any claim to normativity, this was not at all the case in the eighteenth century. As Gadamer points out, taste was thought of as a special way of knowing, one for which rational grounds cannot be given, but which nonetheless involves an inherent universality.[6]

Taste, however, is no longer thought of as a special way of knowing but rather as a form of cultural capital. In his seminal study of the social construction of taste, Pierre Bourdieu foregrounds the interrelations between aesthetics and class hierarchy: "Taste classifies, and it classifies the classifier. Social subjects, classified by their classifications, distinguish themselves by the distinctions they make, between the beautiful and the ugly, the distinguished and the vulgar, in which their position in the objective classifications is expressed or betrayed."[7] Hence for Bourdieu, "taste" is not an ever-changing subjective set of preferences; it is, rather, a way to position oneself in relation to others by acquiring and displaying cultural products.[8] Following this line of argument, our ability to draw pleasure from works of art cannot be considered without first acknowledging the commodification of the eye, "a product of history reproduced by education."[9] In the age in which the audience commodity is described in terms of "eyeballs"—a surprisingly revealing metaphor for what was once known as viewers, consumers, citizens, or simply humans—the ways in which the eye is being reified and reproduced are more wide-ranging than ever.

Bourdieu's definition of taste as a marker of class that is based on the ability to decipher various "cultural codes" is a useful starting point for a discussion of individual taste formation. Ironically, Bourdieu's metaphorical use of the word "code" to imply a process in which both human communication and the consumption of cultural goods are "acts of deciphering, decoding" reinforces a literal sense in the study of Netflix's algorithms for user preferences and the mathematization of taste.

By focusing on the process of taste formation, I therefore hope to achieve three objectives: demystifying *Cinematch* and Netflix's techniques and methods for creating "personal profiles"; contextualizing Netflix's recommendations within a broader historical narrative of "narrowcasting," "personalization," and the rise of niche markets and the "preorder economy"; and, finally, problematizing the celebratory discourse surrounding these new distribution models by foregrounding the tensions, ruptures, and "noise" they seem to deny, as well as the cultural diversity often lost in the process.

The birth of the "taste machine"

The fascination with the ways in which media can be used to shape cultural taste, and by so doing to turn "viewsers" (Dan Harries' amalgam of "viewer" and "user")[10] into eyeballs, can be traced back to the golden age of variety shows during the previous turn-of-the-century.[11] By offering their viewers a collection of short action films, travelogues, spectacles, motion studies, and "gag movies," early programmers tried to appeal to as wide an audience as possible and cater to different tastes.

In its golden years, the variety format enabled filmmakers to market cinema as both an attraction and an educational device. Travelogues, for instance, were promoted as a new kind of "instructive entertainment" based on their promise to offer viewers "a form of attraction that packaged didactic intentions as an aesthetic commodity."[12] As demonstrated by the film historian Jennifer Lynn Peterson, the proliferation of travelogues in the early twentieth century was part of the ongoing attempt to redeem the Nickelodeons from their reputation as "dark dens of vice, where women were molested by 'mashers' and young children were exposed to unsavory influences."[13] Cinema was thus recruited for the "uplift campaign" epitomizing the Progressive Era's belief in the power of education to create a citizenship based on "bourgeois standards of 'temperance, thrift, chastity, social purity, and the accumulation of wealth.'"[14] And so, a new taste machine was born.

To effectively shape taste means to try and appeal to "the universal spectator." As described by Linda Williams, this ideal denies "the heterogeneity of different spectators (of different races, classes, genders, socializations, and subcultural affinities)."[15] In the case of the "uplift campaign," "the universal spectator" indicated the new immigrant. The cinema was thus perceived as an instrument for the "Americanization" of middle- and lower-class audiences who were not yet immersed within the cultural codes of the melting pot. Much later, when television took over the domestic sphere in the 1950s, "the suburban housewife" became the new prototype of broadcast programing in the very moment when newly built houses in the suburbs were hailed as the ideal manifestations of the American dream.[16]

Netflix's viewser, however, is substantially different from the imagined universal spectator. Before Netflix introduced its original content, the service's main competitive advantage was the personal profile and its "Recommended for You" feature. To that extent, the company's business model demonstrates the shift from a mass economy into a niche market of personalized services. In the nascent age of digital personalization, the "You" is neither an immigrant nor a housewife; instead, this signifier stands for the cumulative set of choices made by the viewser, from grading films via the five-star ratings system to meticulously documented viewing patterns and activities (scrolling, replaying, rewinding, binge-watching, and so forth). While Netflix's users might assume that the recommendations they receive are solely based on the star ratings they have previously assigned to titles, since it was launched in 2001 *Cinematch* has evolved into a much more sophisticated system whose logic and mode of operation are increasingly inaccessible to either subscribers or potential competitors.

In fact, *Cinematch* is much more than an electronic matchmaker that can recommend specific titles for each subscriber based on her past choices; it is a system that constantly translates seemingly chaotic behavior into recurring and therefore predictable patterns. It is based on the assumption that human beings are consistently inconsistent—we might watch television on a weekday, but indulge in Hollywood action films during the weekend. More importantly, the algorithmic system is highly adaptive: as our preferences and tastes change, the titles we encounter in our "Recommended for You" section will change as well.

While Netflix was launched in 1997, early versions of *Cinematch* were only developed in 2000. In *Netflixed: The Epic Battle for America's Eyeballs*, Gina Keating explains that since 2010, "subscribers no longer even have to rate movies, because the program embedded in a set-top box or on Netflix website, monitored what shows and movies they watched and how they watched them to figure out whether the selection was memorable, and how to duplicate the experience with films available in the streaming library."[17] Based on Netflix's unprecedented access to the viewing habits of millions of subscribers around the world, *Cinematch* makes informed choices based on the metadata the system collects and analyzes. By using Netflix we are teaching *Cinematch* what we like to watch and when we like to watch it.

This feedback loop can often take the form of homework: in 2009 Netflix launched "Taste Preferences"—an elaborate set of questions in which we are asked to actively provide the service with more information, from the ideal "mood" or "emotional tone" of the title we wish to watch (e.g., feel-good, dark, goofy, gritty, etc.), to its preferred "storyline" (e.g., courtroom, mid-life crisis). Netflix's director of Product Management, Todd Yellin, proudly launched the service on March 26, 2009: "We are rolling out several features to delight our members with a more personalized website that puts an emphasis on movie discovery… the features include taste preferences, more personalized homepages, and customized browsing."[18]

Yellin's use of the magic words "personalization," "preferences," and "customization" epitomizes the celebratory discourse of streaming as a means to enhance viewers' agency and control. In fact, *Cinematch* can be seen as part of a transformation that prompted Lev Manovich to distinguish between "modern media" (typewriting machines, photography, radio, cinema, television, etc.) and digitally based "new media": "New media follows, or actually runs ahead of, a quite different logic of post-industrial society—that of individual customization, rather than mass standardization."[19] The golden role of this new economy can be found in the tautological slogan of a 2014 campaign for Motorola's "Moto X" smartphone: *Choose Choice*. But what exactly do we choose, when we choose choice? Who—and what—is being excluded from this choice-based utopia? And is it still possible to differentiate between our choices and the choices the algorithm is making on our behalf? In order to answer these questions we must first briefly explore the ideas of "collaborative filtering" and "metadata" on which *Cinematch* is based.

The myths of personalization and "on-demand Utopia"

The answers to these questions can complicate the notion of agency and limitless choices in the age of connected viewing. Following Manovich, the media scholar Henry Jenkins explores the move from an "appointment-based model" (i.e., Raymond Williams' "planned flow") to an "engagement-based model" in which the users are no longer dependent on a strict schedule planned by the networks.[20] However, Jenkins warns us against oversimplification of this transformation and foregrounds the paradox embodied within the digital model: "On the one hand, this new 'on-demand' lifestyle can be seen as a utopia, offering us endless choices of personalized content curated to our needs; on the other hand, this never-ending consumption economy is addictive, hyperactive, and unbelievably time-consuming."[21]

While Jenkins is right in recognizing the anxieties evoked by digital media consumption, his argument has at least two drawbacks: the assumption that the choices we are invited to make are, indeed, "endless," and the illusion that the content we consume is uniquely "personalized." As has been repeatedly demonstrated, the idea that our entire cultural world is on its way to digitization is misleading, impracticable, and highly problematic since it denies the difference between analog and digital media.[22] The result of this denial is a platform-agnostic approach that sees film as "pure content" and as "something which exists regardless of its carrier, as information that can be transmitted in a variety of media" while ignoring the inherent qualities of the original format.[23] Since formats and compression methods are constantly changing, numerous cultural products—from DVD extras, booklets, and memorabilia to "paracinema" products described by Jeffrey Sconce as "television ads, government hygiene films, juvenile delinquency documentaries, or soft-core pornography"[24]—are either lost or orphaned due to obsolete technologies. These various manifestations of "bad taste" and "counter-aesthetic" are deemed too niche for family-friendly streaming services such as Netflix, Amazon Prime, or Google Play, and are therefore seldom digitized.[25]

In Netflix's case, the user interface is designed to provide subscribers with the illusion of endless choices, obscuring the fact that the website's content library constantly changes due to expired licensing agreements, leading to the point where "the company can't afford the content that its subscribers most want to watch."[26] Not only can we not find every film or television series we might enjoy on Netflix, the ones we have found may not be there when we look for them again in the future.

Since Netflix's universe is limited and ever-changing, its ability to offer content "curated to our needs" is based on a set of restrictions and criteria. By denying the tension between automating and customizing, the *Cinematch* system presents a form of what we might call "collective personalization." Keating, who bases her research on in-depth conversations with tens of Netflix's programmers and employees, reports that the recommendation system was originally based on the idea of "customer clusters"—namely, people who rated movies similarly. By creating an algorithmic matchmaker, "*Cinematch* noted the overlap in certain subscribers' tastes, then presented films highly rated by cluster members to others in the same cluster who had not previously rented or rated them on Netflix."[27] This "hive-mind" model forces us to rethink the formation of taste as an individual, subjective process. Being part of a "customer cluster" one cannot explore or control is very different from identifying with an imagined community of like-minded cinephiles. And while the VCR era gave birth to new forms of communal experience—from improvised "cine-clubs"[28] to the "Be Kind, Rewind" etiquette of borrowed or rented videotapes—Netflix's subscribers do not share communal responsibility for those who might watch the same titles in the future.

Moreover, in the case of buffering or freeze frames other Internet users might be envisioned as a "bandwidth hog"—competing with us for the same limited resource in a way that invokes an affective economy of anxiety and frustration. These limitations further individualize users' media experiences while instituting a particular kind of class system to media viewing, from viewsers who can afford to pay for "premium services" to those left behind the iron curtain of "the digital divide" and its discriminatory geographies of connectivity and Wi-Fi access.[29]

Netflix's attempts to make the viewing experience more communal by adding features such as "Friends" (which enabled subscribers to share their queue and viewing history with their Facebook friends) turned out to be disastrous due to claims of privacy breach. As a result, "'Friends' gained only a small following—10 percent or less of subscribers—during its six-year existence, since many subscribers said they felt uncomfortable sharing their movie picks."[30] Viewsers, apparently, were far from eager to serve as cultural mediators for their friends and loved ones. While the subscribers forced Netflix to cancel the feature in 2010, they have remained unaware of the ways in which their choices shape the preferences of others—and vice versa. In a narcissistic manner, they confuse the "You" in "Recommended for You" with a unique, complex individual rather than with a group of strangers who all happened to have made similar choices. Ironically, the fact that *Cinematch*'s criteria for recommendations remain hidden serves to sustain the myth of personalization. Since we can't exactly tell why one title was recommended rather than another, we simply assume that Netflix knows us. The god resides in the machine, and it is unknowable and invisible as any other divine and unworldly entity. Netflix, however, did not invent the algorithmic logic of predictive personalization. Digital recommendations and personal profiles emerged in 1994, when Amazon's founder Jeff Bezos developed an economic model based on big data and "collaborative filtering." In his biography, Bezos recalls that the original vision was to transport online bookselling "back to the days of the small bookseller who got to know you very well and would say things like, 'I know you like John Irving, and guess what, here's this new author, I think he's a lot like John Irving.' "[31]

The revolution Bezos envisioned was only made possible in the age of "big data," a term applied to "data sets whose size is beyond the ability of commonly used software tools to capture, manage, and process the data within a tolerable elapsed time."[32] As of 2015, big data sizes tend to range from a few dozen terabytes to many petabytes of data in a single dataset.

Two decades after Bezos established Amazon, personalization has turned into the *raison d'être* of digital commerce. After Google started personalizing its search results on December 2009—using a system of fifty-seven "signals" or variables to determine "who you were and what kinds of sites you'd like"[33]—numerous other digital services have followed suit. In his bestseller *The Filter Bubble*, Eli Pariser argues that "more and more, your computer monitor is a kind of a one-way mirror, reflecting your own interests while algorithmic observers watch what you click."[34] As mentioned, these processes are far from transparent; in fact, most users are either unaware of the fact that their viewing habits are being constantly documented, or are unable to trace, access, and understand the numerous ways in which their actions are being translated into recommendations.

Pariser's alarming account of the rise of personalization and adaptive algorithms warns us that this new economic model creates "parallel but separate universes" in which we are unlikely to encounter anything that might challenge, upset, or provoke us (the very same qualities Sontag attributes to "great films"). While this chapter cannot examine the ongoing debate on privacy and surveillance in the digital age, we should bear in mind that "data mining" forces us into a Faustian contract: "you're getting a free service, and the cost is information about you."[35] Furthermore, the pursuit of "personalization" has been germinating myriad studies of artificial intelligence, machine learning, and the ability to develop algorithms that could predict our future choices. In the words of Google's Eric Schmidt, "the product I've always wanted to build is a Google code that will guess what I'm trying to type."[36] This futuristic terminology of "mind reading" connotes an unmediated reality in which the know-it-all algorithm will be able to read our thoughts before our hand touches the mouse (or activates a sensor either located on our bodies or transplanted in them). This requires writing codes that are meant not only for data collection but also for studying and predicting behavioral patterns.

Early on, Netflix's founder Reed Hastings suggested that a notion of intimacy with the website's interface might be invoked by creating a "digital shopping assistant" that would have "a personality and a photo and could point customers to movies they would like in Netflix's library."[37] Eventually, a nameless algorithmic system turned out to be a much more lucrative solution. Viewers need no shopping assistant named

Mike or Jon to feel an intimate connection with their Netflix's personal profile; all they really need is a sense that the service knows them better than their friends, family, and even marital partners. The overwhelming success of the *Cinematch* model therefore implies that humans attribute intelligence and personality to systems that predict their behavior, rather than the other way around. Netflix's predictive algorithms have been anthropomorphized to a surprising degree by both its subscribers and the popular press. As described by Keating, to its loyal subscribers "Netflix was not only a movie delivery service... it was a friend with whom they shared their deepest secrets about what truly delighted them, and someone they trusted to provide an even better experience the next time they met. To think that it was all just a bunch of algorithms was simply too heartbreaking to bear."[38] To ease the heartbreak and to better understand Netflix's predictive personalization, an exploration of its tagging system is in place.

The algebraic equation of taste

As Alexander Galloway demonstrates in *The Interface Effect*, an algorithm is a translation by way of reduction: "Not only does computer code operate through the definitions of states and state changes, but computers themselves are those special machines that nominalize the world, that define and model its behavior using variable and functions."[39] In Netflix's case, the user's preferences are translated into 76,897 micro-genres as specific as "Emotional Fight-the-System Documentaries" or "Real-Life Period Pieces about Royalty."

As demonstrated by the technology journalist Alexis Madrigal, these "variables" are defined by breaking down every product in Netflix's library into a massive series of tags relating not only to plotlines, locations, or actors but also to much broader philosophical categories such as "tone," "morality," or "emotional effect." Later, these "altgenres"—as Netflix calls them—are juxtaposed with users' viewing habits in a way which gives Netflix's subscribers the uncanny feeling that the streaming portal is, in fact, a fortuneteller.[40]

In other words, Netflix's personalization is based on the twofold process of laborious tagging by humans and computer-based algorithms. In Madrigal's eyes this process results in the very same narrative I wish to challenge:

> [Netflix] recommends genres that are intensely, almost bizarrely personalized. That's because seven years ago, Todd Yellin, a film-obsessed executive at Netflix, set out to break down every movie into data. He hired aspiring screenwriters and paid them to watch movies and rate their levels of romance, gore, quirkiness and even plot resolution. In a sense, Yellin wanted to reverse-engineer all the Hollywood formulas so that Netflix could mathematically show you the movies it knew you would like. Now it's become one of the company's big selling points. Netflix doesn't just provide streaming movies and TV shows; *it knows you* [emphasis in original].[41]

While Madrigal is too eager to adopt Netflix's marketing jargon, his journalistic work is a useful first step in demystifying *Cinematch*. Another useful way to approach this task is by conducting a close reading of Netflix's official "technology blog," an online platform in which senior programmers provide users with a glimpse at the company's agenda and goals. A blog entry posted in 2012 describes the process of taste mathematization by introducing the long-awaited winners in the Netflix Prize, "a machine learning and data mining competition for movie rating prediction" launched in 2006:

> We offered one million dollars to whoever improved the accuracy of our existing system called *Cinematch* by 10%. We conducted this competition to find new ways to improve the recommendations we provide to our members, which is a key part of our business. However, we had to come up with a proxy question that was easier to evaluate and quantify: the root mean squared error (RMSE) of the predicted rating. The race was on to beat our RMSE of 0.9525 with the finish line of reducing it to 0.8572 or less.[42]

Later, the writers provide an example for a personalized ranking function that formulates abstract categories such as "predictability" and "taste" into an algebraic equation: "frank (u,v) = w1 p(v) + w2 r(u,v) + b, where u=user, v=video item, p=popularity and r=predicted rating."[43] For readers who might be baffled by these formulas, Netflix offers a brief explanation stating the company's business model: "Recall that our goal is to recommend the titles that each member is most likely to play and enjoy. One obvious way to approach this is to use the member's predicted rating of each item as an adjunct to item popularity." The fact that Netflix tries to maximize both its number of subscribers and the time they spend streaming content should not come as a surprise. However, what follows is slightly more disturbing: "Using predicted ratings on their own as a ranking function can lead to items that are too niche or unfamiliar being recommended."[44] Netflix is therefore concerned that its subscribers will encounter "too niche" or "unfamiliar" products. This results in what Eli Pariser calls the "filter bubble paradox": the more information you (consciously or unconsciously) provide Netflix, the less likely you will encounter any "great films" outside your comfort zone.[45]

While the company states that it developed and incorporated algorithms to increase the "diversity" of recommended items, the surest way to keep its subscribers happy is to present them with films they might rate at four or five stars, the highest grades possible. Furthermore, the introduction of an instant streaming service in 2007 radically changed the content Netflix's subscribers choose to consume. As explained on the blog:

> For DVDs our goal is to help people fill their queue with titles to receive in the mail over the coming days and weeks; selection is distant in time from viewing, people select carefully because exchanging a DVD for another takes more than a day, and we get no feedback during viewing. For streaming members are looking for something great to watch right now; they can sample a few videos before settling

on one, they can consume several in one session, and we can observe viewing statistics such as whether a video was watched fully or only partially.[46]

This shift foregrounds the unacknowledged difference between the "present self" and "future self" of digital viewers. Simply put, while I like to see myself as the cinephile who binge-watches Claude Lanzmann's *Shoah* and the next day compares it with Joshua Oppenheimer's *The Act of Killing*, the sad truth is that after a long day of library research and a forty-five-minute subway ride during rush hour, *Batman vs. Superman* or an episode of *The Office* may seem more appealing. True, my future self might be embarrassed by these choices; but on-demand culture only exists in the world of the endless now and our immediate choices could prove quite different than our delayed, futuristic taste predictions.

At the same time, the pursuit of the "comfort zone" is based on the denial of the importance of contingency, serendipity, and potentiality within the formation of taste. Throughout the past century, different methods of "audience measurement"—from focus groups to rating systems—gave birth to "the search of the audience commodity"[47] and ideas of predictability and control took hold of the neoliberal market.[48] Being predictable means denying contingency and potentiality—the two principles escaping the logic of "programmability" as described by Wendy Hui Kyong Chun: within the logic of computers the "unknowable" ceases to exist; everything is measurable, quantifiable, and—by extension—controllable and traceable.[49] To that end, Netflix is a symptom of the neoliberal desire to make life a predictive, automatic process.

Following this logic, Netflix does not take into account the unknowable, eclectic, and ever-changing process of individual taste formation. Its algorithm is well suited to the zeitgeist of social media in which we are constantly asked to "like" Facebook status updates or to grade and gives "stars" to our favorite restaurants, shops, or even taxi drivers on a plethora of mobile apps. But, what exactly do we like when we gift our friend a "like"? This, in fact, is a question impossible to answer. As problematized by Bourdieu, "everything seems to suggest that even among professional valuers, the criteria which define the stylistic properties of the 'typical works' on which all their judgments are based usually remain implicit."[50] Following this line of argument, even in the age of big data no algorithm can determine whether we gave *Grizzly Man* five stars because we enjoy dark indie documentaries, nature films, Werner Herzog films, suicide narratives, or all of the above.

Netflix's *Cinematch* system is therefore based on three different methods: the users' personal profile (past choices, the five-star ratings system, scrolling activity, and viewing habits); collaborative filtering via "Costumers Clusters"; and a tagging system meant to group together closely related or "neighboring films" (films made by the same director or featuring the same actor, films in the same alt-genre, films with similar themes, and so forth).

To this triad structure we must add a fourth, no less important, feature: Netflix's own agenda and commercial priorities. Netflix reserves the right to tweak its algorithm to promote the service's original content without informing its customers. In fact, in 2015 the company started to include advertisements for Netflix-produced television series such as *Bloodline* or *House of Cards*. These promos also appear as part of the autoplay feature: once a subscriber is done watching a television series, *Cinematch* instantly plays the promo for one of Netflix's original titles.[51] While Netflix was founded as a movie-focused service, the data collected by *Cinematch* proved this logic wrong: in fact, the service's subscribers tend to watch television series more often than cinematic works. In 2011, Netflix reshaped its catalog to reflect that change, and it has been focusing its efforts in producing television shows ever since. According to Keating, the economic sense is clear: "Each TV series produced tens of hours of viewing compared to the two or three hours for each film—resulting in greater rates of subscriber usage and satisfaction."[52] This is only one example for how recommendation systems such as *Cinematch* effectively create a feedback loop: by documenting viewing habits and consumption patterns, they gradually change these very same activities. What started out as the ideal home for cinephiles has turned into a digital equivalent to cable television.

The decline of the "expert" (or, beyond the ethical principle)

While these different kinds of feedback loops are obscured by Netflix, the myth of personalization is maintained. Hence asking someone to share her Netflix password is a surprisingly intimate—and therefore socially tabooed—act. A look at one's "personal profile" is supposedly a glimpse into one's soul, desires, fantasies, and obsessions. Share your Netflix's password with me—and I'll tell you who are, who you share your life with, and who you wish to become.

This, in turn, leads to a collapse of the distinction between the social and the psychological. As described by the French philosopher Bruno Latour, this is in fact one of the most significant side-effects of the age of "traceability":

> The ancient divide between the social on the one hand and the psychological on the other was largely an artefact of an asymmetry between the traceability of various types of carriers: what Proust's narrator was doing with his heroes, no one could say, thus it was said to be private and left to psychology; what Proust earned from his book was calculable, and thus was made part of the social or the economic sphere. But today the data bank of Amazon.com has simultaneous access to my most subtle preferences as well as to my Visa card. As soon as I purchase on the web, I erase the difference between the social, the economic and the psychological, just because of the range of traces I leave behind.[53]

What, then, happens to taste when the boundaries between the social and the psychological, the collective and the subjective domains, seem to disappear? To begin with, the distinction between the "expert" and the "consumer" collapses. The age of the "preorder economy"—the use of big data in order to predict which products consumers are most likely to purchase—assigned authority and control to algorithmic-based systems. The result is significantly different from the romantic approach to the consumption of cultural goods. Kant, for example, believed that some humans appear to have been born with a talent for superior aesthetic judgment. As we are reminded by Thomas Davenport and Jeanne Harris, the belief that aesthetic sensibility is an inherent and natal talent has prevailed well into the twenty-first century:

> Historically, neither the creators nor the distributors of "cultural products" have used analytics—data, statistics, predictive modeling—to determine the likely success of their offerings. Instead, companies relied on the brilliance of tastemakers to predict and shape what people would buy. If Coco Chanel said hemlines were going up, they did. Feelings, not data, were critical. Harry Cohn, the founder of Columbia Pictures, believed he could predict how successful a movie would be based on whether his backside squirmed as he watched (if it did, the movie was no good).[54]

In late capitalism, the gut feeling of the expert has been replaced by empirical calculations. Paradoxically, the logic of "programmability" imbues the algorithm with the necessary knowledge to dictate the good to us, although—and possibly because of—the fact that it is incapable of any kind of moral or ethical judgment.

Of course, the fact that the underlying assumptions on which the code is based are unknown or unseen to us does not mean that programmers and computer engineers are devoid of ethical commitments and concerns. Code writing is colored by different norms and assumptions concerning human behavior, desires, and needs. But unlike network executives or studio owners, programmers mostly reside in the shadows of the collective imaginary.

The technical and empirical jargon surrounding big data is often used to obscure the fact that algorithms and codes are imbued with sets of underlying assumptions and cultural, social, and racial biases.[55] Systems such as *Cinematch* are the result of a laborious and multifaceted process that can last several years. In the words of Matthew Kirschenbaum, "software is the product of white papers, engineering reports, conversations and collaborations, intuitive insights, professionalized expertise, venture capital (in other words, money), late nights (in other words, labor), caffeine, and other artificial stimulants."[56] The length and complexity of these processes complicate our ability to map and understand accountability in the digital age. If we were to adopt Adrian Mackenzie's definition of "agency" as "an action to which a cognitive dimension is attached,"[57] we can argue that algorithms do not pass "the agential cut."[58] Yet, they now occupy a place that traditionally belonged to human agents.

The logic and underlying assumptions on which the code is based mostly remain inaccessible. While the hardware is unrepairable by design due to the "black box" structure of most electronic products, the software is based on a distinction between the kernel and the shell. Writing about UNIX, Tara McPherson asserts that computer software is always based on what she calls a lenticular logic. It is "a logic of the fragment or the chunk, a way of seeing the world as discrete modules or nodes, a mode that suppresses relation and context. As such, the lenticular also manages and controls complexity."[59] The lenticular logic, in turn, requires a separation of the (invisible) "kernel" and the (visible) "shell" (a logic that paves the way to the myth of digital immateriality that Paul Dourish, Jean-Francois Blanchette and others convincingly refutes).[60] As McPherson writes,

> UNIX's intense modularity and information-hiding capacity were reinforced by its design: that is, in the ways in which it segregated the kernel from the shell. The kernel loads into the computer's memory at startup and is the "heart" of UNIX ... although it remains hidden from the user. The shells (or programs that interpret commands) are intermediaries between the user and the computer's inner workings. They hide the details of the operating system from the user behind the shell, extending modularity from a rule of programming in UNIX to the very design of UNIX itself.[61]

While UNIX and *Cinematch* are substantially different, they follow a similar logic: they are designed in a way that hides the hidden workings and set of underlying assumptions on which they are based. In *Cinematch*'s case, these assumptions are that subscribers strive to remain within the borders of their "comfort zone." The recommendation system functions less as an expert—someone with a unique aesthetic or artistic sensibility—and more as a censor, who constantly redefines the works within our realm of access. It is, however, censorship in disguise; the service's homepage is designed to provide us with the illusion that our entertainment options are endless.

Eventually, Netflix—much like other digital services such as the music provider Pandora or the clothing service Stitch Fix—provides the same recommendations to different people who made similar choices. Since these services learn our histories and habits, the result is often uncannily accurate. That, however, does not mean they were able to intimately map our taste and personality. To quote Manovich, "in what can be read as an updated version of Althusser's 'interpellation', we are asked to mistake the structure of somebody's else mind for our own."[62]

The similarities between Stitch Fix and Netflix are not coincidental. In fact, the clothing company's algorithm was developed by Stitch Fix's "chief algorithms officer" Eric Colson, who previously led Netflix's data science and engineering team. In a recent interview celebrating Stitch Fix's success, Colson declared, "we don't have opinions here, we have hypotheses, and we test them to make sure we're acting in our clients' best interest."[63] In Colson's world, the mouse cursor is a pure embodiment of the viewser's own, singular subjectivity. The gut feeling is dead; long live metadata.

Conclusion

By mapping the set of paradoxes underlying Netflix's logic, I was hoping to move away from the narrative of on-demand utopia and to suggest instead a more complex overview of predictive personalization. As sophisticated as they are, Netflix's tagging process, metadata, and collaborative filters cannot fully imitate individual taste formations. Instead, they make informed choices negotiating the user's viewing history with a content library that frequently changes.

Within this process, many elements are being lost. For one, we are no longer serendipitously exposed to films that regularly violate the norms of storytelling. At the same time, the digital viewing culture is devoid of any sense of community; the intimacy we once shared with follow audience members has been replaced with an intimacy in relation to our gadgets and the "personalized profile" they let us access.

Eventually, the myth of on-demand utopia can only be sustained by denying the moments of failure and breakdown embodied within any encounter with digital media. These include, but are not limited to, buffering; "filter bubbles" creating what Pariser calls "The You Loop"; and a lack of transparency when it comes to Netflix' offerings, algorithms, and recommendations (alongside other, platform-specific obstacles such as bandwidth or battery life).

Most importantly, there exists a contradiction between the notion that we have reached an "on-demand utopia" in which we are finally free to develop our own taste, and the neoliberal reality of filter bubbles, hidden kernels, and various manifestations of digital noise and censorship. The rise of predictive personalization might be good news for the study of artificial intelligence and machine learning, but it is bad news for anyone who wishes to encounter what Sontag calls "great films." True, we are constantly invited to *choose choice*, but only as long as our choices happen to take place in the magical on-demand kingdoms of Motorola, Netflix, Pandora, Amazon, or Netflix.

Notes

1 Pierre Bourdieu, *Distinction: A Social Critique of the Judgment of Taste*, trans. Richard Nice (Cambridge, MA: Harvard University Press, 1984), 3.

2 Sapna Maheshwari, "Stitch Fix and the New Science Behind What Women Want to Wear," *BuzzFeed*, September 24, 2014. http://www.buzzfeed.com/sapna/stitch-fix-and-the-new-science-behind-what-women-want-to-wear (accessed June 15, 2015).

3 Susan Sontag, "The Decay of Cinema," *The New York Times*, February 25, 1996. https://www.nytimes.com/books/00/03/12/specials/sontag-cinema.html (accessed June 15, 2015).

4 The most recent appearance of the term "Cinematch" in Netflix's official technology blog was made on April 6, 2012. The writers, Netflix's engineers Xavier Amatriain and Justin Basilico, described Cinematch as "our existing recommendation system." Despite the fact that, to the best of my knowledge, Netflix does no longer officially use the term *Cinematch*, I will apply it throughout this chapter as shorthand for the service's recommendation system. While Netflix can change the name of its proprietary set of algorithms at any given time without notifying its subscribers, the logic and methods described in this chapter can be consistently found in various discussions of Netflix in the trade presses, as well as in the company's own literature. Ironically, the inability to determine whether the name Cinematch has been replaced can serve to strengthen my argument regarding the transparency characterizing

Netflix's methods and hidden workings. For Netflix's use of the name "Cinematch," see Xavier Amatriain and Justin Basilico, "Netflix Recommendations: Beyond the Five Stars," *Techblog*, April 6, 2012. http://techblog.netflix.com/2012/04/netflix-recommendations-beyond-5-stars.html (accessed July 21, 2015).

5 In a letter written in 1877 Kant mentions he is writing a manuscript to be entitled "Critique of Taste." For the history of *Critique of Judgment* and an overview of Kantian esthetics, see Henry E. Allison, *Kant's Theory of Taste: A Reading of the Critique of Aesthetic Judgment* (Cambridge, UK: Cambridge University Press, 2001).

6 Ibid., 3.

7 Bourdieu, *Distinction*, 6.

8 A similar argument can be found in Thorstein Veblen's conceptualization of "conspicuous consumption"—the acquiring of luxury products to publicly display one's status and wealth. See Thorstein Veblen, *Theory of the Leisure Class: An Economic Study in the Evolution of Institutions* (New York: Macmillan, 1994).

9 Bourdieu, *Distinction*, 3.

10 Dan Harries, "Watching the Internet," in *The New Media Book*, ed. Dan Harries (London: The British Film Institute, 2002), 171–183.

11 For an historical overview of the new sensory experience offered to mass audiences in the early days of cinema, see Jennifer Lynn Peterson, *Education in the School of Dreams: Travelogues and Early Nonfiction Film* (Durham, NC/London: Duke University Press, 2013).

12 Ibid., 2.

13 Ibid., 107.

14 Ibid., 106.

15 Linda Williams, "Introduction," in *Viewing Positions: Ways of Seeing Films*, ed. Linda Williams (New Brunswick, NJ: Rutgers University Press, 1995), 14.

16 See John Hartley, "Housing Television: Textual Traditions in TV and Cultural Studies," in *The Television Studies Book*, eds Christine Geraghty and David Lusted (London: Arnold, 1998), 33–50.

17 See Gina Keating, *Netflixed: The Epic Battle for America's Eyeballs* (London: Penguin Books, 2012), 196.

18 Todd Yellin, "Netflix Launches New Personalization Features." March 26, 2009. http://blog.netflix.com/2009/03/netflix-launches-new-personalization.html (accessed June 3, 2015).

19 Lev Manovich, *The Language of New Media* (Cambridge, MA: MIT Press, 2001), 29.

20 Henry Jenkins, *Spreadable Media: Creating Value and Meaning in a Networked Culture* (New York: NYU Press, 2013), 116.

21 Henry Jenkins, *Convergence Culture: Where Old and New Media Collide* (New York: NYU Press, 2006).

22 For a useful critique of the idea of "on-demand utopia" and the Internet as an infinite archive, see *Film Curatorship: Archives, Museums, and the Digital Marketplace*, eds Paolo Cherchi Usai et al. (Vienna: Österreichisches Filmmuseum, 2008).

23 Ibid., 195.

24 Coined by Sconce, the term "Paracinema" refers to cultural works that are produced and distributed in the margins, and are rarely the focus of scholarly research. For an overview of this concept, see Jeffrey Sconce, " 'Trashing' the Academy: Taste, Excess, and an Emerging Politics of Cinematic Style," *Screen* 36.4 (Winter 1995): 371–393.

25 Initially, Netflix considered offering soft-porn titles to its subscribers, but this intention was abandoned in early 2000 after Reed Hastings was appointed to the California Board of Education. According to Keating, "Hastings believed that distributing adult films could be apolitical liability [...] the engineers worked the rest of that day and through the night delisting each objectionable movie from customers' movie lists and from the inventory." See Keating, *Netflixed*, 57.
26 For an overview of Netflix's content library and a critique of the lack of transparency in regards to the company's offerings, see Felix Salmon, "Netflix's Dumbed-down Algorithms," *Reuters*, January 1, 2014. http://blogs.reuters.com/felix-salmon/2014/01/03/netflixs-dumbed-down-algorithms/ (accessed June 1, 2015).
27 Keating, *Netflixed*, 61.
28 For an historical overview of the emergence of domestic "cine-clubs" in the United States, see Barbara Klinger, *Beyond the Multiplex: Cinema, New Technologies, and the Home* (Berkeley: University of California Press, 2006).
29 Due to the limited scope of this chapter, I cannot explore the various manifestations and definitions of the "digital divide." For an overview of the terms the "digital divide" and the "global digital divide," as well as the differences between them, see Faye Ginsburg, "Rethinking the Digital Age," in *The Media and Social Theory*, eds David Hesmondhalgh and Jason Toynbee (New York: Routledge, 2008).
30 Ibid., 147.
31 Quoted in Eli Pariser, *The Filter Bubble: How the New Personalized Web Is Changing What We Read and How We Think* (New York: Penguin Press, 2011), 25.
32 For an historical overview of the term "big data," see Lev Manovich, "Trending: The Promises and the Challenges of Big Social Data," in *Debates in the Digital Humanities*, ed. Mathew K. Gold (Minneapolis: University of Minnesota Press, 2012), 460–476.
33 Ibid., 53.
34 Ibid., 3.
35 Ibid., 6.
36 Quoted in Pariser, *The Filter Bubble*, 8.
37 Keating, *Netflixed*, 36.
38 Ibid., 254.
39 Alexander Galloway, *The Interface Effect* (Cambridge: Polity Press, 2012).
40 Alexis C. Madrigal, "How Netflix Reverse Engineered Hollywood," *The Atlantic*, January 2, 2014. http://www.theatlantic.com/technology/archive/2014/01/how-netflix-reverse-engineered-hollywood/282679/ (accessed July 21, 2015).
41 Ibid.
42 Amatriain and Basilico, "Netflix Recommendations."
43 Ibid.
44 Ibid.
45 Another manifestation of the cultural obsession with the "comfort zone" is the ongoing debate regarding the need for "trigger warnings" in educational settings and the question of whether students should be exposed to controversial, violent, or otherwise provocative content. For an overview of the "campus war" that has been unfolding since 2014 on these issues, see, for example, Judith Shulevitz, "In College and Hiding from Scary Ideas," *New York Times*, March 21, 2015. http://www.nytimes.com/2015/03/22/opinion/sunday/judith-shulevitz-hiding-from-scary-ideas.html?_r=0 (accessed July 21, 2015).

46 Ibid.
47 For an historical overview of the field of audience measurement, see Ien Ang, *Desperately Seeking the Audience* (London: Routeldge, 1991).
48 Starting in the late 1990s, Queer scholars have richly explored the interrelation between neoliberalism and the need to produce "predictable adults." See, for example, Judith Halberstam, *The Queer Art of Failure* (Durham, NC: Duke University Press, 2011).
49 Wendy Hui Kyong Chun, *Programmed Visions: Software and Memory* (Cambridge: MIT Press, 2011).
50 Bourdieu, *Distinction*, xxvii.
51 Jason Koebler, "What's New on Netflix: Advertisements," *Vice*, June 1, 2015. http://motherboard.vice.com/read/netflix-is-experimenting-with-advertisements?trk_source=popular (accessed June 25, 2015).
52 Keating, *Netflixed*, 256.
53 Bruno Latour, "Beware, Your Imagination Leaves Digital Traces," *Times Higher Literary Supplement*, April 6, 2007. http://www.bruno-latour.fr/node/245 (accessed July 21, 2015).
54 Thomas H. Davenport and Jeanne G. Harris, "What People Want (and How to Predict It)," *Harvard Business Review*, January 1, 2009. https://hbr.org/product/what-people-want-and-how-to-predict-it/an/SMR298-PDF-ENG (accessed March 15, 2015).
55 See, for example, Tara McPherson, "U.S. Operating Systems at Mid-Century: The Intertwining of Race and UNIX," in *Race After the Internet*, eds Lisa Nakamura and Peter Chow-White (New York: Routledge, 2012), 21–37.
56 Matthew Kirschenbaum, *Mechanisms: New Media and the Forensic Imagination* (Cambridge: MIT Press, 2008), 16.
57 Adrian Mackenzie, *Cutting Code: Software and Sociality* (New York: Peter Lang, 2006), 8.
58 The question of whether algorithms or networks can be described as agents stands in the center of actor-network theory and recent writings in object-oriented theory. Mackenzie, for example, asserts that there exists a "secondary agency [...] supporting or extending the agency of some primary agent." For a discussion of the "agential cut," see Karen Barad, "Posthumanist Performativity: Toward an Understanding of How Matter Comes to Matter," *Signs: Journal of Women in Culture and Society* 28.3 (2003): 801–830.
59 McPherson, "U.S. Operating Systems at Mid-Century," 26.
60 See, for example, Paul Dourish, "Protocols, Packets, and Proximity: The Materiality of Internet Routing," in *Signal Traffic: Critical Studies of Media Infrastructures*, eds Lisa Parks and Nicole Starosielski (Urbana: University of Illinois Press, 2015), 183–204; Jean-François Blanchette, "A Material History of Bits," *Journal of the American Society for Information Science and Technology* 62.6 (June 2011): 1042–1057.
61 McPherson, "U.S. Operating Systems at Mid-Century," 29.
62 Manovich, *The Language of New Media*, 58.
63 Colson quoted in Maheshwari, "Stitch Fix."

Part Two

Changing Entertainment

6

"Forward Is the Battle Cry": Binge-Viewing Netflix's *House of Cards*

Casey J. McCormick

Binge structures

With the growing availability of VOD (video-on-demand) and SVOD (subscription video-on-demand) technologies, binge-viewing (aka binge-watching) has quickly become a dominant mode of TV consumption. A recent slew of surveys[1] indicates that a large majority of TV viewers "binge," which many analysts define as watching three or more episodes in a row. The popularity of binging has engendered an entire discourse on the transformation of TV that recalls some of the most central debates in media studies: passive versus active consumption, narrative interactivity, and the shifting power dynamics among media producers and consumers. In this chapter, I'll show how narrative structures and digital interfaces combine to create binge experiences that simultaneously work with *and* against several of the historically defining characteristics of TV. Binge-viewing changes the stakes of narrative engagement by reframing the temporality of viewing experiences to optimize emotional intensity and story immersion. After offering a brief history and theorization of binge-viewing, I'll look at the landmark series *House of Cards* (Netflix, 2013–present) to demonstrate how modes of TV production, distribution, and consumption are changing in an increasingly "on-demand culture."[2] The success of *House of Cards* and the growing prominence of SVOD platforms demonstrate the power—and perhaps the necessity—of binge-viewing for the enjoyment of "complex TV."[3] I argue that *House of Cards* is transformative not only in terms of its nontraditional production and distribution models but also in the kinds of narrative experiences that the series makes possible by explicitly inviting the viewer to binge.

In an interview posted the day before Netflix released *House of Cards* season one in 2013, showrunner Beau Willimon quipped, "Our goal is to shut down a portion of America for a whole day."[4] This hail to binge-viewing represents a drastic shift in TV distribution: by releasing thirteen episodes at once, *House of Cards* invites, even challenges, its viewers to fully immerse themselves in the narrative world and allow the storytelling momentum to take hold. In addition to promoting immersive viewing, simultaneous release of a full season complicates the assumed relationship between distribution method and seriality. As Jennifer Hayward notes, "A serial is, by definition, an ongoing narrative *released in successive parts*."[5] Therefore, *House of Cards* challenges long-standing definitions of narrative categorization, as well as many conventions of TV storytelling. Ted Sarandos, Netflix's head of content acquisition, praises the unique possibilities afforded to the writers of Netflix original series, such as the lack of a need for recaps or forced cliffhangers: "[Y]ou really do get more storytelling, more richness. And by the time you get to 13 hours, you have spent more time with those people."[6] Sarandos' use of *people* is telling; as Michael Newman suggests, binging forges stronger viewer/character attachments than weekly viewing:

> Spending years with characters, they become regular visitors to our living rooms, like pals we see week after week at the same hangout. Binging intensifies the pleasure of this engagement by making characters all the more present in our lives. The relationship becomes more like a passionate but doomed affair, a whirlwind that enlivens us so well for a time, only to leave us empty and lost when it sadly, inevitably, ends.[7]

In contrast to Newman's somewhat bleak outlook on the emotional investment required of binging, Sarandos' positive framing of narrative immersion suggests an ontology of televisual content that moves away from pauses and hiatuses toward a more cohesive textual experience. Sarandos, Willimon, Netflix, and other SVOD content producers are forging new ways of presenting serial narratives that privilege user/text relations over advertising mandates and monolithic, unidirectional structures of programming flow. Binge-viewing along with other forms of time-shifting and mobile consumption are at the core of these new structures of TV experience.

Although the terminology has only become widely used in the past couple of years (see Figure 6.1), "binge-viewing" is not a new phenomenon: VCRs allowed users to record episodes for binging, networks have broadcast single-show marathons of various lengths since the rise of syndication, and DVD box sets have offered full seasons of series since 2000.[8] On-demand cable services, PVRs, and DVRs also facilitate binging and play a major role in the growing ethos of viewing "on your own terms." But the variety of available binge-viewing technologies continues to expand, and scholars are only beginning to scratch the surface of how this shift affects narrative experience. Most of the existing scholarship on binging is based on the DVD box set model, and so I'm interested in how online streaming offers a different kind of experience from other binge technologies. According to Derek Kompare, "the DVD box set plac[es] television programming in a more direct, repetitive, and *acquisitive* relationship with its viewers."[9] Meanwhile, Netflix and other streaming technologies have reconceived VOD with a different ontology: non-material acquisition, repetition via algorithmic suggestion, and (more) mobile consumption.

Jason Mittell notes that "[c]ompiling a serial allows viewers to see a series differently, enabling us to perceive aesthetic values traditionally used for discrete cultural works to ongoing narratives—viewing a DVD edition helps highlight the values of unity, complexity, and clear beginnings and endings, qualities that are hard

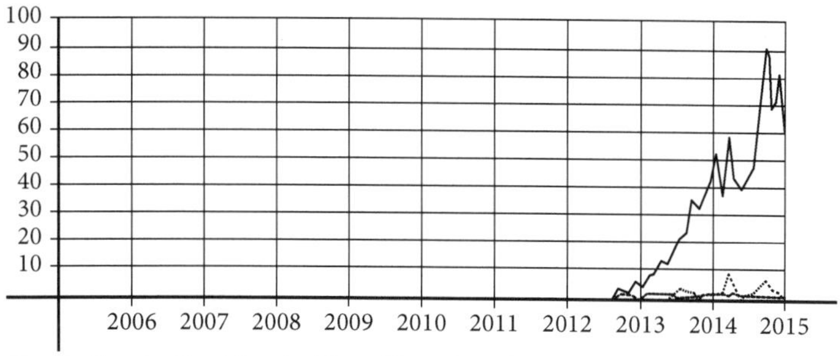

Google Trends: Graphing the Rise of Binge Watching

Search terms:
Binge Watching - ——
Binge Viewing - ·······
Binge-watching - -------

The Y-axis indicates the total number of Google searches relative to the total number of searches at that time. These trends indicate the overall popularity of a search term rather than an absolute number of searches.

Figure 6.1 Trends in search terms—the rise of "Binge Watching" since 2013
Source: Google Trends

to discern through the incremental releases of seriality."[10] However, in considering the difference between binging on a DVD and binging on an SVOD platform, we should analyze how different interfaces encourage (or sometimes hinder) what I call "smooth binging" experiences. DVD menus provide paratextual packaging, usually including special features, but these interfaces are often cluttered. With DVD interfaces that do not include the "play all" button, binge-viewing is marked by pauses that require menu navigation to get to the next episode. On the other hand, SVOD interfaces like Netflix usually default to an "autoplay" structure, in which limited user action is needed to continue the binge. By analyzing how particular interfaces facilitate binging and tracing the development of these interfaces toward smooth binging, we can begin to see how TV viewing operates in "binge culture."[11] Netflix has fully embraced its reputation as a binge platform in its promotional campaigns—most recently with their April Fools PSA videos.[12]

Before going further, it's worth spending some time to parse the "binge" metaphor and how it relates to historical attitudes about TV—and the consumption of fiction more generally. There is no doubt that the term "binge" conjures plenty of negative connotations: addiction, excess, guilt, lack of control, gluttony, and so on. It is foremost a metaphor of *extreme* consumption, of ravenous devouring. The metaphor also reinforces a binary subject/object (and producer/consumer) relationship, working against the rhetoric of narrative interactivity that is so prominent in contemporary media studies. Charlotte Brundson links the "[s]omatic metaphor of 'binging'"[13] to ideas about the addictive nature of fiction, arguing that "there is, in this metaphor . . . , the trace of a persistent shame at absorption in an audio-visual, fictional world."[14] It's true that the stigma of TV as the "idiot box" or "boob tube" continues to persist—despite celebrations over the last decade of the rise of "quality TV" and "the new golden age of TV." I argue, however, that cultural attitudes toward binge-viewing complicate its negative connotations, as viewers engage in self-aware, often ironic discourse regarding loss of control. This conception of binging as a self-conscious practice is at the heart of *House of Cards*: its thematic and structural investment in addiction, combined with Netflix's privileging of binge culture in their promotional campaigns, represents a strategic claim on the relationship between "quality" programming and binge-viewing. Indeed, statistics regarding the "most-binged"[15] shows support this link; and since "quality TV" frequently thematizes addiction,[16] Netflix's overt articulation of this relationship via *House of Cards* sheds light on the bingeability of a variety of other series.

The growing number of TV viewers who utilize "binging" and other terms of obsession to describe their user habits signals a reframing of the discourse of addiction and an assertion of the process as active and intentional. As much as depictions of binge-viewing tend to emphasize (and, often, hyperbolize) a condition of uncontrollable addiction, and as much as we may in fact surrender to the flow of a narrative during a binge, I argue that binging is a productive, often deliberate, and potentially transformative mode of viewing. Therefore, I am not ignoring potential problems with the addictive realities of binging, but I do think the lived experiences of binge-viewing reveal more complex relations of narrative power. As Tim Wu writes in "Netflix's War on Mass Culture," SVOD seeks

> to replace the traditional TV model with one dictated by the behaviors and values of the Internet generation. Instead of feeding a collective identity with broadly appealing content, the streamers imagine a culture united by shared tastes rather than arbitrary time slots. Pursuing a strategy that runs counter to many of Hollywood's most deep-seated hierarchies and norms, Netflix seeks nothing less than to reprogram Americans themselves. What will happen to our mass culture if it succeeds?[17]

The history of binging is unfolding every day, with the development of fleetingly new(er) technologies, shifts in industry and ratings structures, and the writing of media policy that will shape TV's future. Netflix is certainly the primary icon of SVOD, but the growing number of platforms, including Hulu, Crackle, Shomi, Amazon Instant, Yahoo! Screen, etc., means that we'll see a variety of SVOD distribution and consumption methods in years to come.

"Forward is the battle cry": The anatomy of a bingeable show

My reading of *House of Cards*' bingeability relies on structural and thematic analysis, combined with the crucial role of the Netflix interface and distribution model.[18] First of all, *House of Cards*' temporal structure reflects the trajectory of the binge experience: there is a distinct forward momentum in the narrative, with various increments of time passing between episodes, no flashbacks,[19] or flashforwards (also: no "previously on"), and every season amounts to about a calendar year. Furthermore, the show's thematic emphasis on addiction, power, and bodily exhaustion draws attention to the physical and psychological components of a TV binge. *House of Cards* consistently acknowledges the binge experience to incite a form of hyperdiegetic play—the viewer must confront the intensity of her immersion while in the midst of the consumption process. By examining the text and its reception trends, I will demonstrate how *House of Cards* is wholly steeped in binge culture.

From its first episode, *House of Cards* establishes narrative parameters that mark it as a bingeable text. On the level of paratextual framing, episodes do not have unique titles, but are instead represented as "Chapters" by the Netflix interface. This gesture to another narrative medium (books) serves several functions: it links the show to a history of serial fiction, it separates it from the dominant way of organizing TV, and it creates continuity across seasons (season 2 begins with "Chapter 14"). Furthermore, the use of a chapter format implicitly marks the text as a "quality" or "good" cultural object—associating *House of Cards* with the prestige of literature instead of TV. This conflation of media in the formal presentation of the series is echoed by widespread associations of the simultaneous release model with "a 13-hour movie,"[20] again linking the narrative to what has historically been considered a more "quality" medium.[21] Finally, on a basic structural level, the show's narrative complexity, intense seriality, and associations with the political thriller genre, in combination with the Netflix interface, all prime the text for binging.

I posit that complex narrative temporality and temporal play encourage binging by drawing attention to the function of time in the viewing experience. Paul Booth has argued that nontraditional presentations of narrative temporality are a key feature in the broader trend of complex TV.[22] The temporal momentum of *House of Cards* creates story gaps that require negotiation through attentive viewing, since the narrative only provides subtle clues as to the amount of time that has passed since the last episode and what kinds of events may have occurred in those ellipses. Furthermore, the series plays on an interaction between story time and real-world time: each season's narrative begins very close to the actual date of its release, and then propels the viewer into the future, engendering a kind of time travel that evokes the temporality of binging. This accelerated passage of time also draws attention to the way that time works on the body.[23] We see the characters' bodies change at a rate that, on the one hand, contrasts with our own relatively static bodies but, on the other, reflects the bodily exhaustion that might occur while binging. Of course, these temporal effects are dependent upon when and how quickly a viewer consumes the series. If, for example, one were to begin the series now, she would be traveling backward—not forward—in time. And if a viewer chooses *not* to binge, the diegetic gestures to the passage of time do not produce the same effects. The fact that the show's creators have placed such an emphasis on binging as an ideal mode of consumption, however, sets up a preferred reading that is reliant upon accelerated temporality and the play between story time and viewing time.

Another important tactic that amplifies the show's bingeability is the use of Frank's direct addresses, or Shakespearean asides, to the viewer. While these asides were also a part of the British version of the series (and the original source material of *Richard III*), they take on new meaning in the Netflix context. Recent statistics reveal that a growing number of SVOD users watch content on their computers, despite the variety of methods for accessing SVOD services on televisions. Therefore, we can assume a certain degree of *screen intimacy* when analyzing the Netflix audience. The screen is likely closer to the viewer, perhaps even in her lap or bed, and this screen is the same one used for various forms of personal communication. So when Frank looks into the camera and says, "welcome to Washington" just before the opening title sequence of the first episode, the text has already established a particular relationship with the viewer. We might even think of Frank's asides in terms of a *Skype ontology*, that we are video-conferencing with the narrative, or particularly with Frank himself. This structural choice plays on the dream of narrative interactivity—without, of course, actually allowing the viewer to speak back to Frank. Nonetheless, these direct addresses, amplified by Kevin Spacey's gaze, establish a textual intimacy that encourages binging as a means of sustaining the relationship as such.

The thematic elements of the show that evoke binge-viewing are also present from the first episode. In "Chapter 1," after forging his revenge plot,[24] Frank tells his wife Claire, "We'll have a lot of nights like this. Making plans, very little sleep." She responds, "I expected that—it doesn't worry me," and the couple proceeds to share a cigarette. This scene implicates Frank and Claire in a grueling process analogous to binging and acts as a call for psychological (and physical) preparation. The scene also reveals one of their addictions—nicotine—which will become an ongoing motif throughout the series. Another motif that we see in the first episode is Frank's addiction to video games: as he plays, he wears headphones and appears completely focused on the screen. In addition to highlighting themes of attentiveness and immersion, the fact of Frank's gaming emphasizes media interactivity and narrative play—the same kinds of experiences in which the viewer is engaged. Finally, toward the end of "Chapter 1," after he has begun to plant the seeds of his plot to power, Frank looks directly into the camera and tells us, "Forward is the battle cry"; if the episode has done its job, the viewer adopts this battle cry as her own and proceeds to binge the rest of the season.

Other key thematic trends that reflect the binge experience develop throughout season one. In addition to the ongoing theme of addiction, the motifs of consumption, exercise, and fatigue are all prominent. "Chapter 1" ends with Frank agreeing to a second helping of ribs at his favorite BBQ joint, proclaiming, "I'm feeling hungry today." Frank's eating and drinking habits continue to reflect the consumptive desire of the binge-viewer, as he alternates between restraint (eating a salad in "Chapter 4") and gluttony (going on a alcohol bender in "Chapter 8"). In "Chapter 2," Claire insists that Frank take better care of himself and buys him a rowing machine—emphasizing exercise, but also presenting a vehicle for simulated forward momentum. When the rowing machine breaks in the season finale, simulated momentum is exchanged for actual momentum when Frank joins Claire on a run. As the two protagonists jog through a chilly DC evening, the viewer also experiences a sense of renewed freedom of mobility, released from the hold of the narrative—at least until the next season.[25]

One of the most effective and complex devices that *House of Cards* uses to address the audience as binge-viewers is through the deployment of surrogate characters. Surrogates, or characters that stand in for the viewer, are a common narrative device, but they have been understudied in the televisual context.[26] In *House of Cards*, all of our surrogate characters are addicts of one kind or another, and the ways that they deal with their addictions present a spectrum of "good" and "bad" addictive behaviors. This spectrum serves as a kind of instruction manual on how to be a good binge-viewer. As new surrogates are introduced and then killed off, we come to see their failures as warnings, or at least as gestures to the viewer's experience. In season one, for example, Congressman Peter Russo is one of our primary surrogates. His addictive tendencies lead Frank to incorporate him into the main plot, since Frank needs someone he can manipulate. As we watch Peter struggle with his addictions to alcohol, drugs, and sex, the narrative positions him as a regular guy ("Can a corporate sellout roll a joint like this?"[27]). When Frank encourages Peter to run for governor of Pennsylvania, Peter is forced to publicly reveal his addictive past—much like the viewer of *House of Cards* might acknowledge (via social media or not) her own history of binge-viewing, though often with a notable inversion of the accompanying shame. Peter gets clean, but not for long; and once he falls off the wagon, completely succumbing to his addiction, the viewer must also recognize her own immersive behavior as a kind of "giving in." When it becomes clear that Peter is too far gone in his addiction to be of use, Frank takes swift action. As the two men sit in Peter's garage, Frank explains, in a soothing voice:

> I know you're in a lot of pain, Peter. But I don't want you to feel any pain tonight. Here, you can start fresh tomorrow [*hands him the bottle of booze*]. Go ahead, I won't judge ya. Hell, I'll even join you. Just relax. You're home now. Whatever it is you have to face tomorrow, you don't have to face it now. Right now it's just you and me, the rest of the world doesn't matter. Your children, Christina, they will forgive you. Because you're loved, Peter. … Just close your eyes, let it all go. We have all the time in the world.[28]

While this speech might read on one level as an invitation to succumb to addictive viewing, the fact that Frank murders Peter immediately after reveals the disingenuousness of Frank's seemingly comforting words. The camera situates us inside of the car (see Figure 6.2), and the monologue seems addressed as much to us as to Peter (in part because he is more or less unconscious). After Frank stages the suicide scene and exits the garage, the camera remains inside, entombing the viewer with Peter. This cinematic identification thus becomes a warning to the viewer that she cannot "let it all go" and that she does not "have all the time in the world"; rather, this is a moment to refocus attention for the final two chapters of the first season.

Another primary viewer surrogate in season one is Zoe Barnes, the journalist whom Frank uses to manipulate public opinion in the service of his political power grab. In contrast to Peter's straightforward (and more culturally recognizable)

Figure 6.2 Frank Underwood warns the viewer (*House of Cards*, Chapter 11)

substance addiction, Zoe is addicted to information. To emphasize her actions as addictive, we see the consumption metaphor utilized when she asks Frank to "feed her" intel,[29] establishing their salacious relationship in terms of physical and informational voracity. Her desire for knowledge reflects that of the viewer, reinforcing the puzzle nature of the show's complex seriality. Just as Mittell argues that complex TV turns viewers into "amateur narratologists,"[30] identification with Zoe turns viewers into amateur journalists—particularly if that viewer is connected to a second screen, reporting her activities via social media. But as was the case in our identification with Peter, the viewing methods that we see reflected by Zoe are similarly punished. In a major gesture of narrative surprise, Frank pushes Zoe in front of a moving train in the first episode of season two, abruptly severing our tie to her as a viewer surrogate. Mimicking the cinematic tactics of Peter's murder scene, here we are situated even more closely with Zoe's perspective. The camera places us at her level as she and Frank converse on the train platform. Then, when Frank suddenly grabs Zoe and turns her 180 degrees, we get a brief but traumatic point-of-view shot of her falling onto the tracks (see Figure 6.3). This use of a shocking twist in what would traditionally be the "season premiere" suggests an inversion of televisual models of surprise and suspense—it's a narrative move traditionally suited for a season finale. This twist also propels the viewer to binge; by piquing excitement and curiosity at the end of that first hour, Zoe's death becomes the narrative bait for season two. Furthermore, this unexpected character death creates the opportunity for a significant spoiler right off the bat, setting up potential punishment for those who wait too long to watch the season.

Figure 6.3 The abrupt demise of another viewer surrogate (*House of Cards*, Chapter 14)

Doug Stamper, Frank's chief of staff and closest ally, functions as a third viewer surrogate, although his insider knowledge of (and complicity with) Frank's plotting differentiates him from Peter and Zoe. Doug is a former alcoholic, fourteen years sober at the start of the series, and so his initial ability to control addictive tendencies makes him an ideal candidate for model viewership. By season two, however, he becomes obsessed with Rachel, a young prostitute who is implicated in the Peter Russo scheme. In "Chapter 24," Doug attends an Alcoholics Anonymous (AA) meeting and explains to the group:

> I work hard. I keep things simple. I know what my priorities are. There's this … this person. She's not even in my life except on the edges, making things blurrier. It doesn't tempt me to drink. It's more like, more like she feels like what it was like when I was drinking. When I couldn't get enough. No matter how many drinks I had, I wanted another.

During this monologue, the camera starts behind Doug's head, so that we are positioned with and as him, then slowly circles around and stops on a close-up of his face for the final line (creating the illusion of a direct address). This monologue works on two levels: setting up Doug's impending fall off of the wagon, and providing a rather accurate description of the emotional investment of our binge-viewing experience. In the closing moments of "Chapter 26," Doug is literally beaten down by his addiction: after she attempts to run away, Rachel bludgeons Doug in the head several times with a rock. The camera puts us at ground level next to Doug's body, as if we are lying face-to-face with (what appears to be) his corpse.

Over the course of season two, as Doug slides deeper into his addiction to Rachel, a single surrogate character emerges as the apparent embodiment of the ideal viewer: Edward Meechum, the Underwoods' personal security guard. In season one, Meechum undergoes training to become a professionalized addict, and the object of his addiction is the Underwoods themselves. The first words Frank says to Meechum are, "Do you drive fast?,"[31] one of the many references to speed and momentum throughout the series. Then, after failing to protect the Underwoods' home in "Chapter 6" (a mistake that was actually orchestrated by Frank), Meechum begs for a second chance. Frank concedes to rehiring Meechum, but issues the following caveat: "I want you to listen very closely to what I'm about to say. From this moment on, you are a rock. You absorb nothing, you say nothing. And nothing breaks you. Is that clear?" This warning to Meechum and the viewer seems harsh, but it's perfectly in line with the viewer-training motif. Frank is strict with Meechum to prepare him for the challenge, and he eventually rewards Meechum for his attentive dedication. In "Chapter 24," Frank, Claire, and Meechum have a threesome. Similar to the ways that the camera positions the viewer with character surrogates during their deaths, here we are positioned as Meechum in the threesome, and thus become part of their sexual dynamic (see Figure 6.4). So if Meechum is being rewarded with this intimate connection to the Underwoods, the viewer is simultaneously rewarded for her own viewing dedication. However, Meechum's position as primary surrogate and model viewer is undermined by season three, in which he remains a trusted employee of the Underwoods, but is consistently pushed to the fringes of both the story and the visual field. Perhaps Meechum's fade to the background suggests the limitations of

Figure 6.4 Model viewer, Edward Meechum, is rewarded with an unsustainable level of intimacy (*House of Cards*, Chapter 24)

viewer/character relationships—for viewers, the level of intimacy that Meechum achieved with the Underwoods is simply unsustainable.

Frank's position as vice president in season two results in President Garrett Walker playing a more prominent role in the narrative than in season one. While it might seem odd to identify with the "Leader of the Free World," Walker emerges as another potential viewer surrogate, one that represents the most pathetic model of viewership. Despite his position of political power, the narrative reveals Walker as weak, manipulable, and even an addict. The most interesting part about Walker in season two is his trajectory of exhaustion—he simply can't keep up with the narrative. In "Chapter 23," Frank convinces Walker to take a nap on the oval office couch, then turns to the camera and declares, "I've always loathed the necessity of sleep. Like death, it puts even the most powerful men on their backs." Walker continues to look increasingly haggard as the season wears on, reflecting the exhaustion of the viewer while simultaneously warning of the consequences of giving into that exhaustion. Walker faces impeachment and resigns in the season two finale, creating a correlation between giving into exhaustion and losing one's power over the narrative. In turn, Frank ascends to the presidency. It's hard to imagine a more clear narrative telos in a plot about a political power-grab than becoming the leader of the free world, and so Frank's success is a clear closural gesture. Knowing that Netflix guaranteed *House of Cards* two seasons up front, we could conceive of this episode as a potential series finale; however, the show's renewal for a third season was announced before season two was released. Therefore, when Frank enters the oval office, stands behind his new desk, pushes the chair to the side, and gives his trademark knuckle tap, this end becomes another narrative beat, carrying momentum toward season three.

While season two began with the unexpected death of a main character (Zoe), season three begins with an unexpected resurrection. Doug, presumed dead in "Chapter 26" after a chilling shot of his immobile body, eyes open and glazed over, lives on—albeit with severe physical and emotional damage. Excluded from Frank's advisory team, Doug carries out his political goals by watching the news—he becomes an expert TV viewer and the clearest surrogate character in the season. As he oscillates between being off and on the wagon over the course of the season, his trajectory becomes about the process of recovery from bad addictions (Rachel, alcohol) in order to reestablish his connection to the proper object of addiction (Frank). Indeed, he eventually murders Rachel and reclaims his role as Frank's chief of staff; once again, the story emphasizes that loyalty and commitment to Frank, by both characters and viewers, will be rewarded. But at what cost?

As this discussion of surrogate characters has demonstrated, *House of Cards* likes to show us how it feels to be *near* Frank Underwood. But no one is closer to him than his wife, Claire, an equally ruthless—and equally charming—character. Season three gives more story time to Claire than the previous seasons, and it charts a subtle but crucial trajectory of her increasing inability to remain close to Frank. Like many popular TV antiheroes (e.g., Walter White, Dexter Morgan, Tony Soprano, Don Draper), Frank is morally irredeemable. This depravity is why we like watching him, and why we like watching how people around him deal with his actions. As Frank campaigns for reelection in season three, his weaknesses come to the forefront, while the narrative emphasizes Claire's political strengths—as well as her maintenance of a moral code that Frank clearly lacks. Therefore, Claire's decision to leave Frank at the end of season three, made more impactful by an abrupt cut to black as she walks toward the camera, is instructive: she has been our most important surrogate all along, and she holds the most narrative power. Season four will no doubt focus on the fallout of this separation and put further pressure on the audience to reevaluate their processes of character identification.

Digital flows and social binging

House of Cards is as much a social media event as it is a TV show. Season one received an immense amount of press for its groundbreaking production and distribution methods. Season two garnered even more social media hype: by February 2014, the ripple effect of the success of season one (as well as *Orange Is the New Black*, *Arrested Development*, et al.), combined with the growing visibility of binge-viewing more broadly, primed *House of Cards* season two to be a true binge event. The day before the release, President Barack Obama even tweeted, "Tomorrow: @*HouseofCards*. No spoilers, please," acknowledging the fact that many viewers would binge the season quickly and potentially ruin key plot points for those lagging behind. By the 2015 release of *House of Cards*' third season, binge-viewing and simultaneous release of serial programming had become, if not a norm, at least well integrated into the contemporary mediascape. The novelty of the distribution strategy may have worn off, but binging remained a prominent mode of consuming the series—approximately 2 percent of all Netflix subscribers watched the entire season in its premiere weekend. This evidence of *planned* binging represents an interesting variation on the viewing practice, one that is clearly tied to Netflix's brand identity. Most importantly, it reasserts the communal elements of viewing that many scholars and critics argue are lost in on-demand culture. In contrast to the shared experience of watching a serial unfold across weeks and seasons, the planned binge creates different kinds of communal bonds. Social media dialogue is not only about what's happening in the narrative but about what is happening to *us* (physically and emotionally) as we binge the narrative. I posit that there are experiential differences between solo and group binging, and so the mass binge that takes place on the premiere weekend of *House of Cards* brings the sociality of group binging to a global level. Binging has always played a central role in fan practice—we can almost certainly trace the first binge-viewing to the fannish desire to re-watch (or, to think of other media, binging on a particular film director's oeuvre, or rapidly re-reading a favorite book). But with SVOD, and especially with Netflix's simultaneous distribution model, binging can be a typical part of the initial fan experience: although many critics and scholars lament the disappearance of "appointment TV," SVOD viewing patterns indicate that this viewing style persists, with new intensities and interpretive possibilities enabled by binging. In this departure from traditional models of TV distribution and consumption, Netflix and SVOD enable the creation of what I call "digital flows."

In 1974, Raymond Williams reconfigured how we look at TV programming by emphasizing the "mobile concept of flow" in opposition to the "static concept of distribution."[32] He demonstrated that analyzing "sequences" rather than "discrete units"[33] of TV could help us understand how the medium functions as a cultural institution. Through an extension of Williams' conception, we can see how interfaces like Netflix create new kinds of flows, in which viewers gain autonomy over the content of the sequence—but not necessarily over the addictive pull of that content. Binge-viewing represents a shift from a delayed gratification model of narrative relation to one of instant gratification. If televisual flow "establishes a sense of the world,"[34] then binging orders our world in ways that are different from previous media moments. In on-demand and binge cultures, streaming platforms provide interfaces that encourage the user to design her own flow—increasing what Williams calls the "planned" nature of "an evening's viewing."[35] In a similar methodological gesture, William Uricchio proposes "reposition[ing] flow as a means of sketching out a series of fundamental shifts in the interface between viewer and television, and thus in the viewing experience."[36] He argues that with digital interfaces, "Neither the viewer nor the television programmer dominate the notion of flow. Instead, a new factor enters the equation: the combination of applied metadata protocols ... and filters."[37] Therefore, it's important to remember that the apparent user autonomy of digital flows is still subject to the possibilities and limitations of a given technology—as well as the nonhuman logics of algorithms.

Writing in 2004, Uricchio anticipates the telos of VOD: "[T]he envisioned result would seem to be a prime case for flow—a steady stream of programming designed to stay in touch with our changing rhythms and moods, selected and accessible with no effort on our part."[38] He goes on to argue that "[e]xperientially, the new technologies promise to scan huge amounts of programming and in the process package relevant programs into a never-ending stream of custom-tailored pleasure."[39] Uricchio's prediction might have read as somewhat hyperbolic a decade ago, but the reality of SVOD experience in 2015 is not far off from this conception. While platforms like Netflix allow for an array of viewing patterns, this chapter has demonstrated the unique role that binging plays in a transmedia environment that enables diverse narrative experiences. I've argued that *House of Cards* encourages binging through "the reiterated promise of exciting things to come,"[40] linking narrative form and streaming interface in the production of complex digital flows.

SVOD and the practices that have arisen from streaming technologies transform TV culture and the ways in which individuals are interpolated by the media industries. More narrative content and more methods of access to that content allow for the kind of "tailored pleasure" that Uricchio predicted. As Tim Wu argues, "Community lost can be community gained, and as mass culture weakens, it creates openings for the cohorts that can otherwise get crowded out.... Smaller communities of fans, forged from shared perspectives, offer a more genuine sense of belonging than a national identity born of geographical happenstance."[41] This move toward a more dispersed media landscape and the communities that form around nearly every text undermines the mass cultural hegemony that critics and theorists of the nineteenth and twentieth century deemed so toxic. Among the array of new SVOD services being launched,

Netflix has remained a forerunner in the shifting landscape of the media industries. No other service has been credited (or condemned) for changing the face of both film and television so drastically. Similarly, *House of Cards* is now just one of many series that follow the simultaneous release format, but its role as the first to do so should not be downplayed. No text single-handedly alters the course of a medium, but *House of Cards* is certainly one of the most influential series in harnessing the convergence of TV and the internet to produce transformative content.

Notes

1 "'Binging' is the New Viewing for Over-the-Top Streamers," *Nielsen*, September 18, 2013. http://www.nielsen.com/us/en/insights/news/2013/binging-is-the-new-viewing-for-over-the-top-streamers.html; Pamela Marsh, Zeus Ferrao, and Gintare Anuseviciute, "The Impact of Binge Viewing," *Annalect*, July 2014. http://www.annalect.com/impact-binge-viewing; "Can't Stop, Won't Stop: Binge-Viewing Is Our New Favourite Addiction," *Miner & Co., Studio*, April 29, 2014. http://www.minerandcostudio.com/#!binge/cm7c; "Across the Globe, Consumers Seek Increased Personalization from Entertainment," Arris Consumer Entertainment Index, May 28, 2014. http://storage.pardot.com/10832/114254/ARRIS_infographic_May2014.png; Tom Huddleston, Jr., "Survey: Pretty Much Everybody Is Binge-Watching TV," *Fortune*, June 30, 2015. http://fortune.com/2015/06/30/binge-viewing-study (accessed July 17, 2015)

2 See Chuck Tryon, *On Demand Culture: Digital Delivery and the Future of Movies* (New Brunswick: Rutgers University Press, 2013).

3 Jason Mittell, *Complex TV: The Poetics of Contemporary Television Storytelling*, pre-publication edition (MediaCommons Press, 2012–13).

4 Brian Stelter, "New Way to Deliver a Drama: All 13 Episodes at Once," *The New York Times*, January 31, 2013. http://www.nytimes.com/2013/02/01/business/media/netflix-to-deliver-all-13-episodes-of-house-of-cards-on-one-day.html.

5 Jennifer Hayward, *Consuming Pleasures: Active Audiences and Serial Fictions from Dickens to Soap Opera* (Lexington: University of Kentucky Press, 1997), 3 (my emphasis).

6 Ted Sarandos, "Netflix Shows Don't Need Annoying Recaps," *Cnn.com*, June 6, 2014. http://money.cnn.com/video/media/2014/06/06/netflix-no-annoying-recaps-ted-sarandos.cnnmoney/.

7 Michael Newman, "TV Binge," *FlowTV.org*. 9.5 (January 23, 2009).

8 Derek Kompare, *Rerun Nation: How Repeats Invented American Television* (New York: Routledge, 2005), 200.

9 Ibid., my emphasis.

10 Mittell, *Complex TV*, "Complexity in Context."

11 I use the term "binge culture" to expand upon Tryon's "on-demand culture." These concepts are inherently linked, but I conceive of my term as a distinct stage in the evolution of "on-demand culture."

12 On April 1, 2015, Netflix released a series of PSA parodies about the "dangers" of binging. Each lasted about 30 seconds, and many featured actors from Netflix original series.

13 Charlotte Brundson, "Binging on Box-Sets: The National and the Digital in Television Crime Drama," in *Relocating Television: Television in the Digital Context*, ed. Jostein Gripsrud (New York: Routledge, 2010), 64–65.
14 Ibid., 67.
15 Dina Gachman, "Breaking Bad, House of Cards Most Binge-Watched Shows," *Forbes.com*, June 25, 2014. http://www.forbes.com/sites/dinagachman/2014/06/25/breaking-bad-house-of-cards-most-binge-watched-shows/.
16 E.g. *Mad Men* (AMC, 2007–15), *The Wire* (HBO, 2002–8), *Breaking Bad* (AMC, 2008–13), *Deadwood* (HBO, 2004–6), *Dexter* (Showtime, 2006–13), *True Blood* (HBO, 2008–14), *Black Mirror* (Channel 4, 2011–present), and *Orange Is the New Black* (Netflix, 2013–present).
17 Tim Wu, "Niche Is the New Mass," *New Republic* 244.20 (2013): 30.
18 I should note that at the time of this writing, three seasons have aired, and the fourth is in the process of production.
19 The only exception is season three, episode seven, which deploys a "one-month earlier" narrative structure after a flash-forward cold open.
20 Nathan Mattise, "*House of Cards*: The '13-Hour Movie' Defining the Netflix Experience," *ArsTechnica.com*, February 1, 2013. http://arstechnica.com/business/2013/02/house-of-cards-the-13-hour-movie-defining-the-netflix-experience/.
21 As many media scholars have noted, the cultural hierarchy between film and TV has dramatically shifted in the past 5–10 years; but of course, remnants of that hierarchy persist. David Fincher's directorial role in Chapters 1–2 emphasizes the link to film. However, it is important to note that the series' opening credits emphasize that it is "Adapted for Television" by Willimon.
22 Paul Booth, *Time on TV: Temporal Displacement and Mashup Television* (New York: Peter Lang, 2012).
23 The theme of accelerated time is also foregrounded by the opening credits sequence, which is comprised of panning time-lapse panoramas of Washington, DC.
24 Similar to its Shakespearean source text, *House of Cards* follows the story of Frank Underwood's devious rise to power (in his case, after being passed over for a promised position in the newly elected president's cabinet).
25 Season two of *House of Cards* intensifies the narrative tactics of season one that mark the text as bingeable. Consumption becomes a more prominent theme, discourse on addiction becomes more complicated, and the theme of exhaustion plays a central role.
26 Much important work regarding viewer identification has taken place in film studies, emphasizing issues of gender and racial representation (e.g., Mulvey, hooks et al.). In this chapter, I use "surrogate" in a relatively neutral sense to refer to any character that seems to reflect the viewer's perspective.
27 *House of Cards*, "Chapter 2."
28 Ibid., "Chapter 11."
29 Ibid., "Chapter 4"; while "feeding information" is a common idiom, the metaphor is doubled by the foreplay taking place between the two characters.
30 Jason Mittell, "Narrative Complexity in Contemporary American Television," *The Velvet Light Trap* 58.1 (2006): 38.
31 *House of Cards*, "Chapter 3."

32 Raymond Williams, *Television: Technology and Cultural Form*. Ed. Ederyn Williams (London: Routledge, 2005), 71.
33 Ibid., 86–87.
34 Ibid., 110.
35 Ibid., 85.
36 William Uricchio, “Television’s Next Generation: Technology/Interface Culture/Flow,” in *Television After TV: Essays on a Medium in Transition*, eds Lynn Spigel and Jan Olsson (Durham: Duke University Press, 2004), 165.
37 Ibid., 176–177.
38 Ibid., 177.
39 Ibid., 178.
40 Williams, *Television*, 87.
41 Wu, “Netflix’s War.”

7

The Cognitive Psychological Effects of Binge-Watching

Zachary Snider

Jordan M. Carpenter and Melanie C. Green assert the persuasiveness of narrative transportation for viewers: "Social cognitive theory has provided the theoretical basis for much of the work in entertainment-education, which has demonstrated effects on health and social issues around the world."[1] Narrative transportation refers to viewers' emotional self-immersion in a story (specifically for this chapter, the empathetic depth in which viewers become involved in a television series) and the ways that viewers' attitudes, beliefs, and opinions about their own social relationships change because of the stories they experience. Now that so many television series are available on streaming services such as Netflix, viewers' narrative transportation can be sped up by binge-watching: the process of viewing an entire season of a particular series, if not even an entire series, by watching all of its episodes back-to-back for excessive, uninterrupted periods of time.

Carpenter and Green's studies in cognitive psychology explore how effectively fictional narratives offer viewers psychological escape, and also how mass consumption of entertainment medias—like binge-watching television shows, for example—affects one's ability to mentally perceive and process these narratives. Carpenter and Green state that viewers "tend to react to events in the narratives as if they were real, increasing the likelihood of an emotional response,"[2] and that "the kinds of participatory responses that [viewers] have to a narrative can affect their emotional responses, their memory for narrative events, and their real-world judgments."[3] Theories about narrative transportation apply well to the cognitive psychological processes of binge-watchers of Netflix's streaming services. Binge-watching complex dramas such as *Mad Men*, *Breaking Bad*, *Orange Is the New Black*, *House of Cards*, and *Damages*, psychologically affects viewers' perceptions of reality by increasing their rate of empathy for shows' characters, and creates confusion when viewers process these narratives too quickly, which ultimately hinders viewers' real-world judgments and interpersonal relationships.

Television viewing, and binge-watching in particular, serves to illustrate different cognitive functions ranging from one's general "beliefs and behavioral strategies"[4] to how one's "patterns of behavior"[5] are affected by media consumption, and how one's "thinking and belief system" are modified "to bring about enduring emotional and behavioral change."[6] Binge-watching also recalls the type of problem-solving skills that cognitive psychology associates with collaborative forms of "active participation."[7] This means that regardless of whether viewers watch alone or with others, the binge-worthy shows for which Netflix is famous demand a high degree of engagement, a form of participation whereby viewers interact with the story world in order to discern complex plot and character developments.

During a recent three-day stay in a hospital in Brooklyn, New York, I found myself going through this very process: for two nights and three days, I sat in bed with my noise-canceling headphones, sleeping (very) intermittently, unable to eat because I was so ill, and, mostly, binge-watching the first four seasons of Glenn and Todd Kessler's legal thriller *Damages*. My constant escape into *Damages*' evil New York City soon became more realistic to me than my disgusting hospital room. By the time I was released, I wanted to work for Patty Hewes (Glenn Close), so that I could be as powerful and conniving as her, and then maybe kill her, as well. I also wanted to help Ellen Parsons (Rose Byrne) permanently get away from Hewes, and then befriend half of the characters on the show, so that I could warn them about what terrible plights they were in for.

When I was released from the hospital, the streets of Park Slope, Brooklyn, seemed different and much more paranoia-inducing than the morning when I'd been admitted. As fate would have it, the second I stepped onto the Brooklyn sidewalk for the first time in three days, I spotted actor Ben Shenkman, who plays District Attorney Curtis Gates on *Damages*. He stood on the corner with someone who appeared to be his wife and their friends, all waiting for the light to change so they could cross 7th Avenue. I raced over to Shenkman—who at the time I thought was *really* D.A. Gates—and warned him that Patty Hewes was planning to double-cross him and Ellen Parsons, and that his life was in danger. I had not showered in three days, had swollen IV needle holes in both my arms, and was ghost-white from losing all of my bodily fluids and appetite. I looked like a homeless heroin addict. Shenkman at first uncomfortably tried to laugh off my lunacy, but after I insisted that Hewes was going to get him, he thanked me and then quickly ushered his loved ones away from me.

Carpenter and Green might suggest that I was simply trying to help Gates/Shenkman, as he and I were now connected after my *Damages* marathon: "avid viewers of fictional television programs are more likely to believe in a just world: that good deeds are necessarily rewarded and that a person who suffers misfortune somehow deserved [better]."[8] On that morning, I truly believed that I had helped Gates/Shenkman, and I rushed back to my apartment so that I could binge-watch the final season of *Damages* and complete the series.

In their study about how television narratives shape real-world perceptions and personal values, Shrum and Lee report the following: "Heavy television viewing has been shown to be associated with greater anxiety and fearfulness ... and greater interpersonal mistrust."[9] As a paranoid hospital patient, I was not the (usually) sane university professor who lectures about the psychological effects of media; instead, I was stuck in the dangerous, fictional world of *Damages*. It is also important to note that I had binge-watched five seasons *alone*, without any fraternal banter about whether or not the world represented in *Damages* was dramatically effective or even minutely plausible. In solitude, I followed the complex narrative strands of Patty Hewes' intricate scheming, and learned all the twists, turns, and naughty secrets of *Damages*' plotlines. "When people process heuristically," write Shrum and Lee, "they do not carefully consider all information in memory before constructing judgments; instead, they take a cognitive shortcut and consider only a small subset of all information." Likewise, Carpenter and Green explain that

> Transported [viewers] have imaginatively left their immediate surroundings behind and entered the narrative world. Importantly, being transported into a story has strong cognitive and emotional consequences and leaves a [viewer] susceptible to change from the themes of a story they are experiencing.[10]

Transported I indeed was, in this extreme hyper-realistic case, but my situation of desperate escape is not rare. Many viewers binge-watch high-quality, cerebrally challenging television shows on streaming services, like the ones that Netflix offers, as a means of escape—escape from work (stream *Breaking Bad* and, through fictitious escape, become your own vengeful boss!), escape from family and partner problems (binge-watch *Mad Men* and have extramarital affairs and obfuscate your past!), escape from romance troubles (watch every episode of *Orange Is the New Black* and have a male fiancé *and* a jailbird lesbian lover!), escape from objections to the state of American politics (stream *House of Cards* and watch the U.S. government unravel in sin!), and escape from horrible hospital rooms. Escapism through fantastical television narrative is nothing new, of course, but the ability to escape for hours upon hours, or literally *days upon days*, dependent upon how many seasons a series has available to stream, into the same show's unique world *is* a new luxury, one that can also be detrimental to the psyche, to one's interpersonal relationships, to the cognitive psychological understanding of one's reality, and, ultimately, to one's overall happiness and mental well-being.

In February 2015, *Time* referenced "a study from the University of Texas [which found] that people who struggle with loneliness and depression are more likely to binge-watch [more] television than their peers"[11] because "this activity provides an escape from their unpleasant feelings."[12] This study also claimed that "people with low levels of self-control were more likely to binge-watch,"[13] and thus "binge-watching should no longer be seen as a 'harmless addiction,' and [researchers] pointed out that the activity is also related to obesity, fatigue, and other health concerns."[14] Over-immersing oneself in these narratively complex television series becomes detrimental cognitively *and* psychologically because these stories feature characters with whom viewers prefer to spend time. They also engage viewers in emotionally fast-forwarded plots where exciting activity happens more frequently than in the real world. Carpenter and Green state that these narratives "may also create a contrast effect where the real world comes to seem pale by comparison to the exciting or vivid narratives available elsewhere… [which] may in some cases create an overall contrast that causes individuals to devalue their everyday experiences."[15] This devaluation of real life then prompts viewers to binge-watch their preferred series even *more*, and at an even faster consumptive rate, because these complex series offer more pleasure and (faux-)camaraderie that viewers have convinced themselves exists between them and the characters whom they adore.

Peter Vorderer states in his article about the dangers of interactive media consumption such as excessive television viewing: "Every individual has the potential to feel part of a virtual community to which he or she belongs… This feeling of belonging, however, depends on the illusion that the media veridically reflect and depict reality."[16] In other words, the more truthful reality seems, through a television show's plot, characters, production, and so on, the more apt viewers are to binge-watch, thereby ostracizing themselves from actual reality. Similarly, Steven Johnson discusses in his groundbreaking bestseller *Everything Bad Is Good for You* how the cognitive psychological effects of millennial medias (multi-narrative television series, internet streaming services, complex videogame storylines) affect viewers who consume these medias in solitude: "Cognitive psychologists have argued that the most effective learning takes place at the outer edges of a student's competence; building on knowledge that the student has already acquired, but challenging him with new problems to solve."[17] In regards to television binge-watching, Johnson's explanation of cognitive learning means that the writers of television shows which are narratively complex feature many consecutive narrative strands for a multitude of characters that viewers are required to puzzle out. (This includes the aforementioned *Damages*, *Breaking Bad*, *Mad Men*, *House of Cards*, and *Orange Is the New Black*; and may also include *Dexter*, *Friday Night Lights*, and *The West Wing*—all of which can be streamed on Netflix. One might add many of HBO's exclusive drama series to which Netflix does not have streaming rights: *The Sopranos*, *Six Feet Under*, *True Detective*, *The Wire*, etc.). This multitude of cognitively rewarding character arcs thus demands that viewers must mentally file away an overabundance of narrative strands; character interactions; and, most often in shows like these, characters' deceptions, lies, and schemes. Subjecting oneself to any of these series not only requires viewers' full attention in order to memorize all of these narrative complexities; it also means that viewers must become emotionally and psychologically invested enough in the characters to follow them throughout their collective hyper-reality, in order to successfully complete the series—a personal triumph for binge-watchers.

Cognitive psychology's basic tenets focus on how one mentally processes others' behavior, and the effects of these behaviors, particularly in terms of problem-solving ability, deductive personal reasoning, language comprehension, and memory function. When watching a show like Netflix's original dramedy *Orange Is the New Black*, a viewer is required to: psychologically evaluate the many female inmate characters' disparate behaviors; cognitively map out the countless narrative strands through which these aggressive women manipulate each other; emotionally interpret how to feel about these characters' wicked plots (which, for *Orange Is the New Black*, is doubly difficult since each character has both a backstory "reality" *and* a present-day prison hyper-reality); decipher the language use and abuse of each character (e.g., Poussey Washington has two vernaculars—one "real world" with proper diction and another that's a tough-girl "prison language," just as most of the characters do); and, finally, psychologically *and* cognitively make sense of all this. Maier and Gentile propose in their study about psychological analysis of media communication that "humans learn by associating cognitive concepts together, by creating new mental representations of concepts, by creative cognitive maps of spatial arrangements,"[18] meaning that viewers educate themselves about the fictional world of a television series by piecing together a show's many confusing narrative strands. TV viewing has become a puzzle, one that isn't always solvable while binge-watching these particular shows at a rate in which the memory can function effectively enough to make sense of everything. Viewers watch these characters engage in naughtiness and deception for an entire season and, if a viewer shuttles through each season by binge-watching, he runs the risks of cognitive information overload and emotional disturbance about *Orange*'s fictional world versus his own real life.

Binge-watching a cognitively and psychologically complex series like *Orange Is the New Black* is exhausting, and can negatively affect one's otherwise healthy mental stasis. As Maier and Gentile also state,

> Many cognitive concepts also have emotional components associated with them. For example, attitudes and stereotypes are based not only on cognitive "facts" about situations or types of people, but also on our feelings about them ... Furthermore, repeated opportunities to experience or practice certain feeling states can lead to them becoming solidified into traits. This is similar to how cognitive or behavior habits can become personality traits.

While I wouldn't want to adopt this show's characters' personality traits, cognitive psychological research suggests that it could happen. Jane Brown states in her essay about TV's effects on viewers' personalities that "Cognitive Social Learning Theory ... [predicts] that people will imitate behaviors of others when those models are rewarded or not punished for their behavior ... they are likely to learn patterns of aggressive [behavior], as well."[19] Just as Patty Hewes hardly ever has to suffer for her corrupt actions on *Damages*; and Don Draper (Jon Hamm) rarely has to pay for his unethical stumbles on *Mad Men*; and Frank and Claire Underwood (Kevin Spacey and Robin Wright) get away with fraud, libel, and murder on *House of Cards*, the women of *Orange Is the New Black* often go unpunished for illegalities that they ironically commit in prison. To a viewer, this promotes a hyper-reality in which entitlement, illegality, and unethical behavior are permissible.

These psychological relationships that we form with TV characters then become unhealthy, even though, as Johnson says, our empathy for these characters upgrades our understanding of human nature and "activates a component of our emotional IQ, sometimes called our social intelligence: our ability to monitor and recall many distinct vectors of interaction in the population around us."[20] Regarding the adoption of characters' personality traits and our ability to better engage in empathy, Shrum and Lee recall the effects of Cultivation Theory, namely that "the frequent exposure to these [images and characters] results in their internalization: The more people watch television, the more they develop values, attitudes, beliefs, and perceptions that are consistent with the world as it is portrayed on television."[21] In other words, by cognitively processing what happens within the plot of a television series, we psychologically fool ourselves into believing that these characters' reality is also our own.

Although it is certainly possible to apathetically watch one of these narratively complex series and thus be a passive rather than an active viewer, doing so would mean that, as a viewer, I would not be as emotionally enmeshed in the plot and character arcs of a show. While many viewers are presumably not quite as hyper-immersive as I was during my hospital binge-watching, for example, it's important to note that complete engagement in a single series *should* result in one's psychologically altered perception of reality. If a fictional or fact-based television show is successful at construing narrative believability, viewers' cognitive and emotional states will be affected. For example, when I binge-watched *Orange Is the New Black*, I had disturbing dreams for a few consecutive nights that I, a male who is not a criminal, was locked in a women's prison with the show's demented characters. During the day, in between these disquieting dreams, I found myself daydreaming in semiconsciousness about which prison gang I would join and support—Red's (Kate Mulgrew), obviously, as I would need supper and wouldn't want to go hungry until she liked me again—and how guilty I would feel if I cheated on my spouse with my ex while doing prison time for drug possession like Piper did to Larry (Jason Biggs) with Alex (Laura Prepon), and how depressed I'd be during my adjustment period from "real life" to penitentiary living.

Viewer empathy for these troublesome characters only happens because of these series' narrative complexities, which fool our brains into thinking that these characters' lives are more interesting, more complex, more important, and—definitely—more dramatic than ours. According to Johnson,

> Part of that cognitive work comes from following multiple threads, keeping often densely interwoven plotlines distinct in your head as you watch. But another part involves the viewer's 'filling in': making sense of information that has been either deliberately withheld or deliberately left obscure ... You're asked to analyze.[22]

And analyze we do, because we empathize with these characters while feeling a part of *their* lives and vice versa, that is, incorrectly including them as a part of *our* lives. Because we are responsible for "filling in" the blanks of their stories, we want to help these characters, to save them, to kill them, to make sure they get caught, or at least to figure out the puzzles of their past and their wrongdoings. A viewer will rapidly consume seven seasons of *Mad Men* in order to congratulate himself on solving the mystery of Don Draper's past and to psychologically assess his damage. That same viewer will binge-watch *Breaking Bad* for five seasons and become as emotionally involved with Walter White (Bryan Cranston) as with Draper, though these men are vastly different in personality and lifestyle, because the viewer now roots for White's violent tendencies and brilliant methamphetamine-cooking talents. Both of these character examples are featured on shows that require considerable cognitive memory recall, problem-solving skills, and character double-crossings. About this, Johnson says, "In a sense, this is as much a map of cognitive changes in the popular mind as it is a map of onscreen developments, as though the media titans had decided to condition our brains to follow ever larger numbers of simultaneous threads."[23] To watch *Mad Men* or *The Sopranos* or *The Wire* or *Orange Is the New Black* or even *House of Cards* or *Dexter* is to masochistically involve oneself in painful, mind-blowing memory overload. To binge-watch any of these shows is to psychologically torture one's memory function and to abuse one's ability to cognitively process information.

It is difficult to maintain and process all of this plot information so speedily by binging on these character arcs and backgrounds, and side stories, which suggests that, by binge-watching, we're undermining the value and production of these clever programs. Shows that debuted on other channels but are now available to stream on Netflix (like AMC's *Mad Men* and *Breaking Bad*, for example) were not meant to be consumed at such a rapid rate, since they require so much cognitive sorting, emotional empathy, and psychological understanding. Netflix has altered these shows' delivery format for binge-watchers, which in turn affects the way that we bingers receive and process the narratives. So, to make things easier on ourselves, when we binge-watch, we semiconsciously choose what shows to escape into based on our own experiences that now provide us with conditioned emotional empathy and a stronger ability to cognitively process these difficult multi-narrative strands. "[F]rom a psychological perspective,"[24] say Gary Bente and Ansgar Feist in their article about personal media selection, the four characteristics common in public discussion and media criticism are as follows:

- Personalization: The story relates to a particular experience of an individual…
- Authenticity: [seemingly and believably T]rue stories of real, nonprominent people—like you and me…
- Intimacy: Traditional frontiers between the private and public sphere…
- Emotionality: Production methods and interpersonal communication styles within the shows are set up to produce emotional reactions and to reveal personal attitudes.[25]

When we begin streaming a television series, we crave intimacy and emotional connection with the characters and their "truthful" stories; then, once we've garnered this intimacy a few episodes in, the binge-watching process is underway, and thus social and familial ostracization happens, too. Vorderer asserts that "people tend to prefer those [narratives] that fit them personally. This refers not only to their behaviors, but also to their general preferences and tastes. As a result… [engaging with these narratives] individualizes the program even more."[26] These two studies seem rather ironic, considering that most viewers—hopefully—cannot readily identify with serial killers (*Dexter*), 1960s advertising agency philanderers (*Mad Men*), incarcerated women semi-comically fighting for their lives (*Orange Is the New Black*), or corrupt lawyers and politicians (*Damages* and *House of Cards*). I aver that these complicated storylines about deception, murder, adultery, greed, and other unlawful behaviors are of secondary importance to empathetic character connection. I binged *Dexter* to connect with his male aggression and inner rage, and his feelings of isolation, but watching the series never made me a murderer. I binged *Mad Men* for these exact same reasons, and like many other viewers, I enjoy the wardrobe and production design aspects of the show. I binged *Orange Is the New Black* to empathize with the unalterable mistakes these women made that changed their lives forever, as I too have made unalterable mistakes (like any other viewer/human being has). And, I binged *Damages* and *House of Cards* because, unlike these shows' antiheroes, I cannot obtain power through lying, manipulating, and scheming in my career without consequence, so I must instead narratively transport myself into these series to experience the characters' immoral behaviors. For these examples, it's also integral to note that these characters I rapidly consumed have hyperbolized aspects of my own personality traits and fantastical desires. Or, as Bente and Ansgar called it, these characters have an "authenticity"[27] to which I relate that allows me to be "intimate" and "emotional" with them; and, it is not a generalization to presume that this is why most viewers connect with these notoriously naughty characters.

Vorderer's study also notes that viewers have a "tendency not to refer to orientations, values, and goals that are provided for a social regiment of a society as they did in the past, but rather, to choose their orientations individually,"[28] further clarifying that binge-watching and its effects are a solo process that we purposely undergo alone, in efforts to connect with "realistic" people (i.e., television characters) at a consumptively rapid rate. Johnson disagrees with this theory, suggesting that viewing habits are instead "based on the dictates of mass advertising. Word of mouth is often more powerful"[29] and that we choose what to binge-watch based on other consumers who "pride themselves on their pop culture mastery, their eye for new shows and rising talent."[30] Johnson's theory suggests that binge-watching is actually more of a communal experience in which viewers either binge shows together or at least get together and talk about them.

NBC's sitcom *Marry Me*, which debuted in the fall of 2014, satirized this communal television streaming experience, when in one episode the two main characters Jake and Annie both "cheated" on each other by individually streaming their favorite television series that they usually watched together. They hid this information from each other so carefully, and with so much guilt, that they each took a polygraph test to see who had "cheated" on the other.[31] In the spring of 2015, *Time magazine* published an article called "Binge-Watching: Modern Love's New Frontier," in which the journalist Sarah Elizabeth Richards guiltily confessed about her own binge-watching cheating scandal against her husband and also chronicled some of her married friends' cheating behaviors when streaming a mutually beloved series: "Last December, Netflix released the results of a Harris poll that found that 61% of 1,500 respondents regularly watched two to six episodes of the same TV show in one sitting, and more than half of them preferred to do so with company."[32] This suggests that binge-watching with a companion has more in common with the traditional television model of weekly episode delivery, since faithful viewers must wait to catch up on a series' episodes with their viewing partner. The cultural anthropologist Grant McCracken similarly assesses that "People are negotiating agreements when they both find shows they adore. When these rules are broken, it's a source of mild irritation to outright hostility,"[33] while Richards adds that "It doesn't help that Netflix's 'recently watched' feature makes it easy to get caught!"[34]

Still, another demographic study noted that "38 percent [of Netflix viewers who regularly binge-watch] prefer to watch shows for hours on end alone," confirming that approximately two-fifths of Netflix's binge-watchers socially isolate themselves to engage with these series' complex characters and multi-narratives, rather than as a social endeavor. Just as social media—Facebook, Twitter, Instagram, and so on—seemingly promotes unity for its users, overuse of these social networking applications causes isolation, loneliness, depression, and anxiety.[35] Sharon Strover and William Moner state in their study about how streaming services cause binge-witching: "some scholars have suggested reformulating the idea of entertainment to encompass the social nature of media, whether by suggesting a rebranding of interactive TV systems as 'social TV,'"[36] meaning that binge-watching can be just as isolating as popular social networking sites. We don't usually creep through people's Facebook pages or Instagram feeds with others, as this is a solitary activity on our personal devices; thus, when we binge-watch alone, this can stunt our cognitive abilities and negatively affect our psychological progress personally and socially.

This oppositional viewing behavior—individual versus communal—does indeed affect the binge-watcher's comfort with socializing, and his overall psychosocial capabilities. For example, my spouse and I binge-watched the first two seasons of *Breaking Bad* until it became too intense for him, thanks to abundant anxiety while watching the series, and we both also had nightmares that included the show's themes of violence and betrayal and countless images of death. When he abandoned Walter White and Jesse Pinkman, I felt abandoned by him, as I now had to view Walt and Jesse's illegalities on my own, thereby feeling isolated in our own home by my knowing all of *Breaking Bad*'s secrets and lies and him knowing nothing. I was still very intimate with the show, but no longer had anyone with whom to romantically share my anxiety and paranoia. Numerous couples have actually mentioned to us that they were in a similar situation with *Breaking Bad*, in which one spouse found the show too off-putting in its stress- and anxiety-inducing psychological effects, while the other spouse just *had* to continue participating in and empathizing with Walt and Jesse's gruesome debauchery. While my partner mellowed out again after his refusal to continue *Breaking Bad*, my nightmares continued, and I was noticeably more anxious and paranoid after binge-watching consecutive episodes of the show. White and Pinkman had invaded our home and our marriage, but only I was faithful to them. All of this research about committing to a television series by oneself suggests that not only does streaming shows in solitude make viewers more alienated; it also makes us more entitled to consume whatever we want, whenever we want, all by ourselves, with reduced ability to compromise by having a shared, collectively empathetic and social viewing experience.

About such viewing habits and choices, Carpenter and Green state that viewers are "more concerned with plausibility than with real-world truth; if a story 'rings true,' it can influence beliefs even if the events and characters are completely made up… cognitive psychology demonstrates that individuals also learn 'false facts' from fiction."[37] Since I have never been a high school chemistry teacher/drug dealer who cooks meth in his desert trailer, my cognitive comprehension of White's "real life" seemed wholly authentic. Thus, I'd become intimate with him and his story. This intimacy rapidly upgraded the more I binge-watched White's day-to-day activity. As I became generally anxious and tense after binge marathons of *Breaking Bad*, my psychological temperament was faltering in its ability to separate authentic emotion from viewing empathy, since time and television focus demanded that I devote all my empathy and cognitive problem-solving skills to White and Pinkman's crimes. Conversely, when I "dropped out" of *House of Cards*' third season, which I considered far inferior to its first two seasons, my spouse continued watching the series, and found himself alone and anxious while empathizing with Claire Underwood's public embarrassments and hating Frank Underwood's greed. When either of us attempted to talk to each other about our respective shows, the other person could not cognitively assemble any plot points or themes from the show, nor could either of us empathize when one of us spoke at length about our empathy for certain characters. We were ostracized *within* our marriage *because of* television binge-watching. Things became particularly troublesome when I found my spouse walking around, giving short, pointed soliloquies to various corners and furnishings of our home, just as Frank Underwood repeatedly talks to the viewer in this manner. Instead of talking to me, since I could not emotionally empathize, nor cognitively assemble the multi-narratives of the show, my partner went the Underwood route of direct-to-the-camera editorial asides, thereby empathetically connecting with an imaginary viewer, as he'd learned to do from the show's style of breaking the fourth wall.

Just like personal choice of television shows is based on psychological pleasures that are rooted in one's identity and capacity for empathy, we also now get to choose *how* we connect to characters via multiple forms of technology—and Netflix knows this. Because of the way that we now consume our beloved yet short-lived television shows, it's looking more and more impossible to get away from this binge-watching style. "The average user watches five TV shows and three movies per week,"[38] according to *Consumer Reports*' April 2015 assessment, and "Consumers also [seem] to find it easer to stream from Netflix. Its streaming comprised 35 percent of all peak-time U.S. and Canadian Internet traffic." That is, obviously, a lot of cognitive processing and psychological affectation to undertake on a weekly basis, which suggests that we are alienating ourselves more rapidly than we're even aware. We don't have to have friends anymore with whom to chat about our (temporary) favorite series, or what Jeffrey Ulin calls "the water cooler conversation [that helps to] market a show."[39] Ulin also suggests that "Netflix [does] not care whether you [are] accessing your account by a computer, over an Xbox, via a tablet, or through a box."[40] Likewise, according to Strover and Moner's study about the rise of streaming services, which promote binge-watching, "The television industry has reframed its discourse, [and] industries recognize the multimodal delivery systems available to audiences and respond by fragmenting their offerings across multiple devices and multiple modes of viewing."[41]

Netflix shows (both originals and the ones they've licensed to stream) are so "wildly popular,"[42] says Michael Marzec in *Smart Business*, "not because Netflix asks people to alter their viewing behaviors by releasing an entire season of episodes at once,"[43] but "because they give people permission to watch their favorite shows however and whenever they want… The expectations of [viewers] have changed. Customers and prospects no longer want choices in how to interact with [streaming services]; they *expect* them."[44] These staggering statistics will only continue to increase, as entitled younger generations demand entertainment that is curated to their collective personalities and belief systems, in multimodal forms of delivery, and with massive amounts of bundled episodes.[45]

Notes

1 Jordan M. Carpenter and Melanie C. Green, "Flying with Icarus: Narrative Transportation and the Persuasiveness of Entertainment," in *The Psychology of Entertainment Media: Blurring the Lines Between Entertainment and Persuasion*, ed. L.J. Shrum (New York: Routledge, 2012), 187.
2 Ibid., 174.
3 Ibid., 175.
4 Judith S. Beck, *Cognitive Behavior Therapy, Second Edition: Basics and Beyond* (New York: Guilford Press, 2011), 2.
5 Ibid.
6 Ibid.
7 Ibid., 8.
8 Carpenter and Green, "Flying with Icarus," 176.
9 L.J. Shrum and Jaehoon Lee, "The Stories TV Tells: How Fictional TV Narratives Shape Normative Perceptions and Personal Values," in *The Psychology of Entertainment Media: Blurring the Lines Between Entertainment and Persuasion*, ed. L.J. Shrum (New York: Routledge, 2012), 149.
10 Carpenter and Green, "Flying with Icarus," 170.
11 Sarah Begley, "Lonely, Depressed People Are More Likely to Binge-Watch TV," *Time*, February 3, 2015. http://time.com/3689264/lonely-depressed-binge-watching/ (accessed August 6, 2015).
12 Ibid.
13 Ibid.
14 Ibid.
15 Carpenter and Green, "Flying with Icarus," 189.
16 Peter Vorderer, "Interactive Entertainment and Beyond," in *Media Entertainment: The Psychology of Its Appeal*, eds Dolf Zillman and Peter Vorderer (Mahwah, NJ: Lawrence Erlbaum Associates, Inc., 2000), 21–36.
17 Steven Johnson, *Everything Bad Is Good for You* (New York: Berkeley Publishing Group, 2005), 177.

18 Julia A. Maier and Douglas A. Gentile, "Learning Aggression Through the Media: Comparing Psychological and Media Communication Approaches," in *The Psychology of Entertainment Media: Blurring the Lines Between Entertainment and Persuasion*, ed. L.J. Shrum (New York: Routledge, 2012), 280.
19 Jane D. Brown, "Mass Media Influences on Sexuality," *Journal of Sex Research* 39.1 (2002): 42–45.
20 Johnson, *Everything Bad Is Good for You*, 107.
21 Shrum and Lee, "The Stories TV Tells," 148.
22 Johnson, *Everything Bad Is Good for You*, 63–64.
23 Ibid., 70.
24 Gary Bente and Ansgar Feist. "Affect-Talk and Its Kin," in *Media Entertainment: The Psychology of Its Appeal*, eds Dolf Zillman and Peter Vorderer (Mahwah, New Jersey: Lawrence Erlbaum Associates, Inc., 2000), 21–36.
25 Ibid., 114.
26 Vorderer, "Interactive Entertainment and Beyond," 27.
27 Bente and Ansgar, "Affect-Talk and Its Kin," 114.
28 Vorderer, "Interactive Entertainment and Beyond," 27.
29 Johnson, *Everything Bad Is Good for You*, 173–174.
30 Ibid., 174.
31 "Spoil Me," *Marry Me*. NBC, originally aired January 13, 2015.
32 Sarah Elizabeth Richards. "Binge-Watching: Modern Love's New Frontier," *Time*, February 18, 2014. http://ideas.time.com/2014/02/14/binge-watching-modern-loves-new-frontier/ (accessed August 6, 2015).
33 Ibid.
34 Ibid.
35 Jennifer Garam, "Social Media Makes Me Feel Bad About Myself: Reading Facebook and Twitter Streams Can Destroy My Self-Esteem," *Psychology Today*, September 26, 2011. https://www.psychologytoday.com/blog/progress-not-perfection/201109/social-media-makes-me-feel-bad-about-myself (accessed August 6, 2015).
36 Sharon Strover and William Moner, "The Contours of On-Demand Viewing," in *Connected Viewing*, eds Jennifer Holt and Kevin Sanson (New York: Routledge, 2014), 238.
37 Carpenter and Green, "Flying with Icarus," 179.
38 "Video Streaming," *Consumer Reports Money Advisor May 2015*, Vol. 12. Issue 5, 7.
39 Jeff Ulin, *The Business of Media Distribution: Monetizing Film, TV, and Video Content* (Burlington, MA: Focal Press, 2010), 373.
40 Ibid., 396.
41 Strover and Moner, "The Contours of On-Demand Viewing," 236.
42 Michael Marzec, "The Netflix Effect," *Smart Business Northern California* 7.12 (November 2014), 10.
43 Ibid.
44 Ibid.
45 Chuck Tryon and Max Dawson, "Streaming U: College Students and Connected Viewing," in *Connected Viewing*, eds Jennifer Holt and Kevin Sanson (New York: Routledge, 2014), 225.

8

Binge-Watching "Noir" at Home: Reimagining Cinematic Reception and Distribution via Netflix

Sheri Chinen Biesen

Netflix and the home viewing of digitally streamed cinematic new media was certainly not around when French critics in 1946 recognized a new bleak cycle of dark, existential American crime pictures coming out of Hollywood during and just after World War II which they called "film noir," literally "black film," or "dark cinema."[1] However, the brooding shadows, seedy corruption and duplicitous deeds of film noir have come alive in an evolving digital new media viewing environment thanks to Netflix. And these films noir are just as remarkable, compelling, and enthralling as they were on French and American cinema theater screens when classic noir motion picture productions, such as Billy Wilder's *Double Indemnity* (1944), *The Lost Weekend*[2] (1945), *Sunset Boulevard* (1950), and *Ace in the Hole* (1951); Fritz Lang's *The Woman in the Window* (1944) and *Scarlet Street* (1945); Otto Preminger's *Laura* (1944); and Edgar Ulmer's *Detour* (1945) opened to enraptured film going audiences in the 1940s and 1950s. Netflix reimagines the reception context of noir cinema at home, enabling and enhancing the cinematic experience of film noir and neo-noir as digital new media. I will examine how Netflix creates a convergent new media viewing environment that fosters "binge-watching" of film noir in a way that reimagines traditional cinematic reception and distribution.

For over a decade, Netflix has been an influential competitor in the entertainment industry, a company pioneering new directions in film and television, and an exhibitor affecting how media is distributed and received. This is especially pronounced in the realm of home viewing where it has become synonymous with "video-on-demand" (VOD) and instant streaming. Although VOD had been around for years, Netflix quickly dominated the "subscription video-on-demand" (SVOD) streaming video market with enhanced speed, quality, reliability, user interfaces, and algorithms.[3]

Netflix is an important representative of new digital media. It is associated with the new digital technologies that have helped to fundamentally transform distribution and exhibition, and that have changed the way consumers engage with media. In this respect, Netflix would seem to have very little in common with film noir, the well-known 1940s–1950s-period style that emerged in the aftermath of World War II, famous for its shadowy depictions of crime, corruption, and crooked protagonists. In fact, Netflix is at times so closely aligned with the future of media that it appears irreparably divorced from the past and more specifically the kinds of film connoisseurship that gave rise to noir as an important cultural and critical distinction. Despite these appearances, this chapter argues that Netflix and noir have an important connection that goes beyond the streaming service's offering of noir titles. Netflix and noir have created an unlikely synergy—noir in many ways anticipates the current emphasis on transmedia convergence and Netflix has appropriated noir as an important part of its hybrid business model. Additionally, noir as a 1940s–1950s-period style was founded on the emergence of an intensified form of spectatorship (that was stratified by gender as men served in World War II and women held down the home front), a harbinger of what has more recently been labeled binge-watching and its penchant for prolonged engagement. While this dynamic has been mutually beneficial for both Netflix and noir, this relationship also has its drawbacks—the streaming environment developed by Netflix reintroduces the instability and corporate interests that have contributed to noir's elusiveness as classic noir titles disappear. Despite these drawbacks, Netflix is ultimately introducing a new generation to 1940s–1950s noir aesthetics and, in doing so, triggering a curiosity and interest that will help to keep this 1940s–1950s-period style and film history as vibrant as ever.

Yet, even as it introduces contemporary viewers to noir aesthetics and seemingly helps to keep film history alive, Netflix threatens to distort the lineage of these aesthetics by obscuring their historical development and reduce noir to a kind of postmodern pastiche that is inimical to the film culture and historical conditions that created noir. Henry Jenkins' account of transmedia convergence is largely associated with contemporary media, for example, Hollywood blockbusters and media franchises whereby a single property props up variations across multiple formats and platforms. In Jenkins' "convergence culture," "transmedia storytelling" with a "whole new vision of synergy" in the "flow of content across multiple media platforms" provides an innovative "technological, industrial, cultural and social" context where "the art of story-telling has become the art of world-building, as artists create compelling environments that cannot be fully explored or exhausted within a single work or even a single medium."[4] In this sense, transmedia is a deeply commercialized process associated with multiplying a particular brand or commodity across as many commercial opportunities as possible.

With regard to these evolving "convergent" new media issues regarding what Jenkins describes as synergistic "transmedia storytelling," Netflix has been changing media distribution and reception, including the experience of viewing noir and neo-noir, in an era of digital streaming across media platforms, and will continue to affect the way we experience cinema and television in years to come. For instance, Netflix chief technology product officer Neil Hunt predicts that in the future media will continue to transform. He comments on the effect Netflix has already had on television and explains how "Internet TV" liberates filmmakers from traditional weekly half-hour- and hour-long television formats with the imperative to "hook" a viewer in that set time frame. Instead, programs "can be as long or as short as you want, and it doesn't have to tease you into the next episode because you can binge right into the next episode." Hunt argues that ultimately we may not even "recognize TV shows."[5]

However, for Jenkins, transmedia phenomena also provide audiences with new ways to engage with media texts and to create new meanings by virtue of the intersection between different platforms and contexts. In this regard, noir can be seen as a precursor to this new media development. Film genres, especially in the case of film noir, entail audiences identifying narrative and stylistic patterns across multiple texts. Noir fits this description since it was a 1940s–1950s-period style created by audiences and critics (although Hollywood studios and industry trades in the 1940s did have a different marketing rhetoric for noir films).[6] It was not only that viewers recognized stylistic and thematic similarities across a diverse assortment of films but that they recognized noir as a cultural sensibility that spanned different media and social developments. For instance, many key figures in noir—recurring characters like Philip Marlow or Sam Spade—existed in multiple forms and variations (played by different actors in different films while also being featured in multiple narratives that extended beyond the films—to pulp novels, magazines, and comics). Similarly, some of the key actors that helped to distinguish noir—Orson Welles, Humphrey Bogart, and Rita Hayworth—had a strong intertextual persona that served to reinforce key roles like the hard-boiled detective and the femme fatale.

The transmedia quality of film noir is an important part of Netflix's business model. Throughout its early history, Netflix was known for its Long Tail approach. That is, as a DVD-by-mail service, it distinguished itself from leading video chains like Blockbuster by offering a broader overall selection, a deeper catalog that emphasized older films and genres like film noir. Netflix also used its recommendation-filtering software to guide users to films based on their preferences (and, more generally, its interface design made it easier for users to navigate an exponentially more expansive selection than what was commonly found at Blockbuster). In other words, if you enjoyed *Laura* or *Sunset Boulevard*, Netflix made it easier to discover *Raw Deal* and *Scarlet Street*. In a certain sense, what Jenkins describes as transmedia convergence is built into the way Netflix as a platform connects viewers with media. It assumes that its users want to be able to inhabit a certain type of story world, one in which there are common elements that both reinforce and expand one another across individual texts. It also assumes that what is pleasurable about consuming media is the ability to decipher these types of patterns whether they be narrative, thematic, stylistic, or extra-textual. Netflix basically assumes that its users approach media in the same way that the critics and audiences approached film noir in the 1940s and 1950s and how Jenkins argues that contemporary fans engage their favorite forms of popular culture—with a kind of exuberance that can be further intensified and enriched as part of a mutually beneficial and dynamic exchange.

As Netflix shifted from a DVD-by-mail service to one that was devoted primarily to streaming, it turned away from its earlier Long Tail model. Though it continued to offer access to older titles—and in many ways it was easier to license the streaming rights to older noir films than newer Hollywood blockbusters—the emphasis of new VOD platforms was immediacy. As scholars like Chuck Tryon and Charles Acland have noted, these platforms are associated with accelerated distribution and with a general sense of velocity whereby media circulates much faster across different exhibition windows.[7] As in the so-called twenty-four-hour news cycle, this compresses time and stresses the importance of consuming and digesting information at an increasing rate. While this is an important appeal within the current digital media landscape, it has become less important for Netflix. In fact, Netflix has developed several strategies of trying to balance between the drive for immediacy and the financial constraints of licensing newer or premium Hollywood content. Thus far it has had its greatest success in striking this balance with its shift to television programming and a number of original series, many of which have either explicit or implicit ties to noir aesthetics. This is most clearly evident in its signature series *House of Cards*, which follows the shady dealings of a corrupt politician, but is also prominent in more recent series like *Bloodline* and *Daredevil*. The connection to noir is also evident in some of the serial dramas for which cable networks like AMC and FX have been praised and which Netflix has prominently featured. Shows like *Mad Men* and *Breaking Bad*, though less prominently marked by genre, have strong noir elements: flawed or corrupt protagonists, elaborate overlapping plot lines that concern criminal underworlds and immoral debauchery, and a distinct visual style. Even as sun-scorched New Mexico runs counter to general assumptions about noir, *Breaking Bad* uses this as a kind of character element that informs its story world.

These shows have been incredibly valuable to Netflix in multiple ways. Even though licensing rights to stream shows like *Mad Men* and the cost to produce original series like *House of Cards* are growing, this programming is still cost-effective—representing only a small portion of Netflix's overall budget—especially considering the critical praise they have earned and the overall media attention they have generated. More importantly, these shows have been able to parlay elements of transmedia convergence into a new kind of reception, one that intensifies and potentially expands viewer engagement. Television programming is inherently transmedia in that the story extends beyond individual episodes or seasons. In terms of encouraging binge-watching, Netflix allows viewers to consume these shows in an accelerated fashion that highlights the narrative and thematic patterns that span multiple episodes and seasons. More importantly, the success of these recent shows has the potential to drive viewers to earlier noir films—either from the 1940s and 1950s or to more recent cycles of neo-noir from the 1970s and 1980s as well as more recent variations, often independent films that were not heavily promoted and did not spend much time in the theaters. This is important for Netflix in that it needs to optimize the value of its library, and in this way noir creates an unlikely synergy between its current emphasis on television programming and serial dramas in particular and its earlier Long Tail approach of driving users to lesser-known older titles. This is also important in the sense that it provides an expanded example of transmedia convergence—this phenomenon need not be organized around blockbuster franchises but can be developed across different texts through a shared style or thematic patterns. Netflix's current strategy also suggests that this new media phenomenon need not be future oriented—it also has the potential to move backward in time to earlier iterations just as new forms of media engagement can both be accelerated (consuming things faster as with the simultaneous release of entire seasons) and decelerated (the pleasure of deciphering common thematic patterns is spread out over longer periods across multiple episodes and seasons).

Given this shifting context, binge-watching film noir via Netflix at home illustrates how viewers can enter the dark, disturbing nocturnal world of noir cinema—as *Double Indemnity* opens with a black abyss while a car screeches through the shadows—by submerging themselves in a solitary or communal perceptual cinematic experience of intense media immersion.[8] As film noir inspires motion pictures and cinematic television series, Netflix provides an ideal home-viewing environment for binge-watching.[9] Many see Netflix's SVOD streaming (and other competitors like Amazon) eventually replacing conventional television and film viewing.[10] This is especially true when filmgoers have to travel far or in bad weather to see a desirable movie in a theater, or if nothing of quality (or a poor selection) is playing, or if there are disruptions to the cinematic reception experience from others (such as cell phones, texting, noise, lights, loud talking or eating, equipment or projection problems, difficulties with sound). Improved technology and faster computing speed not only improved Netflix's SVOD streaming capability but also enabled significantly better visual quality for viewing and binge-watching noir cinema. Analyzing the film's distinctive formal-aesthetic "look," mise-en-scène, and extraordinary noir style of chiaroscuro lighting, shadowy design, and expressionistic cinematography is especially important and requires sharp clarity, high contrast, and crisp deep focus cinematic images with enhanced audio quality for optimal visuals and sound design.

In the decades since film noir burst into the cinematic imagination in the 1940s, its reception and distribution context has transformed, along with the "look and feel" of noir itself. When film noir was shot during World War II in the 1940s, for instance, it was filmed on jet black nitrate film stock amid the shadows of a blacked out wartime Los Angeles and shown to primarily domestic audiences in theaters on the home front as international film distribution was curtailed due to the conflict overseas affecting foreign film markets (although these noir films were also shown to Allied troops abroad). By the 1950s, Hollywood shot noir films on acetate safety stock that had a different look and feel to the noir picture, and in addition, in later decades films were shown not just in conventional urban "first run" movie theaters but also in suburban outdoor drive-ins, independent "art cinema" revival houses, on television (particularly pre-1948 noir films), multiplexes, and growing international markets (reopened after the conflict).[11] Thus, the look and feel of film noir changed and evolved with the shift from nitrate to acetate film stock; moreover, the media-viewing environment, reception, and distribution climate have transformed since film-going audiences originally experienced noir cinema in theaters in the 1940s and 1950s.

A number of contemporary films and shows on Netflix[12] exude the familiar cinematic terrain of "film noir" and "neo-noir," such as a dark, brooding shadowy atmosphere where no one can be trusted, where so often criminality lurks everywhere, as in a disturbing fatalistic existential noir universe projecting a milieu of corruption that pervades the society, typical in the iconic "urban jungle" setting seen in classic noir films *Scarlet Street* and *Double Indemnity*. As tormented antiheroes and femme fatales brood, plot, and murder in the chiaroscuro shadows of film noir and *House of Cards*, home viewers can "binge-watch," and if the mise-en-scène and visual design are overexposed or the sound design muffled, they can adjust their visual and audio preferences accordingly for the optimal shady suspenseful cinematic experience. It is also worth noting that Netflix's American neo-noir adaptation of *House of Cards* is much more shrouded and expressionistic in its atmospheric noir visual design than the original British series. Like *House of Cards*, *Daredevil* is soaked in shadowy noir cinematography, cloaking a dangerous after-hours' underworld metropolis (New York City).

The recent explosion of noir-influenced long-form original series indicates both the lasting impact of noir cinema and how Netflix has used binge-watching to relocate noir within the home-viewing environment. In this regard, Netflix has created its own personalized "on-demand" cinematic experience for binging noir films and original series reformulated in the image of noir cinema. Netflix promotes its original noir productions such as neo-noir *House of Cards* in theaters, during televised movies and motion picture award shows to simulate the communal noir cinematic experience in a new reception context. This new way of viewing and experiencing noir cinema and media fostered by Netflix can be considered in relation to the shifting mode of cinematic distribution and the way noir films are exhibited in one's own home or on his or her mobile device. Chuck Tryon argues that "digital distribution raises new questions about how, when, and where we access movies and what this model means for entertainment culture. Digital media seem to promise that media texts circulate faster, more cheaply, and more broadly than ever before," suggesting that noir and neo-noir films and programs could be made more widely available for "binge watching."[13] Thus, noir films could conceivably be made available anywhere on-demand to "binge-watch" on streaming platforms such as Netflix. In many cases, Netflix has actually fueled the success and increased the popularity and ratings of certain shows like its original neo-noir production *House of Cards*, as well those produced by other networks such as AMC's *Mad Men* and *Breaking Bad*, aided by the addictive viewing habits of binge-watching. Thomas Schatz writes, "The veritable partnership with AMC in the marketing and dual launch (on cable and the Internet) of its hit series has been crucial to Netflix' climb in recent years."[14]

Whether making it a compulsive all-day, all-night, or all-weekend film noir marathon affair, the Netflix noir binge-watching paradigm is highly addictive. Many, including myself, have spent countless hours binging noir films like *Sunset Boulevard*, *Scarlet Street*, *Raw Deal*, and *Double Indemnity*[15] consecutively on Netflix. Perhaps less satisfying for rabid classic film noir fans but even more addictive in terms of the binge-watching experience is spending a weekend diving into watching a new complete neo-noir original series, such as *House of Cards* or *Daredevil* on Netflix. As a testament to how compelling this noir binge-viewing paradigm is, when recently our household was down with a nasty, miserable bout of bronchitis, we even found a way to binge-watch these films noir and neo-series at home for many hours, into the wee after-hours of the night. However, my ailing spouse, who was too sick to watch with me and fell asleep, later complained on social media that I watched *House of Cards* and *Daredevil* without him, and duly endeavored to catch up on his viewing in my absence later that weekend, but remained disgruntled for missing out on the original noir binge-watching session.

In binge-watching noir films at home, Netflix has also revived a sense of a cinema culture, which I have greatly missed, that has faded in recent years with fewer classic "art cinema" revival theaters or even video rental stores where we live. Movie distribution, as Tryon suggests, is now "characterized by new, more accelerated distribution models in which movies move quickly from theaters (if they play on the big screen at all) to VOD and DVD before landing in DVD remainder bins at big-box stores or, perhaps more likely, archives of videos available for streaming, whether through a subscription service, such as Netflix, or through a pay-per-view option, such as those offered by Mubi.com, Vudu, or Amazon."[16] Moreover, with this changing distribution model, Charles Acland observes that it affects the "velocity of motion pictures as they move from screen to screen, format to format, and hence from a cultural circuit of relative exclusivity to other more accessible circuits."[17] This accelerated velocity of motion pictures moving from screen to screen across platforms has also contributed to the reimagining of the cinematic distribution and reception context for noir films and media via Netflix, thus spurring the personal "binge-watching" home viewing of "noir" cinema and "neo-noir" productions. This immersive experience created a vital sense of a cinema culture and helped film lovers plunge into the worlds of film noir and classic art cinema. Binge-watching noir on Netflix re-creates this intense, immersive cinematic experience in a home-viewing environment, particularly helpful when no classic film theaters are nearby, and fewer DVDs are available to rent or buy.[18] Further, as a film scholar teaching noir cinema, I often find that my own students in recent years frequently watch noir films and neo-noir series for class on Netflix, particularly if they prefer to watch a film noir again to study it, or if they miss a part of a class screening. They often describe indulging in binge-watching film noir when doing late-night studying, which becomes an enhanced bonus activity when studying for a film noir class.

A colleague with a newborn admitted that she and her spouse engaged in intense sessions binge-watching neo-noir series *Mad Men* and *Breaking Bad* in the wee hours while taking turns waking up in the middle of the night with the infant. These late-night noir binge-watching sessions also provided a welcome adult-oriented respite for exhausted parents trying to get the baby to sleep. In this way, these kinds of noir binge-watching experiences are actually quite common occurrences, especially with many new families starting out with young children, who, given the restricted circumstances, would find it very difficult or even impossible to see a film noir in a movie theater with a crying baby, especially if they live far away from major urban or suburban theaters.

Moreover, classic film noir and neo-noir cinema choices are often limited, with very few theaters actually showing film noir unless there is a special noir film series or festival. Thus, in the absence of a film noir series or festival on the big screen, Netflix streaming has become an effective means to augment and access film noir and neo-noir viewing. The implication and upshot of binge-watching noir on Netflix makes for a far more intense and immersive viewing experience while at the same time allowing more latitude and flexibility for how and when and where and in what way which portions of noir cinema and neo-noir media are experienced and consumed in a home-viewing environment.

As Netflix has shifted its focus to producing new original long-form neo-noir television series, the service has transformed what it means to view and experience film [noir] and media. Contributing to this changing noir viewing environment, James Surowiecki recognizes Netflix's influential history of innovation and argues that the media company has "created two markets practically from scratch—online DVD rental, then video streaming." This shift and institutional reinvention by Netflix has, of course, also affected and reframed their noir offerings. As Surowiecki explains, Netflix "obviously has a much bigger catalogue of licensed content, and less original content, than pay-TV services like HBO and Showtime do. But the differences are diminishing: streaming matters more to pay-TV networks now, while Netflix is adding more original shows and movies. Toss in Amazon's streaming service—which has been licensing lots of TV shows and films and has also begun producing its own shows—and you're looking at a crowded marketplace."[19]

Interestingly, or perhaps predictably, the more successful Netflix became, emerging as a popular mode of viewing film and television, the more media conglomerates (including motion picture production studios, distributors, and television cable companies) began to view Netflix as a competitor rather than as a supplemental means of making noir movies and programs available to viewers. As an optimal distributor of fine film noir viewing, in many ways Netflix became a victim of its own success. In earlier years, Hollywood motion picture studios, television media conglomerates, and cable companies (including pay channels such as Starz, a rival competitor of HBO and Showtime) underestimated the lucrative potential and popularity of SVOD streaming and were thus happy to make noir films available on Netflix. As Surowiecki explains, in the early days of streaming, what set Netflix apart was that the company had "far more—and far better—content than anyone else. It was able to build up a sizable catalogue of movies cheaply, because the streaming market was still small and Hollywood was happy to get the extra revenue." Netflix had abundant film titles because it licensed "hundreds of movies from the Starz pay channel for a mere $25 million a year." However, in contrast to this original arrangement which facilitated ample film noir, "Once content providers saw how popular streaming was becoming, they jacked up the price of their content. Netflix's success also attracted new competitors to the market (like Amazon), and encouraged existing competitors (like HBO) to invest more in streaming."[20]

This decline in noir films on Netflix can be attributed to these recent developments because now there is intense competition for streaming viewers, and as Jeffrey Ulin observes, "it's harder to get content... And the content you do get costs more." As a result, many have lamented the loss of classic film noir offerings on Netflix in recent years as Netflix "lost thousands of movies as licensing deals expired." Thus, in terms of viewing noir cinema on Netflix, "Though Netflix still streams plenty of great films, no one really thinks of it as a dream video store in the sky anymore."[21] Starz acquired these rights as part of its pay-TV output deal with Disney and Sony. Starz then licensed the SVOD rights to Netflix. Many studios, including Disney, The Weinstein Company, Paramount, Lions Gate, and MGM, have made SVOD deals directly with Netflix in the aftermath of the Starz deal, which ended in 2012.[22]

As Netflix's deals with film studios lapse, the selection of classic noir films becomes less abundant.[23] There is still a tangible market for a large, vast selection of classic cinema and particularly film noir for streaming and "binging" via home viewing. For classic noir binge viewing, competitor TCM (Turner Classic Movies) finally offered streaming, but it is not actually a stand-alone service (comparable to Netflix) since it requires an additional (and comparatively expensive extra $20 per month) subscription (which simulates a cable bundle) to Dish's "Sling TV" (together with a set-top device like Apple TV or Roku).[24] Thus, its actual cost is significantly higher than Netflix. Moreover, it shows how, regardless of the promise of greater availability of noir films to binge via streaming, as Tryon points out, media conglomerates nonetheless still control "when, where, and how" classic noir films are "circulated" and made available for binge-watching at home.[25] Additionally, Netflix's algorithm is not always intuitive. In many households, different viewers (such as family members) confuse it with conflicting choices, and most users find it a hassle to set up different separate profile accounts to avoid the confusion. As a result, a cheesy TV show or a piece of children's programming might contradict the desirable classic film noir or art cinema choices when Netflix considers which film/TV titles to suggest.[26]

There is also an interesting connection in that film noir initiates the kind of intensified spectatorship that is now common because of VOD streaming services like Netflix. The French critics based their conception of film noir on the American films that flooded into Europe after World War II. This situation created a period of compressed engagement—audiences were able to see a diverse selection in a short amount of time—which in turn enabled the recognition of, or foregrounded the thematic and stylistic qualities that became the basis of, noir. This also happened to some extent with the emergence of television in the 1950s, similarly making a wider variety of films available that were easier to engage. This was especially true of pre-1948 film titles that were licensed for television, including many noir films. For instance, it was easier to note thematic, visual, and extra-textual similarities while watching several crime or detective films in succession as part of a late-night double feature or weekend movie marathon. In France, the appreciation of film noir coincided with the emergence of new forms of film criticism that both continued and expanded an already established penchant for cinephilia. This new criticism emphasized mise-en-scène analysis (recognizing that visual style conveyed thematic insight) and the ability to discern individual distinction within an industrial system of production (as part of auteur criticism). This suggests that intensified spectatorship was beneficial for producing critical insights and as a way to better understand the significance of a genre or cultural style.

Whereas Netflix and noir have formed an unlikely case of transmedia synergy, intensified spectatorship suggests an odd juxtaposition. Though binge-watching has helped to establish Netflix as a prominent media channel and has been vital in promoting certain types of programming, there are certain ways in which VOD services diverge from the original critics that recognized noir. Although the original reception of noir allowed for intensified engagement that was important in being able to identify key traits, it was also premised on cultural dislocation. This was important not only in the sense that noir was a French distinction for Hollywood cinema (often less prestigious or marginalized 'B' movies at that) but also because noir aesthetics were themselves a by-product of cultural dislocation—the influence of exiled European, especially German, filmmakers stemming from the rise of Nazism. This element of dislocation runs counter to much of the rhetoric surrounding the appeal of VOD—that it can be consumed in the comfort of one's home (or bed) and at one's convenience any time across any number of mobile devices. The comfort of home would seem to minimize any sense of dislocation, which may make it more difficult to appreciate that quality within the noirs consumed in this manner. At the same time, while the ability to access media on mobile devices promises to enhance the comfort of home viewing by creating a limitless sense of convenience, this actually reinscribes a sense of homelessness or dislocation. The type of intensified spectatorship made possible by VOD has the potential to amplify the appreciation of noir or of more generally discerning unique traits across multiple texts, as part of Netflix's emphasis on transmedia synergies. But it also has the potential to recall a kind of cultural dislocation or homelessness—the same type of undertone that was a factor in the initial production and reception of noir, but that makes for an uneasy match with the rhetoric surrounding the convenience of VOD media consumption. Despite this juxtaposition, this may very well be the case in that the current media landscape makes it impossible to fully enjoy or view media in a singular context—whether it is the theater or the home, which are increasingly displaced by forms of consumption premised on permanent mobility—instead creating a state of permanent disorientation which may in fact fuel an interest in noir and be the reason for the recent resurgence in neo-noir-ish serial dramas.

There are also some drawbacks to the relationship between noir and Netflix. Watching film noir on smaller video screens makes it more difficult to appreciate some of the formal qualities that stood out so prominently to critics in the 1940s and 1950s—qualities related to the specificity of lighting styles and film stocks. VOD viewing platforms not only diminish the formal richness of the noir aesthetics; but more generally this form of reception shifts noir from a predominantly visual or thematic distinction to more of a narrative dimension. This is why the noir elements in recent serial dramas are overshadowed by other elements and other potential genre distinctions (or lack thereof). Another drawback is that even though the current media environment promises infinite choice and ubiquitous availability, this is not always the case. Netflix is a prominent example of the mutability of availability—its library changes frequently and there is no way to track these changes or know in advance when these changes will take place. This creates a situation of instability and potential scarcity. This recalls, for instance, the way certain DVDs like *Double Indemnity* went out of print—it was impossible to know the reason for this or when it would be reissued and this drove up the price for used copies, making them quite rare. In some ways, this also recalls an earlier era in which film noir was part of a larger film culture that required deliberate and laborious efforts. Throughout the 1970s and 1980s, most film noir was only accessible by venturing beyond the standard multiplex to art house and second-run theaters or to specialized festivals and other one-off screenings. As film noir became available on VHS and DVD, it was more accessible, but was not prominently available at mainstream video outlets—requiring trips to independent video rental stores or to specialized resources like university archives. This extra effort was tied to the fact that film noir had a kind of cachet that required and rewarded extra-textual knowledge and the self-reflexive awareness of that knowledge in relationship to film and media more generally. Online forums can replicate these kinds of fan communities, but at the same time recommendation engines and the internet architecture in general minimize the burden of finding noir and grasping its fundamental significance. This may mean that even as current VOD services like Netflix encourage intensified viewership and transmedia comprehension, they are unlikely to render the same kind of critical insight regarding changing cultural undertones as the critics who identified noir. Lastly, the changing availability of noir titles on services like Netflix points to the fact that there are corporate interests that are trying to maximize the value of these older films. The success of Netflix has prompted others to vie for the licensing rights to titles that were previously considered of little value. As part of this process, new competitors try to exploit exclusivity in order to prop up new platforms. This creates additional barriers and renews the same kind of instability and uneven availability that prevailed in earlier generations.

Media scholars and industry analysts acknowledge the conglomerate Hollywood economic and financial concerns in new media considerations potentially contributing to the (horizontally integrated) global entertainment industry relying on the money it generates from cable company network revenues. However, despite the financial return of this existing paradigm in the short term, as the new media landscape changes and evolves, it seems that given the alternatives, it would actually be in the best interest for studios, as well as binge viewers at home, for film and television companies to make deals with Netflix. Conversely, like Amazon, HBO, CBS, and Sony (streaming via Playstation), several media companies (Showtime, TCM, Apple [i.e., Apple TV, iTunes, Apple Music], ABC, NBC, Starz, Dish [i.e., Sling TV] et al.) are belatedly moving to offer their own streaming products in the wake of Netflix's success. In retrospect, historically, the industry has overcome myriad obstacles (and initial resistance) in adapting to new technology, be it sound film processes, color, widescreen, stereophonic sound, television, VCRs, home video, and now streaming.[27]

In redefining how we see, experience, and interact with cinema and television, Netflix raises an array of considerations about how we project an innovative cinematic vision for the future of viewing (i.e., experiencing, "binging" and engaging, as well as consuming) media. Such convergent new media factors reveal how Netflix's instant streaming service creates an ideal home-viewing environment that fosters "binge-watching" of "noir" media which transforms and reenvisions the traditional cinema experience of how films and TV are seen and shown. Classic noir (and neo-noir) films should be available on Netflix (and in theaters) so that cinephiles can see them.

Ironically, some theater chains want to boycott Netflix feature film releases due to same-day VOD streaming even as that becomes the new primary cinema/television distribution model. The film enthusiast Joseph Walsh, who covers the repertory cinema scene in New York, predicts, "That's the new model: same-day VOD. I'm sure it'll be standard in a year or two. Or less."[28] As we reimagine cinematic reception and distribution via Netflix, this noir cinema lover would certainly embrace binge-watching even more film noir at home in the future.

Notes

1 For more on film noir, see Sheri Chinen Biesen, *Blackout: World War II and the Origins of Film Noir* (Baltimore: Johns Hopkins University Press, 2005); Paul Schrader, "Notes on Film Noir," *Film Comment* 8.1 (1972): 8–10.

2 *The Lost Weekend*, ironically, but also rather aptly describes the intense film noir "binge-watching" experience.

3 Which has encouraged other major global media conglomerates, networks, and studios to make deals to stream film and television programming via Netflix and to try to emulate and compete with the company's successful media distribution model with their own SVOD streaming services (including Amazon, Hulu, Warner Instant, HBO, CBS, Showtime, TCM, ABC, iTunes, Apple TV, PBS, FOX, Sling TV, YouTube, and Café Noir).

4 Henry Jenkins, *Convergence Culture: Where Old and New Media Collide* (New York: New York University Press, 2006), 104, 114.

5 Issie Lapowsky, "What Television Will Look Like in 2025, According to Netflix," *Wired*, May 19, 2014. See also Anirban Mahanti, "The Evolving Streaming Media Landscape," *IEEE Internet Computing*, January/February 2014, 4–6; Mareike Jenner, "Is This TVIV? On Netflix, TVIII and Binge-Watching," *New Media & Society*, Sage Journals, 2014.

6 Biesen, *Blackout*, 2005, 1–10. See also Biesen, "Censoring and Selling Film Noir," *Between* 9 (2015): 1–22.

7 Charles Acland, "Theatrical Exhibition: Accelerated Cinema," in *The Contemporary Hollywood Film Industry*, eds Paul McDonald and Janet Wasko (Malden, MA: Blackwell, 2008), 83–105.

8 If viewers miss a bit of hard-boiled dialogue or get tired, they can stop and re-watch the noir film again at a later time. If they are really addicted and obsessed with a longer-running neo-noir series with seasons of episodes like *House of Cards*, *Mad Men*, *Breaking Bad*, *Bloodline*, or *Daredevil*, viewers can binge at all hours to their hearts' content.

9 Netflix offers optimal sound and picture quality, as well as streaming and user interface, to view and experience noir cinema.

10 As has been readily evident in recent years, the success of Netflix's streaming demonstrates that as technology improved, faster computing led to higher speeds and better quality, which really benefited the company's SVOD capability. Also, as fewer theatrical exhibition venues screen actual celluloid, with 35mm (or 70mm) films no longer shown in movie theaters, there is less incentive for cinema viewers to leave their digital streaming at home for projected digital media in the theater.

11 For more on the changing film stock, aesthetics, technology, production, and reception circumstances of film noir, see Biesen, *Blackout*, particularly for the war years, and Biesen, *Music in the Shadows* (Baltimore: Johns Hopkins University Press, 2014) for the later postwar 1950s shift to acetate and the changing look, style, and viewing conditions of film noir.

12 Including Cary Fukunaga's 2011 BBC remake of gothic *Jane Eyre*, AMC's *Mad Men*, *Breaking Bad*, and Netflix's originally produced *House of Cards* series (set on the shrouded, nocturnal Washington DC city streets of the nation's capital), as well as *Bloodline* and *Daredevil*.

13 However, Tryon cautions, "Despite the promises of ubiquitous and immediate access to a wide range of media content, digital delivery has largely involved the continued efforts of major media conglomerates to develop better mechanisms for controlling when, where, and how content is circulated." Chuck Tryon, *On-Demand Culture: Digital Delivery and the Future of Movies* (New Brunswick, NJ: Rutgers University Press, 2013), 3–4.

14 Netflix has "taken binge-viewing practices to another level—and has pushed the term into the popular discourse—in its promotion of series like *Breaking Bad* and *Mad Men*, and in the strategic coordination of its full-season streaming releases with AMC's rollout of new seasons." Thomas Schatz, "HBO and Netflix - Getting Back to the Future," *Flow*, 19, January 20, 2014.

15 *Double Indemnity* recently disappeared, but was previously available on Netflix.

16 Tryon, *On-Demand Culture*, 2013, 9.

17 Acland, "Theatrical Exhibition: Accelerated Cinema," 94.

18 Moreover, the whole process of consecutively watching noir such as *Sunset Boulevard*, *Scarlet Street*, *Raw Deal*, *House of Cards*, and *Daredevil* on Netflix in a marathon binge-viewing session creates a long-form noir narrative of its own, in considering these noir films as a series, just as the immersive film-student-in-cinema-school experience did years ago in enhancing the intense sense of living and breathing classic noir cinema culture.

19 James Surowiecki, "What's Next for Netflix?" *The New Yorker*, October 20, 2014.

20 Surowiecki, "What's Next for Netflix?" 2014.

21 Significantly, classic noir films began disappearing from Netflix as the company's popularity thrived. Many noir films disappeared with noir-viewing options declining after the Starz agreement ended in 2012. To give you a sense of how much the company is spending to acquire film noir titles, Netflix paid at least $3 billion for content in 2014. Surowiecki, "What's Next for Netflix?" 2014.

22 Many films noir—such as *The Big Sleep*, *The Maltese Falcon*, *Out of the Past*, *Dark Passage*, *The Third Man*, and Alfred Hitchcock's *Shadow of a Doubt* —are available on DVD for rent, but not available to instantly stream on Netflix, which is the more popular choice.

23 To compete with Netflix, in 2015 Amazon added Warner Bros.' *Dark Passage*, with Humphrey Bogart and Lauren Bacall, as a title to stream on Prime, which was not available on Netflix.

24 Moreover, HBO's new streaming service was only made available either as an add-on with this cable-simulating Sling TV bundle or on Apple TV or iPads for its original release (with announcements that it would be added to Roku in the future), so initially the service has been less widely available despite promoting it as a stand-alone offering.

25 Tryon, *On-Demand Culture*, 2013, 3–4.
26 Netflix now offers a children's setting for families.
27 This is worth keeping in mind when considering the pressure studios asserted for Starz to end their agreement with Netflix.
28 Research correspondence, March 2015. Joseph Walsh covers the repertory film scene in New York for nitratestock.net cinema blog. Studios like Paramount are already announcing shorter release windows between theatrical and digital HD home-viewing screens.

9

Netflix and the Documentary Boom

Sudeep Sharma

Along with children's and archival television programming, documentaries have been a major area of interest for subscribers on Netflix's streaming service. Though concrete numbers are difficult to obtain, documentaries are widely seen as a part of the Netflix brand of providing on-demand content viewers want to watch. Part of this appeal is based on the nature of documentary as an edifying, educational, yet still entertaining form. However, another critical reason for the growth of documentary on Netflix has to do with specifics of the documentary film industry. Despite a mature industry with a great number of funders, practitioners, and history, large-scale theatrical success has been elusive except for a handful of titles and broadcast distribution mostly dominated by PBS, HBO Documentary, Discovery Channel, and National Geographic. While feature-length documentary in general shares certain similarities with reality-based television, a catch-all categorization that includes reality television (like *The Real World*, *Survivor*, and *American Idol*), serialized documentary shows (such as *Planet Earth*, *Life*, and *The Hills*), and news programming, documentary film is markedly different from both a historical and industrial perspective. And whereas reality programming has enjoyed great commercial success over the last two decades on television, feature-length documentary has been underutilized and underappreciated as a genre.[1]

Netflix, however, has been one of the few exceptions to this tendency. It has made feature-length documentary a core pillar of its service, both as a way to highlight its connection to quality cinema and to distinguish its catalog from more mundane forms of television programming. This emphasis on documentary has been a major factor in the growth of Netflix and, simultaneously, has led to changes in the documentary film industry. In this chapter, I will examine the complex and changing relationship between Netflix and the documentary film scene. As part of this examination, I detail how Netflix functions more like a newsstand than a library and how its recent increase in "direct buying," as part of its emphasis on original programming, contributes to the evolving character and appeal of documentary film. I further reflect upon these changes by sharing the experience and views of two anonymous professional documentary filmmakers from different ends of the career spectrum. While it is impossible to say what the long-term implications of these changes will be, the experiences of these filmmakers show that the relationship between Netflix and documentary is complex and at times contradictory, a means of greater overall exposure but also a source of new concerns.

Netflix as library versus Netflix as newsstand

The ability of Netflix to increase value for more niche and archival material is something that has been discussed by other scholars, but documentary is a special example of this practice. For documentary films, Netflix's promises of new audiences and possibilities are often presented as nothing less than revolutionary. As a source of streaming documentary, Netflix has been celebrated because the popularly understood model for the service has been that of the *library*. The metaphor of the library works if one considers Netflix as an archive of *all* documentaries allowing its users to take out individual titles as they desire. In fact, Netflix surpasses a library as it is not tied to the physical world of a traditional lending institution.[2] Netflix is a repository for a whole history of a cinematic genre and, through streaming, can serve the needs of an enormous subscriber base that transcends any one location or community.

The problem with the library metaphor for Netflix, however, is that it assumes the service has some larger interest beyond commercial needs. Netflix provides access to various materials, but purely on the basis that access to the material will in some way improve profits for the company. As a commercial entity, Netflix is different from quasi-library-like distribution and exhibition organizations like the National Film Board of Canada, or Women Make Movies, that operate out of a mandate to provide films for some social or national purpose beyond economic gain. Even the more boutique or prestige content Netflix offers is ultimately measured as adding value in other ways to the overall brand. Unlike a library or another nonprofit entity, which maintains collections and material on the basis of scholarly need or historic purpose, Netflix's choices are driven by commercial needs. The library metaphor is particularly problematic for feature documentaries because most audiences only encounter them on the streaming service (in comparison to television shows or major commercial theatrical releases that have limited windows for exhibition, something viewers are already well versed in). Thinking of Netflix as an archive of documentary texts gives users the false impression that the main mandate of the service is access and preservation of the genre and general user education (e.g., as seen in a *Business Insider* article that suggests, "Here's a quick and fun way to enrich your business knowledge: streaming documentaries on Netflix"[3]).

Another important distinction from the library model is that Netflix usually offers a given show or film under some kind of limited time frame. As suggested by monthly articles on popular sites like CNET, *Huffington Post*, and SlashFilm about what is arriving on and departing from Netflix during any given month, the content offered on the service is constantly changing. In this regard, there is a better metaphor for Netflix than that of the library. The service functions more like a *newsstand*, offering material on a rotating basis that is continuously changing based on the availability of material (that can "expire") and the ostensible desires of consumers. Netflix plays the role of "surrogate consumer" for exhibitors. Rather than just simply providing access to texts, they are engaged in what, Timothy Havens and Amanda D. Lotz argue, is an effort to "*push* certain texts on consumers, rather than letting us *pull* what we want."[4]

The distinction between the library and newsstand metaphors helps us understand how Netflix has been able to monetize and build its subscriber base. Despite the fact

Table 9.1 Library versus newsstand

Netflix *as*	Library	Newsstand
Mandate	Access/preservation	Commercial
Materials' availability	Forever/long term	Rotating/short term
Users	Pull texts from	Text pushed on
Success measured by	Scope and representation of collection	Creation of feeling that subscription is necessary

there are no reported ratings in the traditional sense for Netflix, programs on the service have to perform. They have to gain viewership. While Netflix might be in the position right now to experiment with content, the underlying truth of the newsstand model is not going to disappear. The distinction is also critical for documentary because, despite the deep cinematic history of the form, the programming still has to be relevant to viewers in the manner of breaking news reporting. I think that is why the titles that have been the first "original" productions of the service have both an immediacy and broad familiarity in terms of subject matter.

Beyond a thought exercise, these differences have real ramifications for both consumers and producers of content. For consumers, they suggest that Netflix is less invested in the history or the contemporary development of documentary film art than with maintaining viewership. Though Netflix has no real competition in terms of streaming documentary, I believe its lack of an archival approach toward documentary has created a space for alternative services like Mubi, Fandor, and Sundance Doc Club that seek to provide their subscribers a more complete and critical offering of documentary film titles. For filmmakers, Netflix as newsstand highlights the importance of their films gaining and maintaining audiences, particularly if their films are to be renewed on the service. Netflix does not work altruistically in order to preserve documentaries for audiences. Instead, Netflix has done what every exhibitor has ever done, demonstrated "a high degree of selection and shaping of consumer demand."[5] By dominating the feature documentary streaming space, Netflix has been able to add a critical perception of the indispensable nature of the service for many subscribers.

Docs as "being good for you"

Access to exclusive, high-quality, culturally relevant scripted original programming (like *Orange Is the New Black* and *House of Cards*) obviously gives Netflix cachet. However, the often edifying and socially significant nature of documentaries helps further brand Netflix as a meaningful and thoughtful use of time compared with the kind of repetitive viewing that is often portrayed as a sickness.[6] Though "binge" watching is entertaining and a widely shared practice, the term "binge," with its distasteful connotations, suggests that consuming so much television in one sitting is personally destructive. While Netflix does not exist in the same model of "flow" as network television, it leads to a similar experience of time passing as uninterrupted and repetitive. Both traditional television and Netflix keep the viewer engaged in the service and reduce incentives to turn elsewhere; Netflix's main difference is that its programming is not built around the time of day but around the desires of the viewer. Along with providing hours of entertainment for a low monthly fee (with a standard streaming package costing $8.99 a month in 2015, which is comparable to the $8.17 average price for a movie ticket in 2014), a great deal of the focus in Netflix's marketing and self-branding has been its ability to provide choices of entertainment to you that you might not know existed but would want to see.[7] The many articles about the analytics and use of genre tags come back to the idea that the service can and will crack the puzzle of what entertainment you want to consume.[8]

Documentary, on the other hand, creates the feeling of seeing something of the real world and, therefore, learning. Of course this is an illusion in the sense that documentary films are as much as an artifice as fictional filmmaking; however, seeing a reflection of the real world is part of the appeal of documentaries. As Bill Nichols argues, "Documentary shares the properties of a text with other fictions, [but] it addresses the world in which we live rather than worlds in which we may imagine living."[9] While documentaries can clearly be entertaining, they do exist separately from much of the rest of what is offered on the service. Though they are categorized by the same genre-creating formulas, documentaries stand out from the other scripted programming on the service.

Documentaries offer variety on the service, real-world relevance, and, most critically, prestige. Respectability and a feeling of being necessary for the consumer is not something that can be purchased or afforded by a few titles. Considering the industrial lack of a centralized home for feature documentary film, Netflix's presentation of itself as such a home helps make it an important media platform in a way that none of its other named genres do (like romantic comedies or action). In fact, Netflix's position in documentary could be seen as a precursor to its move to original productions, with the important caveat that for feature documentary, Netflix has acted more as a documentary acquisition company than a producer of scripted, original content.

Netflix doc acquisitions and move to "originals"

The traditional and typical financial life cycle of a documentary film would move from the festival circuit to a small theatrical release to some television broadcast and home video distribution. By and large, most documentaries are considered independent productions, and, like other independent films, deal with limited funding budgets and exhibition outlets. Netflix streaming has drastically changed this landscape for documentary film, as they have provided a new widely accessible platform for documentaries to be seen by the public. From the most notable documentaries of the year to films that would only appeal to a specialized audience, Netflix has provided an easy way for home viewers to see the films. Netflix Chief Content Officer Ted Sarandos in a speech reminded audiences that following its Oscar win for Best Documentary, *Born into Brothels* (2005) was only available for audience on their streaming service.[10] Noted documentary producer Dan Cogan has discussed how Netflix has made it easier for audiences to see documentaries, saying "I'm hearing from so many people not in the film industry, 'Oh, I never watch documentaries,' but now, thanks to Netflix, you don't have to make that decision to go to the theater, for instance, to see a documentary. It's not as much of a commitment."[11] Not only is convenience a major factor, but specialty films' very existence on Netflix's platform, including occasional highlighting by Netflix's algorithms, results in more visibility not replicable in other exhibition outlets. The original DVD subscription service already was a benefit due to its somewhat automated nature (setting a queue that would deliver the film to your home) compared to either going to the theater or the local video store. The even more popular streaming service is able to help documentaries perform at levels they simply could not before.

Additionally, Netflix has grown its reputation for documentaries by also moving into directly buying them exclusively for its service. As seen with *Born into Brothels*, there has been a history of exclusive documentary acquisitions, including *The Comedians of Comedy* (2005) and *This Film Is Not Yet Rated* (2006). Following the success of *House of Cards* in 2012 and the company's aggressive expansion into original programming, documentary acquisitions for streaming greatly expanded. Early examples of these were *The Square* (2013), about the Egyptian revolution and directed by Jehane Noujaim (the director of *Control Room*), and *Mitt* (2014), about Mitt Romney's failed 2012 presidential campaign. *Mitt* premiered on Netflix streaming mere weeks after its world premiere screening at the Sundance Film Festival, completely eschewing a theatrical release. Along with other documentaries like *Virunga* (2014), *E-Team* (2014), *Mission Blue* (2014), and *Print the Legend* (2014), Netflix has consciously moved into documentary acquisition while placing them under the larger umbrella of "Netflix Originals," which also includes more traditional scripted, fiction-based television production.

These purchases put Netflix directly in competition with the reigning champion of documentaries for home audience, HBO Documentary. Under the near-three-decade-long leadership of Sheila Nevins, HBO Documentary has developed, produced, exhibited, and distributed documentaries that have won dozens of Emmys, Peabodys, and Academy Awards. Considering its history of backing difficult projects like *Paradise Lost* (1996), its propensity for winning Oscars as with the recent documentary *Citizenfour* (2014); its track record of developing filmmakers like Alex Gibney, Joe Berlinger, Lauren Greenfield, and Nick Broomfield; and its reputation for funding and buying short documentaries that usually had no other market, HBO Documentary has long been the thousand-pound gorilla in the documentary film industry. With HBO Documentary mostly having unchallenged supremacy in the space for several years, Netflix's arrival has been generally greeted as a huge benefit for documentary film because it is another source of revenue and sales. As one industry source told Indiewire, regarding Netflix, "It's all good! As a sales agent, it is one more buyer/platform for the marketplace and one that is known as an outlet for quality documentary films."[12]

Netflix's willingness to spend money in documentary seems to be the primary factor for its embrace by the documentary film community. However, Netflix's spending for documentary has not always been at the level it is today, with some commentators reporting, in 2013, high five-figure deals once offered to filmmakers who had little option but to accept.[13] By 2015 Netflix demonstrated a willingness to spend to acquire films and a considerably evolved mode with documentary filmmakers. Netflix has become known for offering very competitive and, at times, overwhelming deals to filmmakers. Starting in earnest with the 2015 Sundance Film Festival, Netflix and other online competitors like Amazon have been coming to major festivals with the hopes of securing the exclusive rights to independent films (narrative and documentary). Netflix had already purchased the Sundance Day One premiere film *What Happened, Miss Simone?* (2015) ahead of its screening and offered it on the service in summer 2015, again moving a film out of the traditional theatrical route (with the exception of a small Oscar-qualifying run).

Yet, for both documentaries and narrative films, money is not always the deciding factor for exhibition. Multiple reports (confirmed by confidential conversations I have had) have suggested that even when Netflix made higher offers than theatrical distributors, filmmakers sometimes accepted less money and more traditional theater release deals. Considering many filmmakers have day jobs in commercial work that pays the bills, spending the time (often years) and energy on a more personal project made them less likely to simply sell to the highest bidder. Not to say economics are insignificant, but they remain one factor in a more complicated calculus that includes the goal of being part of the national conversation or becoming a must-see commodity—one that can only be achieved through theatrical screenings. As one filmmaker described to me, he saw the audience for his film as people who would pay money to see it in a theater and because of that, he was willing to forgo the guarantee of cash from Netflix for a rollout from a theatrical distributor.

Considering all of this, it is important to note that while varied in subject, Netflix's "Original" documentary acquisitions are very traditional in terms of film style and format—they conform to what an average filmgoer would expect from a documentary. Specifically, these films are often about social issues (environment, international conflict) or biographies of famous people that deploy behind the scenes/archival footage. They are wholly in line with the genre-based expectations of the viewer in the manner of other Netflix categories such as "romantic comedies" and "war film." With some allowance made for creative choices and challenging content, I would argue that these documentaries are overwhelmingly commercial in that they are both easy to market and are often based on some preexisting awareness by audiences. While not commercial in the sense of Hollywood blockbusters, such films are more on the side of accessible and more familiar documentary content, serving in contrast to a more artistic trend in documentary filmmaking that is also gaining in critical attention, such as the films by the Harvard Sensory Ethnography Lab, films like *Leviathan* (2012) and *Manakamana* (2013), and director Joshua Oppenheimer's widely discussed *The Act of Killing* (2012) and *The Look of Silence* (2015). Experimental, more boundary-pushing documentaries are absolutely on Netflix, but they simply are not the focus of its acquisitions, its push in original content, or its presentation to subscribers. In fact, one documentary producer told me Netflix does not invest in producing more "edgy" documentary fare under their belief if the film ends up being successful, it will end up on the service anyway. The emphasis on commercial films, even in this specialized and small genre of feature documentary, highlights the need to see the streaming service as a newsstand in that it reminds us the primary concern for the service is financial and still based on viewership. As I discuss in the next section in my interviews with documentary filmmakers, despite all the positive and supportive actions of the company, the mandate of Netflix is not that of a library, but that of a commercial exhibition service.

Netflix and filmmakers

I interviewed two documentary filmmakers, and both, while eager to talk about Netflix and what it means for them personally and the industry, were very wary of being on the record. I decided to give them anonymity to present the fullness of their thoughts on Netflix and not endanger any future projects they might have with the powerful company. In discussing them here I will use pseudonyms. The two filmmakers are in different places in their career, one (Jules) has just made his first feature and the other (Jim) has made many films and received the industry's highest awards; yet both had remarkably similar, complex views on Netflix. Both were quick to praise the overwhelming positives of Netflix for documentary generally in terms of the industry and specifically for themselves. However, both were also worried about unintended consequences from Netflix's ubiquity.

Jules made his first feature just after film school. Shortly after finishing the film he signed with a sales team that would represent the film on all platforms, including digital downloads, streaming, and VOD. In contrast to the larger "Original" titles, third-party deals like these are how a great deal of content arrives on Netflix. Instead of dealing directly with filmmakers, going to festivals, and developing talent (all of which Netflix is currently doing at a larger scale), in the past the company would partner with independent sales and acquisition companies and make deals with them for the content they represented. In these situations, relationships and reliability were more critical than taste for Netflix. Again, considering the imperative for these titles to perform, Netflix was relying on sales and acquisition companies to know the market and represent the films they think will draw audiences.

Though Jules' project was based on a widely recognizable subject, it had no natural, built-in audience outside of a few dedicated fans. Jules' film played nearly a dozen festivals, and while some were well-known venues for documentary film, they were not among the better-known film festivals. Still, because of the unique subject, high-quality filmmaking, and appealing story, Jules believed there was an audience out there for his film, just not one that would support a traditional theatrical release, which was why he signed with his sales company so early in the life cycle of the project. For him the sales company was the best avenue to help the film get on screens in front of viewers, and with Netflix's eventual interest in his film he felt he reached the best possible outcome. Along with helping place the film on various platforms for download and renting, his sales company helped negotiate the U.S. and international streaming rights for Netflix. In the end, the film was able to get rights fees in the six figures, a huge boon for a first-time documentary filmmaker. While the other streams of income also were helpful, Jules saw Netflix's purchase of rights as the defining financial benefit of making the film. Without hesitation he says, "Netflix is what allowed me to make a living as a filmmaker."

Despite this gratitude, Jules notes a couple of important caveats. First, as soon as the film was available on Netflix, its sales and rentals on other platforms, including its own website, went down. The initial window between the film's availability for purchase and streaming on Netflix was just a week, so while it is hard to say with certainty that the drop was because of its availability on the service, it seems highly probable. Each sale and rental represents direct money to the filmmaker, so the reduction meant lost revenue. Second, the payment from Netflix for the rights did not come in one lump sum, but over financial quarters. While seemingly an insignificant detail of a complex financial transaction, for the filmmaker it can mean the difference between paying back investors and loans immediately and moving on to another project, or instead receiving a kind of small allowance every few months. Third, the manner in which Netflix presents his film to its subscribers, or more specifically the apparent algorithm that functions to presents the film with other, ostensibly comparable films, is completely unknown to him. This is important, considering what will happen at the end of Jules' deal with Netflix.

The deal lasts for three years, at which time Netflix can decide to renew under a new agreement or remove the film from its service. The decision will be made almost entirely based on the viewership numbers for the film, numbers that are seen and known by Netflix alone. Jules is painfully aware that he does not know what will happen at the end of the period, beyond looking for clues based on where the film is placed on the service in relation to other offerings. With other platforms, filmmakers get some meaningful numbers, whereas Netflix is a black box.[14] Further complicating the situation is the fact that, as mentioned earlier, the numbers on other platforms tend to dip when the film is on Netflix. The anxiety is not just that there will be no more revenue for the film; in some ways, the end of the three years could represent the death of the film's life cycle.

So while Jules credits having a career to the streaming service, he also admits they are in a position of complete control over him. This control extends even beyond the current film to his future projects. Due to the success of his first film, his sales agents are anxious to represent whatever his next film will be. With his experience with his first feature and the boon of Netflix money, he has been thinking about projects that are moving, meaningful, but also have some obvious commercial appeal. He feels knowing and reaching an audience is the job of any filmmaker, and he has a sophisticated understanding of balancing commercial realities with creating cinema that can affect culture. In the end, accepting that no one is going to become wealthy making feature documentaries, he is glad Netflix exists to both provide an avenue for his work to be seen and offer a way to make a financial living off of it. Netflix has undoubtedly changed the feature documentary world by allowing for more money and options for filmmakers, however, based on an experience like Jules', I think it is important to note Netflix is not leading to truly groundbreaking and different changes in the genre. The industrial formation and options for new filmmakers like Jules seem radically different (and technologically they are), yet Netflix is similar, and even in a more dominant position, to an older studio model as it has all the power in distribution and exhibition and is itself mainly driven by commercial concerns.

Jim shares a generally positive outlook for what Netflix is doing. He agrees that Netflix has changed the documentary film industry, mainly in taking care of what he labeled the "I have heard of that film, but don't know where to find it" problem that Dan Cogan mentioned. Just being able to point to Netflix as a repository (even if it is a newsstand and not a library) has helped documentary filmmakers with "average" audience members. The other benefit of Netflix to Jim has been its ability to finally provide competition to HBO Documentary's near-total domination of the space for the last decade. Documentarians now have many more options to get a mass audience for their films, in contrast to the situation in the past where any offer HBO Documentary provided was a "must take" deal.

However, as an established, award-winning documentarian with a feature in a recent major film festival, Jim's relationship with Netflix is different than that of Jules. Like other filmmakers and producers, Jim actually turned down larger financial offers from Netflix to go with a more traditional independent theatrical release. Every project has its own reasons for choosing a more risky theatrical strategy, but I think the continued appeal of theatrical release, both financially and artistically, for filmmakers speaks to the continuing values and goals of the industry. For Jim there is the belief that an audience will come to see his particular story and topic in the theater; in other conversations I have had, filmmakers extol a continuing power to being on a big screen in a theatrical space that Netflix cannot duplicate, even with a large amount of money.

Ultimately, Jim looks at Netflix as much more in the mold of a dotcom/tech company than studio. In contrast to seeing the service as being defined by its commercialism, he believes Netflix is much more willing to take risks and try out new production and distribution models than more established companies. With its large amount of money and "newness" of its operation, Netflix is able to think differently and invest in projects that will help more in creating a reputation of quality and innovation than immediate returns. He feels Netflix's original productions and documentary acquisitions demonstrate this. While not immediately profitable and not in the tradition of familiar exhibition and distribution practices, Netflix's programming is building a reputation for quality (and even appealing to a mandate that is not just commercial). However, Jim wonders how sustainable their model will be. Like any dotcom, there is a worry of the inevitable crash or culture change when the demand for revenue arises. Though startups are known for their experimentation and investing large sums of money and time, they are known just as much for crashing when the inevitable bill and commercial needs come due. Also, from my perspective, it is hard to see Netflix taking risks for the kind of "out there," more self-aware artistic documentary features that are developing. Though the impetus might be temporarily delayed at this moment, at some point the underlying commercial mandate of the service will demand its products to perform in some way beyond adding prestige.

Still, both filmmakers see Netflix, for all its good and mostly the worry of the bad, as being an incredibly positive force for documentary. Where Jules saw them as being the driving force in legitimatizing/financing his career, Jim sees them as a revolutionary force in the field. Other models exist for documentary exhibition, but Netflix is alone in its growth and radically new approaches. Though things are "good" now, in terms of money, increased competition and outlets for filmmakers, and a new way to reach audiences, there remains some uneasiness since the underlying commercial demands still remain.

Conclusion

As of 2015, things are changing so quickly that it is hard to say with certainty what the relationship between documentary and Netflix will look like in the future. For example, with the success of HBO's *The Jinx* and National Public Radio's podcast *Serial*, there is a great deal of interest in new documentary formats that could be serialized or generally presented over time rather like long form scripted shows. Netflix is also experimenting with programming like this with *Chef's Table*, perhaps suggesting that the service is becoming less interested in feature-length documentaries and more interested in traditional television programming.

Regardless, the experience of feature documentaries on the service does tell us a great deal about Netflix today and suggests certain future outcomes are more likely than not. Despite the promise of digital technology to create new markets and revolutionize media industries, there is still a great deal of power in the traditional work of distribution and exhibition platforms. In the same way that iTunes used (what Andrew Bard Schmookler would say is the illusion of) choice to gain a stranglehold on the music industry, Netflix can be in the same position for the documentary feature film industry.[15] Today, they are saviors with money and opportunity, but it is not hard to imagine a future where Netflix will charge filmmakers to be on the site, or if not something that extreme, then charge a premium to be on the front section of its digital newsstand when users log in.

Netflix has changed documentary, but this change is more of one of degree instead of kind. Filmmakers and audiences have more options than ever before, but production, distribution, and exhibition decision-making are still dominated by fairly traditional commercial thinking. What has changed is scale and technology, but a lot of Netflix is a reminder of "old" Hollywood with a dependence on a Fordist model of production, including practices like pre-packaging and block-booking. Ultimately films, including feature documentary, have to perform for the service just like any film from any studio since the beginning of the American film industry. Despite being a new frontier, Netflix is a restating of the values and the workings of the past in a new, contemporary, digital dialect. In order to understand our moment then, we need to learn the language.

Notes

1 Whether documentary film can be defined in total as a genre or a form or mode is something beyond the scope of this chapter. The status of documentary as genre has been discussed by Erik Barnouw in *Documentary: A History of the Non-Fiction Film* (New York: Oxford University Press, 1974) and by Bill Nichols, *Representing Reality: Issues and Concepts of Documentary* (Bloomington: Indiana University Press, 1992). I will be describing it as a genre here because doing so both indicates the audience expectations when consuming it and the marketing/exhibition practices in packaging it. Genre also seems most appropriate considering how Netflix categorizes films for its viewers.

2 I am using the library versus newsstand models for distribution as discussed in Timothy Havens and Amanda D. Lotz, *Understanding Media Industries* (London: Oxford University Press, 2011), 153.

3 Jenna Goudreau, "12 Documentaries on Netflix that Will Make You Smarter About Business," *Business Insider*, May 28, 2015. http://www.businessinsider.com/netflix-business-documentaries-to-watch-instantly-2015-5 (accessed August 6, 2015).

4 Havens and Lotz, *Understanding Media Industries*, 153.

5 Ibid., 154.

6 Like the HBO motto "It's Not TV. It's HBO" reminds us, premium television services are often trying to identify themselves as "more than" mere television.

7 Brent Lang, "Average Movie Ticket Prices Increase to $8.17 for 2014," *Variety*, January 20, 2015. http://variety.com/2015/film/news/movie-ticket-prices-increased-in-2014-1201409670/ (accessed August 6, 2015).

8 Alexis Madrigal, "How Netflix Reverse-Engineered Hollywood," *The Atlantic*, January 2, 2014. http://www.theatlantic.com/technology/archive/2014/01/how-netflix-reverse-engineered-hollywood/282679/ (accessed September 25, 2014).

9 Nichols, *Representing Reality*, 112.

10 Ted Sarandos, "Read the Speech That Sent a Wake Up Call to TV and Film Studios: Netflix Chief Ted Sarandos Explains His Company's Success at the FIND Forum," *Indiewire*, October 31, 2013. http://www.indiewire.com/article/read-last-weekends-ted-sarandos-speech-tv-is-where-indie-production-is-happening (accessed August 6, 2015).

11 Paula Bernstein, "What Does Netflix's Investment in Documentaries Mean for Filmmakers?" *Indiewire*, March 9, 2015. http://www.indiewire.com/article/what-does-netflixs-investment-in-documentaries-mean-for-filmmakers-20150309 (accessed May 14, 2015).

12 Bernstein, "Netflix Dives Deeper into Documentaries, Nabbing Award-Winning 'Virunga,'" *Indiewire*, July 28, 2014. http://www.indiewire.com/article/netflix-dives-deeper-into-documentaries-nabbing-award-winning-virunga-20140728 (accessed July 29, 2014).

13 Tom Roston, "Netflix Streaming Deals for Documentary Filmmakers —Some Numbers," *POV Blog | PBS*, June 10, 2013. http://www.pbs.org/pov/blog/docsoup/2013/06/netflix-streaming-deals-for-documentary-filmmakers-some-numbers/ (accessed May 14, 2015).

14 It is interesting to note that the rare release of viewer numbers has only been for Netflix's Original series programming, not all "originals." See Andrew Wallenstein, "Netflix Ratings Revealed: New Data Sheds Light on Original Series' Audience Levels," *Variety*, April 28, 2015. http://variety.com/2015/digital/news/netflix-originals-viewer-data-1201480234/ (accessed May 11, 2015).

15 Andrew Bard Schmookler, *Illusion of Choice: How the Market Economy Shapes Our Destiny* (Albany: State University of New York Press, 1993).

10

Seeing Blackness in Prison: Understanding Prison Diversity on Netflix's *Orange Is the New Black*

Brittany Farr

On July 11, 2013, Netflix premiered its fifth original series, *Orange Is the New Black*, a fictionalized comedic drama based on the memoir by Piper Kerman of the same name. The show follows Piper Chapman, a young, white upper-middle-class woman, after she is sentenced to fifteen months in prison for transporting money for her drug-dealing ex-girlfriend nearly ten years earlier. *Orange Is the New Black* was met with both popular and critical acclaim, and to date has been renewed for its fourth season. The show has made the lives of incarcerated women visible in an unprecedented way. At the time of this writing, the United States has the largest prison population in the world. The number of women in prison increased by 646 percent between 1980 and 2010, while the rate of women's incarceration was almost one and a half times that of men's.[1] So perhaps it should not be surprising that one of the most critically acclaimed shows about women in recent years takes place in a federal women's prison. *Orange Is the New Black* is breaking new representational ground with its diverse, female-led cast and scenes illustrating some of the harsh realities of prison life. In a televisual era where the driving economic logic is that diversity sells, these groundbreaking representations are not quite as revolutionary as they may initially seem. Although *Orange* is representing some of the most vulnerable women in the country, its comedic tone and narrative themes are simultaneously perpetuating some of the most persistent cultural myths about criminality and prison in order to do so.

Focusing on the themes of blackness and visibility, I critically examine the continuities between the show's subject matter (the mass incarceration of women), its political economy (as a Netflix original series), and its critical reception. The show's creators were able to mitigate the risks of content creation, in part, by strategic appeals to diversity. The risks taken at the textual level actually work to temper the risks of Netflix's early forays into content creation. The success of *Orange Is the New Black* proves a point made by Herman Gray and other media scholars: the recognition of difference within contemporary media is good business practice.[2] It is one strategy, of many, used to create marketable representations and manage the riskiness of participating in an ever-less regulated sphere of capitalism. *Orange Is the New Black* is situated at the intersection of the prison and entertainment industries, and by interrogating the logic animating both industries, we can discern a coherency of affective investments across seemingly disparate spheres.

There are two questions guiding my analysis of *Orange Is the New Black*. The first is, as a work of fiction, what kinds of assumptions about our contemporary political and economic climate does the show make most visible? In a recent *American Quarterly* article, Herman Gray encourages media studies scholars to think beyond questions of accuracy, authenticity, or legibility with regard to race in the media and instead "detail exactly how and where media organize and circulate affectively compelling sentiment, attachment, and (dis)identification to public policies, bodies, histories, and cultures."[3] Attending to the premises represented by the show can enable us to more easily see what kinds of sentiment is being organized and circulated by *Orange Is the New Black* about women, about prison and the security state, about Netflix, and about television and storytelling itself. Practices of surveillance cut across our popular and political culture. *Orange Is the New Black* explicitly addresses the security and surveillance in prison. Netflix surveys its users' behavior and uses this data to inform its programming decisions. This intersection of different kinds of security practices provides a unique opportunity to interrogate the many meanings and values of visibility.

The second question is, what do the narratives about the success of the show teach us about the value of racially marked bodies, particularly black bodies, within racial neoliberalism? Within capitalist ideology, mitigating risk and managing vulnerability is a valuable good. *Orange Is the New Black* is able to do so via representations of individuals caught in a system designed to do just that—mitigate risk and manage vulnerability. It is a show with sympathetic characters that have made bad choices, many of whom are characters of color. And what we've seen in the press about the show is that Netflix has made the *right* choice by investing in a show about people (of color) who have made bad choices or the wrong choices.

Reading the fictional world of *Orange Is the New Black*

Even though *Orange Is the New Black* presents a mostly sanitized view of life in prison, it *does* still center its narrative on some the most vulnerable populations in the United States.[4] Part of the show's positive reception is precisely because of the way *Orange Is the New Black* represents some of the least represented injustices of the prison industrial complex. For example, in one episode they show the "humane release" of an elderly prisoner. An elderly woman is released early because her dementia has made her too difficult and expensive to care for. Described as a humane release because of her age, the "humanity" of this act is undercut by the fact that the warden authorizes it for purely economic reasons and it is all but guaranteed that the prisoner in question will end up homeless and completely without resources. Elsewhere in the show we see glimpses of the transphobic violence transprisoners encounter on a regular basis, as well as the cruel institutional response to this violence. The transcharacter Sophia Burset is placed in solitary confinement "for her own protection" after she is attacked by some of the other inmates. *Orange* makes it clear that placing Sophia in solitary is the prison administrators' cruel way of protecting themselves from liability. They are more concerned with their own legal safety. In addition to illustrating the prison system's many hypocrisies, *Orange* has also provided jobs and visibility for the actresses of color featured on the show, many of whom are playing three-dimensional characters, which is still a relative rarity for women of color on television today. Perhaps one of the most remarkable consequences of the show is that Laverne Cox has been able to use her visibility as Sophia Burset to encourage some of the most widespread national conversations about the violence experienced by transwomen, particularly transwomen of color. At the same time, however, *Orange* drastically softens what life in prison is like. The show is more akin to a female workplace comedy than a female version of HBO's *Oz*.[5] Prison is meant to function primarily as a narrative backdrop. And rather than depict the realities of incarceration, the show uses this setting to introduce thematic concerns about the perils and precarity of gendered consumption. The show's writers and creators rely on well-worn stereotypes about the intersection of blackness, Latinidad, poverty, and femininity in order to explore the dangers of incorrectly participating in capitalism.

Flashbacks and failed consumption

In a typical episode of *Orange Is the New Black*, the narrative is interrupted by flashbacks of the women's lives before incarceration. These flashbacks usually show the audience why the women were arrested, and usually in sympathetic terms. In an interview with Terry Gross, Jenji Kohan—*Orange Is the New Black*'s creator and showrunner—implies that she relies heavily on flashbacks within the show in order to keep it from getting too depressing.[6] For Kohan, these flashbacks were necessary for her as a writer because she was unwilling to mentally inhabit the prison the entire time she was writing. Even this mental imprisonment was too big a burden to bear. Many critics have gone on to praise Kohan's use of flashbacks for the ways they humanize the characters, give the viewers insight into the inmates' behavior, and offer opportunities for audience members to empathize with the characters' flaws. Although Piper Chapman is the main character, and consequently gets the most flashbacks, by giving the other characters flashback storylines the show is able to more truly be an ensemble. What we see across all the flashbacks are stories about women struggling to keep up or to "make it" in our consumer society. Although most incarcerated women have been incarcerated as a result of nonviolent drug-related offenses, these are not the majority of the stories that *Orange Is the New Black* represents. In choosing *not* to rely heavily on stories about poverty, institutionalized racism, and sexism (stories that might begin to feel very similar to one another), the show communicates that these kinds of stories are not that relatable. Because each woman's crime is unique, the show provides the audience with a prison full of unique individuals whose crimes are a result of their pursuit of individualism. This criminal individualism is consistent with liberal ideology's privileging of personal responsibility and independence.

There are two primary themes communicated via these flashbacks. The first is about the criminality of improper consumption practices. *Orange Is the New Black* is replete with storylines about women making improper consumer choices and ending up in prison. For example, Sophia Burset is arrested for credit card fraud. She used stolen credit card information to finance her expensive gender reassignment surgeries. Lorna Morello, a woman who obsessively discusses her upcoming wedding, is ultimately revealed to be a delusional stalker. Morello's backstory is featured via flashback in the second episode of season two, and we learn that her fiancé Christopher is not her fiancé, but a man she dated briefly and has subsequently been stalking and harassing her. In this episode Morello's immorality and loose grasp on reality is first communicated via a scene of her committing credit card fraud. Gloria Mendoza—who runs the kitchen in season two—is arrested for welfare fraud even though it was committed in an attempt to save up enough money to leave her abusive boyfriend. Some of the other women are in prison for theft, robbery, drug use, or drug sales; however, these are typically mentioned in passing rather than as the focal point of extended flashbacks. When they are the focal point, these crimes are presented as crimes of passion rather than crimes of circumstance, as in the case of Rosa Cisneros. In season two, we learn that Cisneros is in prison for a spree of armed bank robberies that she committed with her lovers. Cisneros robbed the banks because she loved the thrill of it, not because she needed the money.

The second theme that is present on *Orange* is that black women possess a nonspecific criminality and it is natural for them to be incarcerated. There is a marked difference between the flashbacks provided for the white inmates and the inmates of color. When we learn about the pasts of three of the main black female characters, we are not shown the exact legal transgressions that led to their incarceration. In the first two seasons *Orange* only leaves this sort of narrative ellipses for the black female characters. The criminality associated with blackness or the crime of black sociality is explanation enough.

It isn't just the prisoners who receive the benefit of *Orange Is the New Black*'s humanizing flashbacks either. *Orange* also explores the backstories of several guards, the counselors, and the prison administrators. Consequently, these flashbacks flatten difference. By humanizing everyone, from the inmates, to the guards, to the warden's assistant, *Orange* obscures the power dynamics operating within the prison and minimizes the inequalities that are actually at play within the prison industrial complex. To use a phrase from Herman Gray, the flashbacks make the struggles of the show's inmates "visible, but emptied," thus providing the cachet of diversity without having to ask hard questions.[7] The flashbacks give the impression that all the characters are stuck in the prison together—much like all the characters in a workplace comedy are stuck with each other. This is clearly not the case; the prisoners do not have the option of leaving.

The prison economy

In seasons two and three, the focus is less on the characters' past acts of improper consumption and more about the smuggling and embezzling happening in the show's present. The embezzlement in season two forces tough decisions about the prison's finances in the following season. The focus of season two is the prison economy—both the illegal exchange of contraband between inmates and the financial dealings of the prison writ large by the warden's executive assistant. The assistant to the warden embezzles money from the prison's budget in order to finance her husband's senate campaign. She justifies her embezzlement by reasoning that the legislative changes her husband can enact will have a greater impact on the incarcerated women's lives than spending the budget on plumbing and better snacks. In the third season, the illicit economy within the prison and the economy of prisons more generally continue to drive a lot of the show's narrative action. In the wake of season two's embezzlement, Litchfield is out of money and scheduled to be closed. The new warden's assistant Joe Caputo manages to convince MMR—a private corporation—to take control of the prison's operations. Responsibility for the prison's inhumane practices, both toward its inmates and its employees, is now displaced onto the profit-only motives of the private corporation. For example, in the interest of cutting costs, MMR provides the women with less expensive and less appealing food. The show goes to great lengths to show just how disgusting and inedible the new prison slop is. Unlike on *Orange Is the New Black*, however, the problems with prisons in the United States are not solely attributable to corporate greed. As Ruth Wilson Gilmore writes in *Golden Gulag*, although U.S. prisons have become increasingly privatized, 95 percent of the United States' prisons are still state or federally operated.[8] Despite what season three of *Orange Is the New Black* suggests, many of the problems Litchfield faces as a result of MMR's profit-centric decision making are not exclusive to privately owned prisons. Prisons are inhumane whether they are privately or federally operated.

Both of these story arcs represent the prison as a porous, flawed economy. Within the world of *Orange Is the New Black*, Litchfield Penitentiary's facilities are outdated and the prison is barely getting by financially. The show treats the warden's assistant's flawed attempt to help change the prison system not just as disingenuous but also as irrelevant. And it is here that we see how *Orange* allows for an easy metonymic reading between the prison system in the show and the televisual landscape that both *Orange Is the New Black* and Netflix are operating within. Litchfield's prisoners suffer because the powers that are within the prison choose to do things the way they have always done them. Those (and they are almost all men) who run the prison care very little about the consumer desires of their female inmates. The prison administration is unwilling to take risks on running the prison differently, and when they do, as one counselor does in season two, early signs of failure easily discourage them. Litchfield can easily serve as a metaphor for the outmoded world of network and cable television. The system is broken. But the show does not suggest that the prison system should be revolutionized, just that it should be run more efficiently and more sensitively. As I will discuss later, this sentiment is remarkably similar to the one expressed by Kevin Spacey in a highly circulated speech about Netflix. If the people running the prison knew how to appropriately distribute the control and the freedom, then perhaps everyone would get what they want. The stories presented on *Orange* take our surveillance and security state as a given, as part of our common sense. Surveillance—in the form of big data—has now become an important tool for creating stories. *Orange Is the New Black* naturalizes prison as a fact of life, and (re)produces the idea that this visibility in the form of surveillance is not just necessary, but is good.

In the section that follows I map out a theoretical framework for understanding the relationship between common-sense beliefs about blackness and the ways in which the visibility of blackness matters not just in the United States' entertainment industry but in its governance and economy as well. These thematic premises about criminality, consumption, and blackness can be productively understood as an example of Gramscian common sense. From there I situate Netflix's attempt to brand its entry into content creation within the longer historical relationship between blackness and branding in the United States, and consider *Orange Is the New Black's* role in Netflix's brand development. The show is the most diverse of Netflix's original series and one of its most successful, and its success is due in no small part to the black characters.

Blackness, common sense, and visibility

Many scholars in visual studies, cultural studies, and African American studies alike have written about the ways in which visual culture in the United States has been impacted by the legacy of slavery.[9] Put simply, blackness is an overdetermined symbol in U.S. visual culture; blackness and/or the black body can stand in for sexuality, aggression, criminality, passivity, weakness, pathology, coolness, authenticity, and the list goes on. The hypervisibility of black bodies allows blackness to "be transplanted to new arenas that both displace its historicity and abstract certain values, feelings, or ideas associated with its historical context to new audiences and settings."[10] In other words, blackness is an incredibly mobile and adaptable icon, one that has the potential to be profitable if utilized properly. In this representational context, Herman Gray's argument for rethinking our investment in representation is a compelling one. When difference and diversity become marketing strategies, increasingly diverse televisual representations don't guarantee equality outside of the televisual sphere. With *Orange Is the New Black*, we see very clearly how "diversity" sells the show. Because capitalism is adaptive, it has incorporated calls for more diverse, fairer, representations into its logic. Calls for "better" representation no longer have the same potential to effect systemic change as they did in the civil rights era.

Gramsci's notion of common sense is useful here. Rather than considering a representation's authenticity, or whether it is "good" or "bad," we can ask what kinds of common sense the representation (re)produces or makes most visible.[11] Common sense is a set of shared assumptions about the world that is shared by the majority of people in a social order. There are multiple kinds of common sense within a given society; they can be contradictory and incoherent. And they have a powerful ability to shape and support our worldview. Ideology can remain unnoticed because it can operate most effectively and most powerfully as common sense. The film scholar Kara Keeling takes up Gramsci's notion of common sense in *The Witch's Flight*. Keeling's work highlights the ways in which consolidated common sense corresponds to sets of socioeconomic relations. The common sense we perceive across various media communicates beliefs about the appropriateness and the naturalness of existing socioeconomic relations. Keeling's use of the term "consolidation" in her discussion of common sense speaks to the ways in which these representations build on one another; their power is cumulative.[12]

Colorblindness is an example of common sense that has become one of the dominant ways of seeing and understanding racial diversity within neoliberalism.[13] It situates racism as something that occurred in the past *and* it celebrates the visibility and recognition of racial difference without an acknowledgment of historical legacies of suffering and the continued existence of unequal systems of privilege. Whether it is in "multiculti" United Colors of Benetton ads or arguments decrying the continuing need for affirmative action policies, an "I don't see color" sentiment is pervasive in American popular culture. Through the lens of colorblindness the structural racism that contributes to the United States' racialized income inequality becomes insensible. Colorblind ideology prevents contemporary racism from making sense *as racism*. Within this colorblind common sense we can celebrate a representation of women in prison for its diverse cast without having to "see" the racism that fills American prisons with "diversity" in the first place.

Colorblind discourse facilitates these calls for visible diversity by discouraging investigations into the ways in which the visibility of bodies of color has been a long-standing technique of power in the United States.[14] Although Michel Foucault's theorization of the panopticon is often evoked in discussions of visibility and power, the logics of racial neoliberalism described by Gray and others clearly extend beyond (though still incorporate) a panoptic logic. Foucault's notion of security offers a way of thinking about the relationship of visibility and power beyond his oft-used panoptic metaphor. To the extent that the mechanisms of the security state—surveillance, incarceration, and militarization—are both common*place* and common *sense* within contemporary U.S. society,[15] Foucault's notion of security provides one possible avenue for understanding the vectors of relation between the visibility of blackness within both the security state and the entertainment industry. Foucault writes that security is "a matter of maximizing the positive elements, for which one provides the best possible circulation, and of minimizing what is risky and inconvenient... while knowing that they will never be completely suppressed."[16] For Foucault, security is a problem of managing the future. Security is about the management of risk and the promotion of circulation, particularly in the service of capitalism. Because circulation necessitates vulnerability, within a logic of security, the goal is not to eliminate vulnerability but to keep it within an acceptable statistical occurrence. Appealing to certain common-sense ideas is perceived as making shows more accessible and less risky, more circulateable. Blackness is valuable for the ways in which it minimizes the risks associated with cultivating brand culture, which I explain more fully in the next section. This logic very clearly underpins Jenji Kohan's claim that *Orange Is the New Black* needed its white female lead as a Trojan horse in order to get made, reach audiences, and be successful.[17]

For Foucault, security is the system of power that follows the disciplinary regime of power, within which the panopticon was the primary metaphor for the way power operates. Within panopticism visibility has a disciplinary effect; power's gaze, whether external or internalized, disciplines and normalizes subjects. In a post-panoptic era, visibility is no longer primarily disciplinary. Security is a post-panoptic regime, wherein power operates via circulation. We can understand the rapid expansion of the prison system within this complex of Foucauldian security. We can think of security as "panopticism plus," it is a scenario of both/and: *both* panopticism *and* security. In other words, power still operates via a panoptic model but not *only* via a panoptic model. Prisons have been situated at the intersection of juridico-legal and disciplinary power. The disciplinary gaze is still present in the prison *and* their commodification is part of a larger trend toward treating security as an industry and private good in the United States. Security is about managing populations rather than people. The prison-industrial complex with its profit margins and risky populations is an institution whose function is to manage the consequences of the vulnerabilities necessitated by capital's circulation.

The marketplace functions as a structure of vision within capitalism. If circulation is the primary technique of power, then the facility and manner of circulation are a measure of one's access to power. The visibility of goods, services, and consumers within the marketplace is essential to its functioning, as is the circulation of all three elements. And with the circulation of these elements comes risk and vulnerability, which are in turn managed by increased visibility, often in the form of surveillance. Visibility is a necessary precursor to participation in the market, and subjects work to make themselves visible as the right kind of consumer, or the right kind of "good," as is the case with self-branding. Those who hold the most power within the market, like multinational corporations or governments, in turn have the most power to legitimate or acknowledge the visibility of participants in the market or, as is often the case, to privilege and value certain forms of visibility over others.

In the case of *Orange Is the New Black*, by investing in a show with an ensemble cast featuring many women of color, Netflix demonstrates that the stories of women of color are a valuable investment. This investment is made less risky because the main character is a "safe" televisual representation—a young, attractive, middle-class white American woman. The visibility of blackness on *Orange* simultaneously aligns with a hegemonic common sense about the authenticity of a criminal blackness. In the first two minutes of the first episode the show uses the character Taystee—a large black woman—to introduce the audience to Piper's harsh new reality. Dressed in a *mumu* with her hair in disarray, Taystee sexualizes and objectifies Piper's vulnerable and naked body while Piper attempts to shower in the prison for the first time. Unlike the safe, wealthy, white spaces that Piper declares are her "happy place," Taystee and the prison showers embody the absolute difference and otherness of the prison and establish Piper's fall from grace. The racial and sexual dynamics of these first two minutes are meant to be intriguing enough to keep audience members watching. This juxtaposition between Piper's old and new life, between her previous comfort and her newfound vulnerability as a rich, white, fish out of water, are shown before the show's title and title sequence. Piper's voiceover in these shots establishes that this is Piper's story, told from Piper's point of view.

Although the emphasis on Piper's point of view wanes as the season progresses, her viewpoint was integral to the show's initial conception, its sale to Netflix, and to its initial positive reception and success. The common-sense beliefs about the natural associations of blackness and criminality that we see in these first two minutes undergird much of *Orange*, and the same common sense provides the justification for the mass incarceration of black people and the continued expansion of the prison industry. It goes something like this: blackness and black people are unruly and threatening, and are particularly threatening to white, middle-class propriety. As Herman Gray demonstrates in *Watching Race* (2004), televisual representations of black criminality in the 1980s and 1990s both reflected and reinforced conservative politician's largely successful attempts to dismantle "progressive notions of racial entitlements."[18] Similarly, there is a de facto acceptance, naturalization, and normalization of the pathologization and surveillance of poor people and people of color on the show that can be found throughout the techniques and ideology of the security state.

Blackness and branding in the United States

Advertising permeates U.S. visual culture. Since the 1980s, the goal of advertising has shifted from selling a product to selling a brand and its attendant brand culture. Because selling a brand is about selling authenticity, the long-standing association of blackness with authenticity situates blackness at the center of the creation and expansion of branding and brand cultures in the United States.[19] Consequently, blackness, and a co-opting of a black aesthetic have been integral to the development of brands and brand cultures in the United States.[20] Once folklorists in the nineteenth and early twentieth centuries determined that black music was only truly authentic when performed by black musicians, ideas about the meanings of authenticity changed.[21] Black culture and by extension black people were believed to be more authentic because black people were closer to their primitive, folk roots. The primitivism associated with blackness meant that blackness and black culture were more "real" more "natural," less refined, less polished, and less commercialized. The folkloric conception of authenticity (which has become the hegemonic understanding of authenticity) counterposes authenticity to commodity culture and the marketplace. Because primitive black culture was believed to be a window into a less civilized world, a world less touched by capitalism, it was thus deemed to be more authentic. Unsurprisingly, we can trace brands' attempts to be seen as more authentic with their attempts to signify blackness.

The practice of branding itself was developed to help mitigate the risk of participating in capitalism. Because a brand's meaning cannot be fixed, it is always in an insecure position. Having a strong brand means that your brand is highly visible and recognizable in the marketplace. It means that you have cultivated a series of positive feelings with your recognizable brand. A successful brand or brand culture helps to mitigate the risks associated with the marketplace. In Todd Gitlin's now canonical *Inside Prime Time*, he details the lengths broadcast networks would go to in order to try and predict what kinds of shows audiences wanted. These techniques ranged from focus groups and audience testing, to relying on ratings widely understood to be inaccurate, to imitating successful shows on other networks. Broadly, what Gitlin's analysis of the television industry demonstrates is that the industry's primary goal is not quite to make a hit show but to mitigate the risk of attempting to create a hit show. To put it another way, the industry is structured around "the problem of uncertainty."[22] Television networks' attempts to cultivate a strong brand identity are a direct response to this problem of uncertainty.

Although Gitlin's research on the television industry took place during the eve of the cable revolution, many of his insights about the problem of uncertainty still hold true today. Netflix's entry into content creation has been marked by uncertainty. One of the ways in which Netflix has attempted to manage this uncertainty is by imitating the branding and content strategies of HBO.[23] In the words of Netflix's chief content officer, Ted Sarandos, "The goal is to become HBO faster than HBO can become us."[24] Netflix's brand is less focused on creating shows for one particular audience and more about revolutionizing storytelling. In this way it is very similar to HBO, whose slogan "It's Not TV. It's HBO" emphasizes the qualitative differences between HBO's shows and shows on broadcast networks and other cable channels. Netflix is trying to build its brand as a renegade player in the television game, one that is able to successfully take risks, and do things that other, conventional, boring networks are "afraid" to do.

Revolutionizing storytelling

The image of Netflix as an innovative and disruptive agent in the television industry relies primarily on the success of its original programming. Netflix's CEO Reed Hastings, as well as chief content officer Ted Sarandos, don't just want to make successful television shows; they want to reshape what television shows look like, what kinds of stories get told on "television," and the kinds of storytelling that can take place within a television format. Netflix's marketing switch from DVD mailing service to on-demand content provider—streaming both old favorites and original content—helped the company revive and recast its brand image and company value after the disastrous announcement of price increases and the creation of Qwikster in 2011.[25] The originality of Netflix's in-house programming is crucial for this brand narrative, and it did not take long for Netflix's original content to transition from "novelty to expectation among subscribers."[26] Just three years after Netflix's first rollout of its original content, in January 2015, the cost efficiency of these shows was a central component of Hastings' quarterly letter to shareholders.

Netflix's branding strategies are remarkably similar to those undertaken by HBO in the early history of the network.[27] Freed from the television set itself, Netflix is able to construct a vision of itself as doing HBO better than HBO. *House of Cards* star and executive producer Kevin Spacey spoke highly of Netflix's approach to television, in a widely circulated speech given at the Edinburgh Television festival. According to Spacey, "Clearly the success of the Netflix model, releasing the entire season of *House of Cards* at once proved one thing. The audience wants the control. They want the freedom.... The audience has spoken, they want stories, they're dying for them."[28]

Netflix is simultaneously the underdog, the rebel, and the visionary. They are the upstart looking to shake up a dying and out-of-touch industry not just for the sake of money but for the sake of storytelling and authenticity. At least that's the kind of narrative Netflix executives like to tell about their brand.

A "ballsy" use of big data

The media's reception of Netflix's shows similarly emphasizes Netflix's role as a disruptor in the television industry. Netflix's strategic use of the data it has on its users' viewing habits is a critical part of the narrative told by Netflix's executives, its content creators, as well as journalists and critics. In the case of *Orange Is the New Black*, the data-based research done for the show is especially important to the narrative about the show because of the show's success. *Orange Is the New Black*'s success is credited in large part to Netflix's ability to accurately interpret data.[29] Unlike Netflix's other hit series, *House of Cards, Orange Is the New Black* did not benefit from extensive marketing and does not have an Academy-Award-winning lead actor. Consider this *Rolling Stone* review of the show from August 2013 titled "How 'Orange Is the New Black' Became Netflix's Best Series":

> Aside from four or five male characters, nearly every player on *Black* is female.... For television fans, it's a welcome change, one that *only a ballsy outfit like Netflix* would have the marbles to broadcast.... Despite the lack of pre-release hype, early buzz and big-name stars, *Black* is the very best original series Netflix has released so far. (emphasis added)[30]

Part of Netflix's brand narrative is that extensive data is critical for the successful display of difference on a show like *Orange Is the New Black*. According to various reports, Netflix chose not to market *Orange Is the New Black* in the way it marketed *House of Cards* and *Arrested Development* because it *knew* audiences would watch the show without marketing. This knowledge was based upon an analysis of data collected from users' viewing habits. This data led Netflix executives to the conclusion that viewers enjoy dark comedies, shows about crime and/or prison, and shows with a "likeable" female lead.[31]

While this story of *Orange Is the New Black*'s conception is slightly different from the one Jenji Kohan tells, what is consistent across all stories of the show's creation is the predictive intent of the show's creators—a desire to manage probabilities and risk. And while this is true for TV shows in general, the difference is Netflix's "ability" to predict its viewers' desires. The difference is data. The story Netflix tells with *Orange Is the New Black* is about the risk of making choices. The more one knows, and the more data one has, the better one is able to minimize the risk of decision-making and minimize the risk of investments. It is a story told at the level of both form and content with *Orange Is the New Black*. It is a story that allows Netflix to build the power of its brand and contributes to its identity as a brand that successfully makes "risky" investments. It is also a story that is crucial to the justification of security and racial neoliberalism.

Whereas network and cable television make money from advertising revenue, which is linked to ratings, Netflix's revenue is entirely subscription based. Netflix's content must be desirable enough to encourage new people to sign up and start paying its monthly fee. Netflix doesn't need all of its users to watch its original programming in order to be successful. It just needs enough people to watch, or discuss, or report on its shows in order to convince other people in the entertainment marketplace to buy into its network. And in the fall of 2013, Netflix had more subscribers than HBO, making it the largest pay-TV service in the United States.

Clearly, based on the buzz generated from its casting choices and storylines, this proliferation of difference is economically advantageous. This is precisely the operation of racial neoliberalism Gray addresses. He writes, "The alignment of markets, digital participation, and difference is making visible and translating the rich and multiple differences in tradition, history, and circumstance into marketable brand distinctions and consumer choices for self-reliant citizens."[32] In other words, a brand culture is successful when it is able to translate difference, however defined, into marketable brand distinctions. For Gray, the marketplace is designed in such a way that a consumer's desire and ability to choose between distinct brands/brand cultures becomes evidence of his or her self-reliance and democratic participation. Consumer choices become duties of citizenship, and properly making these choices is akin to performing one's status as a citizen-subject. What this means for Netflix and for *Orange Is the New Black* is that we cannot and should not understand viewership and Netflix's consumption solely at the level of individual taste and the economy. As reviews of the show demonstrate, Netflix's deployment of difference on *Orange* has been interpreted not just as a willingness to take risks but as evidence that they are the only network who could *successfully* take such risks. For example, the *Rolling Stone* review mentioned earlier stresses that "*only* … Netflix would have the marbles to broadcast" a show like *Orange*.[33] A similar sentiment is expressed in the following *Washington Post* review of the show: "Watching the show, one begins to realize that *all the good parts for women truly have been kept locked up somewhere*; now, here they all are, free. … Each episode contains fascinating revelations about the prison world, almost like a documentary report from within."[34]

For the reviewer, the prison setting imparts a documentary-style authenticity that makes the show qualitatively good. He uncritically asserts that these great roles have been locked up and congratulates Netflix for setting them free. This is exactly what Herman Gray is referring to when he describes the translation and flattening of difference and circumstance into marketable brand distinctions. "Showcasing" black and Latina actresses and the "harsh reality" of prison casts Netflix as an intelligent and progressive brand.

Representational politics can begin to feel like an echo chamber, where the calls for (and representations of) diversity exist as answers in themselves to the problem of racial inequality. It takes more than just representation to explode common sense—from the inside or out—but occasionally representations can light the fuse. While I do not want to let *Orange Is the New Black* off the hook, per se, for the ways in which it normalizes prison and plays prison violence for laughs, the show's goal is entertainment, not progressive politics. At a political level, in many ways the show is largely a failure. If we measure political success by changes in power dynamics, it is hard to argue that *Orange* has incited a prison revolution. If we're looking for the ways in which the show challenges oppressive common sense(s) about the necessity of prison, there is little of that to be found either. The show does succeed, however, in creating sympathetic portraits of incarcerated women. *Orange*'s most important success is probably Laverne Cox's activism; Cox's role and storyline on the show were a signal boost for transgender issues. Her commitment to highlighting the violence and structural inequalities faced by transwomen of color during press interviews for *Orange Is the New Black* is one way in which visibility and representation can attempt to reach beyond the representational sphere.

Notes

1 "Incarcerated Women," Washington, DC: The Sentencing Project, 2012. www.sentencingproject.org (accessed June 21, 2015).

2 For more on the value of selling difference and diversity, see bell hooks, "Eating the Other: Race and Resistance," in *Black Looks: Race and Representation* (Boston, MA: South End Press, 1992), 21–39; Sarah Banet-Weiser, *Authentic™: The Politics of Ambivalence in a Brand Culture* (New York: New York University Press, 2012); Kristal Brent Zook, *Color by Fox: The Fox Network and the Revolution in Black Television* (New York: Oxford University Press, 1999).

3 Herman Gray, "Subject(ed) to Recognition," *American Quarterly* 65.4 (2013): 793. doi:10.1353/aq.2013.0058.

4 A woman who was incarcerated at Danbury Federal Prison—the real-life basis for Litchfield—writes, "Take it from me, prison life isn't funny. Nor is it anything like the comic-book portrayal of prison as exemplified in the Netflix rendition": Beatrice Codianni, "Former Prisoner: 'Orange Is the New Black' Is Not Funny," *Truthout*, September 3, 2014. http://www.truth-out.org/opinion/item/25957-former-inmate-orange-is-the-new-black-is-not-funny (accessed July 15, 2015). In a BuzzFeed article written by a formerly incarcerated senator, however, the author praises the show for the things it "gets right" about life in prison: Jeff Smith, "A Former Prisoner on What 'Orange Is the New Black' Gets Right —And What It Doesn't," *BuzzFeed*, August 22, 2013. http://www.buzzfeed.com/jeffsmithmo/a-former-prisoner-on-what-orange-is-the-new-black-gets-right (accessed July 15, 2015).

5 *Oz* (1997–2003) was known for its unflinching, often gratuitous representations of prison life.

6 Terry Gross, "'Orange' Creator Jenji Kohan: 'Piper Was My Trojan Horse,'" *National Public Radio*, August 13, 2013. www.npr.org.
7 Gray, "Subject(ed) to Recognition," 782.
8 See Ruth Wilson Gilmore, *Golden Gulag: Prisons, Surplus, Crisis, and Opposition in Globalizing California* (Berkeley: University of California Press, 2007).
9 For more on this topic, see Nicholas Mirzoeff, *The Right to Look: A Counterhistory of Visuality* (Durham, NC: Duke University Press Books, 2011); Sasha Torres, *Black, White, and in Color: Television and Black Civil Rights* (Princeton, NJ: Princeton University Press, 2003); Herman Gray, *Watching Race: Television and the Struggle for Blackness* (Minneapolis: University of Minnesota Press, 2004); Nicole R. Fleetwood, *Troubling Vision: Performance, Visuality, and Blackness* (Chicago: University of Chicago Press, 2011); bell hooks, *Black Looks: Race and Representation* (Boston, MA: South End Press, 1992).
10 Fleetwood, *Troubling Vision: Performance, Visuality, and Blackness*, 37.
11 Although several media scholars have made similar arguments, in the interest of space, I focus primarily on Gray's article. See also Sarah Banet-Weiser, *Authentic™*.
12 Kara Keeling, *The Witch's Flight: The Cinematic, the Black Femme, and the Image of Common Sense* (Durham: Duke University Press Books, 2007).
13 Gray, "Subject(ed) to Recognition," 785.
14 See Gray, *Watching Race*; Saidiya V. Hartman, *Scenes of Subjection: Terror, Slavery, and Self-Making in Nineteenth-Century America* (New York: Oxford University Press, 1997); Mirzoeff, *The Right to Look*.
15 For more about the history and mechanisms of security states, see Paul Amar, *The Security Archipelago: Human-Security States, Sexuality Politics, and the End of Neoliberalism* (Duke University Press, 2013); Judith Butler, *Precarious Life: The Power of Mourning and Violence* (New York: Verso, 2006); Vijay Prashad, *Keeping up with the Dow Joneses: Stocks, Jails, Welfare* (Cambridge, MA: South End Press, 2003).
16 Michel Foucault, *Discipline and Punish: The Birth of the Prison*, trans. Alan Sheridan (New York: Random House, 1992), 19.
17 When asked by Terry Gross why she seems interested in stories about privileged white women and criminality, Kohan responded, "In a lot of ways Piper was my Trojan Horse. You're not going to go into a network and sell a show on really fascinating tales of black women, and Latina women, and old women and criminals. But if you take this white girl, this sort of fish out of water, and you follow her in, you can then expand your world and tell all of those other stories. But it's a hard sell to just go in and try to sell those stories initially. The girl next door, the cool blonde, is a very easy access point, and it's relatable for a lot of audiences and a lot of networks looking for a certain demographic. It's useful." See Gross, "'Orange' Creator Jenji Kohan: 'Piper Was My Trojan Horse,'" *National Public Radio*, August 13, 2013. www.npr.org.
18 Gray, *Watching Race*, 16.
19 The logic being that customers will most identify with authentic brand cultures, and as members of these brand, cultures will exhibit brand loyalty. For more on the relationship between authenticity and branding, see Sarah Banet-Weiser, *Authentic™*.
20 See Zook, *Color by Fox*; Robert E. Weems, *Desegregating the Dollar: African American Consumerism in the Twentieth Century* (New York: New York University Press, 1998).
21 See Karl Hagstrom Miller, *Segregating Sound: Inventing Folk and Pop Music in the Age of Jim Crow* (Durham, NC: Duke University Press Books, 2010).

22 Todd Gitlin, *Inside Prime Time* (Berkeley: University of California Press, 2000), 14.

23 In the late 1990s, HBO executives decided that creating original shows would differentiate HBO from its competitors. With the slogan "It's not TV, it's HBO," HBO built a brand identity based on a critique of contemporary television. HBO was a television for viewers with taste who were tired of the conventionality of TV programming. See Gary R. Edgerton and Jeffrey P. Jones, *The Essential HBO Reader* (Lexington: University Press of Kentucky, 2008).

24 Nancy Hass, "Reed Hastings on *Arrested Development, House of Cards*, and the Future of Netflix," *GQ*, January 29, 2013.

25 The reaction to the announcement that the DVD mailing service would continue as the newly created Qwikster was so negative that Netflix reversed its decision, though the price increase for streaming remained.

26 Victor Luckerson, "2015 Will Be the Year Netflix Goes 'Full HBO,'" *Time*, January 20, 2015. http://time.com/3675669/netflix-hbo/ (accessed July 15, 2015).

27 See Deborah L. Jaramillo, "The Family Racket: AOL Time Warner, HBO, the Sopranos, and the Construction of a Quality Brand," *Journal of Communication Inquiry* 26.1 (2002): 59–75. doi:10.1177/0196859902026001005.

28 "Kevin Spacey Mactaggart Lecture—Full Text," *The Guardian*, August 22, 2013. http://www.theguardian.com/media/interactive/2013/aug/22/kevin-spacey-mactaggart-lecture-full-text (accessed July 15, 2015).

29 The following quote from a 2014 *The Guardian* article about Netflix exemplifies this assumption: "Instead of making a show and then hoping it catches on with a big audience, Netflix crunches its subscriber base viewing data to identify fans of specific genres and then looks at TV formulas that it already knows are likely to appeal to them." Mark Sweney, "Netflix Gathers Detailed Viewer Data to Guide Its Search for the next Hit," *The Guardian*, February 23, 2014. http://www.theguardian.com/media/2014/feb/23/netflix-viewer-data-house-of-cards (accessed July 15, 2015).

30 Scott Neumyer, "How 'Orange Is the New Black' Became Netflix's Best Series," *Rolling Stone*, August 13, 2013. http://www.rollingstone.com/tv/news/how-orange-is-the-new-black-became-netflixs-best-series-20130813 (accessed July 15, 2015).

31 Andrew Hirsh, "Netflix: Using Big Data to Hook Us on Original Programming," *Technology Advice*, September 7, 2013. http://technologyadvice.com/business-intelligence/blog/how-netflix-is-using-big-data-to get people-hooked-on-its-original-programming/ (accessed July 15, 2015).

32 Gray, "Subject(ed) to Recognition," 782.

33 Neumyer, "How 'Orange Is the New Black' Became Netflix's Best Series.'"

34 Hank Stuever, "Netflix's 'Orange Is the New Black': Brilliance Behind Bars," *Washington Post*, July 11, 2013. http://www.washingtonpost.com/entertainment/tv/netflixs-orange-is-the-new-black-brilliance-behind-bars/2013/07/11/d52f911e-e9aa-11e2-8f22-de4bd2a2bd39_story.html (accessed July 15, 2015).

Part Three

The Business of Media Convergence

11

Questioning Netflix's Revolutionary Impact: Changes in the Business and Consumption of Television

Cameron Lindsey

In a climate of sweeping change, traditional broadcast and cable television sit at the heart of the storm. According to the Nielsen Total Audience Report for 2014, roughly 2.6 million American households are broadband only.[1] This means these households consume all of their media through nontraditional models including online viewing, subscription services, apps, and so on, but they do not have a cable subscription nor do they watch broadcast television. This number represents an increase of 113 percent from 2013,[2] and the number continues to grow. *Time* reported that 40 percent of households subscribe to some kind of video-on-demand service (Netflix, Hulu, etc.)—which represents an increase from 35 percent in 2013.[3] This is not to suggest that broadcast and cable television have already lost the battle against new media; far from it, as that same Nielsen report indicates the average viewing time per week ranges between just under sixteen and a half hours to more than forty-seven hours on traditional television.[4] Clearly broadcast and cable still hold a tight grip on the distribution of televisual content, but the effects of time-shifted viewing (digital video recorder [DVR] and video on demand [VOD]), mobile and app viewing, online networks and subscription services, and the ever-increasing number of ways to watch content illegally or extra-legally on the web are becoming more evident in the numbers year after year.

Of these new media competitors, Netflix holds a particularly coveted position thanks to its strong brand identification, large user base, critically acclaimed original content, and much more. *Forbes* reported that Netflix's subscriber base grew by 4.33 million in the last quarter of 2014, reaching a global total of 57.4 million—an amazing growth since the company's founding in 1997.[5] While Netflix currently stands as the biggest success story in this transition away from traditional television media, many of the same aspects that have contributed to its success could, when implemented by others, lead to Netflix's demise. By first investigating the ways in which broadcast and cable television are losing ground in this media battle, and then analyzing why Netflix has become the biggest winner, this chapter aims to illuminate how Netflix's current success has created a media environment that may yet endanger its long-term survival. The chapter will then go on to discuss some ways Netflix might avoid this fate and maintain its position as a leader among a growing assortment of online viewing options.

Before delving into Netflix's hypothetical future, it is worth considering the other components that are contributing to the evolution of broadcast and cable television. The most important factor in this changing environment is the phenomenon known as "time-shifting." Initially introduced as part of the legal defense for videocassette recorders (VCRs), the term is now associated with DVRs like TiVo and with various VOD options offered by cable and satellite providers or through over-the-top (OTT) services like Netflix. In general, time-shifting now refers to any method of watching television whereby viewers watch programming at a time other than when it originally aired. As it is still connected to the traditional model of television, this does not seem to present a problem, and time-shifted television is not entirely an issue as VOD and certain playback features have ingrained advertisements that viewers cannot skip. DVR and Tivo, however, have caused cable and broadcast networks to rethink their programming despite not undermining television's bottom line or its ability to generate advertising revenue. As both allow viewers to record programs and watch them later at their own leisure, audiences no longer sit through commercial breaks while watching their favorite shows but fast-forward through them instead. Largely, though, the response to time-shifted television by cable and broadcasting has mirrored the way Hollywood responded to home video. The suggestion is that broadcast and cable are concerned about the effects of time-shifted television, but they are not necessarily changing their format entirely, and the practice is certainly not revolutionizing the way we consume media.

Although companies still pay dearly for these commercials spots, the value of these spots has decreased significantly as fewer and fewer people watch them.[6] Perhaps this has contributed to the increase in shows emphasizing "liveness" including spectaculars, sports, and reality television with interactive aspects. Even in these scenarios, though, audiences are not guaranteed to watch the advertisements. In contrast, online viewing promises advertisers a captive audience. Typically only one advertisement appears before a given program, thus fewer spots exist for revenue. However, the audience must watch the advertisement in order to see the program, barring additional ad-blocking software. If most viewers prove willing to accept ad-supported online platforms, advertisers may begin to favor this model due to its captive audience.[7]

Many viewers prefer to see zero advertisements but still want to watch network and cable content. To do this, many viewers download programs illegally or opt for extralegal, morally gray means of accessing content. Though these options undermine the commercial logic of media advertising, some of these options engage the viewer better than even the original broadcasts might. For example, some sites maintain a constant stream of their television screens to a limited number of online viewers. Each stream has its own appeal, but hosts will often engage their community of viewers by having a chat room, asking questions or hosting a discussion during commercial breaks, or even playing games with the viewers. These kinds of activities encourage viewers to watch online as opposed to watching the same content on broadcast or cable. This type of viewing, however, negatively affects the program's ratings and the ability of the program to increase its advertising revenues. Broadcast and cable have tried to replicate this engagement to a certain extent with "second screen" activities and by pushing viewers to engage with their programming through social media, extra footage, or behind-the-scenes clips online at the network's website, but these pale in comparison to the level of involvement offered by these extralegal sites. Altogether, these illegal options, the rise of subscription services like Netflix and Hulu and online streaming sites like YouTube or Twitch, as well as the spread of mobile apps have acclimated audiences to the benefits—namely greater accessibility and convenience—of time-shifted media consumption. Terms like "binge-watching" are now more ubiquitous for the common viewer than the notion of the family gathering around the home's television set to watch that week's newest episode of primetime television.[8]

Broadcast and cable television have been largely unsuccessful in keeping up with these new forms of media consumption and what audiences now think television should be. The clearest indicator of this failure is the spectacular rise of Netflix. As stated before, Netflix now boasts over 50 million subscribers worldwide, and that number increases every quarter.[9] As impressive as these numbers may be, a more detailed look at Netflix's strategic advantages will better illuminate why Netflix has had such success. Netflix's success is especially surprising when considering its competitors. Besides broadcast and cable networks, Netflix also competes with Amazon's VOD service and premium channels like HBO. Netflix, however, has a penchant for beating out bigger, notable competitors. Most obviously, Netflix's success played a large role in the demise of video store giant Blockbuster. Many will tally this success up to the fact that brick-and-mortar stores, like Blockbuster, cannot hope to succeed when customers have another service that sends them the product by mail or streams it directly to their computers. However, those same people forget that Blockbuster also offered a DVD-by-mail service (a service that was, in some ways, superior to Netflix's as it allowed users to bring the DVDs into a store to exchange them for a faster turnaround). Furthermore, Blockbuster also offered an instant streaming service that was almost identical to the structure of Netflix's model. Not only that, but retail giant Walmart also offered a DVD-by-mail service,[10] and it even currently offers an instant viewing option through its partnership with Vudu. In both of these battles, against Blockbuster and against Walmart, Netflix managed to continue its financial success, and its success can be attributed to a number of things. Blunders at Blockbuster, including a poor relationship between investors and the company's CEO, deserve some of the blame,[11] but Netflix deserves its own credit. While Walmart had to apologize for such mistakes as suggesting the movie *Planet of the Apes* to users of their service looking for films related to Black History Month,[12] and while Blockbuster struggled to find a way to get their DVDs to users and back again in a timely manner, Netflix flourished. Netflix's prediction algorithm is somewhat legendary and they refuse to share many details surrounding its huge success, and their mailing system, closely connected with the U.S. Postal Service, had users consistently receiving their next DVDs within just a couple of days of sending their last one back.

This success in competing with larger, more established companies helps to contextualize Netflix's relationship with some of its current rivals. Today, Netflix competes against two similar services again backed by much larger entities: Amazon Prime and Hulu, the latter of which is a joint venture between the NBC/Universal Television Group, the Fox Broadcasting Company, and the Disney/ABC Television Group. As before, Netflix leads in number of subscribers, and does so by tens of millions.[13] Even for its paying subscribers, Hulu Plus users must sit through numerous advertisements before, and sometimes even during, their viewings. For users accustomed to the Netflix model, these advertisements can seem burdensome and annoying. For many Netflix users, the only advertisements they watch are when they choose to view the newest trailer for a Netflix original series. Amazon Prime does not have any advertisements, but the majority of Amazon's library consists of a la carte viewing options where the user must pay a fee for each movie or episode rental—albeit a generally reduced rate for Prime subscribers. For users that are already paying a monthly subscription fee, this additional price for some content causes frustration, and Netflix's model of offering an enormous library of movies and shows, all covered by the one monthly cost, has attracted a large number of subscribers away from the more established Amazon brand.

Perhaps the most discussed rivalry for Netflix, however, is with HBO. In an interview with the *New York Times*, Netflix's CEO, Reed Hastings, described the rivalry between HBO and Netflix as "like the Yankees and the Red Sox."[14] This should not come as much of a surprise to anyone closely following Netflix's trajectory. The company began by distributing movies and programming from other companies. It then moved forward to financing and creating its own original content, and now the name Netflix is synonymous with quality content. In fact, this trajectory closely follows that of HBO's but on a different platform. Now, both companies intend to compete with one another by offering better content and better methods of watching that content. HBO launched HBO Go in 2010 as a "watch anywhere" service that allowed audiences that already paid for an HBO subscription to watch a catalogue of content, including movies and past HBO shows and documentaries, on a variety of devices. Accessing HBO Go required users to have a cable subscription as it was the only means of having the required HBO subscription to use the service, but in 2014, the company announced plans to launch HBO Now, which allows potential viewers to sign up for an HBO subscription without any cable contract whatsoever. Here it would seem that HBO, boasting the powerful Time Warner as its parent company, is poised to beat Netflix, but so far the battle has played in Netflix's favor.[15] Perhaps the most obvious reason for this is the accessibility of Netflix. Netflix comes preloaded on most mobile devices and tablets today as well as on many gaming systems, set-top boxes, and computers. The same cannot be said for HBO Go and HBO Now. These services are simply not accessible on certain gaming devices, set-top boxes, and mobile devices. Unless HBO becomes as ubiquitous an app as Netflix already is, this rivalry will seem more of a blowout in Netflix's favor. It is also possible, though, that premium subscription services could pair up with already existing streaming services, as HBO has done with Amazon and Showtime with Hulu, in order to beat out Netflix, but the current pairings have not had a noticeable effect on Netflix.

Finally, the dark horse competitor against Netflix remains the illegal downloading and extralegal streaming sites. I use the phrase "extralegal streaming sites" here to refer to sites that host streams of content they do not own. These differ from sites offering content to download because, while it is illegal to download or distribute for profit content one does not own, one has not necessarily committed a crime by viewing a stream of pirated material. Other sites and services, such as the popular Popcorn Time or Project Free TV, operate legally by providing viewers with an accessible layout and interface that directs them to streams or downloads hosted by other sites, but these other sites may be of questionable integrity. That being said, though these sites offer a practically unlimited library of content from around the world as soon as (and sometimes even before) it is available to the public, questions surrounding legality scare away many potential viewers. Furthermore, without heavy virus protection, visiting some of these sites can result in malware and other hazardous additions to computers. Finally, these streams and downloads are often unreliable. Frequently the quality is so atrocious that the content is practically unrecognizable. For these reasons, viewers opt for the safer, more reliable, and legal option of paying for a Netflix subscription despite the illegal downloads and extralegal sites offering as much, if not more, content. In fact, Netflix's chief content officer, Ted Sarandos, said in an interview with Stuff.tv that "the best way to combat piracy was not legislatively or criminally but by giving good options," and also noted that traffic drops at BitTorrent, a popular cyberlocker of sorts known as a hub for questionable media distribution, when Netflix enters a new territory.[16]

Even considering all of these benefits and advantages Netflix has over the other services, it offers yet more unique, individual selling points. Most obvious among its advantages, Netflix offers a plethora of high-quality original content unavailable on any of the other services. From noteworthy titles such as *House of Cards* and *Orange Is the New Black* to less acclaimed fan favorites such as *Hemlock Grove* and the reboot of *Arrested Development*, Netflix provides numerous shows on par with a broadcast or cable network. This even overlooks the many titles sporting the "Netflix Original" logo in the top corner—a moniker that Netflix uses to refer to any program to which it has sole distribution rights within the United States. These same programs, though bringing in an unreported number of viewers,[17] sport an impressive amount of praise from critics and numerous awards—Netflix programs boasted an impressive 14 Emmy nominations in 2013. Furthermore, these programs reach audiences around the globe as Netflix continues to expand into other countries and regions and offers a variety of programs in other languages and with high-quality subtitles. These advantages set Netflix apart from its rivals and other emerging alternatives. They also explain why it has had such success amidst the changing landscape of broadcast and cable television.

Even with this success, there are still questions as to whether Netflix will remain on top. While Netflix has helped change the ways companies distribute media, their long-term success is still in question. As opposed to a sustainable, revolutionizing force behind media distribution, Netflix may simply be one of its early instigators or innovators. A revival of the 2014 debates surrounding net neutrality, and more importantly any change in legislation, could prove a death sentence for Netflix. Netflix users expect content to stream seamlessly. Changes in regulatory policies such as net neutrality could result in disruptions to Netflix's service and prompt subscribers to watch broadcast, cable, or time-shifted television instead. Moreover, the same aspects of Netflix's service that currently appear as benefits and advantages could become threats in different hands. That is to say, what makes Netflix great now will continue to be co-opted by its competitors. These rivals may also be able to use their size and access to additional resources—via their media conglomerate affiliations—to beat Netflix at its own game. Today, Netflix faces increasing costs for content licensing. According to *Forbes*, Netflix spent over $1.3 million dollars per episode for one of AMC's hit shows, *The Walking Dead*. Furthermore, the same report notes that "content costs have been rising steadily for Netflix. According to its third quarter 2014 results, streaming content obligations increased from around $7.2 billion at the end of 2013 to more than $8.8 billion as of September 30, 2014," and importantly emphasizes that content expenses account for over 70 percent of Netflix's total expenses.[18] These content costs do not show signs of decreasing, and Netflix has few options if they intend to make a profit amidst these rising costs. As one option, Netflix could increase the cost of its monthly subscription; however, history has shown that this could easily backfire. In 2011, when Netflix raised its subscription costs for users that wanted both instant streaming and DVD-by-mail services, they lost roughly 800,000 subscribers.[19] Though Netflix recovered from the debacle, a price hike could cause similar effects or worse. In this hypothetical future where content costs force Netflix to seek extra revenue to make a profit, advertisements or pay-per-view options could prove useful. As mentioned previously, though, both options would make Netflix nearly indistinguishable from its competitors, Hulu and Amazon Prime, both of which have the support of their larger parent companies. Furthermore, when Netflix recently began testing trailers for their original content in front of programs for some users, there was a large public outcry, and Netflix executives had to act fast to reassure users that third-party advertising was not being added.[20]

All of this speculation assumes, however, that Netflix will falter amidst rising content costs, but there are additional problems that may arise for Netflix in the future. Free viewing options, both existing and potential, will likely present major hurdles for Netflix in the years to come. A particularly difficult challenge comes from the broadcast and cable networks themselves. CBS currently offers a service called CBS All Access.[21] For a monthly price that is less than Netflix's, users have access to a plethora of CBS shows including current prime-time shows, cult classics, and oldies. Furthermore, CBS All Access includes the ability to watch live programming such as NCAA men's basketball, game shows, award shows, and reality television. These programs can also be live streamed through an app on most computers, tablets, and smart phones. CBS All Access offers a huge library of shows and event programming as well as the ability to stream live TV anywhere at a monthly cost that undercuts

Netflix, Hulu, and Amazon by dollars per month. Now imagine if a broadcast or cable network were to offer this same kind of service for free. The service would almost certainly require advertisements to play before programs, but Hulu subscribers and other online viewers have shown their willingness to watch a small number of advertisements. Not only would this hypothetical service provide a safe and legal way to watch the network's programs, but it would also mean prospective viewers would more likely see that network's programs at the source, viewing that network's advertisements and further benefiting its overall ratings. In this hypothetical, the network could still sell licensing rights to Netflix and other services (just as CBS does now with many of the programs on CBS All Access). To take this hypothetical a step further, imagine if Fox uploaded every episode of their hit animated show *The Simpsons* onto their website in an easy-to-access format. This would not require a cable subscription to login or watch; it could be streamed on most devices, and a single advertisement played before each episode. The implications are huge. The rights to *The Simpsons* could still be sold to Netflix (and Hulu Plus, Amazon Prime, and as many other streaming sites as possible) for millions of dollars per episode, but Fox would also profit from their own showing of the program as well. Netflix taught its users to watch programming online. It instilled users with the notion that television doesn't have to be watched on a TV. So far, Netflix has profited from this shift while other more dated models have lagged behind. But if the broadcast and cable networks develop a way to easily access and stream their content on a variety of devices, new and old alike, even with some advertising, Netflix could see its hold on online viewing quickly disappear.

Another evolving aspect of online watching behavior involves the aforementioned extralegal streaming options. As ad-blocking and antivirus software continues to improve, content seekers may feel more comfortable going to these sites and seeing the same content that Netflix offers for a monthly fee. Besides the lower price, many of these sites also offer better ways for viewers to engage in the content they're watching, and entire communities form around the shared, online viewing experience offered as part of the moderated chats and forums linked to certain extralegal streams. In *Shadow Economies of Cinema: Mapping Informal Film Distribution*, Ramon Lobato suggests that many of these extralegal sites exist solely to draw viewers to a cavalcade of advertisements before directing viewers to links or downloads that may or may not work, and may or may not be legal.[22] More often, though, sites will offer streaming content at no cost and with no advertisements. For example, I watched much of the popular series *Breaking Bad* on an extralegal online stream. While searching for ways to engage with others during the show, I stumbled across a site that showed the program via a live stream from a person's television, but the stream's host would mute the television during advertisements, speculate on the show with other viewers in a chat, and even play games with viewers. What's more, all of this was done with no cost and featured no advertising of any sort. This site, then, was a superior way to watch *Breaking Bad* because of the way I was able to engage with the show, and I found myself preferring the stream even though I paid for a cable subscription and could watch the show in better quality on AMC.

On the subject of engagement, sites like YouTube and Vimeo, which allow users to curate their own sites, have seen a surge of new and quality content including a plethora of original series, all of which offer users numerous free options for engagement through comments, replies, voting, and so forth. YouTube alone has networks of corporate-managed channels and programs that provide free content to different audiences. Cartoon Hangover, for example, offers a variety of animated programs from the creators of popular shows like *Adventure Time*, and the Public Broadcasting Service even has its own channel called PBS Digital Studios, which produces numerous programs every week.

Netflix's biggest potential downfall, however, comes from two sources that are already well-established foes. First, Netflix has set itself apart by offering, along with its generous library of other shows and movies, its own programs as well. Now, however, some of its competitors have begun producing their own content too. Amazon recently released *Transparent* to significant acclaim, and the company has produced other programs including *Alpha House* and *Mozart in the Jungle*—though none received as much attention as *Transparent*. Hulu has also begun producing original programs for sole distribution through their service. One can only assume that both companies will continue making original programs, and a major hit could draw some Netflix's subscribers to another service just as earlier subscribers chose Netflix over other services for their original content. Furthermore, newcomers such as Yahoo Screen are following this same model, though it currently offers its programs for free. Yahoo has begun creating new episodes of the popular series *Community*, which previously aired on NBC. As more and more potential eyes turn to their computer, phone, and tablet screens for content as opposed to broadcast and cable television alone, more companies will see the potential in producing original programming distributed over the web. Such a diversification of media will devalue Netflix by comparison if viewers opt more for a cheaper smorgasbord approach to their online viewing than the more costly one-stop-shop offered by Netflix.

As Netflix pushes into international markets, the popularity of streaming sites dedicated to content tailored to specific genres and even niche audiences has the potential to disrupt Netflix's progress. In the case of anime, this alternative streaming site already exists. Crunchyroll offers streaming anime (as well as manga, news, forums, a store, and more) with no ads and early access to shows premiering in Japan for $6.95 a month. Many readers familiar with the site, however, likely know it as a free way to access a massive library of high-quality streaming anime with small ads before content, as the majority of its content does not require a subscription. This kind of site and community is not specific to the anime genre either. TV dramas, which is another particularly popular genre, especially in the East Asian markets that Netflix hopes to move into,[23] has many websites and services dedicated to streaming content. Between DramaFever, Viki, and even user-curated sites like YouTube and its counterparts, viewers seeking high-quality streams of TV dramas, be they Korean, Japanese, Chinese, or even the popular Mexican telenovelas, have numerous free options to choose from. Many of these sites run completely legally and maintain themselves through short ads before the content. While this might not work for all genres and types of television (it seems hard to imagine a free site dedicated to streaming American sitcoms), the simple fact that these sites exist, providing high-quality content without undue cost, should give Netflix pause as they attempt to move into other global markets.

Clearly, Netflix has a variety of issues on the horizon. Emerging niche markets, the advancement of its competitors, subscribers' preferences for cheaper or free options, as well as other unforeseen possibilities could arise to topple Netflix in this post-broadcast, post-cable world. First, and perhaps foremost, Netflix must continue releasing high-quality, original content. More exclusive content will elevate Netflix from a simple streaming service to a full-blown network of its own that not only competes with HBO and other premium channels but with the broadcast and cable networks as well. Netflix clearly recognizes this. In the aforementioned *New York Times* article, the author noted that Netflix plans on releasing 320 hours of original programming in 2015.[24] Surprisingly, though, Netflix does not own licensing rights to many of its best-known programs. Netflix, for example, does not own *House of Cards*—instead the production company Media Rights Capital owns these rights. This too will change, and should, if Netflix plans on keeping its competitive edge. In an interview with *Bloomberg Business*, CEO Reed Hastings said that the company plans on taking a larger role in its original programming including production and ownership.[25] This, of course, would mean high risk for Netflix. If a program were to underperform, this type of move puts Netflix at the mercy of rising content costs. If Netflix owns its own programs, it can decide to offer them on its own service and cash out through distributing licensing rights to others. It could also begin making money through the small, though not negligible, DVD sales of its programs. In short, just as networks are emulating Netflix and moving online, Netflix should draw on the networks' earlier strategies to monetize programming in all possible ways.

Netflix may yet take other, less predictable steps. In the aforementioned Nielsen Total Audience Report, research showed that kids and teens between the ages of two and seventeen watch a sizable amount of television, but they watch very little of it outside traditional broadcast and/or cable television.[26] While most children and teens likely cannot subscribe to Netflix themselves, Netflix should consider marketing more to parents. More optional parental control features could entice parents to subscribe to the service as an alternative to the complicated and confusing parental controls of cable. Netflix does currently have a "kids" section when creating users, and children likely find the image-heavy menu easy to use, but parent-geared features as well as more exclusive programming geared directly to children, such as the popular *Turbo FAST* and *All Hail King Julien* (both adaptations of DreamWorks animated films), could drive up subscription with this audience that is otherwise undervalued in the internet watching market.

In this same vein, Netflix should develop better ways for its users to engage with the content and one another. The community-building aspects of current extralegal streaming sites keep viewers engaged, and encourage them to share their experience with others. While any such attempts by Netflix should remain optional—many users will simply want to watch their content uninhibited—forums, chat rooms, live commentary by users and/or content creators, connection through social media platforms, and any other number of possibilities could only benefit Netflix. The company has attempted to do this in some ways through a connection with users' Facebook accounts, but the service has been hindered by problems and it does little to actually connect subscribers together. Considering the number of (somewhat facetious) articles suggesting Netflix double as or team up with a dating site,[27] it would seem that many Netflix subscribers would welcome some kind of interactivity with the service, as well as with their fellow subscribers, beyond a "see what your Facebook friends are watching" section on their Netflix menu. Finally, perhaps the best suggestion for Netflix moving forward comes in the form of things not to do. As mentioned before, other regions already have favored streaming services, and many of the services elsewhere offer their programming for free or with minimal advertising. Making a costly move into another market without heavily investigating the preexisting online viewing habits could prove dangerous and costly for the company. Innovation, however, is key. None of Netflix's competitors have chosen complacency as their tactic moving forward, and Netflix would be wise to continue innovating and continue pushing the traditional definition of televisual media as it has since its creation in 1997. This is how Netflix helped start the trend toward digital media, and this is how Netflix will successfully come out of this dynamic time as a revolutionary force is media distribution and viewing and not simply an early innovator.

Change remains constant in the hectic realm of television. Now, the very definition of television seems up for debate. With how ingrained Netflix and online viewing has become in the day-to-day lives of many people, it is hard to imagine a future without them. Looking back, though, Netflix burst onto the media scene quickly, and with all of its competitors, it may disappear just as quickly. Or it may not. Netflix may lead the pack in the new era of internet distribution and online viewing of media as it is doing presently. On the other hand, traditional broadcast and cable television may play a larger role in the online viewing market and displace Netflix altogether. It is also possible that extralegal, or even illegal options, will usher viewers into a new realm that overturns everything we know about mass media distribution, consumption, and even production. There is much to speculate on. What can be said with certainty is that in the years to come, what we, as viewers, consider television will see changes.

Notes

1 "The Total Audience Report," *Nielsen*, December 3, 2014. http://www.nielsen.com/us/en/insights/reports/2014/the-total-audience-report.html (accessed July 27, 2015).

2 Victor Luckerson, "Fewer People Than Ever Are Watching TV," *Time*, December 3, 2014. http://time.com/3615387/tv-viewership-declining-nielsen (accessed July 27, 2015).

3 Ibid.

4 "Total Audience Report."

5 Lauren Gensler, "Netflix Soars on Subscriber Growth," *Forbes*, January 20, 2015. http://www.forbes.com/sites/laurengensler/2015/01/20/netflix-soars-on-subscriber-growth (accessed July 27, 2015).

6 Jim Edwards, "Brutal: 50% Decline in TV Viewership Shows Why Your Cable Bill Is So High," *Business Insider*, January 31, 2013. http://www.businessinsider.com/brutal-50-decline-in-tv-viewership-shows-why-your-cable-bill-is-so-high-2013-1 (accessed July 27, 2015). As the article succinctly puts it, "As the number of big, unfragmented audiences declines, [TV advertising spots] become more valuable," and, "So now advertisers are paying much more, for much less."

7 Pamela Marsh, Zeus Ferrao, and Gintare Anuseviciute, "The Impact of Binge Viewing," *Annalect*, July 2014. http://www.annalect.com/impact-binge-viewing (accessed July 27, 2015).

8 Kelly West, "Unsurprising: Netflix Survey Indicates People Like to Binge-Watch TV," *CinemaBlend*, 2013. http://www.cinemablend.com/television/Unsurprising-Netflix-Survey-Indicates-People-Like-Binge-Watch-TV-61045.html (accessed July 27, 2015). This survey points out that 61 percent of respondents claimed to binge-watch regularly—thus suggesting it is not a trend but "the new normal."

9 Gensler, "Netflix Soars on Subscriber Growth."

10 Gina Keating, *Netflixed: The Epic Battle for America's Eyeballs* (New York: Portfolio, 2012). See especially: 159 and 225. When this service ended in 2005 (and then ended its download service entirely in 2008), Walmart effectively gave all of its subscribers to Netflix.

11 Ibid.

12 Ylan Q. Mui, "Wal-Mart Website Makes Racial Connections," *Washington Post*, January 6, 2006. http://www.washingtonpost.com/wp-dyn/content/article/2006/01/05/AR2006010502176.html (accessed July 27, 2015).

13 Jillian D'Onfro, "Amazon Prime Versus Netflix Versus Hulu Plus: Which Should You Pay For?" *Business Insider*, April 25, 2014. http://www.businessinsider.com/amazon-prime-versus-netflix-versus-hulu-plus-2014-4 (accessed July 27, 2015). The actual number of subscribers for each service can be difficult to pinpoint as each company chooses to release it's numbers at different times, but this *Business Insider* article from 2014 estimates that Netflix had 35.67 million subscribers, Hulu Plus had 5 million subscribers, and Amazon Prime has "at least" 20 million users (though this does not indicate the number of users that are engaging with Amazon Prime Instant Viewing).

14 Emily Steel, "Netflix Is Betting Its Future on Exclusive Programming," *The New York Times*, April 19, 2015. http://www.nytimes.com/2015/04/20/business/media/netflix-is-betting-its-future-on-exclusive-programming.html (accessed July 27, 2015).

15 Emily Steel, "Netflix, Amazon and Hulu No Longer Find Themselves Upstarts in Online Streaming," *The New York Times*, March 24, 2015. http://www.nytimes.com/2015/03/25/business/media/netflix-amazon-and-hulu-no-longer-find-themselves-tvs-upstarts.html (accessed July 27, 2015). According to this article, Netflix beats out HBO in number of U.S. subscribers at 40 million to 30 million.

16 Luke Edwards, "Netflix's Ted Sarandos Talks *Arrested Development*, 4K and Reviving Old Shows," *Stuff.tv*, Haymarket Media Group, May 1, 2013. http://www.stuff.tv/news/netflixs-ted-sarandos-talks-arrested-development-4k-and-reviving-old-shows (accessed July 27, 2015).

17 Those who watch Netflix closely know that the company infamously holds most of its audience numbers secret, and this is especially true of the numbers regarding its original programs.

18 Trefis Team, "Why Growing Content Costs Are a Necessary Evil for Netflix," *Forbes*, December 29, 2014. http://www.forbes.com/sites/greatspeculations/2014/12/29/why-growing-content-costs-are-a-necessary-evil-for-netflix (accessed July 27, 2015).
19 Julianne Pepitone, "Netflix Hikes Prices for DVDs + Streaming," *CNN Money*, CNN, July 12, 2011. http://money.cnn.com/2011/07/12/technology/netflix_unlimited_dvd (accessed July 27, 2015).
20 Mike Snider, "Netflix CEO: No Advertising Coming to the Streaming Service," *USA Today*, June 2, 2015. http://www.usatoday.com/story/tech/2015/06/02/netflix-ceo-reed-hastings-no-advertising/28367663 (accessed July 27, 2015).
21 "CBS All Access," CBS, 2015. http://www.cbs.com/all-access/ (accessed July 27, 2015).
22 Ramon Lobato, *Shadow Economies of Cinema: Mapping Informal Film Distribution* (London: British Film Institute, 2012), 95–109. I have cited all of Lobato's discussions on "The Grey Internet" which goes into great detail on the various kinds of legal, extralegal, and illegal sites that distribute media. It also discusses their reasons for existing and the ways they are shaping media distribution on a larger scale.
23 Elsa Keslassy, "Mipcom: Netflix's Ted Sarandos Eyes Asia Expansion, Talks Recent Movie Deals," *Variety*, October 14, 2014. http://variety.com/2014/tv/global/mipcom-netflix-ceo-ted-sarandos-talks-about-potential-expansion-across-asia-move-into-original-feature-films-and-recent-launch-across-continental-europe-1201329381 (accessed July 27, 2015).
24 Steel, "Netflix Is Betting Its Future on Exclusive Programming."
25 Lucas Shaw, "Netflix's Pursuit of TV Domination Has a New Step: Ownership," *Bloomberg Business*, April 21, 2015. http://www.bloomberg.com/news/articles/2015-04-21/netflix-s-pursuit-of-tv-domination-has-a-new-step-ownership (accessed July 27, 2015).
26 Ibid.
27 These suggestions float around both Tumblr (with several thousands of reblogs and shares) and Reddit's "crazyideas" subreddit, but it seems to be mostly tongue-in-cheek.

12

Individual Disruptors and Economic Gamechangers: Netflix, New Media, and Neoliberalism

Gerald Sim

In many ways television is being disrupted in a dramatic way and Netflix is a perfect example of that.

Ken Auletta, *Charlie Rose*, January 29, 2014

In the final week of January 2014, Netflix's stock price surged an incredible 21 percent on news in the company's quarterly earnings report that the service had added more than 4 million new subscribers worldwide.[1] Those shares grew by another 36 percent over the next month. It represented a stark turnaround from a pricing and public relations debacle approximately two years earlier, when an unwelcome price increase amid plans to charge customers separately for its "Netflix Instant" streaming service incurred the wrath of subscribers and investors. Netflix aborted the idea, but was forced to claw its way out of a sustained nightmarish period when it lost customers and the faith of market watchers. But claw its way out it did, which was reflected in both its latest news and forecasts of future business. Two weeks later, Ken Auletta, media writer for *The New Yorker*, published a 6,100-word article titled "Outside the Box: Netflix and the Future of Television," documenting Netflix's major role in slaying Blockbuster Video, popularizing mobile platforms of media consumption, and radically altering the television business.[2] Auletta promoted the story with an appearance on the *Charlie Rose* show. Much of what he reported in the magazine can be gleaned from various industry studies undertaken in various quarters over the last decade[3]; Auletta's account, however, rubberstamped by the imprimatur of Rose's late-night sobriety, is noteworthy. I spotlight it less as a definitive record than an ossified popular narrative of putative discourses situating Netflix in media history. In many ways it also underlines the current and possibly future ways with which scholars grasp Netflix's impact.

Auletta's lede takes his readers to a 2000 meeting in Dallas between Netflix CEO Reed Hastings and executives from Blockbuster, long-time leader in the video rental business. Hastings offered to sell 49 percent of his company in exchange for running Blockbuster's online service. Blockbuster spurned the deal, a fateful decision in light of Netflix's steady advances on the home video market since then and the inverse trajectory of Blockbuster's fortunes over the same period. Auletta's article was published merely two months after the chain shuttered its remaining 300 outlets, and forty months after it filed for bankruptcy.[4] From its prior hegemonic position as cultural institution, Blockbuster's demise felt momentous. Its postmortems usually run through the company's litany of strategic indecision and missteps. But Auletta lauds Hastings' nous and foresight regarding online streaming as the catalysts in a zero-sum game between the companies. Here lies a key turning point in his version of the tale. Post-Blockbuster, historians are negotiating the larger cultural impact of online content distribution and mobile exhibition platforms. That Netflix killed its dithering and overly cautious rival is a closed debate.[5] Instead, this chapter litigates aspects of how historians and media users are coming to terms with Netflix's second act, namely in regard to the social significance and economic workings of digitally enabled consumption.

Defined as an online video platform, Netflix is categorically associated in popular as well as scholarly historical accounts with services such as Apple's iTunes, Amazon's Instant Video, and Hulu—a cohort of technological peers and business competitors. Having vanquished Blockbuster, Netflix now ostensibly faces them as fresh adversaries. Herein I rethink the tendency to comprehend Netflix this way, and posit that the predilection is encouraged by the lure of autonomy and mobility that new media ostensibly affords to both spectators and content creators. I argue that the inherent populism in particular is ideologically inflected. On the one hand, it is hard to deny that a cultural shift toward convergence and new habits of spectatorship is irreversibly underway; the media industry is also without question realigning. For example, Netflix recently became the latest attempt to unsettle Hollywood's norms by narrowing the theatrical release window. Its plans to stream its production of *Crouching Tiger Hidden Dragon II: The Green Destiny* (2016) during its theatrical run was met with threats by major theater chains to boycott the film.[6] In any event, the outsized role frequently attributed to Netflix in effecting these changes is ideologically if not politically fraught. Specifically, writers are codifying a history where Netflix and, by extension, Hastings are institutional and individual change agents within a narrative laden with individualist tropes favored by neoliberalism.

If the history of Netflix were to be scripted as an overblown biopic movie, the storyline would write itself. The protagonist in that telling is naturally Hastings the visionary, whose invention slayed a corporate behemoth, changed the business, and eventually altered the way that the world consumes and interacts with media. This chapter in fact contemplates how these tropes appear in key productions associated with Netflix, *Breaking Bad* (2008–13) and *House of Cards* (2013–). The historical stakes are multifold. Besides the interests of balance, if not accuracy, we must remember that neoliberalism is not merely an economic doctrine. It subtends a cultural mythology and political hermeneutic that conditions how we perceive new media spectatorial practices such as time-shifting and binge-watching. Consider Auletta's account, which quite assiduously hews to predictable types, beginning with the title, "Outside the Box."

The pun denotes the main topic, television, and designates Netflix as innovator. On *Charlie Rose*, Auletta furthers his narrative by referring to the company as a "disruptor," a marketing *mot à la mode* (of expiring utility, as it were[7]). Confluence between historical discourse and what Madison Avenue manufactures and releases into our cultural ecosystem further presses the case to reconsider accepted wisdom, especially when it echoes neoliberal jingoism.

Few works of new media history are more important than *Convergence Culture*, in which the author Henry Jenkins diagnoses a cultural shift rooted in more active consumer participation.[8] He argues that technologically empowered audiences, "occupying a space at the intersection between old and new media, are demanding the right to participate within the culture."[9] These hopes have been alive at least since Walter Benjamin wrote that famous essay about the work of art. According to Jenkins, convergence might be a bidirectional process—both "top-down corporate-driven and bottom-up consumer-driven"—where media consumers have wrestled away from the industry the power to control their experience and are now able to drive cultural change from below. Media producers, Jenkins believes, will either reexamine their relationships with audiences or suffer the economic consequences.[10] Where Netflix is concerned, Hastings evidently agrees. Auletta reports as follows:

> Hastings has succeeded, in large part, by taking advantage of what he calls viewers' "managed dissatisfaction" with traditional television: each hour of programming is crammed with about twenty minutes of commercials and promotional messages for other shows. Netflix carries no commercials; its revenue derives entirely from subscription fees. Viewers are happy to pay a set fee, now eight dollars a month, in order to watch, uninterrupted, their choice of films or shows, whenever they want, on whatever device they want. "Think of it as entertainment that's more like books," Hastings said. "You get to control and watch, and you get to do all the chapters of a book at the same time, because you have all the episodes."[11]

Do we? We might have all the episodes but do we hold all the cards? Given Netflix's market penetration, my reader is also a likely subscriber. If that is so, do you feel more in control of the experience than you were before, or might you merely be enjoying more customer satisfaction than is possible with a cable monopoly? My cynicism arises partly from the tidy consistency of Jenkins, Hastings, and Auletta's testimonies.

Nonetheless, the purpose is not to question the presence of change or the propositions offered by *Convergence Culture*. Change is definitely afoot, but this chapter pauses and reflects in the midst of much excitement, where an era is being consigned to the past and celebrations are kicking off for the digital future. Jenkins charts a progression where online video services alter modes of consumption, change textual forms, and move media culture into a new era. Although he does not name Netflix, it is easy to transpose the discourse surrounding the company onto his narrative. In that context, I reconsider the degree to which "disruptive," "gamechanging," or "transformational" are truly appropriate adjectives.

It all sounds pretty familiar. Christopher Anderson's important work in *Hollywood TV* provides adequate warning about the tendency to go along with the idea of "seismic shifts described in ... epic accounts of the industry's demise."[12] Wracked with uncertainty after the Paramount Decrees, the film industry perpetuated a mythology about its postwar business. "Under conditions that threatened the very existence of the studio system, television served many in the Hollywood community as a convenient stock villain," when television production in fact turned out to be a crucial source of revenue. It turned out that the film and television industries were symbiotic. "The motion picture industry during the 1950s was less an empire on the verge of ruin than one struggling, under unsettling conditions, to redefine its frontiers."[13] Anderson's findings reduce the temptation to see Netflix as a rival bringing the television industry face to face with its demise, and more of a symbiotic partner with the networks. Even Auletta cites the case of the CBS Corporation where the drop in revenue from commercials is being partly offset by licensing fees that parties such as Netflix pay for its programming. Still, CBS continues to monitor the hovering specter of an existential threat posed by so-called cord-cutting audiences who opt for streaming services over traditional cable subscriptions.[14]

Anderson argues that depicting cinema and television as distinct industries in competition with each other is discursively reinforced by perceptions of the latter's technological inferiority, susceptibility to commercial pressure, and lack of artistic sophistication. Mobilized within a marketing strategy of product differentiation, "movie industry discourse has often implied that the cinema exists in an autonomous sphere outside the corrupting influence of the marketplace."[15] The Netflix-versus-television story updates that construction too. This time, it is the upstart that offers autonomy to consumers with the freedom to choose what they want and when they want it, as well as creative freedom to artists to develop riskier and more demanding shows. Furthermore, Netflix is able to offer what Jason Jacobs terms the "pure" text, free of "adverts, promotional material, and other pollution."[16] The ballyhooed phenomenon of "binge-watching" multiple television episodes uninterrupted, especially serials, is central. It is an offshoot of "time-shifting," the original practice of recording programs for later viewing at consumers' convenience. Do they truly transform viewing practices in the wake of Anderson's reformulation of the film–television binary and his cautionary tale of overstating change?

A further corollary exists between the film–television dynamic in the 1950s and that of Netflix–television today—recourse to "quality television." Binge-watching on Netflix is routinely associated with the series *Breaking Bad* because of how the streaming service helped the show expand the audience for the cable network AMC. *Breaking Bad* is commonly taken as an exemplar of the current "Golden Age" of television, a term that associates the present with "quality" reminiscent of the past. Since these monikers are discursive constructions, what is the historical significance of their contingencies? In other words, what may we glean from "quality television" such as *Breaking Bad* and its place in Netflix history? Economically, Mareike Jenner argues that Netflix produced "quality" specifically to brand itself as source and venue of binge-worthy programming.[17] Ideologically, "quality" is a shiny result that burnishes the company's achievements, validating capitalism's promise that productivity and innovation arrive via an "invisible hand" that guides individualist effort.

The final consequence is historiographical. Anderson points out that the original "Golden Age" of the 1950s, brought about by movie producers' venture into prime-time programming, is important for understanding how the film and television industries intersected.[18] Reflecting on the new Golden Age as a meeting between Netflix and television can be comparably instructive. The perceived role of Netflix in encouraging networks to produce "quality" shows strikes at a similar sweet spot, a coming together that ironically draws contrast within the Netflix–television binary. To the extent that the term "Golden Age" is presently invoked out of yearning for prestige, pining for quality during this period of realignment is indirectly deployed as an impetus for change brought by Netflix and as a reason to encourage the media industries to follow its lead and collectively evolve.[19] It is as if to say, Netflix can make television as good as it used to be, if not better. But underneath the hype and luster, is Netflix truly the change agent that everyone wants it to be?

The false promise of creative autonomy

Film and media scholarship usually takes note of Netflix as part of the epochal transition from old to new media.[20] B. Ruby Rich believes that as cinema rolls through the "post-celluloid era ... in which film is on the verge of becoming a generic term, a signifier devoid of any fixed category," television faces its own seismic challenges.

> Television addresses a fundamental shift in viewer habits and public consumption: the desire for the episodic, a refusal of the one whole organic object, the reliance on continuity and replicability into an uncertain but newly reassured existence. Further, new digital platforms have altered television's seriality: now it's possible to be immersed in marathon viewings that stitch together epics out of once-parsed chapters. Such new viewing habits affect the narrative power of television and reset cinematic expectations. With Netflix, iTunes, and Amazon Prime as studio and distributor, an update is overdue.[21]

Encapsulating other writings in television—and new media studies—the passage articulates the links between technological change, evolving viewing practices, and textual transformations, while situating Netflix specifically.[22] Streaming platforms such as Netflix enable consumers to alter the nature of their experience. As a consequence, they lead producers to tailor their programs for binge-watching, or at least incentivize a structural redesign of episodic narratives. Rich's characterization darkens the ink even further on Jenkins' oft-repeated account of empowered audiences who now enjoy a right of refusal—of commercial interruptions, or of having to watch at the pleasure of predetermined programming schedules.[23] For some critics, liberation also arrives in the form of random and unplanned encounters with media objects and new meanings.[24] Audiences today can call the shots on what they watch, when they watch it, and how. Mobile platforms and lowered price points have additionally led to rapid market penetration by devices such as tablets and smartphones. Consumers are not only able to time-shift; they are also unbound to living rooms or desktop screens.

This represents the new reality confronting producers and distributors; this is the disruption that the industry must navigate. Nonetheless, by associating the nature of Netflix usage as Jason Hill and Elisa Schaar do, with words like "dialogical" and "usurp," the current historical view seems to conflate its consumption with a strong hint of political bearing.[25] Rich goes so far as to argue that accessibility to film archives via new media channels can "democratize."[26] It would be unfair to accuse these writers of trying to equate consumption with meaningful political activity. However, questions should still be posed regarding the newfound control that new media's denizens are claimed to possess. What is the nature of Netflix users' autonomy? To what degree is it significant? Even if the industry is being forced to reassess their revenue streams, are questions being asked of the *culture industry*?

To hear the brigade from Netflix tell it, the company stands squarely as a comrade marching arm in arm with newly empowered spectators.[27] As if heeding a clarion call, Netflix continues its mission to rescue traditional viewers from the indignities of "managed dissatisfaction." Hastings elaborates in a corporate and personal profile published in *GQ*.

> "The point of managed dissatisfaction is waiting. You're supposed to wait for your show that comes on Wednesday at 8 p.m., wait for the new season, see all the ads everywhere for the new season, talk to your friends at the office about how excited you are." If it's a movie, he adds, you wait till the night it opens, you wait for the pay-channel window, you wait for it to come to cable. Waiting means pent-up demand, millions of people watching the same thing at the same time, preferably at night, when they're pliant with exhaustion and ready to believe they need the stuff being hawked in all those commercials. Waiting, Hastings says, is dead.[28]

According to Netflix's chief content officer Ted Sarandos, the company's designs for culture extend even further. It speculates openly about how liberating customers from managed dissatisfaction can "radically alter the way stories get told."[29]

On this score both Netflix and media historians place high premiums on ideas of individual freedom and flexibility. But where consumers are concerned, the notion of an alliance propagated by public relations exercises such as the *GQ* article obscures the materially transactional nature of their relationship with Netflix. Customers are not comrades. Beyond that, the individualism implicitly defined bears the contours of a neoliberal subject, which as David Harvey points out, neither possesses nor seeks the sort of ideals and freedoms capable of threatening corporate power.[30] At a minimum, Harvey's critique prompts an assessment of whether the hype emanating from corporate headquarters holds up under scrutiny.

The popular and largely unchallenged view of Netflix positions the company as a hero to both users and creators of media content. It has supposedly brought about a new economic model and mode of consumption understood to benefit television programs in particular. Because Netflix revenues stem from membership subscriptions, it becomes easier to believe in a direct correlation between the nature of its content and what customers desire, part of which is the luxury of time-shifting and the related fetish of binge-watching. Producers are thus freed from the dictates of decency standards and of corporate risk aversion on the part of those who purchase advertising time. As a result, content is less constrained by rigid conventions routinely imposed on narrative content and episodic structure. Afforded creative autonomy and serial formats, so the logic goes, producers now possess license to construct lengthier story arcs and deeper, more complex plots to house fuller and more nuanced characters, ushering in the new Golden Age of television. "Quality TV" never had it so good, and Netflix seems at the heart of it all. Its flagship of original programming, the political drama *House of Cards*, enjoys all these benefits. Netflix outbid HBO and AMC by discarding the usual requirement of a pilot episode for prior testing; it committed long term to two 13-episode seasons in March 2011.[31] Showrunner Beau Willimon was all too ready to give Netflix credit in an interview with *Variety*, which also hailed the company for "forcing the entertainment industry to reexamine the very definition of a TV series."

> I think it's the smartest business model out there. When you give artists the opportunity to make what they want to make, place faith in them, allow them to take risks, to push boundaries, to even flirt with failure and take those risks, then you're going to get the best possible work, because that's what they thirst for.[32]

"Faith," "risk," and willingness to "flirt with failure," however, rarely constitute wise economic strategy. Contrary to what the party line articulates, Netflix financed *House of Cards* with a defined risk abatement strategy.

Willimon is probably sincere in his romanticization of how much creative freedom he enjoys with Netflix, but highlighting the company's gamble requires a concomitant de-emphasis of the rationality mitigating the financial risk. Netflix's faith in *House of Cards* was not blind, but methodically guided by conclusions based in turn on its trove of usage statistics compiled on an unprecedentedly extensive level for years. One aspect of this database consists of tagging each and every title in its catalog with an elaborate system of labels. This produces a complex taxonomy of traits, including genre, content, tone, character attributes, narrative resolutions, and so on. Dubbed the "Netflix Quantum Theory," this document is layered with user profiles and metadata generated by tracking subscriber behavior—how they scroll through its menu, select titles, and play videos. Devised primarily to generate personalized recommendations, the data has proven useful elsewhere.[33] Netflix had in fact explicitly declared its intention to apply that knowledge in its foray into original programming.

> Netflix's data indicated that the same subscribers who loved the original BBC production also gobbled down movies starring Kevin Spacey or directed by David Fincher. Therefore, concluded Netflix executives, a remake of the BBC drama

> with Spacey and Fincher attached was a no-brainer, to the point that the company committed $100 million for two 13-episode seasons.[34]
>
> Netflix has created a database of American cinematic predilections. The data can't tell them how to make a TV show, but it can tell them what they should be making. When they create a show like *House of Cards*, they aren't guessing at what people want.[35]

What people want, therefore, is both quantified and commodified. The freedom of choice exercised by what Theodor Adorno and Max Horkheimer of the Frankfurt School term "pseudoindividuals" resembles Harvey's depiction of the neoliberal subject, who prizes "the liberty of consumer choice, not only with respect to particular products but also with respect to lifestyles, modes of expression, and a wide range of cultural processes."[36] The "Netflix Quantum Theory" renders abundantly clear, the literal existence of a system fashioned to feed "differentiated consumerism," "individual libertarianism," and "consumer niche choices."[37]

House of Cards began its run on Netflix eight months before *Breaking Bad* aired its final episodes on AMC. The two shows feature prominently in historical accounts of Netflix and the industrial reorganization brought on by its success. Those reports consider Netflix an important instrument of time-shifting and binge-watching—along with DVDs, video on demand (VOD), and even illegal downloading—that enabled *Breaking Bad* to develop an audience over time, reducing the traditional pressure on shows to hit ratings targets during initial broadcast.[38] Viewers whose interest developed gradually from a combination of word of mouth, critical praise, and high-profile award show victories could binge-watch and get caught up in time for new episodes airing on AMC. The showrunner Vince Gilligan even credits Netflix with keeping the drama on the air while its broadcast ratings lagged.[39] But ascribing causal recognition to Netflix in this instance discounts AMC's strategic commitment to a show that underlined the cable channel's own investments in original programming. AMC had been trying for at least a decade to establish its own slate of original programming, as other cable networks had successfully done. *Breaking Bad* and *Mad Men* (2007–15) merely represented the culmination of those efforts to accrue brand equity as a destination for quality television and consequently, if not more importantly, good films. AMC president Charlie Collier explained it thus in 2008:

> The mission is to make sure we build a breadth of originals that really complement what we do best—present a diverse array of the best movies of all time. We know very well what we want. We want our brand, when we do originals, to be as high-end and high-quality as the films we're airing.[40]

These objectives do not override the imperative for these shows to succeed either commercially or critically, but they do alleviate some of the usual pressure to garner ratings. For that matter, not all ratings points are equal. Advertisers more greatly covet a show's audience if it skews richer, younger, or more male as it was in *Breaking Bad*'s case.[41] And before its final run of episodes began, the Film Society of Lincoln Center stamped its cultural imprimatur by indulging in some binge-watching of its own, feting the production with an entire week of events, including a marathon of all previously aired installments. The show also enjoyed significant and high-profile critical acclaim from its very first season, all of which represents the "third-party validation" that Collier and the network craved. In short, binge-watching did play an important role in building the show's audience for its final season. But the enduring belief furthered by Gilligan that Netflix and its subscribers saved *Breaking Bad* from cancellation is also outlandish.

Binge-watching in the neoliberal economy

We should therefore not be as cavalier in thinking that Netflix empowers audiences against the industry. New media technologies are far more likely to advantage owners of production before they benefit consumers. If the history of *Breaking Bad* illustrates how AMC's corporate decisions can be elided in favor of an admittedly more inspiring populist narrative, the data-driven rationale behind the important choice to greenlight of *House of Cards* calls the very idea of autonomy into further question. Consumer sovereignty in the realm of programming decisions is a manufactured fantasy, just as creative control was limited by rationalized parameters determined prior to production.

It might also be presumptive to equate the practice of binge-watching with consumer autonomy. Empirically speaking, time-shifting, made exponentially easier since the advent of video cassette recorders that gave audiences greater ability to avert their eyeballs from commercials, represents an unmistakable transformation. Still, the relevance of "appointment" television remains vital. Research commissioned by the digital video recorder seller TiVo suggests that "binge-viewing is primarily a function of playing catch-up … [53 percent of its subscribers] binge in order to be sufficiently caught up in time for the next season premiere."[42] Indeed, the important benefit AMC derived from the binge-watching of *Breaking Bad* was the ratings momentum and higher ad rates that Netflix, along with other platforms such as VOD and iTunes, helped to generate for the show's final run of original episodes.

An audience of 50,000 watched the entire fourth season of *Breaking Bad* in the twenty-four hours before the show's fifth season premiered on AMC.[43] Are these small windows of time not "events" for all intents and purposes? The cultural writer Graeme McMillan concurs that even though television networks are not responsible for staging these events.

> Technology may have freed us from the restraints on our viewing schedules placed on us by television networks, but it turned out to be a zero sum game; at the same time as one hand offered us freedom, the other was ensuring that we'd have to keep up to date and fall under an equally artificial schedule created by our online communities.[44]

Eulogies for appointment television specifically prompted by *House of Cards*, blamed indirectly on Netflix, thus seem premature.[45] The 10.3 million viewers for the *Breaking Bad* series finale outdrew the program's previous record by 56 percent.[46] From that point of view, the result of binge-watching *Breaking Bad* was ultimately the creation of a television "event" and cultural phenomenon. *Variety* reported on elaborate viewing parties around the United States for "perhaps the most anticipated scripted TV event of the social media era."[47] AMC reaped a windfall when the cable network's top ad rates for the finale matched those of broadcast series.[48]

Moreover, binge-watching is etymologically associated with indulgence, compulsion, and loss of self-control—behaviors conceptually antithetical to autonomy.[49] TiVo discovered that approximately 74 percent of its subscribers watched at least one full season of a television show over a number of days.[50] Two percent of Netflix subscribers in the United States watched *House of Cards*' entire second season within its first weekend of release. In other words, 634,000 viewers consumed thirteen hours of programming over three days.[51] According to Jacobs, for digital television's time-shifting spectators, it is a Kantian "question of will," that is to say, of control, intention, or choice.[52] We can condense it further and consider the integrity of those choices. Are they made autonomously, as it were? Beyond pseudoindividuality, Adorno likens the mental state of those living in standardized mass culture to that of fascistically manipulated subjects. These "members of contemporary masses are, at least *prima facie* individuals, the children of a liberal, competitive and individualistic society," but are in fact "largely robbed of autonomy and spontaneity, instead of setting goals the realization of which would transcend the psychological status quo no less than the social one."[53]

The strength that Netflix provides consumers to disrupt is illusory. Even if we generously estimate the limits of their autonomy and available choices, we would be well advised to consider talk of revolution and gamechange carefully. But the temptation to adopt optimistic lines of individualist discourse can be irresistible. Their neoliberal truthiness is additionally reinforced by the company's public image, corporate practices, and the ideology of its most prominent shows. Netflix is famous within Silicon Valley for its constitution (labeled "Netflix Culture" on its website or known alternatively as its "Culture Deck") that rewards performance over effort, and encourages employees to assume personal responsibility and adopt appropriate ethics when utilizing uncommon perks. Netflix does not track vacation days, sick days, or expensing.[54] Peppered with terms from the neoliberal lexicon such as "freedom," "responsibility," "flexibility," and "market," the document grants Netflix's staff uncommon freedom to determine where, when, and how they labor. And if they successfully eradicate "managed dissatisfaction," they will permit subscribers to consume media where, when, and how they desire.[55] The corporate ethos comes full circle.

Its celebrity CEO, profiled in *GQ* as an ascetic rogue and free-spirited visionary, personifies those values. Hastings' paternalistic position in the imaginary recapitulates Adorno's Freudian theorization of fascism's sadomasochistic subject, who idealizes and succumbs to the leader even if doing so is "irreconcilable with his own rational interests as a private person as well as those of the group or class to which he actually belongs."[56] Readers and customers alike are called to identify with the peripatetic figure.

> Hastings is a rangy, goateed 52-year-old with a master's in computer science from Stanford who left the Marine Corps officers' training program to teach in the Peace Corps in Swaziland.[57]

House of Cards showrunner Willimon apparently internalized the culture when he was brought on board. He describes the early phases of the venture to *Variety*:

> We were all excited about this possible programmatic shift. None of us had really done television before and neither had Netflix. So we were all in the same boat of experimentation, trying something different. We didn't know what the rules were, so we were completely ready to break them.[58]

We chance upon an iconographical mirror in Frank Underwood, protagonist in *House of Cards*, who is likewise a fearless rule-breaker. An even stronger parallel to Hastings is Walter White, the high school chemistry teacher turned meth dealer in *Breaking Bad*. When the Netflix founder displayed his well-known brashness in early 2014, joking publicly during an earnings call that HBO copresident Richard Pepler's password is "netflixbitch," he harkened back to White's famous declaration, "I am the one who knocks!"[59]

These connections do not prove that the productions are manifest irruptions of corporate speech—especially since Netflix did not produce the AMC hit. Without extrapolating too eagerly from text to economic base, an ideologically critical reading of *Breaking Bad* demonstrates nevertheless the pervasiveness of neoliberal discourse from which media history can be more critically distant. Readers of Adorno will inevitably wonder about the extent to which history is reified in the show. As scientist, innovator, sociopath, and entrepreneur in artisanal meth production, White embodies the type of personality prized by the present economic era (Figure 12.1).

Figure 12.1 The final shot of *Breaking Bad*

Conclusion

Over the course of five seasons, Walter White struggled continually to find newer and more extensive distribution channels, perpetually hindered by one established network after another. As the camera pulls away in the series' wistful final crane shot, somewhere in that world, Madrigal Elektromotoren GmbH remains intact, a massive German industrial conglomerate fronting a multinational drug operation. The hero was defeated after having vanquished a slew of economic adversaries. In a way, where he fails to become a mogul with mass distribution, Netflix has succeeded, primarily by dominating the video-streaming market.[60]

Netflix reached that zenith by way of Amazon Web Services, a cloud-computing platform used for vital operations such as delivering content and managing customer accounts.[61] The corporate partnership may seem strange, but only if one perceives Netflix and Amazon as direct competitors, a predilection exacerbated by those who privilege spectatorship as the variable with which to chart media history. Studies that measure industrial realignment or technological development through the impact on modes of spectatorship habitually clump streaming video services together as a result: Netflix, Amazon Instant Video, iTunes, HBO Go, Hulu, VOD, Google Video or YouTube, and others. This customary list implicitly equates those services, and when famous corporate names are cited interchangeably with their popular products (e.g., Amazon and Instant Video, Apple and iTunes, Google and YouTube), the companies can appear economically comparable and competitive when they are fundamentally not. Netflix's reliance on Amazon Web Services should not strike anyone as peculiar. Every company on the list derives its biggest source of revenue from different businesses; each is also of vastly different size.[62] Apple is essentially a smartphone manufacturer whose dalliance in the media business with Netflix and Amazon merely involves the so-called hobby revenue.[63] Amazon is a retailer that dangles Instant Video as a perk for Amazon Prime members. Google's main interest in advertising moved it to acquire YouTube, but more as a source of metadata than a source of profit, which in fact remains elusive.[64] Looking behind the businesses reveals that although these companies have horses on the same track, they may in fact be running different races. These material relations can be obscured when media are historicized through spectatorship and consumption.

This tendency attests to the intellectual influence of thinkers like Carolyn Marvin who believe that media are defined by how society uses them. In her classic text, *When Old Technologies Were New*, she declares that media "are constructed complexes of habits, beliefs, and procedures embedded in elaborate cultural codes of communication. The history of media is never more or less than the history of their uses, which always lead us away from them to the social practices and conflicts they illuminate."[65] Her argument's attractiveness in this case is intensified by the optimistic allure of greater agency within the culture industry, against its indomitable ideologies. A media landscape experiencing tectonic shifts causes enough turmoil to offer hope of conjuring some autonomy. It is an understandable impulse. The expansion of broadband internet access, initially through hardwires, then wirelessly, enabled online streaming platforms to reshape mass media industries. Diversity within screen culture proliferated, and software and interfaces advanced alongside those developments, all of which has changed how we consume media. Unprecedented encounters with films and television shows can recontour interpretation, generating new meanings in unpredictable ways. Opinions currently differ on whether streaming platforms including Netflix encourage intertextuality, for example. Against J.M. Tyree's belief that they cultivate "fluid" enjoyment of "interlinking" "points of reference," Jonathan Nichols-Pethick reminds us that "pure agency" is elusive because those points are preselected according to usage history.[66] Counterintuitively, Caetlin Benson-Allott has also observed viewing practices on online platforms narrowing in a sense, toward "stripped down, feature-only convenience."[67] In the clamor to make sense of it all, we should neither overestimate individual agency nor misread where subjective autonomy is headed. If they are moving toward neoliberalism, under the very regime that nurtures the digital era's trajectories, it would be ironic to understand Netflix or its users as "gamechangers." The term matches the discursive fabric, but may be inaccurate in substance, and therefore warrant some disruption of its own.

Notes

1 Netflix, letter to shareholders, January 22, 2014. http://ir.netflix.com/results.cfm (accessed July 9, 2015).

2 Ken Auletta, "Outside the Box: Netflix and the Future of Television," *The New Yorker*, February 3, 2014. http://www.newyorker.com/magazine/2014/02/03/outside-the-box-2 (accessed June 3, 2015).

3 See, for example, Kevin P. McDonald, "Digital Dreams in a Material World: The Rise of Netflix and Its Impact on Changing Distribution and Exhibition Patterns," *Jump Cut* 55 (2013). http://ejumpcut.org/archive/jc55.2013/McDonaldNetflix/index.html (accessed May 5, 2015).

4 Alex Barinka, "Blockbuster Video-Rental Chain Will Shut All U.S. Stores," *Bloomberg Business*, November 6, 2013. http://www.bloomberg.com/news/articles/2013-11-06/blockbuster-video-rental-chain-will-shut-remaining-u-s-stores.

5 See also Gina Keating, *Netflixed: The Epic Battle for America's Eyeballs* (New York: Penguin, 2012).

6 Brent Lang and Marc Graser, "Amazon Movies May Crack Theatrical Windows, but It Won't Break Them," *Variety*, January 19, 2015. http://variety.com/2015/film/news/amazon-movies-may-crack-theatrical-windows-but-it-wont-break-them-1201408849 (accessed July 14, 2015); Brent Lang and Dave McNary, " 'Crouching Tiger 2' Fallout: AMC, Regal Won't Play Imax Release," *Variety*, September 30, 2014. http://variety.com/2014/film/news/crouching-tiger-2-fallout-regal-cinemark-wont-play-imax-release-1201317183 (accessed July 14, 2015); Brent Lang, "AMC Entertainment Chief Talks Netflix's 'Crouching Tiger' Sequel, MoviePass Trial and Theater Innovations," *Variety*, February 18, 2015. http://variety.com/2015/film/news/amc-entertainment-chief-talks-netflixs-crouching-tiger-sequel-moviepass-trial-and-theater-innovations-1201436114/ (accessed July 9, 2015).

7 Simon Dumenco, "Eight Media and Marketing Buzzwords That Must Die," *Advertising Age*, July 28, 2014. http://adage.com/article/the-media-guy/media-marketing-buzzwords-die/294333/; Dumenco, "Six More Media and Marketing Buzzwords That Must Die," *Advertising Age*, August 11, 2014. http://adage.com/article/the-media-guy/media-marketing-buzzwords-die/294521/ (accessed June 3, 2015).
8 Henry Jenkins, *Convergence Culture: Where Old and New Media Collide* (New York: New York University Press, 2006), 3.
9 Ibid., 24.
10 Ibid., 18, 24.
11 Auletta, "Outside the Box."
12 Christopher Anderson, *Hollywood TV: The Studio System in the Fifties* (Austin: University of Texas Press, 1994), 6.
13 Anderson, *Hollywood TV*, 2, 5, 13.
14 Auletta, "Outside the Box."
15 Anderson, *Hollywood TV*, 16, 18.
16 Jason Jacobs, "Television, Interrupted: Pollution or Aesthetic?" in *Television as Digital Media*, eds James Bennett and Niki Strange (Durham, NC: Duke University Press, 2011), 257.
17 Mareike Jenner, "Is This TVIV? On Netflix, TVIII and Binge-Watching," *New Media and Society* (July 7, 2014): 11.
18 Anderson, *Hollywood TV*, 11–12.
19 A parallel case is found in Roger Ebert's declaration of the present as a "golden age" of film criticism, where critics can develop and disseminate their craft through new media. Online streaming platforms such as "Netflix, Amazon, Hulu, MUBI, the Asia/Pacific Film Archive, Google Video or Vimeo" provide unprecedented access to films, while blogs offer easy means to self-publish and potentially find a massive audience. Roger Ebert, "Film Criticism Is Dying? Not Online," *The Wall Street Journal*, January 22, 2011. http://on.wsj.com/1w7vKmD (accessed July 14, 2015).
20 For film studies, see Chuck Tryon, *On-Demand Culture: Digital Delivery and the Future of Movies* (New Brunswick: Rutgers University Press, 2013); B. Ruby Rich, "Film [*sic*]," *Film Quarterly* 67.2 (2013): 5–7; Lucas Hilderbrand, "The Art of Distribution: Video on Demand," *Film Quarterly* 64.2 (2010): 24–28; Jenna Ng, "The Myth of Total Cinephilia," *Cinema Journal* 49.2 (2010): 146–151; Caetlin Benson-Allott, "Cinema's New Approaches," *Film Quarterly* 64.4 (2011): 10–11; J.M. Tyree, "Searching for Somewhere," *Film Quarterly* 64.4 (2011): 12–16; Jonathan Nichols-Pethick, "Going with the Flow: On the Value of Randomness, Flexibility, and Getting Students in on the Conversation, or What I Learned from Antoine Dodson," *Cinema Journal* 50.4 (2011): 182–187; Alisa Perren, "Rethinking Distribution for the Future of Media Industry Studies," *Cinema Journal* 52.3 (2013): 165–171; Jason E. Hill and Elisa Schaar, "Training a Sensibility: Notes on American Art and Mass Media," *American Art* 27.2 (2013): 2–9.
21 Rich, "Film [*sic*]," 6.
22 For television and new media studies, see Jenner, "Is This TVIV?"; Jason Mittell, *Complex TV: The Poetics of Contemporary Television Storytelling* (New York: New York University Press, 2015); Sidneyeve Matrix, "The Netflix Effect: Teens, Binge Watching, and On-Demand Digital Media Trends," *Jeunesse: Young People, Texts, Cultures* 6, 1 (2014): 119–138.

23 See also Jenner, "Is This TVIV?"; Matrix, "The Netflix Effect," 120; Ng, "The Myth of Total Cinephilia," 150.
24 Nichols-Pethick, "Going with the Flow," 183–184.
25 Hill and Schaar, "Training a Sensibility," 7.
26 Rich, "Film [*sic*]," 7.
27 Netflix similarly places itself within a popular alliance in the political debate over net neutrality. Anne Marie Squeo, "What Netflix CFO David Wells Really Said About Net Neutrality and Title II Yesterday," *Official Netflix Blog*, March 5, 2015. http://blog.netflix.com/2015/03/what-netflix-cfo-david-wells-really.html (accessed June 21, 2015).
28 Nancy Hass, "And the Award for the Next HBO Goes to … " *GQ*, February 2013. http://www.gq.com/entertainment/movies-and-tv/201302/netflix-founder-reed-hastings-house-of-cards-arrested-development?printable=true (accessed May 19, 2015).
29 Hass, "And the Award for the Next HBO Goes to … "
30 David Harvey, *A Brief History of Neoliberalism* (New York: Oxford University Press, 2005), 42.
31 Andrew Wallenstein, "Netflix Seals 'House of Cards' Deal," *Variety*, March 18, 2011. http://variety.com/2011/tv/news/netflix-seals-house-of-cards-deal-1118034117/ (accessed April 24, 2015).
32 Laura Prudom, " 'House of Cards': Beau Willimon on Netflix's Rule-Breaking Creativity," *Variety*, June 20, 2014. http://variety.com/2014/tv/awards/beau-willimon-house-of-cards-netflix-1201229981/ (accessed July 15, 2015); Jenner (2014) argues that the "business model" Willimon mentions is part of a branding strategy to associate Netflix as a destination for quality television, "Is This TVIV?" 7.
33 Alexis C. Madrigal, "How Netflix Reverse Engineered Hollywood," *The Atlantic*, January 2, 2014. http://www.theatlantic.com/technology/archive/2014/01/how-netflix-reverse-engineered-hollywood/282679/ (accessed July 2, 2015); see also Seth Fiegerman, "Netflix Knows You Better Than You Know Yourself," *Mashable*, December 11, 2013. http://mashable.com/2013/12/11/netflix-data/ (accessed June 26, 2015).
34 Andrew Leonard, "How Netflix Is Turning Viewers into Puppets," *Salon*, February 1, 2013. http://www.salon.com/2013/02/01/how_netflix_is_turning_viewers_into_puppets/ (accessed June 26, 2015).
35 Madrigal, "How Netflix Reverse Engineered Hollywood."
36 Harvey, *A Brief History of Neoliberalism*, 42.
37 Ibid., 42, 47.
38 Josef Adalian, "What Networks Can Learn from Breaking Bad's Ratings Explosion," *Vulture*, August 16, 2013. http://www.vulture.com/2013/08/lessons-from-breaking-bads-ratings-explosion.html (accessed May 28, 2015).
39 Jon Weisman, "Emmys: Vince Gilligan Credits Netflix for AMC's 'Breaking Bad' Surviving, Thriving," *Variety*, September 22, 2013. http://variety.com/2013/tv/news/breaking-bad-amc-vince-gilligan-credits-netflix-1200660762/ (accessed May 28, 2015).
40 David Bianculli, "AMC's Brand-Smart Strategy," *Broadcasting & Cable*, September 26, 2008. http://www.broadcastingcable.com/news/news-articles/amcs-brand-smart-strategy/85213 (accessed June 6, 2015).
41 Tom Lowry, "How Mad Men Glammed up AMC," *Bloomberg Business*, July 23, 2008. http://www.bloomberg.com/bw/stories/2008-07-23/how-mad-men-glammed-up-amc (accessed July 15, 2015).

42 Anthony Crupi, "Study: Nine Out of 10 Americans Are Binge-Viewers," *Advertising Age*, June 30. 2015. http://adage.com/article/media/study/299284/ (accessed July 2, 2015).

43 Georg Szalai, "Edinburgh TV Fest: Netflix's Ted Sarandos Defends International Expansion, Content Spending," *The Hollywood Reporter*, August 23, 2012. http://www.hollywoodreporter.com/news/netflix-ted-sarandos-edinburgh-tv-festival-365002 (accessed June 26, 2015).

44 Graeme McMillan, "Why Do People Still Watch Live TV?" *Time*, March 4, 2014. http://time.com/12431/appointment-viewing-spoilers-live-tv/. McMillan's allusion to online communities of viewers also weighs against the axiom that "digital television threatens the universal experience of television's social function" (Jacobs, "Television, Interrupted," 267), as well as the empirical trend of lone binge-watching (Crupi, "Study: Nine Out of 10 Americans Are Binge-Viewers").

45 David Zurawik, "The Year Appointment Television Died," *The Baltimore Sun*, December 27, 2013. http://articles.baltimoresun.com/2013-12-27/entertainment/bal-the-year-appointment-television-died-20131227_1_amazon-prime-vince-gilligan-public-tv (accessed July 13, 2015); Katie Collins, "*House of Cards* Producer Declares Appointment TV 'Dead,'" *Wired*, November 6, 2014. http://www.wired.co.uk/news/archive/2014-11/06/house-of-cards-netflix (accessed July 13, 2015).

46 Rick Kissell, "AMC's 'Breaking Bad' Returns to Record 5.9 Million Viewers," *Variety*, August 12, 2013. http://variety.com/2013/tv/news/amcs-breaking-bad-returns-to-record-5-9-million-viewers-1200576953/ (accessed July 2, 2015); "'Breaking Bad' Finale Soars to Series-Best 10.3 Million Viewers," *Variety*, September 30, 2013. http://variety.com/2013/tv/news/breaking-bad-finale-ratings-1200681920/ (accessed June 6, 2015).

47 Allegra Tepper, "'Breaking Bad' Finale Viewing Parties Sweep the Nation," *Variety*, September 29, 2013. http://variety.com/2013/tv/news/breaking-bad-viewing-parties-1200671090/ (accessed June 6, 2015).

48 Jeanine Poggi, "The Cost of 'Breaking Bad': AMC Asks $400,000 for Finale," *Advertising Age*, September 27, 2013. http://adage.com/article/media/cost-breaking-bad-amc-asks-400-000-finale/244442/ (accessed June 7, 2015).

49 For a brief discussion of Netflix watching and spectatorial control, see Ariane Lebot, "Netflix and Rethinking Ritualized Consumption of Audiovisual Content," *In Media Res*, December 3, 2013. http://mediacommons.futureofthebook.org/imr/2013/12/03/netflix-and-rethinking-ritualized-consumption-audiovisual-content (accessed July 13, 2015).

50 Crupi, "Study: Nine Out of 10 Americans Are Binge-Viewers."

51 Andrew Wallenstein, "'House of Cards' Binge-Watching: 2% of U.S. Subs Finished Entire Series Over First Weekend," *Variety*, February 20, 2014. http://variety.com/2014/digital/news/house-of-cards-binge-watching-2-of-u-s-subs-finished-entire-series-over-first-weekend-1201114030/ (accessed July 6, 2015).

52 Jacobs, "Television, Interrupted," 264.

53 Theodor W. Adorno, "Freudian Theory and the Pattern of Fascist Propaganda," in *The Culture Industry*, ed. and trans. J.M. Bernstein (London: Routledge, 1991), 135, 150.

54 Hass, "And the Award for the Next HBO Goes to … "; Netflix, Inc., "Netflix Culture: Freedom and Responsibility," https://jobs.netflix.com (accessed July 9, 2015).

55 Charles Tryon connects this flexible consumption with the flexible labor prized by neoliberalism.

56 Adorno, "Freudian Theory and the Pattern of Fascist Propaganda," 139.

57 Hass, "And the Award for the Next HBO Goes to … "

58 Prudom, "'House of Cards': Beau Willimon on Netflix's Rule-Breaking Creativity."

59 Sam Thielman, "Reed Hastings Takes a Loud Shot at HBO: 'His Password Is Netflixbitch,'" *Adweek*, January 22, 2014. http://www.adweek.com/news/technology/reed-hastings-takes-loud-shot-hbo-155140 (accessed May 26, 2015); "Cornered" (director: Michael Slovis) *Breaking Bad*, AMC, August 21, 2011. Television.

60 Todd Spangler, "Amazon Streams More Video Than Hulu or Apple, But It's Still Miles Behind Netflix," *Variety*, April 8, 2014. http://variety.com/2014/digital/news/amazon-streams-more-video-than-hulu-or-apple-but-its-still-miles-behind-netflix-1201154130/ (accessed June 6, 2015).

61 Brandon Butler, "Amazon and Netflix: Competitors Who Need Each Other," *Network World*, July 24, 2013. http://www.networkworld.com/article/2168433/cloud-computing/amazon-and-netflix–competitors-who-need-each-other.html (accessed June 20, 2015).

62 Even when Netflix's valuation was highest, Apple, Google, and Amazon were more than 19, 9, and 5 times as large. HBO is a division of Time Warner Inc., a media conglomerate perhaps most similar to Netflix, but whose market capitalization is 82 percent larger. Market capitalization figures were based on stock prices at the end of June 5, 2015. The share price of Netflix, $633.22, is only $0.55 off its record high, and more than 50 percent greater than its value after the surge in early 2014.

63 John Martellaro, "Apple Reveals Movie & TV Sales in Billions—Is This Really a Hobby?" *The Mac Observer*, July 23, 2013. http://www.macobserver.com/tmo/article/apple-reveals-movie-tv-sales-in-billions-is-this-really-a-hobby (accessed June 20, 2015).

64 Rolfe Winkler, "YouTube: 1 Billion Viewers, No Profit," *The Wall Street Journal*, February 25, 2015. http://www.wsj.com/articles/viewers-dont-add-up-to-profit-for-youtube-1424897967 (accessed May 29, 2015).

65 Carolyn Marvin, *When Old Technologies Were New: Thinking About Electronic Communication in the Late Nineteenth Century* (New York: Oxford University Press, 1988), 8.

66 Tyree, "Searching for Somewhere," 14; Nichols-Pethick, "Going with the Flow," 184–185.

67 Benson-Allott, "Cinema's New Appendanges," 10.

13

From Online Video Store to Global Internet TV Network: Netflix and the Future of Home Entertainment

Kevin McDonald

In 1995, Ken Auletta described the formation of a new kind of software giant. The recent combination of Paramount, Viacom, and Blockbuster Video formed a media conglomerate that was organized largely around programming assets—or content—and primed to strike strategic alliances wherever possible. For example, Blockbuster promised to give "preferential, eye-level shelf space to movies from Paramount" or to "offer ten free rentals to new Showtime subscribers."[1] There was even talk of reinventing Showtime as the Blockbuster Channel, using the video store's database of customer information to generate recommendations or personalized promotions.[2] Though it was not the period's foremost example or the last deal of its kind, this new software giant was an exemplary case of what Jennifer Holt terms structural convergence, the drive for corporate synergies through "a mixture of vertical and horizontal integration and conglomeration."[3]

Of course for all of its ambition, the Viacom deal and several others like it would end in disappointment. Viacom spun off Blockbuster in 2004, which then began the rental retailer's descent into bankruptcy. Two years later Viacom split its film studio and cable channels from broadcast networks like CBS, which it had acquired in 1999. Altogether, such unlikely twists and turns seem to offer another illustration of William Goldman's Hollywood truism: "nobody knows anything."[4] This is not to question Holt's characterization of modern media and entertainment industries as an oligopoly in which both hegemonic and economic power are consolidated in the hands of a select few. However, the demise of what was supposed to be a key representative in this new era of conglomeration foregrounds the instability that remains, despite a general concentration of power. By extension, cases like this stress the importance of further detailing how and why certain types of corporate power persevere while others falter amidst heightened economic pressures, complicated and uneven partnerships, and conflicting business priorities.

Netflix, in this regard, offers an especially interesting case study. It is in many ways the company that most clearly illustrates the changing state of media in the twenty-first century and the challenges that hamper claims of either technological utopianism or absolute corporate control. First, Netflix remains an outlier within the media and entertainment industry, an intermediary that succeeded precisely because of the major conglomerates' inability to negotiate the transition from DVD to digital on demand. Netflix is at the same time closely associated with "cultural convergence" in Henry Jenkins' more general sense of the term.[5] Netflix, for example, was at the forefront of accelerating cross-platform accessibility, promoting its ability to allow users to access its service by computer, television, or mobile devices. The rise of platform agnosticism has likewise encouraged a broader blurring of media formats—Netflix, for instance, no longer counts the number of films or television programs that it offers but instead measures its service in terms of "hours of entertainment." As a result of these innovations, Netflix has gained significant stature as an enviable hybrid business model, one that synthesizes the technological savvy of an internet company with the leverage of a vertically integrated media company, combining the control of programming content with favorable access to interlinked distribution and exhibition networks.

Despite all of this success, Netflix is simultaneously viewed as perpetually vulnerable. There are concerns that it will end up, like its predecessor Blockbuster, technologically obsolescent, or that it will simply acquiesce to the growing demands of either the major media conglomerates or the cable and data providers that control distribution. To understand the basis of these forecasts, this chapter examines three developments that both coincide with and help to contextualize what Amanda Lotz designates the "post-network era," a period that closely parallels Netflix's transition from an online video store to a self-proclaimed global internet TV network.[6] First, media and entertainment throughout this period follow the broader trend of financialization whereby companies like Netflix are evaluated primarily on market performance. This development overlaps with a growing emphasis on the so-called Long Tail economics and the ability to leverage niche or undervalued assets either within or against larger corporate structures. The second development concerns the rise of branded entertainment, the way that services like Netflix and high-profile channels like HBO and ESPN stress the importance of a distinct brand identity that is then reinforced through programming and other strategic features. Third, and again in line with broader economic trends, there is a shift in focus to international expansion. These three developments are of course deeply intertwined, and a large part of Netflix's current success is tied to its ability to simultaneously navigate these different challenges. Its ability to remain a leader in home entertainment will likewise depend on how well it continues to do so while also confronting new competitors.

Long Tail markets

While finance capital has played an important role throughout the history of Hollywood and other media industries, this role has intensified significantly over the course of the past three to four decades.[7] In the aftermath of World War II, a number of social and regulatory changes—stemming from the antitrust Paramount

Decrees—destabilized Hollywood's standard business practices. This resulted in a period of market volatility that in turn prompted an industry-wide series of corporate reorganizations. As part of an initial wave of conglomeration, major companies from outside of the entertainment industry merged with or acquired major studios like Paramount and United Artists. These companies were interested in Hollywood because of the promise of diversification or because they believed the studios were temporarily undervalued. The logic of these earlier mergers accelerated in the 1980s as government deregulation and the emergence of new technologies allowed for the formation of a new wave of larger, yet more media-focused, conglomerates (like the one mentioned above which combined Paramount, Viacom, and Blockbuster). One of the key catalysts during this period, as Jennifer Holt details, was the ongoing growth of cable and, more specifically, the ability of cable to attract higher risk forms of financing.[8]

During the 1990s, in conjunction with the growing convergence between film, broadcast, and telecommunications, much of this highly speculative venture capital began to extend beyond the cable industry to new internet-based companies. Though many of these companies failed to ever turn a profit, Chris Anderson introduced the idea of "Long Tail economics" to explain those that eventually did.[9] While the concept is fairly imprecise, it quickly became a staple of twenty-first-century business terminology and continues to evoke the dramatic changes that took place as digital technologies reshaped the economics of entertainment. For Anderson, the Long Tail signifies the growing importance of niche markets and the subsequent shift from relying exclusively on massively successful commodities to more modestly successful commodities that generate value over longer periods of time. Anderson, moreover, associates this transition with the declining costs of production and distribution—which he primarily attributes to the democratizing effects of new digital technologies—and the increased efficiency in synchronizing supply chains with consumer demands—which he equates with new filtering programs and interface designs made possible as an extension of different internet technologies. In these ways, the Long Tail is framed as a positive development for consumers and businesses alike, especially for upstart companies like Amazon and Netflix which served to illustrate the Long Tail premise throughout Anderson's case.

Although the Long Tail is mainly characterized as a twenty-first-century technological innovation, it can be applied in a much broader sense. Joseph Turow, for instance, discusses the rise of niche markets as part of the "breaking up" of America that takes place over a long term and across multiple industries. In publishing, there was a switch in the 1960s and 1970s from mass-circulation titles like *Life* to more narrowly focused magazines catering to select lifestyles and demographic criteria.[10] Similarly, the cable industry encouraged more narrowly defined channels—devoted either to specific genres like news and sports or demographic segments like African Americans and women—as an alternative to broadcast networks' mass appeal model.[11] Though the benefits of these developments, like Anderson's account of the Long Tail, were partly cast in terms of democratic progress, they were mainly driven by economics. Advertisers were willing to pay to access a more delineated target audience.

In the case of cable, an even more important factor was that individual channels were tied to the expansion of larger multisystem operators (MSOs) which often owned a partial stake in many different programming assets. In this regard, niche markets were part of a complicated arrangement of interlocking interests. Individual channels relied on the carriage fees—a per subscriber fee paid by the MSO—to supplement advertising revenues. MSOs, in turn, used these channels to promote their overall cable package as part of their aggressive expansion efforts.[12] In other words, niche markets were not only established long before the internet arrived but were also fully compatible with the logic of horizontal integration.

Another dimension of the Long Tail is evident in two other ancillary markets. Although Anderson contrasts Netflix with its predecessor Blockbuster, the entire conceit of the video rental industry was to unlock the long-term value of movies after their theatrical release. More specifically, video rental was profitable because retailers were able to continue generating value from a product after amortizing its cost.[13] The main difference between Blockbuster and Netflix, at the time of Anderson's book at least, was that as the rental industry matured, Blockbuster shifted its focus to new releases and to partnering with the Hollywood studios in profit-sharing agreements that lowered wholesale costs. Netflix, meanwhile, did indeed place greater emphasis on driving customers to the further reaches of its catalog in lieu of new releases, but it did this as much as anything as a way of differentiating itself from the likes of Blockbuster and because of the need to limit costs as an upstart. What was unique about the video rental industry in an overall sense was that the studios did not control it themselves—this was partly the result of their resistance to the VCR. The studios were certainly not unaware, however, of the benefits of the Long Tail. The clearest evidence of this is perhaps in the windfall they generated through the important ancillary market of television syndication.[14] Although syndication was contingent on developing hit shows, the real value of these programs was in their ability to generate additional profits long after their initial broadcast.

In a certain sense, television syndication complicates the idea of Long Tail economics in that it shows how hits and long-term profitability are not mutually exclusive.[15] Another, much more convoluted, divergence arises in terms of the differences between the video rental model and the syndication example. The former succeeds by virtue of minimizing or controlling the cost of its inventory. There is a key difference in this regard between a business that retails manufactured commodities while dealing directly with consumers and a company like Google that simply harvests user-generated information as if it were a naturally occurring resource—one that can then be exploited or monetized at the expense of consumers. This difference is exacerbated in that the syndication model emphasizes how the entertainment industry is committed to controlling intellectual property rights and to maximizing the value of those rights as part of a long-term investment. The video rental industry grew because these interests were temporarily muted—home entertainment was still in its nascent stage, meaning that market values were not definitively established, and more importantly because the "first sale doctrine" allowed physical media to be redistributed on secondary markets without having to further compensate the rights holder.[16] Over time, the value of these goods changed and it became more difficult for retailers like Blockbuster or Netflix to simply aggregate undervalued content. For Blockbuster, these difficulties began with the transition from VHS to DVD. For Netflix, it was the transition from DVD to streaming. In both cases, the combination of changing market conditions and new technologies significantly altered the efficacy of Long Tail economics.

Whereas Netflix ultimately overcame the challenges of its transition from DVD-by-mail delivery to digital on-demand streaming, Blockbuster's efforts to adapt precipitated its demise. There is some irony to this since Blockbuster recognized from the outset the limitations of the video rental industry's Long Tail premise. It hedged against these limitations by committing to all-out growth—believing that its dominant position would allow for other benefits, for instance, economies of scale, and cross-industry partnerships—and to utilizing financial mechanisms as part of that strategy. For example, Blockbuster used stock swaps in its acquisition of competing regional chains, and, similar to the dot-com boom that followed, its executives' salaries were sweetened with various stock options.[17] The company's stock continued to increase throughout this period, winning over investors and financial analysts with the rate of its expansion and its status as a clear market leader. But as the video rental industry matured amidst persistent speculation that new technologies would soon displace it, Blockbuster began looking for new business opportunities. These included international expansion and acquiring programming assets, establishing in effect a blueprint that Netflix would follow a decade later.[18] In its most aggressive move, Blockbuster joined with Viacom in its contentious bidding war for Paramount. Initially, the deal consisted of Blockbuster investing in Viacom, providing the consortium of cable channels with the additional capital it needed to raise its bid for Paramount. As the deal evolved, however, Viacom acquired Blockbuster as part of a complicated stock exchange, mainly to service the new conglomerate's debt load.[19] Despite the widespread discussion by Ken Auletta and the business media more generally, the deal did not yield the much-touted synergies that the merger had promised.[20]

In fact, the deal did not merely fail to clinch Blockbuster's effort to move beyond the limits of Long Tail economics, but it increased the rental retailer's financial instability, triggering a downward spiral that eventually ended in bankruptcy. In the years immediately following the merger, the chief executive Sumner Redstone blamed Blockbuster for the new conglomerate's underwhelming financial performance.[21] Viacom, as a result, moved rather quickly to rid itself of Blockbuster, first spinning off 20 percent in 1999 and completing the disunion in 2004.[22] The terms of these transactions were largely unfavorable for Blockbuster. First, throughout this interim period Viacom refused to support additional expenditures, for instance, setting up a DVD-by-mail service to compete with fledgling competitors like Netflix. This was part of an effort to enhance Blockbuster's bottom line so as to attract potential buyers. After failing to do so, however, the 2004 spin-off was structured in a way that Blockbuster took on over $1 billion in debt. At the same time that technology was radically transforming media and entertainment, Blockbuster was handcuffed primarily because of its financial limitations—not because of a failure in its primary business model. This situation was further compounded as the "activist shareholder" Carl Icahn ignited a proxy battle to seize control of Blockbuster's board of directors, in turn prompting a series of embarrassing public feuds regarding the company's direction.[23]

Although Blockbuster and Netflix have been largely depicted as competitors, they also share a deeply intertwined history that illustrates the different, and sometimes divergent, aspects of the Long Tail. In general, the video rental industry illustrated the potential of niche content. From a business standpoint, the importance of this content was not about serving consumer demand or expanding choice. Instead, it was about leveraging an undervalued commodity within an emerging market. This advantage encouraged rapid expansion, which then determined control of the market. These developments were closely tied to their perceived financial value. That is, the rise of the video rental industry coincided with investors' willingness to gamble on higher risk opportunities and on the promise of exponential stock increases. As these emerging markets mature, however, retailers—whether online services like Netflix or the brick-and-mortar variety like Blockbuster—necessarily shift away from Long Tail economics. In many cases, diversification or horizontal integration through mergers and acquisitions promises to replace the declining benefits of the Long Tail with new advantages. The cable industry is an example of how niche content can be strategically coordinated to support larger corporate interests from the outset. Blockbuster, by contrast, demonstrates the difficulty of combining complementary services within a conglomerate structure. While Netflix enjoyed tremendous growth throughout its first decade, essentially replicating the same pattern established by Blockbuster, it faced increased marketplace scrutiny amidst its efforts to move beyond the Long Tail. Most famously, Netflix's stock fell by 70 percent in 2011 after the company announced a price increase and an ill-fated plan to separate its streaming service from its DVD-by-mail service—set to be rechristened Qwikster.[24] In October 2014 Netflix's stock again fell 20 percent following announcements that both HBO and CBS would be introducing stand-alone over-the-top (OTT) services.[25] Even without the burden of conglomeration, Netflix, like its predecessor, remains vulnerable to increasing financial instability, especially now that its initial growth phase has come to an end.

Branded entertainment

The shift away from Long Tail economics coincided with a growing emphasis on developing a recognizable brand identity. This was true for Blockbuster as it began to diversify beyond the video rental industry, and it was even more pronounced in the cable industry, where, according to Michael Curtin and Jane Shattuc, the most significant development of the 1990s was the way niche channels transformed themselves into brands.[26] In select cases, a brand identity was built into the channel from the outset. For instance, the Disney Channel was as recognizable as the major broadcast networks due to its parent company's status.[27] Other channels like MTV, CNN, and ESPN adopted distinct genre identities—music, news, sports—that then became the basis of their brands. Branding became especially important at this time because cable and direct satellite services were expanding significantly. Individual channels had to prove that they could cut through the clutter of an increasingly crowded marketplace to ensure that they were carried as part of these services' basic subscription plans. By and large, niche-oriented channels demonstrated their value to cable operators not through ratings but by formulating a brand that appealed to particular audience segments. Sarah Banet-Weiser, for example, details how Nickelodeon's distinct orange splat logo took precedence over individual shows as part of its appeal to children viewers.[28] Many other scholars have likewise noted how the memorable slogan "It's Not TV. It's HBO" was a deliberate attempt to court a more discerning or elite audience.[29] Although there is less of an imperative for Netflix, as a stand-alone service, to differentiate itself, its $1 million prize contest to improve a recommendation algorithm is tantamount to a public relations gimmick that functions as another kind of branding strategy. Altogether, the growing emphasis on branding was an indicator that the business of media and entertainment was not reducible to a rational economic logic, Long Tail or otherwise, and that marketing and promotion were an important means of combating the financial pressures that came with Wall Street's exorbitant expectations.

While logo design and marketing rhetoric were valuable in creating a distinct brand identity, the most decisive factor for cable channels was programming. In some cases, cable channels like Bravo, MTV, and A&E created signature programming as an extension of Long Tail economics. These channels created low-cost unscripted or reality programs that then became the basis for extensive franchises or for a format that extended across multiple channels. By contrast, for more general-interest cable networks like TNT, USA, and FX, original programming signified a move away from cheaper content like reruns, older movies, and syndicated materials, a move that did not necessarily translate into additional advertising revenues but did provide leverage in negotiating with cable operators.[30] For HBO, original programming became a way of further distinguishing itself as a quality or premium brand, a service for which cable subscribers were willing to pay an additional fee. Beginning in the early 2000s, several cable networks mimicked this strategy. The success of FX's *The Shield* and AMC's *Mad Men* proved that prestige—by way of winning industry awards, garnering critical praise, and developing an intense following—was incredibly valuable in generating "buzz," or promotional currency, despite these shows' relatively low ratings.[31]

For several channels, the brand equity provided by original programming was also a way to hedge against the rising cost of other forms of content. HBO, for instance, was created as a premium movie service, one that provided subscribers with exclusive access to recent Hollywood films. Although it has always had to supplement this feature with other forms of programming, it was only in the 1990s that it made a conscientious effort to develop serial dramas that more closely resembled traditional network television.[32] In part, this was a way to offset the rising costs of licensing premium Hollywood films and the financial risk implicit in long-term output deals that had become the industry standard. More recently, ESPN has followed a similar course. After an aggressive effort to acquire the broadcast rights for a wide range of sporting events—considered lucrative because they are predominantly viewed live, seemingly immune to the time-shifting technologies that have bedeviled linear television more generally—the cost of these rights began to skyrocket.[33] ESPN aims to mitigate these costs with cheaper in-house productions like its staple *Sportscenter* program and its recently developed branded documentary series *30 for 30*. In the same way that HBO's dramatic series opened up ancillary revenues with DVD sales, ESPN has licensed these documentaries to secondary exhibition platforms like Netflix.[34] This programming thereby enhances the channel's brand identity while providing additional value, generating another source of revenue, and also saving on additional programming costs. The economic benefits of original programming were also a major factor as Netflix navigated the transition from DVD delivery to streaming. The deal Netflix struck with the premium channel Starz was invaluable in facilitating this transition, but it also served to dramatically inflate the cost of subscription video-on-demand (SVOD) rights. As a result, Netflix quickly shifted its focus to acquiring the streaming rights to television programming and eventually to developing its own original programming very much in the same vein as HBO and AMC.

Signature shows like *House of Cards* and *Orange Is the New Black* were certainly a boon to the service's marketing and promotion efforts, but original programming was also part of Netflix's larger, and in some ways more complex, brand strategy. Television programming was a bargain in that Netflix paid less for more hours of content. At the same time, it represented a different form of consumption, one in which viewers were likely to be more engaged in both a quantitative and qualitative sense. This was especially true for serial dramas, which provided an added benefit as a new source of Long Tail economics. *The Sopranos*, *Sex and the City*, and *24* generated impressive DVD sales, but as the DVD market began to decline in 2007, these programs demonstrated less long-term value.[35] Netflix provided a convenient trade-off, with SVOD licensing basically replacing DVD sales for these types of programs. More importantly, serial dramas like *Lost*, with its complex narrative arcs and prolonged character development, illustrate what M.J. Clarke describes as a beneficial addictive good or what he more generally terms transmedia television. As Clarke further elaborates it, these are the shows in which the more you watch, "the more consumption capital is accrued and the more valuable are subsequent encounters with the text in all its forms."[36] Netflix used this logic in its aggressive acquisition of ongoing programs like *Mad Men*, *Breaking Bad*, *The Walking Dead*, and *Sons of Anarchy*. It was willing to pay a higher premium for these shows and create what amounts to a new "catch-up" market that precedes traditional syndication, believing that these deals made for a mutually beneficial partnership. As Netflix generated additional interest in these shows, leading to higher ratings as additional seasons premiered on broadcast television, the increased popularity of these shows enhanced the value of its catalog.[37]

Original programming for Netflix, then, is part of a larger brand identity that it designates internet TV. This concept revolves around encouraging extended periods of viewer engagement, something Netflix reinforces with its decision to release its own programs en masse as entire seasons. This isn't only a matter of further differentiating the Netflix brand, but emblematic of its overall approach to content. As Ted Sarandos, chief content officer, explains it, "What I really want you to do is find a show in which you'll get lost, a show that makes you want to watch 'just one more episode', even though you know you have to get up early tomorrow morning."[38] This idea of internet TV is often promoted as part of Netflix's technological advantage—its ability to escape the restrictive confines of linear television and empower viewers to watch what they want when they want. Despite the suggestion that viewers are granted additional control, Sarandos' explanation hints at something different. He continues, "We are restoring a sense of connection between consumers and content. I think audiences have lost that emotional investment in content because television can no longer provide them access in the way they want it."[39] This type of extended emotional engagement is further likened to the time and effort required to either play certain video games or read a novel. However, the less flattering and more common term for this phenomenon is "binge-watching." As a key part of Netflix's effort to deepen its connection with consumers, this term, as several authors in this collection have noted, suggests something more problematic. In some respects, it recalls Henry Jenkins' account of affective economics as a marketing ploy that pays lip service to the sensate force of consumers' desires but that, ultimately, merely endeavors to transform information about consumer behavior into a better return on investment.[40] And insofar as Netflix aims to replicate the addictive qualities that some serial dramas engender, its personalization algorithms contribute to what Mark Andrejevic describes as a digital enclosure. That is, the data generated as part of a subscriber's activity on the Netflix site predetermines and constrains future behavior, compelling certain choices while foreclosing others.[41]

The development of branded entertainment in the 1990s and 2000s speaks to the efforts of cable channels and entertainment services like Netflix to create a distinct identity that went beyond Long Tail economics or niche markets. This was a matter of simply evolving as part of the media and entertainment industry as well as a way of defending against fluctuating market speculation. Despite the success of Netflix and others in establishing a recognizable brand identity, there are still many instances of tension or instability. This is most commonly evident as different stakeholders lay claim to and negotiate the value of programming assets. For instance, there are questions regarding which brand—Netflix or AMC benefits most from programs like *Mad Men* and *Breaking Bad* and this leads to disagreements in terms of licensing rights across different windows.[42] This type of tension is even more pronounced in the case of ESPN, the cable channel that has made the most concerted effort to expand its brand across multiple platforms. These strategies stem from the rising cost of sports programming and the growing competition from professional sports leagues—which have all created their own networks—for control of this content. But, in trying to monetize its programming assets through online on-demand streaming and mobile apps, ESPN runs the risk—even when using apps developed as part of the TV Everywhere initiative that authenticates the user's cable subscription—of undercutting its traditional ratings and advertising revenues. More importantly, these strategies may jeopardize ESPN's relationship with cable operators and the carriage fees—nearly $6 per subscriber—that remain its main source of income.

HBO faces similar challenges as it moves into internet TV with its 2015 introduction of a stand-alone OTT service, HBO Now. Many have long speculated that this would mean doom for Netflix. These types of transitions, however, are rarely seamless. The new service requires that HBO set up its own billing, customer service, and marketing operations, all of which had been delegated to cable providers. Also, HBO has set the price for HBO Now at virtually the same price as its cable service, in an effort to avoid upsetting its existing cable partners, perhaps limiting its potential market to the 10 million households that currently pay for high-speed internet but not cable.[43] As channels like HBO and ESPN move to compete more directly with Netflix, some worry that this may trigger a more fundamental collapse of the current system and this may have unexpected consequences. An "a la carte" system, in which consumers only pay for the channels they want, was supposed to mark a major improvement. But now it may mean that consumers pay more for less, especially considering internet services are mainly controlled by cable providers.

Another larger issue involves the $70 billion in advertising spent each year as part of the current system of television. This may not directly concern subscription services like HBO and Netflix, but others remain deeply invested in preserving some form of the current system. Finally, in addition to all of this, there is speculation that the rise in original programming—as an extension of individual channels' branding efforts—has reached a saturation point. *Variety* reporter Cynthia Littleton notes that there has been an exponential "spike" in the number of scripted series developed by HBO, FX, and AMC since 1999. This increase is the direct result of cable channels building brand equity through signature programming as well as the emergence of new Long Tail markets like SVOD licensing. The rapid increase of these shows, according to Littleton, produces a kind of bubble effect in which ballooning production costs, thinning quality, and diminishing returns threaten to render these channels unviable in the long term.[44]

International expansion

In 2011, Netflix surpassed 20 million subscribers. In doing so, it recognized that its business model was maturing and that domestic growth would begin to slow. Similar to Blockbuster and HBO in the 1990s, Netflix responded by rapidly expanding its service to a number of international markets. It began by testing the waters in 2010 with a streaming-only service in Canada before expanding to over forty countries in Latin America in 2011. Netflix then launched its service in the UK, Ireland, and Scandinavia in 2012, and by the end of 2014 it was available throughout most of Continental Europe including major markets like France and Germany. While Netflix has grown significantly because of these efforts, to over 60 million subscribers worldwide, international expansion has also compounded some of the cross-purposes already evident in the two previous sections.

The increasing number of total subscribers has buoyed Netflix's overall financial performance, though this also means that the company remains vulnerable to investor speculation and ongoing market turbulence. For example, in the fourth quarter of 2012, Netflix reported losses of over $100 million as a result of its global expansion plans and the upfront costs of original programming. This sent the company's stock down 16 percent.[45] At the start of 2015, though its stock had recently plunged on news of HBO's OTT service, Netflix quickly rebounded with higher-than-expected international subscriber growth. Again in April 2015, Netflix shares increased 12 percent to $534, raising the company's market value to almost $29 billion despite the fact that its profits amounted to only $24 million, far less than the $1.8 billion in profits that HBO accrued in 2013.[46] These fluctuations simultaneously encourage a riskier overall approach. For example, Netflix in 2013 raised $400 million in credit to cover its growing expenditures but also as interest rate relief on its existing $500 million in debt.[47] While the company maintains that it will complete its international expansion by 2016, it is also now exploring the possibility of introducing its service in Russia and China following its 2015 expansion into Australia, New Zealand, and Japan. As one financial analyst sums up the logic of Netflix's strategy, "If they don't expand quickly enough overseas, investors are going to hammer the stock."[48] This begs the question of what will happen when there is nowhere else to expand.

In addition to intensifying the existing financial pressures of perpetual growth, international expansion engenders numerous difficulties as Netflix recasts itself as a global brand. Many of these are the result of the logistical challenges that come with moving into new and less familiar markets. Although Netflix makes a concerted effort to only expand into markets with a sufficient existing technical infrastructure, there are still unforeseen obstacles. In 2011, Latin America appeared lucrative because of its more than 40 million broadband subscribers and because of its manageable language barrier.[49] Growth proved to be slower than expected, however, because consumers were wary of Netflix's payment system. Protective regulatory policies in France, local variations like Germany's preference for dubbing, and data caps in Australia create similar complications, forcing Netflix to carefully tailor its operations to each individual territory. This creates a larger disadvantage in that international subscribers are less profitable for Netflix. That is, while it is able to streamline its service for the U.S. market, internationally, Netflix devotes a higher percentage of operating costs to a lower percentage of its overall subscriber base.

The much bigger challenge, however, concerns programming content and securing the necessary rights to these properties. In many cases Netflix does not control exclusive international rights—not even to the original programming that has played such a significant role in establishing its domestic brand identity. This is true not only for Netflix but for competitors like HBO as well. The international rights to important programming assets like *House of Cards* and *Game of Thrones* were forfeited not out of any kind of a miscalculation but because of the complexity of the international market. In most cases these rights were sold to markets prior to arrival of Netflix or HBO, in an effort to maximize their value and because competitors were willing to pay a premium for them as a way to legitimate their own entry into VOD.[50]

While HBO has a stronger overall global position, with 100 million international subscribers, its standing is somewhat more complicated because its service is available across different platforms—as part of satellite or terrestrial cable system in some territories and as a stand-alone streaming service in others. Because of these types of complications, both HBO and Netflix are at times forced to compete against content that they are promoting in other territories as their own. And in lieu of their own signature programming, they are compelled to develop marketing campaigns around other content, sometimes a motley patchwork notable only because it is an American export. Altogether this makes for a crowded and confusing marketplace with no dominant business model and the possibility that overall growth may be limited—one 2014 forecast anticipates that streaming video market for all of Western Europe will reach $1.1 billion by 2017 (as compared to $14 billion in the United States).[51]

Since embarking upon international expansion, Netflix has become more conscientious both in securing exclusive rights and in appealing to global consumers. But this in turn exposes another conflict of interests. In late 2014 Netflix announced its plans to finance a sequel to the 2000 film *Crouching Tiger, Hidden Dragon* along with a deal to produce four feature films through Adam Sandler's Happy Madison Productions. As in its initial efforts to extend itself beyond the Long Tail economics of the video rental industry, this move amounts to a diversification of programming, one that is aimed more explicitly at a mass audience. As one commentator explains, "When you want to get to be in 50 million homes, you have to be all things to all people. You have to appeal to the 10-year-old who wants to watch a racing snail, but you also have to appeal to the college student who gets his laughs from Adam Sandler or the action fan who wants to see some cool fight scenes."[52] In a way, this logic is a kind of corollary to the disproportionate costs of international expansion—as the per-subscriber costs increase on an international basis, it is necessary to lower the overall cost of content. Be this as it may, this logic runs counter to Netflix's earlier programming investments. It would certainly seem that its latest signature series *Marco Polo*, widely panned as anything except a hollow allegory of Netflix's global ambitions, undermines the critical acclaim generated by *House of Cards* and *Orange Is the New Black*.[53] While this type of programming may make sense as part of the economics of global internet TV, it may leave something to be desired in terms of extending or intensifying viewer engagement with the Netflix brand—which will be all the more important as the company runs out of new markets.

Conclusion

The last three decades have given rise to a handful of incredibly dominant media conglomerates. And yet this same period has been one of the most dynamic and innovative in terms of media, technology, and especially home entertainment. Netflix is an example of how new business models emerged during this period and how, even amidst the constraints of structural convergence, there are fleeting gaps or limits that can be exploited by others. Though the Long Tail concept is often overstated and imprecise, it helps to explain the role that new markets play in providing newcomers like Netflix the advantage they need to compete with more established business interests. One of the reasons that Netflix is perpetually under threat of the so-called disintermediation is that the advantages of Long Tail economics change quickly both as a matter of larger market conditions and heightened investor scrutiny. Netflix has been adept in navigating these circumstances, evolving its business model and building a brand identity as internet TV. Regardless of its success, pressure remains as competitors like HBO and other high-profile cable networks adopt the premise of internet TV for their own purposes and as international expansion threatens to compromise Netflix's ability to focus on its key strategic advantages.

These pressures further indicate the degree to which media and entertainment are intertwined with market economics. This means that even while these industries are more fluid—in terms of fluctuating formats, platforms, technologies, and business models—they also favor the large conglomerate structures that are capable of withstanding perpetual instability. This of course doesn't mean that all companies are immune to failure—simply recall the fate of Blockbuster—but it suggests that even amidst dramatic change the basic landscape remains largely the same. While Netflix has succeeded in maintaining its place thus far, its future depends on consumers' insatiable demand for media and entertainment. In the case that this demand should ever dwindle, Netflix is well versed in fortifying demand with its own algorithmic machinations. More generally, the future of media and entertainment will remain bright so long as such things can be tethered to the various profit-engines that serve existing global economic interests.

Notes

1 Ken Auletta, *The Highwaymen: Warriors of the Information Superhighway* (New York: Random House, 1997), 102.
2 John Dempsey, "Showtime/Encore Meld Could Be a Blockbuster," *Variety*, September 26, 1994. http://www.lexisnexis.com/hottopics/lnacademic (accessed July 8, 2015).
3 Jennifer Holt, *Empires of Entertainment: Media Industries and the Politics of Deregulation, 1980–1996* (New Brunswick, NJ: Rutgers University Press, 2011), 3.
4 Quoted in Richard Maltby, *Hollywood Cinema*, 2nd ed. (Malden, MA: Blackwell, 2003), 205.
5 Henry Jenkins, *Convergence Culture: Where Old and New Media Collide* (New York: New York University Press, 2006), 2–3.
6 Amanda Lotz, *The Television Will Be Revolutionized*, 2nd ed. (New York: New York University Press, 2014), 27–34.
7 These developments have been widely detailed by a number of media scholars. For further discussion, see Tino Balio's *Hollywood in the New Millennium* (London: BFI, 2013); Holt's *Empires of Entertainment*; Paul McDonald and Janet Wasko's collection *The Contemporary Hollywood Film Industry* (Malden, MA: Blackwell, 2008); Maltby's *Hollywood Cinema*; Stephen Pince's *A New Pot of Gold: Hollywood Under the Electronic Rainbow, 1980–1989* (Berkeley: University of California Press, 2000).

8 Holt, *Empires of Entertainment*, 15. See also Patrick R. Parsons, *Blue Skies: A History of Cable Television* (Philadelphia: Temple University Press, 2008), 438–441.
9 Chris Anderson, *The Long Tail: Why the Future of Business Is Selling Less of More* (New York: Hyperion, 2008), 22–24.
10 Joseph Turow, *Breaking Up America: Advertisers and the New Media World* (Chicago: University of Chicago Press, 1997), 30.
11 For further discussion, see Parsons, *Blue Skies*, 448–469.
12 Ibid., 523–537.
13 Janet Wasko, *Hollywood in the Information Age: Beyond the Silver Screen* (Austin: University of Texas Press, 1994), 132–135.
14 For further discussion, see Derek Kompare, *Rerun Nation: How Repeats Invented American Television* (New York: Routledge, 2005), 69–71.
15 Anderson actually considers a number of earlier examples of the Long Tail model (e.g., the Sears Roebuck mail order catalog). For the most part, however, the Long Tail has been associated with new internet technologies. This tends to overshadow or obscure the continuities that link older business models to newer ones like Netflix.
16 Paul McDonald, *Video and DVD Industries* (London: BFI, 2007), 115.
17 Gail DeGeorge, *The Making of a Blockbuster: How Wayne Huizenga Built a Sports and Entertainment Empire from Trash, Grit, and Videotape* (New York: Wiley, 1996), 151–158 and 121–123.
18 Ibid., 161–163 and 199–207.
19 Ibid., 264–304. Others tend to characterize the deal as a straightforward acquisition, but the complications associated with this merger were a key factor in why it did not succeed in the way it was supposed to.
20 See Anthony Ramirez, "In Terms of Technology, Viacom Might Have an Edge," *New York Times*, January 19, 1994. http://www.nytimes.com/1994/01/19/business/company-news-in-terms-of-technology-viacom-might-have-an-edge.html (accessed July 8, 2015). See also Calvin Sims "'Synergy': The Unspoken Word," *New York Times*, October 5, 1993. http://www.nytimes.com/1993/10/05/business/the-media-business-synergy-the-unspoken-word.html (accessed July 8, 2015).
21 See, for example, the first chapter, "Blockbuster Tanks," in Sumner Redstone and Peter Knobler, *A Passion to Win* (New York: Simon & Schuster, 2001), 29–40.
22 Eric Dash and Geraldine Fabrikant. "Payout Is Set by Blockbuster to Viacom," *New York Times*, June 19, 2004. http://www.nytimes.com/2004/06/19/business/payout-is-set-by-blockbuster-to-viacom.html (accessed July 8, 2015). See also Andres Ross Sorkin and Geraldine Fabrikant, "Viacom Close to Deciding to Spin Off Blockbuster," *New York Times*, February 2, 2004. http://www.nytimes.com/2004/02/02/business/ viacom-close-to-deciding-to-spin-off-blockbuster.html (accessed July 8, 2015).
23 This part of Blockbuster's history is discussed in detail in Gina Keating's *Netflixed: The Epic Battle for America's Eyeballs* (New York: Portfolio, 2012). In particular, see: 71–83, 86–97, 110–138, 151–164, 169–170, and 205–210.
24 See Holman W. Jenkins, "Netflix Isn't Doomed," *Wall Street Journal*, October 26, 2011. http://www.wsj.com/articles/SB10001424052970204644504576653182551430322 (accessed July 8, 2015). See also, Nick Wingfield and Brian Stelter, "A Juggernaut Stumbles," *New York Times*, October 25, 2011. http://www.nytimes.com/2011/10/25/technology/netflix-lost-800000-members-with-price-rise-and-split-plan.html (accessed July 8, 2015).

25 Meg James, "CBS Offers Streaming Service," *Los Angeles Times*, October 17, 2014. http://www.latimes.com/entertainment/envelope/cotown/la-et-ct-streaming-breakthrough-20141017-story.html (accessed July 8, 2015).
26 Michael Curtin and Jane Shattuc. *The American Television Industry* (London: BFI, 2009), 82.
27 For a more general discussion of branding and Disney in particular, see Paul Grainge's *Brand Hollywood: Selling Entertainment in a Global Media Age* (New York: Routledge, 2008), 8–15.
28 Sarah Banet-Weiser, "The Nickelodeon Brand: Buying and Selling the Audience," *Cable Visions: Television Beyond Broadcasting*, eds, Sarah Banet-Weiser, Cynthia Chris, and Anthony Freitas (New York: New York University Press, 2007), 242.
29 For further discussion, see Janet McCabe and Kim Akass, eds, *Quality TV: Contemporary American Television and Beyond* (London: I.B. Tauris, 2007); Marc Leverette, Brian L. Ott, and Cara Louise Buckley, eds, *It's Not TV: Watching HBO in the Post-Television Era* (New York: Routledge, 2008); Gary R. Edgerton and Jeffrey P. Jones, eds, *The Essential HBO Reader* (Lexington: University Press of Kentucky, 2008).
30 Curtin and Shattuc, *American Television Industry*, 76.
31 Scott Collins, "Cable Networks Are TV's Biggest Stars," *Los Angeles Times*, October 1, 2012. http://articles.latimes.com/2012/sep/30/entertainment/la-et-st-homeland-market-20121001 (accessed July 8, 2015).
32 Edgerton and Jones, "Introduction: A Brief History of HBO," *Essential HBO Reader*, 9–10.
33 Kurt Badenhausen, "The Value of ESPN Surpasses $50 Billion," *Forbes*, April 29, 2014. http://www.forbes.com/sites/kurtbadenhausen/2014/04/29/the-value-of-espn-surpasses-50-billion (accessed July 8, 2015). See also Matthew Futterman, "Pay-TV Providers Bid to End Sports Networks' Win Streak," *Wall Street Journal*, July 15, 2013. http://wsj.com/articles/SB10001424127887323823004578595571950242766 (accessed July 8, 2015).
34 Richard Sandomir, "Once Specials, Documentaries Are Now TV Staples," *New York Times*, March 22, 2015. http://www.nytimes.com/2015/03/22/sports/documentaries-are-the-go-to-players-of-sports-television.html (accessed July 8, 2015).
35 Curtin and Shattuc, *American Television Industry*, 114 and 139.
36 M.J. Clarke, *Transmedia Television: New Trends in Network Serial Production* (New York: Bloomsbury, 2013), 5.
37 Ted Sarandos interview in Michael Curtin, Jennifer Holt, and Kevin Sanson, eds, *Distribution Revolution: Conversations About the Digital Future of Film and Television* (Berkeley: University of California Press, 2014), 134–135.
38 Ibid., 135.
39 Ibid.
40 Jenkins, *Convergence Culture*, 62.
41 Mark Andrejevic, *Reality TV: The Work of Being Watched* (Lanham, MD: Rowman & Littlefield, 2004), 36–37.
42 See, for example, Andrew Wallenstein, "Are Binge Viewers Killing Shows?" *Daily Variety*, November 19, 2012. http://www.lexisnexis.com/hottopics/lnacademic (accessed July 8, 2015). See also Andrew Wallenstein, "Inconsistent Availability of Cable Programs Frustrates Viewers and Hampers Growth," *Daily Variety*, August 2, 2012. http://www.lexisnexis.com/hottopics/lnacademic (accessed July 8, 2015).

43 Meg James and Ryan Faughnder, "HBO to Offer Its Programs Online," *Los Angeles Times*, October 16, 2014. http://www.latimes.com/entertainment/envelope/cotown/la-et-ct-hbo-time-warner-internet-online-program-20141016-story.html (accessed July 8, 2015).
44 Cynthia Littleton, "How Many Scripted Series Can the TV Biz and Viewers Handle?" *Variety*, September 16, 2014. http://variety.com/2014/tv/news/new-television-fall-season-glut-of-content-1201306075 (accessed July 8, 2015).
45 Dawn Chmielewski, "Netflix Third-Quarter Profit Falls 88% on Global Expansion Costs," *Los Angeles Times*, October 24, 2012. http://www.latimes.com/2012/oct/23/entertainment/la-et-ct-netflix-earnings-20121023 (accessed July 8, 2015).
46 See Ryan Faughnder, "Netflix Gets Boost from Global Push," *Los Angeles Times*, January 21, 2015. http://www.latimes.com/entertainment/envelope/cotown/la-et-ct-netflix-earnings-20150121-story.html (accessed July 8, 2015). See also Emily Steel, "Though Profits Fall, Netflix Stock Surges on Subscriber Growth," *New York Times*, April 16, 2015. http://www.nytimes.com/2015/04/16/business/media/though-profits-fall-netflix-shares-surge-on-subscriber-growth.html (accessed July 8, 2015). For HBO's profits, see David Carr and Ravi Somaiya, "Punching Above Its Weight, Upstart Netflix Pokes at HBO," *New York Times*, February 17, 2014. http://www.nytimes.com/2014/02/17/business/media/punching-above-its-weight-upstart-netflix-pokes-at-hbo.html (accessed July 8, 2015).
47 Paul Bond, "Netflix Announces Plan to Raise $400 Million," *Hollywood Reporter*, January 29, 2013, www.hollywoodreporter.com/news/netflix-announces-plan-raise-400-416528 (accessed July 8, 2015).
48 Quoted in Andrew Wallenstein, "World Orders: Netflix Takes Wing with Global Goal," *Variety*, April 11, 2011. http://variety.com/2011/digital/news/netflix-shifts-toward-new-world-orders-1118035178/ (accessed July 8, 2015).
49 See Andrew Wallenstein, "Netflix Expansion Plan Sends Stock Soaring," *Variety*, July 5, 2011. http://variety.com/2011/digital/news/netflix-expansion-plan-sends-stock-soaring-1118039439 (accessed July 8, 2015).
50 See Sam Schechner and Amol Sharma, "Europe's Media Giants Prep for Netflix Landing," *Wall Street Journal*, January 29, 2014. http://wsj.com/articles/ SB10001424052702303277704579348774128548520 (accessed July 8, 2015).
51 Quoted in Ibid. For estimated U.S. revenues, see Joe Battaglia, "Report: Revenue from Online Video Streaming to Surpass Box Office," *Newsmax*, June 5, 2014. http://www.newsmax.com/US/Netflix-Hulu-video-movies/2014/06/05/id/575369/ (accessed July 8, 2015).
52 Quoted in Ryan Faughnder and Yvonne Villarreal, "Netflix Film Deals Reflect Its Growing Clout," *Los Angeles Times*, October 4, 2014. http://www.latimes.com/entertainment/envelope/cotown/la-et-ct-netflix-theaters-crouching-tiger-20141001-story.html (accessed July 8, 2015).
53 See Emily Steel, "How to Build an Empire, the Netflix Way," *New York Times*, November 30, 2014. http://www.nytimes.com/2014/11/30/business/media/how-to-build-an-empire-the-netflix-way-.html (accessed July 8, 2015).

14

Streaming Transatlantic: Importation and Integration in the Promotion of Video on Demand in the UK

Sam Ward

At the 2014 BAFTA (British Academy of Film and Television Arts) Television Awards, two of the four nominees in the International category had not actually been aired in their entirety on a British channel. Since its introduction in 2007, the category—for imported programs of any genre—had been dominated by two of Britain's biggest television companies: the BBC and Sky.[1] But a change in the rules allowing web-based content to be considered in the awards meant that this year *Breaking Bad* (American Movie Classics [AMC]; 2008–13) was able to take the prize. It had been six years since the British version of Fox (then called FX) had dropped the show after its first season had failed to attract adequate viewing figures. It was then briefly given a late-night slot by the public service Channel 5 for its second season, before disappearing altogether from the schedules. The basis for the show's nomination was, instead, the reception that all of its five seasons had enjoyed more recently as a flagship attraction for Netflix. Meanwhile, fellow nominee *House of Cards* (Netflix; 2013–) had not appeared on *any* traditional channel, having been made exclusively and directly available via its producer-distributor's online streaming service. As well as competing in the International category, perhaps even more notably, *House of Cards* was also in the running for the publicly polled *Radio Times* Audience Award (although it lost out here again to the fiftieth-anniversary special episode of *Doctor Who* [BBC; 1963–]).

This apparent acceptance of Netflix by the British television establishment is especially notable given the challenge that the British marketplace had posed when it launched in January 2012. The digital television industry in Britain was already dauntingly diverse and well populated, with over 150 services fitting the regulator's definition of video on demand (VOD).[2] Moreover, the most popular of these were extensions of old broadcaster brands with solid market standings. As one commentator put it at the time, "The whole nation's video on demand is already carved up.... It's already a relatively mature market, and we're not short of choice."[3] At the same time, web-based pay-TV as a whole was still a relatively marginal means of viewing. In fact, Netflix's most obvious rival, Lovefilm, which had been acquired by Amazon twelve months before Netflix launched, had seen a 13 percent *fall* in unique users during

2011.[4] Netflix's considerable level of penetration in Britain during its first three years is therefore striking. Attracting 1.2 million subscribers within two months of its launch,[5] it went on to overtake Lovefilm (since renamed Amazon Instant Video) as the country's most used streaming site and is now estimated to be present in more than 10 percent of households, compared to Amazon's 4.5 percent.[6]

Given that Britain was one of the first testing grounds for Netflix's ongoing international expansion (and, with Ireland, its first venture into Europe), its launch in the country provides a key insight into the approach it has taken to bringing its "post-broadcast" platform to new national territories. This chapter will argue, however, that this approach has been characterized more by *assimilation* and *integration* with the existing local television ecosystem, rather than on any claim to supersede it. In order to demonstrate this, I will compare the promotional strategies that have emerged around VOD in Britain before and as part of Netflix's launch. Three interconnected reasons for Netflix's relative success in Britain are identified by this analysis. First, despite the continuing predominance of broadcast viewing, the fact that streaming content was already a familiar consumer option (if not an everyday activity) for a significant portion of the British public gave Netflix its opening. Second, Netflix has presented itself explicitly as an importer of content, with its promotional discourse working to conflate *transnational* and *technological* connectivity. But rather than signaling a lack of local viability, this reliance on imported content represents the continuation of a broader trend in Britain's digital television culture. Third, Netflix has sought partnerships with domestic television platforms that have allowed both its software and its brand to be integrated with existing domestic services. These partnerships have given material and technical form to the broader promotional presentation of Netflix as continuous with established viewing habits, rather than as an interruptive alternative.

My main point of comparison will be with the leading pay-TV provider Sky, which the first half of the chapter will discuss as a representative example of how VOD had been presented to British viewers in the years leading up to Netflix's arrival. Sky's strategies provide an important point of comparison to the development of Netflix, not least because it was identified by Netflix personnel as the newcomer's key rival at launch, rather than their more natural counterpart Lovefilm/Amazon.[7] More importantly, though, analyzing Sky's promotional texts from 2011 onwards helps to illuminate the central place given to both specifically televisual culture—made clear by a range of television personalities used in promotions—and imported content in the discourse surrounding VOD in Britain. I will then go on to trace how these themes recur in Netflix's marketing as it launched in Britain. Finally, I will explain how a strategy of affiliation with established service providers has further helped to position Netflix as part of the nationally specific televisual experience.

Before I focus on the comparison between Sky and Netflix, it is nevertheless necessary to summarize some of the broader market developments leading up to Netflix's arrival. The range of viewing choices presented to the average British viewer had increased rapidly in the decade or so before 2012. Until the emergence of pay-TV services in the late 1980s, virtually all viewing had been done via terrestrial aerials that received open, free-to-air signals. Limited to a handful of public service channels, this was by far the most common way of watching television. The only firmly established pay-TV option to emerge before digitalization was Sky's satellite service. Sky offered multichannel packages that included the public service broadcasters as well as a range of exclusive channels (some operated by Sky), but these packages were only taken up by a small section of the public. Television signals were digitalized through the 2000s, culminating in a nationwide analogue switch-off between 2008 and 2012. The more spacious digital spectrum allowed for many more free-to-air channels to be broadcast, and its standardization brought the proportion of households with access to multichannel television up to 98 percent, compared to around 45 percent a decade earlier.[8] In the same decade, the audience share of the main public service channels fell from 78 percent[9] to a little over half of all viewing[10] as audiences got used to browsing the multichannel listings, which included several spin-off brands from the public service broadcasters themselves.

Another layer of consumer choice was also created by the fact that the new digital signals had to be decoded, meaning that all viewing was now done via a service provider that supplied the necessary equipment and software. Several new services—both subscription-based and free-to-air—emerged, each with their own set-top box and branding (see Table 14.1). The main way of watching television without paying a subscription fee was via the digital terrestrial television (DTT) service Freeview, which was established in 2002 by a nonprofit consortium that included the major public service broadcasters and Sky. Freeview offered a more limited range of channels than pay-TV, including all of those under the public broadcasters' brands. Meanwhile, for the first time, Sky was seriously challenged in the pay-TV market by new digital services offered by rival telecommunications operators like Virgin Media and British Telecom (BT).

There are two important points to draw out here about the impact of digitalization in the UK. First, it has not been accompanied by the same prospect of "cord-cutting" as has been observed in the United States. Instead, the most notable shift in television consumption has been a surge in subscriptions to pay-TV packages. Given the strong tradition in Britain of public service broadcasting that is free at the point of use, Sky's penetration in the analogue era had not reached levels that were anything like comparable with cable in the United States. Since digitalization, however, pay-TV subscriptions have become the most important source of revenue for the national industry as a whole, accounting for nearly as much as advertising and public funds combined.[11] Since 2009, more viewers have subscribed to pay-TV than have used free-to-air services,[12] with Sky reaching over 10 million subscribers by the time Netflix launched.[13]

Second, by 2012 VOD viewing in Britain was dominated by several established brands that were already widely familiar. *Service providers* like Sky and Freeview are to be distinguished from the VOD *platforms* that emerged during the same period, but crucially there are several overlaps and interconnections between these two sets of brands. For example, all the pay-TV service providers added on-demand, catch-up, and digital recording facilities to their packages through the 2000s. Meanwhile, in 2007 the BBC launched the iPlayer, which quickly became the most used VOD

Table 14.1 The main television services available in Britain by 2012

Platform	Owner(s)	Main delivery system[1]	Pay structure	VOD facilities
Freeview	BBC, ITV Channel 4, Sky, and Arqiva	Digital Terrestrial Television (DTT)	Free	None
YouView	BBC, ITV, Channel 4, Channel 5, British Telecom (BT), TalkTalk, and Arqiva	DTT and Internet	Free	iPlayer, ITV Player, 4OD, Demand 5, STV Player, and Now TV
Sky	BSKyB (controlled by News Corp.)[2]	Satellite	Monthly subscription	Sky On Demand
Virgin Media	Liberty Global	Fiber Optic Cable	Monthly subscription	Virgin On Demand, BBC iPlayer, ITV Player, 4OD, and YouTube
BT Vision[3]	BT	Internet (via BT Broadband)	Monthly subscription	BT Vision
BT YouView	BT	DTT and Internet	Monthly subscription	As YouView with BT Vision Player
TalkTalk Plus TV	TalkTalk Group	DTT and Internet	Pay-per-view and one-off "boosts"	As YouView with TalkTalk Player

1 The table lists the technology used for each provider's main delivery system at the time of their introduction. Several platforms now use internet-based delivery alongside earlier delivery methods such as broadcast

2 In 2013, BSkyB came under ownership of the newly spun-off 21st Century Fox. In 2014, BSkyB was renamed as Sky, in line with the branding of its television service, and merged with Sky Italia and Sky Deutschland.

3 BT Vision and BT's YouView service were merged in 2013 to form BT TV, which combines the content of both under a single brand.

platform.[14] The other public service broadcasters ITV, Channel 4, and Channel 5 each followed with similar platforms. Tracking by the regulator Ofcom showed that in the first quarter of 2011, 35 percent of the population had watched television using an internet connection,[15] but this was almost entirely accounted for by these free catch-up platforms.[16] As Elizabeth Evans and Paul McDonald have found, the older terrestrial broadcasters "remain the key focal point for connected viewing" in Britain, thanks to their existing familiarity among the population and their dominance of *scheduled* viewing that gives them valuable cross-promotional opportunities.[17] This was further consolidated by the 2012 launch of YouView, which offered the same channels as Freeview but with the addition of a broadband internet connection. This made all the free-to-air platforms accessible on the viewer's television set, rather than only via computers and tablets.

Even for subscribers to pay-TV services, VOD has been encountered primarily as part of a *package* with scheduled channels rather than as "over-the-top" products, given that the requisite broadband internet connection and digital video recorder (DVR) equipment is usually included in their standard subscription deals. The enduring association between the television set and connected viewing is also underlined by the strong increase in ownership of "smart" TVs, sales of which represented a 45 percent share of the market in 2014,[18] up from 10 percent when Ofcom started measuring it in 2010.[19] Several web-based platforms have also been introduced as offshoots from existing pay-TV companies. For example, Sky's Now TV was launched a month after Netflix, allowing Sky to further exploit its valuable movie, drama, and sports rights via the internet. Now TV costs much less than Sky's main service and does not bind viewers to a long-term contract. Therefore, it was generally received as Sky's answer to Netflix, described as "aiming to sweep up the Netflix generation—those customers who do not want to pay up to £850 a year for satellite TV."[20] Finally, besides Netflix and Amazon, several over-the-top VOD platforms *without* preexistent brand awareness *have* entered the race, some lasting longer than others. The British-owned Blinkbox, which offers downloads to rent and purchase, and the Spanish-owned Wuaki.tv are two that have made modest inroads. These various ventures may prove to be the start of a "cord-cutting" shift, but numbers of viewers opting *only* for web-based content remain negligible.[21]

Importation on demand: Sky, "quality" American drama and VOD

The rapid upsurge in competition for viewers' attention was, as we would expect, accompanied by an intensification of branding strategies across the industry.[22] Specifically, several channels have sought to develop distinct brands based on the acquisition of exclusive rights to imported—usually American—drama.[23] Digital channels spun off from the public service broadcasters have been eager to make use of such content in order to focus their specific demographic appeal and compete with pay-TV rivals. For Channel 5's spin-off 5USA (originally Five US), for example, imports have been an explicit *raison d'être*. More recently, BBC Four has bolstered its claim to a share of the public license fee through a Saturday night slot dedicated to subtitled European drama.[24] Meanwhile, several brands have appeared in the listings that are *themselves* imported, such as the Universal Channel and a range of CBS channels.

The most significant investment in transatlantic flows since the switchover (at least in terms of financial expense) was made by Sky when it launched its new channel,

Sky Atlantic, in February 2011. In preparation, Sky secured exclusive rights to most of HBO's fiction back catalogue and first refusal on all its future productions, which would make up a large portion of Sky Atlantic's prime-time programming. At a reported cost of $233 million, the unprecedented magnitude of the deal drew heavy press coverage as Sky Atlantic was launched with the subtitle "The Home of HBO in the UK."[25] All marketing for the channel featured this slogan and HBO's logo alongside that of the channel itself. Branding agency Heavenly was commissioned to design the channel's idents (brief sequences shown between programs that display the channel logo), which, as their creative director explained, were "inspired by the thought that Sky Atlantic is the channel that bridges the best of US and UK culture."[26] They presented more metaphorical variations on the theme of transnational connection, consisting of alternating scenes from British and American settings spliced together to look like a continuous panning shot. So one sequence blended shots of the Tyne Bridge in Newcastle (in the north-east of England) with Brooklyn Bridge in New York, while another showed trains speeding through the contrasting terrain of the two nations—one across dusty Midwestern plains, the other surrounded by green rolling hills.[27]

Sky Atlantic exemplifies the key role played by imports in pushing the uptake of pay-TV to more consumers and new demographics. The channel was introduced as standard in all Sky's subscription packages and as such it has been perceived as a key asset in the recent surge in its customer base. Sky's director of programs Stuart Murphy explained that the channel was intended to attract a "more upmarket audience—basically, people who have Freeview and who have never considered pay TV before and think that there is nothing on Sky for them."[28] Other commentators used the more specific shorthand of the "BBC viewer—one who generally tends to shy away from commercial channels in the search of 'quality broadcasting.'"[29] With Sky's new channel, then, access to imported content was purposefully associated with a shift in the perception of pay-TV and used to poach the same ABC1 viewers who would form Netflix's main source of custom.[30]

Foreshadowing Netflix more specifically, though, was the central role played by the "quality" American drama boasted by Sky Atlantic in the promotion of Sky's VOD service. As Sky Atlantic's flagship shows were revealed in the run-up to its launch, it was also announced that the content would feature heavily on the new Sky Anytime+ service, which would be rolled out between October 2010 and February 2011. Now renamed Sky On Demand, the service offers content for download via an internet connection, which is then stored on the subscriber's Sky+ DVR device. Sky Atlantic's imports have been far more prominent than any of Sky's domestic shows in the promotion of Sky On Demand, helped by the fact that the deal with HBO also ruled out any launch of HBO Go in Britain. The received wisdom in the trade press saw the on-demand availability of the content as crucial in ensuring Sky Atlantic's appeal. For example, one commentator pointed out that "UK fans of HBO's output are likely to look to DVD boxsets or online to get their fix and may not be used to paying a monthly subscription to pay-TV services, so Sky will have to play heavily on the added-value it can offer."[31] I will return below to the pressure from online services hinted at here. For now, the crucial point here is that imports have served as a pivotal form of content in attempts to engineer the flow of viewers between scheduled channels and VOD technologies.

Indeed, Sky Atlantic was the first of Sky's channels to be offered *as a channel* on the mobile and tablet app Sky Go, which had so far only been used for individual sports events. That this move came a month after the arrival of Netflix fueled press predictions of a collision between the two companies.[32] The channel's content soon became more overtly associated with Sky's time-shift facilities in the promotion of On Demand. Advertisements for the facility increasingly featured the motif of a seemingly infinite shelf full of DVD box sets representing the different series available via the service. The metaphor was made all the more literal when Sky released an advertisement featuring the British actor Idris Elba (who starred in HBO's *The Wire* [2002–8]) wandering around an expansive library (actually the all-white minimalist architecture of Stuttgart City Library) stacked with rows of box sets (see Figure 14.1). While the On Demand "library" includes both domestic and imported content, Sky Atlantic's "quality" American series invariably appear as more numerous and more prominent in this physicalized representation. Conversely, these imports have been especially successful via VOD viewing. One of Sky Atlantic's most viewed shows, *Game of Thrones* (HBO; 2011–), has proven a key case in point, with season three being viewed 2.3 million times via Sky Go and downloaded one million times via On Demand.[33] According to Sky's 2013 Annual Review,

> The epic fantasy series ... typifies our commitment to bringing customers the best TV from around the world. Thanks to our partnership with HBO, Sky customers enjoyed new episodes of the dramatic third season less than 24 hours after they were broadcast in the US. [...] The success of *Game of Thrones* illustrates the growing variety of ways in which our customers now choose to watch.[34]

Figure 14.1 Idris Elba explores the Sky On Demand library in a February 2013 promotional spot

So we see here a close alignment between flagship imports and the value of the service as a whole as it combined broadcast and time-shift technologies. The reduction of the lag between U.S. and UK airings (several other high-profile imports were also given near-simultaneous airings) is incorporated into a *general* discourse of connectivity, and VOD viewing itself is framed as integral within a repertoire of viewing options across which the imagined viewer moves actively and fluidly. Far from functioning as a viable *replacement* to "traditional" television, here VOD has been incorporated as both a commercial and technological *extension* to Sky's scheduled channels.

The promotional positioning of Sky On Demand makes two things clear about Netflix's prospects as it moved into the British market. On the one hand, although scheduled television remained by far the most common form of viewing, by 2012 many Brits would have been at least acquainted with the idea of watching nonscheduled television, and more and more were paying a subscription fee for the pleasure. Coupled with the relatively high level of access to broadband internet in the country,[35] this potentially made Netflix's integration less of a leap than might have been the case elsewhere. On the other hand, Sky's aggressive marketing of the service, and the expensive acquisition of content on which that marketing relied, reflects the overwhelmingly competitive marketplace that had already emerged for the British viewer wishing to time-shift, space-shift, download, or stream content. The means by which Netflix has reacted to this challenge can be split into two key strategies, both of which echo those of Sky, and which I examine respectively in the following two sections. First, the platform has been promoted predominantly in terms of its flagship American drama. Second, Netflix has pursued intercorporate partnerships—not with American distributors like HBO, but with British television service providers.

From bridges to interstellar gateways: Netflix as importer

In the run-up to its launch in Britain, Netflix joined major British broadcasters like Sky, the BBC, and Channel 4 at the Los Angeles Screenings, where deals for the international distribution of American content are negotiated. As a result their first offering to British viewers included the only chance to see the remaining seasons of *Breaking Bad*, as well as a range of older American shows that were already popular among Brits, such as *Arrested Development* (Fox/Netflix; 2003–). *Breaking Bad* appeared in virtually every advertisement for Netflix around the time of its launch, cementing its reception as a "Netflix hit,"[36] despite it not being a Netflix production. A year later, Netflix took the exclusive UK rights to *The Killing* (AMC; 2011–14) from Channel 4, which had aired the first two seasons, as well as a range of new lesser-known series such as the comedy *Portlandia* (IFC; 2011–). Alongside acquisitions, another important factor was the timing of Netflix's UK launch soon after it had started commissioning its own original programming. This allowed for maximum association between the high production values of *House of Cards* and its overall brand. By contrast, in countries where Netflix launched later, preexisting deals for the rights to its original productions have made this less clear-cut (as Christian

Stiegler explains elsewhere in this volume, regarding Sky Deutschland's purchase of *House of Cards* in Germany).

Writing about the promotional discourse surrounding the acquisition of *Lost* (ABC; 2004–10) by British broadcasters, Paul Grainge argues that such content functions as "emblematic property" for the importing channel.[37] A handful of shows have served a similarly emblematic function for Netflix, not simply for their textual characteristics but in collectively constituting a signal of the company's proactive approach to the global content marketplace. This investment represented a significant risk for a new venture with only nascent brand recognition. But the perception of the newcomer's content buyers as "serious contenders for first-run rights at LA" alongside "traditional" domestic broadcasters was more valuable than the number of sign-ups that individual acquisitions may have brought.[38] As an executive from a rival British company told the trade magazine *Broadcast*, "Netflix had to establish itself and come into the market with a statement. It overpaid for rights and that's probably unsustainable, but it is now at the table."[39] So the value of the Netflix service has been presented to British viewers not so much for its place as a technological trailblazer, but more as a means of access to specific non-British television content.

It is important to add that Netflix has not relied *solely* on imports in its bid to lure British subscribers. Before its launch, the company secured licensing deals with BBC Worldwide, ITV, and Channel 4, presumably to give a local flavor to its menu of content. In 2014 it even announced it had commissioned an original series, *The Crown*, from British production company Left Bank Pictures. However, as of 2015 it has not acquired first-run rights to any domestic content, and British programming rarely appears in its advertising. The effect is that Netflix's place in the British television landscape has been *presented* primarily as that of an importer, making it directly comparable with broadcast channels like Sky Atlantic. This has been encoded in its marketing, moreover, through a similar promotional discourse as that utilized by Sky Atlantic, emphasizing metaphors of physically expansive choice and transportation between the domestic sphere and the global content marketplace.

At first its on-screen spots were reedited versions of those used in the United States. However (perhaps with an eye on the planned British launch), one featured a quintessentially *English* aristocratic housewife (played by the British television actor Susan Tracy) showing off the new "interstellar gateway" in her ornate Georgian living room.[40] Through the retro sci-fi hole in her wall leaps a Victorian-era explorer, a Roman soldier, and a leg-warmer-clad dancer. As it becomes apparent that the portal is malfunctioning, the elderly early adopter decides that "Netflix will more than suffice," and settles down on her sofa with the eclectic congregation of characters to choose something to watch on her flat-screen television. This pastiche reimagining of VOD technology clearly plays on the same bridge metaphor employed in Sky Atlantic's idents, albeit with more comic overtones. However, Netflix itself is dissociated from the clunky, indiscriminating portal and represented instead as a traditional televisual experience.

As Netflix started to make ground in Britain, their marketing continued to play on the theme of physical transportation, but focusing increasingly on specific content.

A 2014 spot saw the British comedian Ricky Gervais promoting Netflix as a whole. Gervais (for whose sitcom *Derek* [Channel 4; 2012–14] Netflix had secured second-run rights) is presented in the spot as a TV "superfan." He is found watching *House of Cards*—again on a wide-screen television from his sofa—as he addresses the viewer: "You know when you're watching your favorite Netflix show and after five straight episodes it's like you want to be in it?"[41] He is accordingly transported into the action of several of Netflix's most high-profile shows. He appears in the place of Kevin Spacey as Frank Underwood in *House of Cards* before bumping into Steve Van Zandt in his role as Frank Tagliano in *Lilyhammer* (NRK; 2012–),[42] and then wanders onto the set of *Orange Is the New Black* (Netflix; 2013–). The scenes make use of Gervais' trademark comic awkwardness in dramatizing the incongruity of a Brit trying to "make it" in the various settings: Underwood's confidant Doug Stamper (Michael Kelly) questions his attempt at an American accent, while Tagliano and the inmates from *Orange* scare him off set, leading Gervais to conclude "maybe I'm better off just watching." Finally, his own titular character from *Derek* is glimpsed momentarily waiting on set for Gervais to turn up there too.

For all its playful irony, this spot explicitly places Netflix UK—and its projected subscriber—in a position of transnational connectedness. But whereas Sky Atlantic's idents drew more metaphorically on images of real travel and transition, Netflix's *content* becomes the mode of transport here. Gervais' couch-potato persona and the insertion of his British program (for which Netflix wasn't even the first-run distributer in the UK) at the end tether the image of the service solidly to the domestic (in both senses of the word), allowing the two strategies of localization and importation to function cooperatively. Also note how Gervais' "five straight episodes" is presented (however accurately) as a consumption habit that is taken for granted among British viewers, picking up on the same appeal to "bingeability" as found in the promotion of Sky On Demand as an endless library of DVD box sets.

In fact, the combination of Netflix's position as an importer of content and its offering of whole series availability has been key in forming its status as a "game changer" since it began its international expansion. A 2014 report by the market analyst firm IHS Technology, incidentally entitled *The Netflix Effect*, predicted that Netflix's strategy of simultaneous worldwide release would lead other distributors to supply content to importing territories more quickly in order to compete.[43] As we have seen, Sky had started to address the task of closing the transatlantic lag with its HBO deal. But with its increasing activity on the acquisitions market and the simultaneous release of its own productions, Netflix has presented a challenge to one of the fundamental conditions of the global trade in content: namely, the country-by-country basis on which deals are made. At the same time, though, it has sought direct integration with the nationally specific technical infrastructure and branded spaces of British television. While I have explained above how the promotional rhetoric made possible by importation has helped to frame Netflix as locally valuable, I will finish the chapter by turning to the intercorporate affiliations through which Netflix has extended these efforts.

Just another channel? Brand integration and Netflix intercorporate partnerships

As we have seen, by 2012 television in Britain amounted to a broad and complex ecology consisting of a multitude of channels, services, and technologies. In practical terms, when shopping for a new DVR set-top box or smart TV, the British consumer has increasingly to choose from a growing range of service providers that are not simply distinguished by differently designed interfaces, giving access to a more or less extensive range of traditional channels. They might also be drawn by additional built-in apps that connect to the internet, some of which include the iPlayer, YouTube, and, indeed, Netflix. Clearly, all these services are distinct in terms of both technology and finance, but they are increasingly being packaged, in the form of such smart devices, as part of a single consumer product.

Other services are available via these devices, but this has had specific relevance in the case of Netflix inasmuch as its rapid penetration has been facilitated by the integration of its software and brand with the set-top boxes provided by various platforms. Netflix had been made available via a variety of web-connected games consoles at its launch (as had Amazon Instant Video). But more importantly, in September 2013, it became the first online-only platform to be made available via television sets as it entered into a partnership with Virgin Media.[44] Virgin already had a partnership in place with TiVo to supply its DVR software, but the inclusion of the Netflix app in Virgin's electronic program guide (and the offer of six months of free Netflix membership) specifically made streamed content easily accessible for Virgin's 3.7 million subscribers. The partnership was announced in advertisements by the actor David Tennant, the long-standing promotional face of Virgin Media. Tennant's phrasing reflects the complex (and, for the consumer, somewhat confusing) layering of brands and technologies produced by such intercorporate collaboration: "TiVo from Virgin Media has thousands of hours of box sets available on demand—including Netflix—so you never have to watch another cat video again."[45] Here again we have a well-known television personality used to position Netflix as closely integrated with established televisual habits. Like Gervais, Tennant is watching *House of Cards* from his sofa, which is littered with cats. Here the gap between Netflix and its content is collapsed altogether, with a similar effect to Sky's shelf full of box sets. The brand itself is synonymous with a valuable collection of content that is added on to Virgin's overall menu, while the technical difference between the Netflix and Virgin services is made invisible. At the same time, Netflix is jokingly legitimized above nontelevisual content—here specifically identified as (user-generated) web video—and thus closely aligned with a *televisual* experience on an ideological as well as a technical level.

While this partnership saw Netflix made available as an extra product within an existing subscription service, an even more complicated situation arose when it was also added as an optional extra to YouView in November 2014. This was especially significant in the British context, as it blurred the division between free-to-air and pay-TV that has underpinned the national industry ever since the emergence of the latter in the 1980s. Although YouView had been set up to allow access to free-to-air VOD services such as the BBC's iPlayer, with the addition of the Netflix app viewers could pay to access content via their existing YouView set-top box. YouView chief executive Richard Halton described the deal itself as a "game changer": "Freeview homes can pay £5.99 for Netflix, which feels like a really good first step compared with the £30 or £40 they would pay for Sky or Virgin."[46] One of the most significant effects of Netflix's integration in Britain, then, has been to intensify the previously tentative overlapping of the pay and free sectors of the industry.[47]

Notwithstanding the financial distinction drawn by Halton, Netflix's partnership with YouView is comparable with Sky On Demand insofar as its promotion has been primarily based on the salability of imported drama. The press release announcing the new app promised it would give "YouView audiences even more choice," before listing content that was exclusively American (with the one exception of the James Bond film *Skyfall* [Sam Mendes, 2012]).[48] Interestingly, YouView also celebrated its new partnership by setting up a real-life version of Gervais' immersive viewing experience described above, with a "giant set-top box" built on London's Southbank. Passersby were invited to enter and have their picture taken in the costumes and on the sets of *House of Cards*, *Breaking Bad*, and *Orange Is the New Black*. None of Netflix's British content featured in the exhibition.[49]

These deals have made it possible for Netflix to be presented as a mark of added value rather than yet another alternative in the increasingly numerous options on offer to British viewers. As one journalist wrote in reaction to the latest estimate of Netflix's subscriber numbers in August 2013, "Netflix is growing not by changing traditional viewing habits but by establishing itself as another channel, an 'extra choice option' after viewers have checked what is on live television or stored in the digital video recorder."[50] The persistence of the television set as the main device of choice for accessing audiovisual content in Britain suggests this has been a necessity for Netflix, but the centrality of the televisual devices (rather than the laptop or tablet) in the promotional videos described above shows that it is one that the company has accepted proactively. More broadly, its partnerships with established service providers reflect a trend in the British media and telecommunications industries: the strong grip on viewer *access* by a few large companies like Sky and the major public service broadcasters has yet to loosen significantly, but the more open trade in *content* can be utilized by smaller, newer entrants in the market in order to generate leverage that allows them to *join* rather than attempt to *beat* those established giants.

Conclusion

Netflix has continued and adapted to promotional and viewing patterns already in place before it launched in Britain. In this way, it epitomizes the combination of two mutually supportive forms of bridging that are increasingly definitive of the national digital television system: between domestic and international television markets; and between familiar viewing behaviors and emergent new ones. It has not relied on any straightforward localization of its service or its range of content. Instead, it has fostered the flow of viewers from traditional channels to its new service most purposefully through the promotional appeal of *imported* drama. As such it has behaved more like a domestic channel taking advantage of the global content marketplace than a new media game changer. However, it has also sought to integrate its service with the everyday technological objects of British television viewing through its partnerships with Virgin and YouView.

It should be stressed that the relative success of Netflix in Britain has not exactly tipped the balance toward on-demand and web-based television becoming the norm. In 2014 the combined amounts of free and paid-for VOD still only represented 8 percent of all viewing.[51] Among VOD users, meanwhile, two-thirds of long-form viewing (i.e., films and TV episodes rather than clips) was done via services that did not cost extra (on top of the license fee as with iPlayer, or on top of subscription fees as with Sky On Demand).[52] As suggested by its recent announcement of an increase in non-American productions,[53] Netflix's status as a global brand looks set to develop in more complex ways, which might aid attempts to challenge more directly the stronghold of companies like Sky. However, further success at awards ceremonies (*House of Cards* and *Orange Is the New Black* were both nominated for BAFTAs in 2015) and the fastest growing subscription numbers of any VOD platform[54] show that integration and importation have proven a valuable combination for Netflix in securing its place in the British television ecosystem.

Notes

1 The category had been won by imports aired on Sky or BBC channels every year since 2008. In recent years, most or all of the nominations had aired on either Sky Atlantic or BBC Four.

2 In April 2011 there were 154 services in Britain that fell within the regulatory definition of "on demand service providers," rising to 184 a year later (see ATVOD's *Annual Report 2011/12*. http://atvod.co.uk/uploads/files/Annual_Report_2012.pdf [accessed January 19, 2014], 9–10), although this included all the various outlets for a single service. Following a redefinition of ODSPs to address this, there are now 111 services counted (see ATVOD's *Annual Report 2013/14*. http://www.atvod.co.uk/uploads/files/Annual_Report_2014.pdf [accessed January 19, 2014], 10–11).

3 Emma Halls, "Does Netflix Have Anything New to Offer U.K. Viewers?" *AdAge.com*, January 12, 2012. http://adage.com/article/global-news/netflix-offer-u-k-viewers/232056/ (accessed December 9, 2014).

4 Ofcom, *Communications Market Report, 2011: TV and Audio-Visual*, 149. http://stakeholders.ofcom.org.uk/binaries/research/cmr/cmr11/UK_Doc_Section_2.pdf (accessed December 19, 2014).

5 Ofcom, *Communications Market Report 2012*, 175. http://stakeholders.ofcom.org.uk/binaries/research/cmr/cmr12/CMR_UK_2012.pdf (accessed January 10, 2014).

6 See Joe Lewis, "Netflix—Friend or Foe?" *Barb.co.uk*, Blog Post, July 21, 2014. http://www.barb.co.uk/whats-new/329 (accessed April 5, 2015).

7 See Nate Lanxon, "Behind Netflix's UK Launch: Why Now, Why No DVDs, and What's Next?" *Wired*, January 9, 2012. http://www.wired.co.uk/news/archive/2012-01/09/netflix-reed-hastings-feature (accessed November 10, 2014).
8 Ofcom, *Digital Television Update: Chart Pack for Q4 2012*, 4. http://stakeholders.ofcom.org.uk/binaries/research/tv-research/tv-data/dig-tv-updates/2012Q4.pdf (accessed November 10, 2014).
9 Ofcom, *Communications Market Report 2006*, 233. http://stakeholders.ofcom.org.uk/binaries/research/cmr/tv1.pdf (accessed April 5, 2015).
10 Ofcom, *Communications Market Report 2012*, 127.
11 Ofcom, *Communications Market Report 2014*, 127. http://stakeholders.ofcom.org.uk/binaries/research/cmr/cmr14/2014_UK_CMR.pdf (accessed April 5, 2015).
12 Ofcom, *Communications Market Report 2011*, 133.
13 BSkyB, *Annual Review 2013*, 32. http://www.atvod.co.uk/uploads/files/Annual_Report_2014.pdf (accessed January 19, 2014).
14 Ofcom, *Communications Market Report 2014*, 145.
15 Ofcom, *Communications Market Report 2011*, 103.
16 Ibid., 106.
17 Elizabeth Evans and Paul McDonald, "Online Distribution of Film and Television in the UK: Behavior, Taste, and Value," in *Connected Viewing: Selling, Streaming, and Sharing Media in the Digital Era*, eds Jennifer Holt and Kevin Sanson (New York: Routledge, 2014), 167.
18 Ofcom, *Communications Market Report 2014*, 132.
19 Ofcom, *Communications Market Report 2011*, 101.
20 Henry Mance, "Sky: All to Play For," *Financial Times*, December 22, 2014. http://www.ft.com/cms/s/0/d83a8000-851a-11e4-ab4e-00144feabdc0.html#axzz3OdEcfO98 (accessed January 10, 2014).
21 In 2014, Ofcom estimated that paid-for online content represented only 3 percent of all viewing (Ofcom, *Communications Market Report 2014*, 128).
22 See Catherine Johnson, *Branding Television* (New York: Routledge, 2012), 63–111.
23 Paul Rixon, *American Television on British Screens: A Story of Cultural Interaction* (Houndmills, Basingstoke: Palgrave Macmillan, 2006), 162–183; Johnson, *Branding Television*, 91–96; Elke Weissmann, *Transnational Television Drama: Special Relations and Mutual Influence Between the US and UK* (Houndmills, Basingstoke: Palgrave Macmillan, 2012), 186–192.
24 See also Sam Ward, "Finding 'Public Purpose' in 'Subtitled Oddities': Framing BBC Four's Danish Imports as Public Service Broadcasting," *Journal of Popular Television*, 1.2 (2014): 251–257.
25 Andreas Wiseman, "Sky Announces Sky Atlantic as 'Home of HBO' in UK," *Screen Daily*, January 5, 2011. http://www.screendaily.com/sky-announces-sky-atlantic-as-home-of-hbo-in-uk/5021990.article (accessed April 5, 2015).
26 Quoted in Colm O'Rourke, "Heavenly Crosses the Atlantic for Sky," *TheTVRoomPlus.com*, February 2011. http://tvdesignnews.thetvroomplus.com/2011/feb/heavenly-crosses-the-atlantic-for-sky (accessed July 20, 2015).
27 All the idents are viewable at http://heavenly.co.uk/brand-development-work/sky-atlantic/ (accessed February 17, 2014).
28 Quoted in Alex Farber, "Sky Goes Upmarket with Atlantic," *Broadcast*, January 7, 2011. http://www.broadcastnow.co.uk/sky-goes-upmarket-with-atlantic/5022019.article (accessed July 20, 2015).

29 Emily Smith, "Sky Targets Beeb with Atlantic Launch," *Brand Republic*, February 7, 2011. http://www.brandrepublic.com/television/article/1052487/think-br-sky-targets-beeb-atlantic-launch/ (accessed December 12, 2014).
30 Lewis, "Netflix—Friend or Foe?"
31 Smith, "Sky Targets Beeb with Atlantic Launch."
32 See David Crookes, "Sky Atlantic Goes Mobile in Battle for Viewers," *Independent.co.uk*, January 31, 2012. http://www.independent.co.uk/news/business/news/sky-atlantic-goes-mobile-in-battle-for-viewers-6297348.html (accessed February 18, 2014).
33 BSkyB, *Annual Review 2013*, 9.
34 Ibid.
35 In 2011 there were an estimated 77 fixed broadband connections per 100 households in Britain. This placed Britain fourth, behind only the Netherlands (93), Canada (86), and France (81), out of 17 countries for which data was available (see Ofcom, *International Communications Market Report 2012*. http://stakeholders.ofcom.org.uk/binaries/research/cmr/cmr12/icmr/ICMR-2012.pdf (accessed January 10, 2013), 191.
36 Nigel Farndale, "Why a Night in Front of the TV Is a Family Favourite Once Again," *The Telegraph*, December 14, 2014. http://www.telegraph.co.uk/culture/tvandradio/11291145/Why-a-night-in-front-of-the-TV-is-a-family-favourite-once-again.html (accessed July 20, 2015).
37 Paul Grainge, "*Lost* Logos: Channel 4 and the Branding of American Event Television," in *Reading* Lost: *Perspectives on a Hit Television Show*, ed. Roberta Pearson (London: I.B. Tauris, 2009), 102.
38 Peter White, "Rise of the OTT Providers," *Broadcast*, May 31, 2013. http://www.broadcastnow.co.uk/news/international/rise-of-the-ott-providers/5056895.article (accessed July 20, 2015).
39 Quoted in White, "Rise of the OTT Providers."
40 The UK version can be viewed at https://www.youtube.com/watch?v=4Z4kOhYunJo and the U.S. version at https://www.youtube.com/watch?v=o4XBxmi8Zos (both accessed 9 December 2014). The only significant difference is the woman's viewing selection. Notably, though, in both she is watching an *American* movie.
41 The spot can be viewed at https://www.youtube.com/watch?v=a2RY14Zqdvw (accessed December 9, 2014).
42 The acquisition of the Norwegian made *Lilyhammer*, starring Steve van Zandt of *The Sopranos* (HBO; 1999–2007) fame, is a particularly notable move by Netflix just as it started work on its global expansion, given the mixture of associations with HBO prestige and BBC Four's "Nordic Noir" imports mentioned above.
43 Morgan Jeffrey, "US TV Shows Take Average of 95 Days to Air in UK, Report Claims," *DigitalSpy.co.uk*, February 21, 2014. http://www.digitalspy.co.uk/ustv/news/a552828/us-tv-shows-take-average-of-95-days-to-air-in-uk-report-claims.html#~oXnCOmMiRzFQC1 (accessed December 3, 2014).
44 At the same time as its appearance as part of Virgin's service, Netflix agreed similar deals with pay-TV providers in Denmark and Sweden, where it was integrated into packages offered by Waoo! and ComHem, respectively.
45 The spot can be viewed at https://www.youtube.com/watch?v=uWpx5CHe2-o (accessed January 13, 2015).
46 Quoted in David Benady, "YouView Adds Netflix and Sky Sports to Its Armoury," *Campaign*, November 14, 2014. http://www.campaignlive.co.uk/news/1321622/ (accessed January 12, 2015).

47 This incorporation of internet-based subscription services seems to be a key project for YouView. It has since added access to Sky's Now TV service, and in 2014 it purchased the loss-making Blinkbox from the supermarket giant Tesco, announcing that it would eventually rebrand the service under its own name.

48 "Netflix Now on YouView," *YouView Press Release*, November 4, 2014. http://www.youview.com/news/2014/11/04/netflix-now-on-youview/ (accessed January 19, 2014).

49 The resultant video can be viewed at https://www.youtube.com/watch?v=rZ6ykzjAXks (accessed January 10, 2015).

50 Juliette Garside, "Netflix Reaches 1.5m UK Subscribers for Its Internet Video Service," *The Guardian*, August 21, 2013. http://www.theguardian.com/media/2013/aug/21/netflix-uk-subscribers-internet-video (accessed November 10, 2014).

51 Ofcom, *Communications Market Report 2014*, 145.

52 Ibid., 64.

53 As well as *The Crown* (forthcoming in 2016), Netflix has funded *Marco Polo* (2014–), which was shot in Kazakhstan, Malaysia, and Italy, and featured a multinational cast (prompting it to be billed as Netflix's answer to *Game of Thrones*). In August 2014, Netflix announced *Marseille*, a new in-house production that would be set and shot in France, and in January 2015, they agreed a partnership with Danish channel TV 2 to finance the third series of their comedy drama *Rita* (2012–).

54 Ofcom, *Communications Market Report 2014*, 145.

15

Invading Europe: Netflix's Expansion to the European Market and the Example of Germany

Christian Stiegler

Introduction

As in most European countries, Germany's media industry structure is defined by a mixed mandate system in which state-supported public broadcasters compete with a growing commercial sector. Since the emergence of this system in the 1980s, the commercial sector has developed steadily as a result of ongoing deregulation, changing consumer preferences, and the introduction of platforms that individualize media reception. These trends are likely to continue following the introduction of Netflix into the German market in Fall 2014. Although Germans are sensitive to issues of conglomeration and the consolidation of media ownership, the announcement that Netflix was expanding to Germany was received surprisingly well by local media and audiences. In fact, the success of Netflix in the United States and elsewhere made it appear as a sort of a faraway utopia that, once available, would provide German audiences with content that was otherwise impossible to see on local television. These expectations were heightened by the heavy promotion of Netflix's premium series like *House of Cards* or *Orange Is the New Black* in German mass media, even while there was no legal way to watch them.

Although Germany, in this respect, couldn't wait to get "netflixed," there were also a variety of challenges that complicated Netflix's entry into the German market and that have the potential to undermine the biggest expansion in the company's history. For example, the promotion of shows like *House of Cards* created a perplexing situation for audiences. There was high demand for something that was in short supply. This encouraged audiences to access Netflix's premium content through illegal streaming options. Major newspapers even provided tips and guidelines that explained how to trick Netflix by using virtual private networks (VPN) and other location-masking software to access the service in places where it was not legally available. Thus far Netflix has taken a quite liberal position regarding the issue, but it has to be careful to not jeopardize its relationship with content providers or its ability to add more

Thanks to Charlotte Rund for her inspiring assistance in writing this chapter.

subscribers.[1] This illustrates the challenge Netflix faces not only in competing with existing industry leaders but also in navigating a patchwork of different technological infrastructures as well as different national and regional regulatory policies. Currently, many countries utilize the so-called geo-blocking in order to uphold legal restrictions such as copyright protections.[2]

In order to address these complications, this chapter analyzes Netflix's German expansion by using the Industrialization of Culture framework introduced by Timothy Havens and Amanda Lotz.[3] This framework suggests that media industries involve different economic, social, and cultural factors and, more specifically, it identifies mandates, conditions, and practices as key components in understanding how contemporary media industries function. In drawing on this framework, this chapter examines how these components have affected Netflix and how the media texts produced as part of this process relate to larger social trends, tastes, and traditions of the German public. This approach emphasizes that these different influences are deeply intertwined and dependent on one another. To illustrate this point, Havens and Lotz suggest that culture is like a pinball game. As they describe it,

> The large bumpers that deflect the balls, determining their speed and trajectory, represent "Mandates" in our model. The various smaller bumpers, spinners, ramps, and chutes that alter a ball's speed and direction in less dramatic ways represent "Conditions." Finally, the "Practices" of the industries and the people who work in them are represented by the players themselves, who demonstrate varying degrees of skill operating the plunger and the flippers to initiate and redirect each pinball.[4]

In this analogy some factors—like the bumpers, spinners, and flippers—are relatively stable. Other factors—like the speed and direction of the pinball—are entirely variable. For Havens and Lotz, this indicates the importance of taking both variables into account in order to thoroughly analyze the creation of individual media texts and their producers. In following the Industrialization of Culture model, this chapter argues that it is necessary to develop a similarly interdisciplinary, multiperspective approach to understand Netflix's international expansion and, more specifically, its relationship to local media cultures, competing business models, and preexisting technological parameters (Figure 15.1).

Contexts and mandates

Netflix functions under a commercial mandate, meaning that the company's strategic decisions both in general and as a content producer are based on profitability. This is the largest motivation behind its recent international expansion. As a new competitor within the German market, however, Netflix has had to negotiate the earlier mandates that inform or frame the country's media and entertainment industries. In this regard, it is worth recounting a brief overview of the German marketplace.

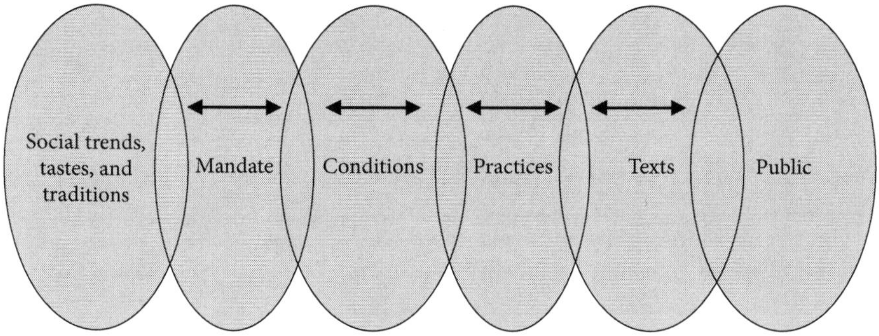

Figure 15.1 Variables in the industrialization of culture model
Source: Timothy Havens and Amanda D. Lotz (*Understanding Media Industries* 4)

About 85 million people live in Germany and 38 million households have at least one television set. Germany shares the German language together with Austria and the German-speaking part of Switzerland resulting in a total market of about 100 million people. After World War II, the Basic Law of 1949 established Germany's postwar media system, specifically stipulating principles to ensure freedom of the press. As one of the biggest European media markets, Germany eventually developed a mixed or dual mandate system with a strong public broadcasting system operated by ARD (Arbeitsgemeinschaften der öffentlich-rechtlichen Rundfunkanstalten der Bundesrepublik Deutschland, since 1950) and ZDF (Zweites Deutsches Fernsehen, since 1963), which own various TV and radio channels throughout the country. In public broadcasting, the so-called *Länder* (or individual states) play a strong role, since the German Federal Constitution states that the sole responsibility for broadcasting rests with the *Länder* as part of their cultural sovereignty. This leads to individual and joint acts of public service broadcasters as a creation of the *Länder*. The only exception is the broadcaster Deutsche Welle, designed to provide their broadcasting services to foreign countries only.

Public service broadcasters are set up as a noncommercial service financed primarily by license fees (approximately €18 per month/household). Quite similar to the BBC in the UK system, the public service broadcasting organization (*Anstalt*) provides a state ("Land") with public service radio, television, and online services. For example, SWR (Southwest Broadcasting) serves the southwestern German states Baden-Württemberg and Rhineland-Palatinate while the NDR (North German Broadcasting) serves the states Lower Saxony, Mecklenburg-Vorpommern, and Schleswig-Holstein. Because of this decentralization, there are many media centers in the country, for example, Cologne, Munich, or Hamburg—all financed primarily by license fees.

With the introduction of private broadcasting in 1981, ARD and ZDF began diversifying their portfolio. They started several youth-orientated channels (EinsPlus, EinsFestival, ZDFneo, ZDFkultur) in order to introduce younger audiences (an important target group for advertisers) to their content, emphasizing digital and social media as a way to compete with commercial channels for prime-time ratings.[5] Although these public broadcasters are nonprofit institutions by design, they exist in a fragmented and multifarious media landscape that spans from TV to video on demand (VOD) and online media. Because of this, the ordinary media consumer in Germany does not necessarily differentiate between public and private broadcasting providers.

Two media groups or *Senderfamilien*, literally translated as "broadcaster family," control Germany's commercial television sector. One of these, formerly owned by Leo Kirch, is named ProSiebenSat.1 Media AG. It consists of the channels Sat.1, Pro 7, N24', and Kabel 1, among others, and in 2014 it had 22 percent of the overall market. Bertelsmann, the largest media company outside of the United States, controls the other broadcaster family: the RTL Group. This group owns TV channels in about a dozen European countries. In Germany, it includes RTL, RTL II, Super RTL, VOX, and n-tv for a total of 24 percent of the television market.[6] There are other privately owned channels, some of which are subsidiaries of international conglomerates like Viacom, Disney, and NBC Universal, but these represent a much smaller percentage of the overall market. In addition to the two major media groups, there are well-established regional commercial broadcasters in large cities like Berlin, Munich, Hamburg, and Cologne.

Germany has an above-average percentage of cable-using households. Among the country's 38 million households, approximately 19 million of them access television through a cable service. Nearly 15 million households access television via satellite service, leaving a very small number of households still using terrestrial reception. As indicated above, public service broadcasters continue to dominate—accounting for 44 percent of all viewing (with ARD and ZDF each accounting for at 13 percent of the market)[7]—while private channels are becoming more significant—with RTL, Sat.1, and ProSieben being the most prominent. As private channels gain market share, advertising revenues are becoming more important, however, because public broadcasters still control such a large part of the market these revenues are less prominent than in other territories like the United States.

In terms of the noncommercial mandates, an independent Broadcasting Council or *Rundfunkrat* governs Germany's broadcast corporations. According to a Federal Constitutional Court ruling, the council advocates on behalf of the German public and other relevant social groups. With the advent of commercial broadcasting in the 1980s, the *Länder* drafted new media laws to supplement the existing broadcasting laws. These laws specifically regulate electronic media produced outside of the rubric of public broadcasting, mainly by issuing commercial radio and television licenses and by regulating the programming that airs on cable systems. As part of these laws, new supervisory bodies (*Landesmedienanstalten*) were created, each with a council resembling the *Rundfunkrat*. Private channels are also subject to the European Union, which primarily aims to unify or coordinate regulatory policies across different countries.

While public and private broadcasters are an important contextual factor for Netflix, the service is more commonly compared to pay-TV providers. These are services that require an additional subscription fee. Pay-TV is currently dominated by Sky Deutschland AG (formerly known as Premiere until 2009), which, along with ProSiebenSat.1 Media AG and the RTL Group, is considered one of the largest commercial forces in contemporary German media industries. Although Sky is part of much larger global conglomerate, it has been limited to a relatively modest role in the German market where pay-TV remains a minor segment. Sky currently has 3.7 million of the country's 6 million pay-TV subscribers, but that is only approximately 10 percent of the overall market. By contrast, in the UK, Sky Deutschland's sibling BSkyB has 11 million of the 14 million pay-TV customers, which is closer to 40 percent of the overall market.[8] One reason for German's resistance to pay-TV may be the license fee that they are required to pay in to the public broadcasting system. The €17,50 per month fee is currently required regardless of whether a household actually owns or uses a television. If a TV connection exists, you have to pay the fee. This is something that Germans regularly lament and suggests a general unwillingness to pay extra to supplement free TV.[9]

Both Sky and Netflix are attempting to gain market share by providing access to premium content that is not currently available through existing public or private broadcasters. This has created a more competitive market for high quality content. For example, Sky Deutschland has secured the exclusive rights for well-known HBO shows like *Game of Thrones* and *True Detective* as well as Showtime's *Masters of Sex*. Netflix aims to attract subscribers by emphasizing its original productions. In some cases this has created confusion. Netflix sold the rights to the first three seasons of *House of Cards*, its most popular in-house production, to Sky. Some critics suggest that this will hurt Netflix's ability to succeed in Germany. It is possible however that the media hype surrounding the show will help to better establish Netflix's reputation (Table 15.1).

Table 15.1 North America and Europe–subscribers and available titles

	Millions of subscribers	Total titles available	Available on Netflix				
			Breaking Bad	*House of Cards*	*Lost*	*Mad Men*	*The Office* (U.S.)
United States	37.7	8,522	Yes	Yes	Yes	Yes	Yes
Canada	3.1	4,306	Yes	Yes	Yes	Yes	No
Britain	3.3	3,186	Yes	Yes	No	No	Yes
Sweden	1.1	2,342	Yes	Yes	No	Yes	No
Netherlands	0.94	2,127	Yes	Yes	Yes	Yes	No
Norway	0.9	2,359	Yes	Yes	No	Yes	No
Denmark	0.79	2,349	Yes	Yes	No	Yes	No
Finland	0.54	2,284	Yes	Yes	No	Yes	No
Germany	0.47	1,646	Yes	Yes	No	No	No
France	0.51	1,686	Yes	No	No	No	No
Ireland	0.18	3,189	Yes	Yes	No	No	Yes
Switzerland	0.14	1,842	Yes	Yes	No	No	No
Austria	0.05	1,602	Yes	Yes	No	No	No

Source: Stephen Heyma, "Netflix Taps into a Growing International Market," *The New York Times*, May 12, 2015.

Table 15.2 VOD competitors in Germany

Provider	Price per month	Flatrate	Service options			
			Purchase to own	Rental	Offline mode	Monthly notice
Netflix	€7,99–11,99	Yes	No	No	No	Yes
Maxdome	€7,99	Yes	No	No	Yes	Yes
Snap by Sky	Sky TV + €3,99	Yes	No	No	Yes + €6,99	No
Amazon Prime	€49/year	Yes	Yes	Yes	Yes	No
iTunes	–	No	Yes	Yes	Yes	–
Watcher	€8,99	Yes	No	No	Yes	Yes

Despite the limited growth of the pay-TV market, VOD platforms have shown greater promise having increased at a steady rate from 2008 to 2012.[10] These platforms include iTunes, Amazon's Prime Instant Video (previously Lovefilm), and ProSiebenSat.1's Maxdome, which is the current market leader. Netflix may have entered the market later than these other options, but it also has some clear strengths. These include the publicity surrounding its original programming, the appeal of its interface design, and its experience in collecting data and using predictive algorithms to personalize the user experience. The growing importance of the VOD market (German business consultancy Goldmedia predicts the German market will grow with the entry of Netflix to €300 million in 2018[11]) was evident in the significant increase of television advertising for these services around the time Netflix introduced its service.[12] See Table 15.2 for further details of the different services and how they differentiate themselves within the market.

Technological practices

As the previous section details, Netflix's German expansion involves many different contextual factors—these include shifting commercial and noncommercial mandates and different economic contexts related to the development of pay-TV and the VOD markets. These factors will play a significant role in whether Netflix is successful. Technological practices are a more specific concern since they impact Netflix's operations from both an internal and external standpoint. Netflix has built a strong overall reputation based on its innovative approach to technology. It is perhaps best known for its recommendation software and its ability to create an enhanced user-oriented service. It has also utilized a software program known as the Chaos Monkey System. This software generates a series of failures in order to test how well the overall system's architecture is able to respond and avoid a more serious outage. Although

Netflix has maintained a successful record with its internal technological practices, it is also dependent on numerous external technologies. In order to watch Netflix on a television, for example, it is necessary to use an internet-connected device. Netflix has made a concerted effort to ensure that it is available on a wide assortment of devices including video game consoles, DVD and Blu-ray players, and stand-alone streaming players.

Of course, the most important technology for Netflix is the internet itself. This is also the clearest example of how politics and legal regulations define the conditions and practices that affect how media industries function. As mentioned earlier, the use of VPNs illustrates how technology is at odds with an existing legal framework.[13] Media like film and television programming have been licensed on a region-by-region basis and different windows or platforms are typically licensed separately. Rights holders use exclusivity as a way to drive up the value of licensing. Exclusivity is also valuable for distributors because it allows them to differentiate themselves from competitors. VPNs have become more common, and recent studies indicate that Netflix is a major part of the trend, accounting for 29 percent of all VPN usage, with up to 20 million of those users in China where Netflix is not legally available.[14] These put Netflix under a steadily increasing pressure from series and movie right holders as Netflix's license agreements vary based on each country. As a result, rights holders are pressuring services like Netflix to implement technical measures in order to detect and block proxy users. Netflix CEO Reed Hastings wants to remedy this by licensing rights on a global basis.[15] Rights holders are wary, however, since this might hurt their ability to optimize value through exclusive windows. If this continues to be a problem, it may affect how Netflix deals with media producers and the content it is able to license.

Another major technological practice associated with the internet concerns the regulation of net neutrality. In contrast to the United States, European regulators have taken a stronger position on net neutrality, affirming the principle that telecommunication companies and cable operators must treat internet traffic equally.[16] According to a report by the Global Internet Phenomena, Netflix and YouTube are responsible for half of North America's downstream traffic during peak hours in the evening and on weekends. Netflix is the largest contributor to internet traffic accounting for up to 35 percent during peak hours. In comparison, Amazon Prime Instant Video accounts for less than 3 percent. This means that Netflix will be at the center of future debate about this issue and that its success depends heavily on how the political system responds to it. Some critics fear that unless net neutrality is enacted in a stronger manner, major media conglomerates, including companies like Netflix, will be able to prioritize their content, and thereby undermine the principles of an open internet.

As of 2015, Germany and the rest of the European Union have upheld the principles of net neutrality. The continuation of this policy will be crucial if Netflix is to succeed in its European expansion. In some cases, regional communication providers like Unitymedia Kabel BW, Deutsche Telekom, Kabel Deutschland, Vodafone, or O2 have been suspicious of Netflix's agenda. The huge amount of bandwidth used by Netflix puts pressure on these providers to improve and expand their networks.[17] They are averse to the additional financial expenditures that these improvements require. Rather than antagonize these companies, Netflix is seeking to develop strong alliances with powerful telecommunications providers like Telekom or Vodafone. As part of these promotional partnerships, new customers are offered temporary free access to Netflix when subscribing to services through Telekom or Vodafone.[18]

These arrangements promise to promote Netflix and acclimate German consumers to the benefits of the service. More importantly, they allow Netflix to create strategic partnerships with Germany's existing telecommunications providers. The most significant aspect of these deals may be that they align Netflix with these other companies as they both try to influence the regulations and political policies that will shape future technological conditions and practices. Though Germans have traditionally opted for free TV, the VOD market is expected to grow significantly in the near future. Netflix needs to be in a position to advocate for favorable circumstances like net neutrality while also ensuring that VOD platforms become more attractive to German audiences. These aims are intertwined with its ability to offer premium content as part of its service. Although negotiating access to this type of content remains difficult, if Netflix continues to successfully expand into new markets, then the costs of licensing the global rights to films and television programs will be become more favorable.

Media texts

As much as Netflix would like to secure exclusive global streaming rights for all of its content, it has had to adjust its strategy as part of its expansion into international territories. In Germany, for example, audiences prefer to watch original content that has been dubbed in their native language. This preference is part of a well-established tradition, but it is one that presents a challenge to Netflix. Dubbing requires an additional expense and the process of re-recording dialogue takes additional time. This can be a significant problem considering that Netflix needs to make content available as quickly as possible in order to differentiate itself from competitors. Even though you can always choose between dubbed and original version, Netflix tries to stick to traditional consumer behaviors in Germany, for example, using the same German dubbing actors known already from previous non-Netflix productions (e.g., Till Hagen for dubbing Kevin Spacey[19]). Another challenge is that there is high demand for premium American content and many of the rights to these materials have already been licensed. When first introduced in Germany in 2014, Netflix offered the Hollywood blockbuster *The Hobbit* (2012) and select smaller, critically acclaimed films like Jim Jarmusch's *Only Lovers Left Alive* (2013). However, the service did not offer any major Hollywood new releases—films with a 2014 or later theatrical release. This is partly because competitors like Maxdome already had an exclusive distribution deal with all major U.S. film studios as part of its affiliation with ProSiebenSat.1 AG. This made it difficult for Netflix to promote its film selection as a reason to sign up for the service.

As a result, Netflix is making "quality" television more of a focus and it is mainly promoting its original series to attract subscribers.[20] For example, there is a tendency to emphasize Netflix originals like *Orange Is the New Black*, *Unbreakable Kimmy Schmidt*, *Hemlock Grove*, *Penny Dreadful*, *Bojack Horseman*, and *Marco Polo* in all of the company's marketing materials. As part of the December 2014 release of the historical epic *Marco Polo*, Netflix Germany launched an interactive map on its official Instagram account. Netflix is using these social media sites as part of a larger campaign to engage users and promote its shows. Netflix has also licensed nonoriginal serial dramas like *Ripper Street*, *Bates Motel*, *Fargo*, and *Top of the Lake*, all recent television programs, primarily American and often well received by critics.

While Netflix is known for releasing all episodes of a new season at the same time as a way to encourage "binge-watching," they are also adopting new ways of expanding the service's association with quality television. Contrary to its earlier release strategy, Netflix used an episodic format in releasing the first season of the *Breaking Bad* spin off *Better Call Saul*. The show was uploaded weekly every Tuesday shortly after its original broadcast on AMC in the United States. In addition, Netflix's licensing deal allows them to label *Better Call Saul* a Netflix original outside of the United States. This creates a more general connection between Netflix, rather than AMC, and quality programming. There was further evidence of this strategy in the German marketing campaign in which *Better Call Saul* was featured as regularly as *Orange Is the New Black* on both television advertisements and billboards.

Although Netflix has emphasized its original series and other imported programming, it has also made some effort to cater its service to localized German preferences. The site includes, for example, a "Deutsch" search category that features German films and television programs. This section highlights shows like *Stromberg* (2014), a German movie-remake of the British comedy series, *The Office*, which previously aired on Pro 7, one of the flagship channels of ProSiebenSat.1 AG. Other local content includes German blockbusters with the famous actor Til Schweiger (*Kleinohrhasen*, *Kleinohrkücken*, and *Kokowääh*) and TV classics for children such as *Sendung mit der Maus*. This type of content suggests that Netflix wants to appeal to mainstream audiences. This may explain why there are not many independent films—by critically acclaimed German directors like Christian Petzold or internationally renowned auteurs like Michael Haneke—currently available. This strategy is also evident in its genre categories. It offers standard categories like "Crime," "Romantische Filme" (Romantic films), and "Preisgekrönte Filme" (award-winning films, mostly Oscar related). Interestingly, some genres that feature on Netflix's U.S. site are not found on its German counterpart. For example, even though Netflix Germany offers films like *The Beginners*, *Brokeback Mountain*, and *In and Out*, they are not classified as part of a broader category like "Queer Cinema." It may be that Netflix does not want to provoke or antagonize German audiences. As Netflix develops plans to produce German-based original programming in the future—perhaps using the data it collects from current users and their preferences[21]—these strategies indicate that it seeks content that strikes a balance between international flair and local appeal. Netflix also wants content that is safe and easy for most viewers to consume.

Social trends, tastes, and traditions

Germany is going through a massive transformation right now. Cultural and aesthetic traditions are changing rapidly. This is particularly clear in media and television. In contrast to the quality television associated with new platforms like Netflix, consider one of Europe's largest and most successful shows of the 1980s and 1990s, *Wetten, dass..?* First broadcast in February 1981, the show and its legendary host Thomas Gottschalk became one of the highlights of Saturday night television six to eight times a year. It was the basis for similar shows such as *Wanna bet?* in the United States and featured the simple premise that audience guests were there to perform bizarre and unusual tasks. Celebrity guests then decided to bet on the outcome of these tasks. The show had its peak in 1987, when over 23 million viewers watched it live in Germany, Austria, and Switzerland. Though it began to decline after that, it was still doing well throughout the 1990s. A horrible on-air accident in 2010[22] led to its eventual cancellation in December 2014.

As *Wetten, dass..?* began to lose momentum, the television host Stefan Raab introduced an interesting successor, *Schlag den Raab* or *Beat the Host*. In creating a series of bizarre competitions, Raab attracted a sizable audience with an original German format. As with *Wetten, dass..?*, this show quickly became an example of successful Saturday night prime-time programming, before Stefan Raab announced his retirement from television at the end of 2015, making it "the end of an era."[23] These types of shows illustrate the socializing function of media in post–Cold War Germany. Families and friends were drawn to these shows as a kind of Saturday night social event. The show sometimes lasted for over three hours and very often ran up to 45 minutes longer than scheduled. The emergence of new technologies and changing consumer behaviors eventually made these types of shows obsolete. Although Germany remains an unusual example in the degree to which many viewers continue to access only free TV, Netflix has the potential to mark an interesting turning point. VOD platforms individualize media consumption; they cater to individual tastes and preference, they prioritize immediacy and convenience, and they shift the focus to a user-oriented experience. The socialization function of media no longer occurs at the moment of media consumption, but rather at secondary points of communication through exchanges on social media and elsewhere on the internet. While program structures and listings degenerate and media audiences become more and more autonomous, the premises of traditional television and media consumption fall apart. These developments can be seen with Netflix as well as related services like Spotify.

Internet-based services such as Netflix are expected to triple between 2014 and 2019. The growing demand for VOD marks a shift away from live programming like *Wetten, dass..?* to serial dramas like the type that Netflix is promoting as the centerpiece of its service. Netflix, however, is not alone in this new market. Other VOD platforms and competitors in pay-TV promise intense battles in licensing the rights to premium American content. This will encourage services like Netflix to continue to develop its own original series (as well as with regional appeal to target markets, e.g., Germany), especially since this may be the best way to secure exclusive distribution rights on a global basis. There are other larger technological considerations that will also be a factor as Netflix moves forward. It may be difficult to maintain an advantage like net neutrality in the long term, and technology brings together a particularly volatile combination of public and private mandates. Despite all these concerns, the German media market was too big for Netflix to ignore. Now that it has a foothold there, it will learn to adapt to the social, economic, regulatory, and technological factors that shape its culture and media.

Notes

1 Alex Hern, "Why Netflix Won't Block VPN Users—It Has Too Many of Them," *The Guardian*, January 9, 2015. http://www.theguardian.com/technology/2015/jan/09/why-netflix-wont-block-vpn-users (accessed June 28, 2015).

2 Josh Taylor, "How Netflix Wants to End Geoblocking," *ZDNet*, January 20, 2015. http://www.zdnet.com/article/how-netflix-wants-to-end-geoblocking/ (accessed June 28, 2015).

3 Timothy Havens and Amanda Lotz, *Understanding Media Industries* (Oxford: Oxford University Press, 2012), 4–9.

4 Havens and Lotz, *Understanding Media Industries*, 8.

5 Sebastian Schneider, "TV Formats for Young People. Public Television Fighting for the Younger Audience," *Goethe Institut*, May, 2014. https://www.goethe.de/en/kul/med/20392577.html (accessed July 1, 2015).

6 Arbeitsgemeinschaft der Landesmedienanstalten (ALM), *Privater Rundfunk in Deutschland* (Berlin: vistas, 2015).

7 Ibid.

8 Sky Deutschland, *Q2 Report 2014/15*. http://ir.sky.de/sky/pdf/2015/Q2201415bericht_en.pdf (accessed July 1, 2015).

9 "*330,000 Sign Up Against TV Licence Fee*," *The Local*, April 14, 2015. http://www.thelocal.de/20140414/330000-sign-up-against-new-licence-fee (accessed June 21, 2015).

10 Dirk Martens and Jan Herfert, *Der VoD-Markt Deutschland* (Berlin: House of Research, 2013), 104.

11 Christian Grece et al. "The Development of the European Market for On-Demand Audiovisual Services," *European Audiovisual Observatory*, March 2015, 174.

12 Ingo Renz, "So wirbt der Streamingdienst in Deutschland," *Horizont*, September 17, 2014. http://www.horizont.net/medien/nachrichten/Spot-Premiere-So-wirbt-Netflix-in-Deutschland-130421 (accessed June 21, 2015).

13 Taos Turner, "Video Streaming Geo-Blocking Gets Workaround," *Wall Street Journal*, April 16, 2015. http://www.wsj.com/articles/video-streaming-geo-blocking-gets-workaround-1429234440 (accessed July 1, 2015).

14 Alex Hern, "Why Netflix Won't Block VPN Users—It Has Too Many of Them."

15 Josh Taylor, "How Netflix Wants to End Geoblocking."

16 European Commission, "Our Commitment to Net Neutrality," *Digital Agenda for Europe*, June 29, 2015. https://ec.europa.eu/digital-agenda/en/eu-actions (accessed July 11, 2015).

17 "Germany ISP Speed Index Netflix May 2015," http://ispspeedindex.netflix.com/germany (accessed on June 16, 2015).
18 Jörn Krieger, "Vodafone to Add Netflix in Germany," *Broadband TV News*, November 11, 2014. http://www.broadbandtvnews.com/2014/11/11/vodafone-to-add-netflix-in-germany (accessed June 28, 2015); Peter Steinkirchner, "Netflix kooperiert mit Telekom und Vodafone," *WirtschaftsWoche*, September 14, 2014. http://www.wiwo.de/unternehmen/dienstleister/internetfernsehen-netflix-kooperiert-mit-telekom-und-vodafone/10693414.html (accessed June 28, 2015).
19 See, for example, http://www.sprechersprecher.de/synchronsprecher/till-hagen (accessed July 1, 2015).
20 Laura Slattery, "*Netflix Steps Up Release of Originals in Push for 'Must Have' Status*," *Irish Times*, February 12, 2015. http://www.irishtimes.com/business/media-and-marketing/netflix-steps-up-release-of-originals-in-push-for-must-have-status-1.2097076 (accessed July 11, 2015).
21 Jörn Krieger, "Netflix to Produce German Series," *Broadband TV News*, August 31, 2014. http://www.broadbandtvnews.com/2014/08/31/netflix-to-produce-german-series/ (accessed July 11, 2015).
22 "Stunt Jumper Student Seriously Injured After Leaping over Moving Cars on Spring Stilts on Live TV," *Daily Mail*, December 6, 2010. http://www.dailymail.co.uk/news/article-1335851/Samuel-Koch-stunt-Student-seriously-injured-stilts-jump-moving-cars-live-TV.html (accessed May 28, 2015).
23 "German Media Star Stefan Raab Says Goodbye to TV," *DW.com*, June 17, 2015. http://www.dw.com/en/german-media-star-stefan-raab-says-goodbye-to-tv/a-18523666 (accessed July 1, 2015).

Index

Note: The letter 'n' following locators refers to notes